INTRODUCTION TO
AFRICAN CIVILIZATIONS

Books and Pamphlets by John G. Jackson

Christianity Before Christ (1938)
Ethiopia and the Origin of Civilization (1939)
Pagan Origins of the Christ Myth (1941)

With Dr. Willis N. Huggins:

A Guide to the Study of African History (1934)
An Introduction to African Civilizations (1937)

1. Aries. 2. Taurus. 3. Gemini. 4. Cancer 5. Leo. 6. Virgo. 7. Libra. 8. Scorpio. 9. Sagittarius. 10. Capricornus. 11. Aquarius. 12. Pisces.

INTRODUCTION TO AFRICAN CIVILIZATIONS

By
John G. Jackson

Introduction and additional Bibliographical Notes by:
John Henrik Clarke

A CITADEL PRESS BOOK
PUBLISHED BY CAROL PUBLISHING GROUP

A Citadel Press Book
Published by Carol Publishing Group
Citadel Press is a registered trademark of Carol Communications, Inc.
Editorial Offices: 600 Madison Avenue, New York, NY 10022
Sales & Distribution Offices: 120 Enterprise Avenue, Secaucus, NJ 07094
In Canada: Canadian Manda Group, P.O. Box 920, Station U, Toronto,
Ontario, M8Z 5P9, Canada
Queries regarding rights and permissions should be addressed to:
Carol Publishing Group, 600 Madison Avenue, New York, NY 10022

Manufactured in the United States of America
ISBN 0-8065-0420-X

20 19 18 17 16   15 14 13 12

Carol Publishing Group books are available at special discounts
for bulk purchases, sales promotions, fund raising, or
educational purposes. Special editions can also be created to
specifications. For details contact: Special Sales Department,
Carol Publishing Group, 120 Enterprise Ave., Secaucus, NJ 07094

This book is dedicated to everybody with an African ancestry—the whole human race!

CONTENTS

	Introduction by John Henrik Clarke	3
I	Africa and the Origin of Man	37
II	Ethiopia and the Origin of Civilization	60
III	Egypt and the Evolution of Civilization	93
IV	Africa and the Civilizing of Europe: The Empire of the Moors	157
V	The Golden Age of West Africa	196
VI	Africa and the Discovery of America	232
VII	Mariners and Merchants of the Eastern Coast	264
VIII	Zimbabwe, Monomotapa, and Other Kingdoms of the Interior	283
IX	The Destruction of African Culture	296
X	Africa Resurgent	319
	Bibliography	351
	New Bibliographical Approach to African History by John Henrik Clarke	366
	Index	376

INTRODUCTION TO
AFRICAN CIVILIZATIONS

INTRODUCTION

One thing should be completely understood before entering into the main body of this book. Mr. Jackson has not written this volume on African history to tell benevolent stories about so-called savages and how the Europeans came to civilize them. Quite the contrary, in many ways he has reversed the picture and proved his point. Civilization did not start in European countries, and the rest of the world did not wait in darkness for the Europeans to bring the light. In order to understand how this attitude came about, one needs to look at the sad state of what is called "world history." There is not a single book in existence with a title incorporating the words "world history" that is an honest commentary on the history of the world and its people. Most of the history books in the last five hundred years have been written to glorify Europeans at the expense of other peoples. The history of Asia has been as shamefully distorted as the history of Africa.

Most Western historians have not been willing to admit that there is an African history to be written about, and that this history predates the emergence of Europe by thousands of years. It is not possible for the world to have waited in darkness for the Europeans to bring the light because, for most of the early history of man, the Europeans themselves were in darkness. When the light of culture came for the first time to the people who would later call themselves Europeans, it came from Africa and Middle Eastern Asia. Most history books tend to deny or ignore this fact. John G. Jackson has examined this fact and its dimensions with scholarly honesty. He has also examined the origins of racism and its effects on the writing of history.

It is too often forgotten that, when the Europeans emerged

and began to extend themselves into the broader world of Africa and Asia during the fifteenth and sixteenth centuries, they went on to colonize most of mankind. Later, they would colonize world scholarship, mainly the writing of history. History was then written or rewritten to show or imply that Europeans were the only creators of what could be called a civilization. In order to accomplish this, the Europeans had to forget, or pretend to forget, all they previously knew about Africa.

In his booklet *Ancient Greece in African Political Thought* (1966), Professor Ali A. Mazrui of Makerere University in Uganda observes, after reading the book *A History of the Modern World* by R. R. Palmer and Joel Colton, that:

> As Africans begin to be given credit for some of their own civilizations, African cultural defensiveness would gradually wane. Not everyone need have the confidence of Leopold Senghor as he asserts that "Negro blood circulated in the veins of the Egyptians." But it is at any rate time that it was more openly conceded not only that ancient Egypt made a contribution to the Greek miracle, but also that she in turn had been influenced by the Africa which was to the south of her. To grant all this is, in a sense, to universalise the Greek heritage. It is to break the European monopoly of identification with ancient Greece.

And yet this is by no means the only way of breaking Europe's monopoly. In order to cope with the cultural offensive of the Graeco-Roman Mystique, African cultural defenders have so far emphasized the Africanness of Egypt's civilization. But a possible counteroffensive is to demonstrate that ancient Greece was not European. It is not often remembered how recent the concept of "Europe" is. In a sense, it is easier to prove that ancient Egypt was "African" than to prove that ancient Greece was "European." In the words of Palmer and Colton:

There was really no Europe in ancient times. In the Roman Empire we may see a Mediterranean world, or even a West and an East in the Latin and Greek-speaking portions. But the West included parts of Africa as well as of Europe, and Europe as we know it was divided by the Rhine-Danube frontier, south and west of which lay the civilized provinces of the Empire, and north and east the "barbarians" of whom the civilized world knew almost nothing.

The two historians go on to say that the word "Europe," since it meant little, was scarcely used by the Romans at all.

Even as late as the seventeenth century, the notion that the land mass south of the Mediterranean was an entity distinct from the land mass north of it had yet to be fully accepted. Melville Herskovits has pointed out how the Geographer Royal of France, writing in 1656, described Africa as "a peninsula so large that it comprises the third part, and this the most southerly, of our continent."

In the years when the slave trade was getting effectively under way, some Europeans were claiming parts of Africa— especially Egypt—as an extension of their "continent" and their "culture." During this period, most history books were written to justify the slave trade and the colonial system that followed. Therefore, any honest writing of African history today must take this fact into consideration and be, at least in part, a restoration project.

The distinguished Afro-American poet, Countee Cullen, began his poem "Heritage" with the question: "What is Africa to me?" The new writers of African history must extend this question by asking, "What is Africa to Africans and what is Africa to the world?" Asking these questions emphasizes the need for a total reexamination of African history. A new approach to African history must begin with a new frame of reference. We will have to discard a number of words that have been imposed on African history. There is a need to reject the term "black Africa" because it presupposes that there is a "white Africa." There is an urgent need to discard the term "Negro Africa" and the word "Negro" and all that it implies. This word grew out of the European slavery and colonial systems and it fails to relate the people of African descent to land, history, and culture. There is no "Negroland." When one hears the word "France" or "French," it is easy to visualize the land, history, and culture of a people. The same thing is true of the words "English" or "Englishman." When one hears or reads the word "Negro," the only vision that comes to mind relates to a condition.

There are many physical varieties of African peoples. The complexions of Africans are mainly black and brown. Most of the light-skinned people in Africa today are latecomers or interlopers. They have little or no relationship to Africa's ancient history. The Egyptians are a distinct African people. They did not originally come from Europe or Asia. Their history and their culture started in what is now Ethiopia and the Sudan. It is incorrect to refer to them or any other African people as Hamites. There is no such thing as a Hamite people. This is another term that was imposed upon African history by Europeans who wanted to prove that everything good in African history was brought in from the outside. The Hamites are supposed to be "black white people." Western historians move the so-called Hamites around in Africa as they see fit in order to prove that the rest of Africa has no history worthy of its name.

In a recent speech on "The Significance of African History," the Caribbean-American writer Richard B. Moore has observed:

> The significance of African history is shown, though not overtly, in the very effort to deny anything worthy of the name of history to Africa and the African peoples. This widespread, and well nigh successful endeavor, maintained through

some five centuries, to erase African history from the general record, is a fact which of itself should be quite conclusive to thinking and open minds. For it is logical and apparent that no such undertaking would ever have been carried on, and at such length, in order to obscure and to bury what is actually of little or no significance.

The prime significance of African history becomes still more manifest when it is realized that this deliberate denial of African history arose out of the European expansion and invasion of Africa which began in the middle of the fifteenth century. The compulsion was thereby felt to attempt to justify such colonialist conquest, domination, enslavement, and plunder. Hence, this brash denial of history and culture to Africa, and, indeed, even of human qualities and capacity for civilization to the indigenous peoples of Africa.

Mr. Moore is saying, in essence, that African history must be looked at anew and seen in its relationship to world history. First, the distortions must be admitted. The hard fact is that most of what we now call world history is only the history of the first and second rise of Europe. The Europeans are not yet willing to acknowledge that the world did not wait in darkness for them to bring the light. The history of Africa was already old when Europe was born.

In an essay, "The Nations of Black Africa and Their Culture," written in 1955, the Senegalese historian Cheikh Anta Diop makes the following observation:

In our time it is customary to ask ourselves all kinds of questions; so we must ask if it was necessary to study the problems dealt with in this work. Even a superficial examination of the cultural situation in Black Africa justifies such an undertaking. Indeed, if one must believe western works, it is useless to look in the interior of the African forest for a single civilization which, in the last analysis, might be the product of blacks. The civilizations of Ethiopia and Egypt, the express testimony of the ancients notwithstanding, the civilizations of the Ife and Benin, of the Chad Basin, of Ghana, all those referred to as neo-Sudanese (Mali, Gao, etc.) those of Zimbabwe (Monomotapa), of the Congo on the Equator, etc. . . . according to the coteries of western scholars, were created by mythical whites who then vanished as in a dream, leaving the blacks to perpetuate the forms, organizations, techniques, etc., which they had invented.

The explanation of the origin of an African civilization is only logical and acceptable, serious, objective and scientific if one, by what distortion whatsoever, leads up to this mythical white man. One does not bother to provide proof of his arrival or his settling in these parts. It can be readily understood how scholars could not help being led to the extreme from their reasoning, from their logical and dialectical deductions, to the notion of "whites with black skins," a notion quite widespread in the circles of European specialists. Such modes of thought obviously cannot persist forever since they are completely lacking in any substantial foundation. They are explained only by the passion which consumes those who create them and shows through their appearances of objectivity and calm.

But these "scientific" theories on the African past are highly consistent; they are utilitarian, pragmatic. Truth is what is good for something and, in this instance, good for colonialism: the aim is, under cover of the mantle of science, to make the black man believe that he has never been responsible for anything at all of worth, not even for what is to be found right in his own house and home. In this way, it is made easy to bring about the abandonment and renunciation of all national aspirations on the part of those who are wavering, and the reflexes of subordination are reinforced in those who have already been alienated. It is for this reason that there exist numerous theorizers in the service of colonialism, every one more clever than the other, whose ideas are spread abroad and taught on a popular scale as fast as they are worked out.

The use of cultural alienation as a weapon of domination is as old as the world itself; every time one people in the world have conquered another, they have used it. It is edifying to underline that it is the descendants of the Gauls against whom Caesar used that weapon who, today, are employing it against us.

Many white students of African history are now willing to admit that, according to most of the evidence we now have available, mankind started in Africa. The same students are not also willing to admit that it is logical to assume that human cultures and what we refer to as civilization also started in Africa.

In a lecture on "Early African Civilizations," Professor William Leo Hansberry calls attention to the long search for the origin of man:

> Between the years 1834 and 1908, there occurred a revolution in academic thinking about Africa's place in the outlines of world geography and world history. And in the past 150 years, European explorers and archaeologists have found in the valleys of the Niger, Benwezi, Limpopo and Nile Rivers, in the basin of Lake Chad and the Sahara, extensive remains of hundreds of ruins which bear witness to the existence of former civilizations hundreds and thousands of years ago. This knowledge of the facts about the African past when combined with the known history of other continents reveal that these also are the stories of triumphs and failures of mankind, and form many chapters in the history of the human race.

When and where did living things and human life first appear on earth? Who built the first human civilization? For centuries these questions have been raised in the minds of poets, philosophers, and myth makers among most of the world's peoples. Specifically, the Athenians thought that the first men sprouted from Attic soil; the ancient Hebrews and their spiritual descendants were of the opinion that Adam, the supposed primal parent of mankind, was made in the Garden of Eden six days after the creation of the world. According to

Pindar the poet, the ancient Libyans believed that Iarbas, the earliest of men, sprang into existence in the heart of Libya. Ancient Egyptians contended that it was in their country, the oldest in the world, that the gods fashioned the first of all human beings out of a handful of mud moistened by the life-giving water of the "Blessed Nile." Likewise, Creation stories have come from many other parts of Africa (Ethiopia, Tanzania, Rhodesia, Congo, Ghana, Nigeria, etc.).

One of the oldest of such stories told by Africans to account for the origin and early development of man and his culture survives in a Greek version of the thesis first advanced by the ancient Kushites. This remarkable people flourished in olden times in the region called Kush in the Hebrew scriptures and marked on present-day maps as Sudan. The great historian, Diodorus Siculus, wrote that the Kushites were of the opinion that their country was not only the birthplace of the human race and the cradle land of the world's earliest civilization, but, indeed, the primal Eden where living things first appeared on Earth, as reported by the Scriptures. Thus, Diodorus was the first European to focus attention on the Ethiopian claim that tropical Africa was the cradle land of the world's earliest civilization, the original Eden of the human race.

In John G. Jackson's chapter on "Ethiopia and the Origin of Civilization," the reader is literally challenged to reconsider the prevailing definition of civilization and the story of its origin. In the book *Progress and Evolution of Man in Africa*, Dr. L. S. B. Leakey states: "In every country that one visits and where one is drawn into a conversation about Africa, the question is regularly asked by people who should know better 'But what has Africa contributed to world progress?' The critics of Africa forget that men of science today are, with few exceptions, satisfied that Africa was the birthplace of man himself, and that for many hundreds of centuries thereafter, Africa was in the forefront of all world progress."

In his book *Egypt*, Sir E. A. Wallis Budge says: "The prehistoric native of Egypt, both in the old and in the new Stone
Ages, was African and there is every reason for saying that
the earliest settlers came from the South."

He further states: "There are many things in the manners
and customs and religions of the historic Egyptians that suggest that the original home of their prehistoric ancestors was
in a country in the neighborhood of Uganda and Punt."
(Some historians believe that the Biblical land of Punt was in
the area known on modern maps as Somalia.)

European interest in "Ethiopia and the Origin of Civilization" dates from the early part of the nineteenth century and
is best reflected in a little-known, though important, paper on
"Karl Richard Lepsius' Incomparable Survey of the Monumental Ruins in the Ethiopian Nile Valley in 1843–1844."

The records found by Lepsius tend to show how Ethiopia
was once able to sustain an ancient population that was
numerous and powerful enough not only to challenge, but on
a number of occasions to conquer completely, the populous
land of Egypt. Further, these records showed that the antiquity
of Ethiopian civilization had a direct link with the civilization
of ancient Egypt.

Many of the leading antiquarians of the time, based largely
on the strength of what the classical authors, particularly Diodorus Siculus and Stephanus of Byzantium, had to say on the
matter, were exponents of the view that the ancient Ethiopians
or, at any rate, the black people of remote antiquity were the
earliest of all civilized peoples and that the first civilized inhabitants of ancient Egypt were members of what is referred
to as the Black Race who had entered the country as emigrants
from Ethiopia. A number of Europe's leading writers on the
civilizations of remote antiquity have written brilliant de-
fenses of this point of view. Some of these writers are Bruce,
Count Volney, Fabre, d'Olivet, and Heeren. In spite of the

fact that these writers defended this thesis with all the learning at their command, and documented their defense, most of the present-day writers of African history continue to ignore their findings.

In 1825, German backwardness in this respect came definitely to an end. In that year, Arnold Hermann Heeren (1760–1842), Professor of History and Politics in the University of Göttingen and one of the ablest of the early exponents of the economic interpretation of history, published, in the fourth and revised edition of his great work *Ideen Über Die Politik, Den Verkehr Und Den Handel Der Vornehmsten Volker Der Alten Weld*, a lengthy essay on the history, culture, and commerce of the ancient Ethiopians, which had a profound influence on contemporary thought respecting such matters, not only in Germany, but throughout the learned world. In 1850, an English translation of Professor Heeren's *Historical Researches into the Politics, Intercourse and Trade of the Carthaginians, Ethiopians and Egyptians* was published. This book gave more support to the concept of the southern African origin of Egyptian civilization. Professor Heeren joined other writers in the conclusion that it was among these ancient black people of Africa and Asia that international trade was first developed, and he thinks that as a by-product of these international contacts there was an exchange of ideas and cultural practices that laid the foundations of the earliest civilizations of the ancient world.

Mr. Jackson's chapter on "Egypt and the Evolution of Civilization" calls to mind the fact that the study of Egyptology developed in concurrence with the development of the slave trade and the colonial system. It was during this period that Egypt was literally taken out of Africa, academically, and made an extension of Europe. In many ways Egypt is the key to ancient African history. African history is out of kilter until ancient Egypt is looked upon as a distinct African nation.

The Nile River played a major role in the relationship of Egypt to the nations in southeast Africa. During the early history of Africa, the Nile was a great cultural highway on which elements of civilization came into and out of inner Africa. Egypt's relationship with the people in the south was both good and bad, depending on the period and the dynasty in power.

Egypt first became an organized nation about 6000 B.C. Medical interest centers upon a period in the Third Dynasty (5345–5307 B.C.) when Egypt had an ambitious pharaoh named Zoser; and Zoser, in turn, had for his chief counselor and minister a brilliant noble named Imhotep (whose name means "he who cometh in peace"). Imhotep constructed the famous step pyramid of Sakkarah near Memphis. The building methods used in the construction of this pyramid revolutionized the architecture of the ancient world.

Egypt gave the world some of the greatest personalities in the history of mankind. In this regard, Imhotep is singularly outstanding. In the ancient history of Egypt, no individual left a deeper impression than the commoner Imhotep. He was probably the world's first multi-genius. He was the real father of medicine. In his book *Evolution of Modern Medicine* (London, 1921, page 10), Sir William Osler refers to Imhotep as "the first figure of a physician to stand out clearly from the mists of antiquity." Imhotep, the Wise, as he was called, was the Grand Vizier and Court Physician to King Zoser and architect of the world's earliest stone building, after which the Pyramids were modeled. He became a deity and later a universal God of Medicine, whose images graced the first Temple of Imhotep, mankind's first hospital. To it came sufferers from all the world for prayer, peace, and healing.

Imhotep lived and established his reputation as a healer at the court of King Zoser of the Third Dynasty about 5345–

5307 B.C., according to the book *A Scheme of Egyptian Chronology* by Duncan Macnaughton (1932). From a study of the period in which he lived, Imhotep appears to have been one of the most versatile men in history. In addition to being the chief physician to the king, he was sage and scribe, Chief Lector Priest, architect, astronomer, and magician. He was a poet and philosopher. One of his best-known sayings, which is still being quoted, is "Eat, drink and be merry for tomorrow we shall die."

Imhotep's fame increased after his death. He was worshiped as a medical demi-god from 2850 B.C. to 525 B.C., and as a full deity from 525 B.C. to 550 A.D. Kings and queens bowed at his shrine.

When Egyptian civilization crossed the Mediterranean to become the foundation of what we think of as Greek culture, the teachings of Imhotep were absorbed along with the precepts of other great African teachers. When Greek civilization became predominant in the Mediterranean area, the Greeks wanted the world to think they were the originators of everything. They stopped acknowledging their indebtedness to Imhotep and other great Africans. Imhotep was forgotten for thousands of years, and Hippocrates, a legendary figure of two thousand years later, became known as the father of medicine. As regards Imhotep's influence in Rome, Gerald Massey, noted poet, archaeologist, and philologist, says that the early Christians worshiped him as one with Christ.

It should be understood that, while the achievements of Egypt are the best known among African nations, these are not the only achievements that African nations can claim. The nations to the south called Kush, Nubia, and Ethiopia developed many aspects of civilization independent of Egyptian influence. These nations gave as much to Egypt as Egypt gave to them.

Trade was the basis for the earliest contact of Egypt with

the rest of Africa. Gold was obtained from Nubia. Trading expeditions were sent to visit the nations along the east coast of Africa, and the city-state of Meroe. These trading expeditions also helped to spread Egyptian ideas. Egypt, in turn, observed and took ideas from other nations within Africa.

Mr. Jackson's chapter on *Africa and the Civilizing of Europe: The Empire of the Moors* challenges two standard myths about Africa: One is that the Africans played no part in introducing civilization into Europe; the other myth is that the "Empire of the Moors" was a white North African achievement and had no relationship to what is referred to as Black Africa. This assumption prevails because most students of the subject, including most so-called African scholars, have no detailed knowledge of the interrelationships of African nations. North Africa did not develop out of context with the rest of Africa, and early Europe did not develop out of context with Africa in general.

There was a considerable African influence on what later became Europe in the period before the Christian era. Africans played a major role in the formulative development of both Christianity and Islam.

Many aspects of the present-day Christian church were developed in Africa during the formative years of Christianity. One of the more notable of African contributions to the early church was monasticism. Monasticism, in essence, is organized life in common, especially for religious purposes. The home of a monastic society is called a monastery or a convent; the inhabitants are monks or nuns. Christian monasticism probably began with the hermits of Egypt and Palestine about the time when Christianity was accepted as a legal religion.

Professor J. C. deGraft-Johnson gives us the following information on the rise of monasticism in Africa:

It was left to another Egyptian Christian to be the founder

of the monastic life. I refer to Pachomius, who established the
first Christian monastery on an island in the Nile in the Upper
Thebaid. Monastic life became very popular in Egypt and
tended to undermine the military and economic life of the country; and in A.D. 365, we find a law of the Valens which decreed
that all who left the cities of Egypt for the monastic life of the
desert should be compelled either to return to discharge or perform their civic duties, or else to hand over their property to
relatives who would be under obligation to perform those duties.

In the Emperor Valens' day the persecution of the African
Church had ceased. The persecution of African Christians came
to an end with the rise of Constantine as the undisputed master
of Rome and the West in A.D. 312.

From the north the church continued to spread southward
and eastward. Ethiopia received Christianity at an especially
early date. Part of tradition suggests that St. Matthew, who
wrote one of the Gospels, preached in Ethiopia.

When an Ethiopian emperor was converted from a "wor-
shiper of Michren" to Christianity in the middle of the fourth
century, this transformation marked a turning point in the
history of the century. Eventually, the national church that
emerged became the strongest supporter of Ethiopian independence.

Hadzrat Bilal ibn Rahab, a tall, gaunt, bushy-haired, black
Ethiopian, was the first High Priest and treasurer of the Mohammedan empire. After Mahomet himself, that great religion,
which today numbers upwards of 300,000,000 souls, may be
said to have begun with Bilal. He was reputed to be the
Prophet's first convert. Bilal was one of the many Africans
who participated in the establishment of Islam and later made
proud names for themselves in the Islamic wars of expansion.

Zaid Bin Harith, another convert of Mahomet, later became
one of the Prophet's foremost generals. Mahomet adopted him
as his son and made him governor of his tribe, the proud

Koreish. He was later married into the Prophet's own family —the highest honor possible. Zaid Bin Harith was killed in battle while leading his men against the armies of the Byzantines. The Encyclopedia of Islam hailed him as one of the first great heroes of that faith.

In writing about the nations on the Mediterranean, Harold Peake, the English scientific writer, has this to say:

> The first light that burst in upon the long night of Europe's Dark Ages and heralded the dawn of a new day was from Moorish Spain, and from their Saracenic comrades who had settled in Sicily and Italy. Light first dawned on Europe from Spain, by means of the foundation by the Moors in the 9th century of a Medical School at Salerno, in Southern Italy. This developed into a university about 1150 A.D. and received a new constitution from Emperor Frederick II in 1231. Thence the new civilization spread up through Italy then to France and soon penetrated all parts of Europe except the north-eastern section.

All over the Arab-Moorish Empire a brisk intellectual life flourished. The Khalifs of both the East and West were, for the most part, enlightened patrons of learning. They maintained immense libraries and offered fortunes for new manuscripts. Khalif Harun-al-Rashid founded the great University of Baghdad, at which the most celebrated professor was Joshua ben Nun, a Jew. Here Greek classics were translated into Arabic. In other fields of science the Arabs and Moors were equally brilliant. Geber, in the eighth century, was an outstanding chemist. He has been called the founder of scientific chemistry. The names of some other savants and their fields of study will further show us the extent of Arab-Moorish erudition.

The outstanding characteristic of the Arab-Moorish rulers was tolerance. Their relations with the most distant nations were most cordial. The Moslem traveler journeyed with utmost freedom in such widely separated lands as China and the Sudan. When the Mohammedan merchants reached the western Sudan (now West Africa) in the year 1000, or our era, they found well-developed kingdoms flourishing in this region. The commercial relations that they established with these kingdoms lasted for more than five hundred years.

The period covered by the chapter "The Golden Age of West Africa" has a special significance for the whole world. Europe was lingering in her Dark Ages at a time when western Africa was enjoying a Golden Age. In the non-European world beyond Africa, Asians built and enjoyed an age of advancement in technology before a period of internal withdrawal and isolation permitted the Europeans to move ahead of them.

It should be realized that during the Middle Ages oriental technology was far more advanced than European technology, and that until the thirteenth century Europe, technologically, was but an appendage of Asia. While the Greeks and Romans were weaving subtle philosophies, the Chinese were busy inventing gunpowder, paper, alchemy, vaccinations, plastic surgery, paint, and even the pocket handkerchief, which was unknown to the fastidious Greeks.

For more than a thousand years the Africans had been bringing into being empire after empire until the second rise of Europe, internal strife, and the slave trade turned what was an "Age of Grandeur" of the Africans into an age of tragedy and decline. Certain events in Europe and in Africa set this historical period in motion. In this respect no year was more important than 1492.

The fifteenth and the sixteenth centuries were both good and bad for Africa. The great nation states in Africa, especially in western Africa, rose to their height and began to decline. Europe partly recovered from the trouble of the Middle Ages and began to expand into the broader world.

Christopher Columbus opened up the New World for European settlement. The combination of Africans—Moors, Arabs, Berbers, and some Africans who came from south of the Sahara—lost their power in Spain after ruling that country for nearly eight hundred years.

In the great Songhay Empire of West Africa, the Emperor, Sunni Ali, died in 1492. This event brought to power Muhammad Touré, better known in African history as Askia the Great. This man, the last of West Africa's great rulers before the Europeans penetrated the hinterland of Africa, took inner West Africa through the last of its Golden Age after the slave trade had already started.

The story of the African slave trade is essentially the story of the consequences of the second rise of Europe. In the years between the passing of the Roman Empire in the eighth century and the partial unification of Europe through the framework of the Catholic Church in the fifteenth century, Europeans were engaged mainly in the internal matters within their own continent. With the opening up of the New World, after the expulsion of the Moors from Spain during the latter part of the fifteenth century, the Europeans started to expand beyond their homeland. They were searching for new markets and materials, new manpower, and new lands to exploit. The African slave trade was created to accommodate this new expansion.

Had there been no market for the slaves there would have been no slave trade. The market and the motive were the opening up of the New World and the creation of the vast plantation system that followed.

The slave trade had far-reaching repercussions that are acutely apparent today. In fact, there is no way to understand the social, political, and cultural history of black Americans without understanding what happened before and after the slave trade.

Africans were great storytellers long before their first appearance in Jamestown, Virginia, in 1619. The rich and colorful history, art, and folklore of West Africa, the ancestral home of most Afro-Americans, present evidence of this, and more.

Contrary to a misconception which still prevails, the Africans were familiar with literature and art for many years before their contact with the Western world. Before the breaking up of the social structure of the West African states of Ghana, Mali, and Songhay, and the internal strife and chaos that made the slave trade possible, the forefathers of the Africans who eventually became slaves in the United States lived in a society where university life was fairly common and scholars were beheld with reverence.

There were in this ancestry rulers who expanded their kingdoms into empires, great and magnificent armies whose physical dimensions dwarfed entire nations into submission, generals who advanced the technique of military science, scholars whose vision of life showed foresight and wisdom, and priests who told of gods that were strong and kind. To understand fully any aspect of Afro-American life, one must realize that the black American is not without a cultural past, though he was many generations removed from it before his achievements in American literature and art commanded any appreciable attention.

I have been referring to the African origin of Afro-American literature and history. This preface is essential to every meaningful discussion of the role of the Afro-American in every major aspect of American life, past and present. Africans did not come to the United States culturally empty-handed.

I will elaborate very briefly on my statement to the effect that "the forefathers of the Africans who eventually became slaves in the United States once lived in a society where university life was fairly common and scholars were beheld with reverence."

During the period in West African history from the early part of the fourteenth century to the time of the Moorish invasion in 1591, the city of Timbuktu and the University of Sankore in the Songhay Empire were the intellectual center of Africa. Black scholars were enjoying a renaissance that was known and respected throughout most of Africa and in parts of Europe. At this period in African history, the University of Sankore at Timbuktu was the educational capital of the western Sudan. In his book *Timbuctoo the Mysterious*, Felix DuBois gives us the following description of this period: "The scholars of Timbuctoo yielded in nothing, to the saints in their sojourns in the foreign universities of Fez, Tunis and Cairo. They astounded the most learned men of Islam by their erudition. That these Negroes were on a level with the Arabian Savants is proved by the fact that they were installed as professors in Morocco and Egypt. In contrast to this, we find that the Arabs were not always equal to the requirements of Sankore."

I mention here only one of the great black scholars referred to in the book by Felix DuBois.

Ahmed Baba was the last chancellor of the University of Sankore. He was one of the greatest African scholars of the late sixteenth century. His life is a brilliant example of the range and depth of West African intellectual activity before the colonial era. Ahmed Baba was the author of more than forty books; nearly every one of these books had a different theme. He was in Timbuktu when it was invaded by the Moroccans in 1592, and he was one of the first citizens to protest the occupation of his beloved home town. Ahmed Baba, along with other scholars, was imprisoned and eventually exiled to Morocco. During his expatriation from Timbuktu, his collection of 1,600 books, one of the richest libraries of his day, was lost.

Now, West Africa entered a sad period of decline. During the Moorish occupation, wreck and ruin became the order of the day. When the Europeans arrived in this part of Africa and saw these conditions, they assumed that nothing of order and value had ever existed in these countries. This mistaken impression, too often repeated, has influenced the interpretation of African history for over four hundred years.

In order to understand the chapter on "Africa and the Discovery of America," it will be necessary for most students of the subject to suspend all that they think they know about the presence of the Africans in the New World. After reading Mr. Jackson's documented analysis of this little-known aspect of history, it will be difficult for anyone to hold to the old assumption that the Africans just came to the New World as slaves. This assumption will be easier to discard if we look first at the formative development of Africans at the dawn of history. We need to look again and again at this African man and see how he developed and what he contributed to himself and mankind.

In the pamphlet *African Contribution* by John M. Weatherwax (published by the Bryant Foundation of Los Angeles, California, 1964), the following information about early Africa is revealed:

> The languages spoken in Europe and America today have roots in (and may in basic respects be traced to) the languages spoken by Africans ages ago. Those early Africans made hooks to catch fish, spears to hunt with, stone knives to cut with, the bola, with which to catch birds and animals, the blow-gun, the hammer, the stone axe, canoes and paddles, bags and buckets, poles for carrying things, bows and arrows.
>
> The last few hundred thousand years of the early prehistory of mankind is called the Old Stone Age. It may have lasted half a million years.
>
> The bola, stone knives, paddles, spears, harpoons, bows and arrows, blow-guns, the hammer and the axe—all of them invented first by Africans—were the start of man's use of power.

Today's cannon, long-range missiles, ship propellers, automatic hammers, gas engines, and even meat cleavers and upholstery tack hammers have the roots of their development in the early African uses of power.

Africans gave mankind the first machine. It was the fire stick. With it, man could have fire any time. With it, a camp fire could be set up almost any place. With it, the early Africans could roast food. Every time we light a match, every time we take a bath in water heated by gas, every time we cook a meal in a gas-heated oven, our use of fire simply continues a process started by the early Africans: the control of fire.

Knives and hammers and axes were the first tools. It is the making of tools that sets man apart from and in a sense above all living creatures. Africans started mankind along the tool-making path.

Of course those early Africans were the first to discover how to make a thatched hut. They had to be the first because for hundreds of thousands of years they were the only people on earth. They discovered coarse basket-making and weaving and how to make a water-tight pot of clay hardened in a fire.

In cold weather, they found that the skins of beasts they had killed would keep them warm. They even made skin wraps for their feet. It was from their first efforts that (much later) clothing and shoes developed. We owe the early Africans much, much more.

They domesticated the dog. They used digging sticks to get at roots that could be eaten. They discovered grain as a food, and how to store and prepare it. They learned about the fermentation of certain foods and liquids left in containers. Thus, all mankind owes to Africans: the *dog* that gives us companionship and protection, the *spade* the farmer uses, the *cereal* we eat at breakfast-time, the *fermented liquids* that many people drink, the woven articles of *clothing* we wear and the *blankets* that keep us warm at night, the *pottery* in which we bake or boil food, and even the very *process* (now so simple) of *boiling water*—a process we use every time we boil an egg, or make spaghetti, or cook corned beef. Canoes made it possible for man to travel farther and farther from his early home. Over many centuries, canoes went down the Nile and the Congo and up many smaller rivers and streams. It was in this way that the early peopling of Africa took place.

From the blow-gun of ancient Africa, there followed, in later ages, many devices based on its principle. Some of these are: the bellows, bamboo air pumps, the rifle, the pistol, the revolver, the automatic, the machine gun—and even those industrial guns that puff grains.

African hunters many times cut up game. There still exist, from the Old Stone Age, drawings of animal bones, hearts and other organs. Those early drawings are a part of man's early beginnings in the field of Anatomy.

The family, the clan, the tribe all developed first in Africa. The family relationships which we have today, they fully understood then. The clan and the tribe gave group unity and strength. It was in these groups that early religious life and beliefs started.

When a great tribal leader died, he became a god to his tribe. Regard for him, appreciation of his services to the tribe, and efforts to communicate with him, became *worship*.

The first formal education was spoken tradition given during African tribal initiation ceremonies. The leaders of these ceremonies were medicine men. From their ranks the priests of following periods came. Ceremonial African ritual dances laid the basis for many later forms of the dance. Music existed in prehistoric Africa. Among instruments used were: reed pipes, single-stringed instruments, drums, gourd rattles, blocks of wood and hollow logs. Many very good prehistoric African artists brought paintings and sculpture into the common culture. The early Africans made a careful study of animal life and plant life. From knowledge of animals, mankind was able to take a long step forward to cattle raising. From the knowledge of plants and how they propagate, it was possible to take a still longer step forward to agriculture.

Today, science has ways of dating events of long ago. The new methods indicate that mankind has lived in Africa over two million years. In that long, long time, Africans and people of African descent migrated to other parts of the earth. Direct descendants of early Africans went to Asia Minor, Arabia, India, China, Japan and the East Indies. All of these areas to this day show an African strain.

Africans and people of African descent went also to Turkey, Palestine, Greece and other countries into Europe. From Gibraltar, they went into Spain, Portugal, France, England, Wales and Ireland.

Considering this information, the pre-Columbian presence of Africans in the New World is highly possible and somewhat logical.

The first Africans to be brought to the New World were not in bondage, contrary to popular belief. Africans participated in some of the earliest explorations by Spanish people into what is now the United States. The best known of these African explorers was Estevanico, sometimes referred to as Little Stephen. He accompanied Cabeza de Vaca during his six years of wandering, 1528–1530, from Florida into Mexico. In 1539, as guide to the Niza expedition, Estevanico set out from Mexico City in the party of Friar Marcos de Niza, in search of the fabled Seven Cities of Cibola. When the others wearied, Estevanico went ahead alone, except for Indian guides, and opened up to European settlers the rich land that is now Arizona and New Mexico.

There were Africans with Christopher Columbus, Balboa, and with Cortez in Mexico.

Most historians writing about the subject have attributed the civilizations of East Africa to every known people except the East Africans. Mr. Jackson's chapter, "Mariners and Merchants of the Eastern Coast," and a recent book by Basil Davidson *A History of East and Central Africa* (Doubleday, Anchor Books) will help to put some of the main historical facts in order.

The early civilizations of this part of Africa are splendid with achievements that most European writers have not been able to accept as evident African accomplishment. The influence of Islam and the Arabs in East Africa has been highly overstated. This influence was not always for the better. In fact, the Arabs, like all of the other invaders of Africa, did more harm than good. They, like the Europeans of a later day, destroyed many African cultures that they did not understand. Their role in the East African slave trade brought wreck and ruin to the nation states in this part of Africa. They were not without achievements, but their achievements are outweighed by the harm they did.

For the last five hundred years of recorded history, East Africa has had one troublesome invader after the other. Following the Arabs, the Portuguese came with a new crew of vandals.

The nations of central and southeast Africa have only recently been given some of the attention by historians that should have been given all along. There was less Arab influence in this area than in the nations of Africa further north. These nations have succeeded in keeping most of their culture intact. This is especially true of Zimbabwe, Monomotapa, and the kingdoms of the interior. The remarkable thing about these African states is that, in most cases, they had a resurgence of development in nation building and in the arts after the slave trade had already started. These were, in the main, landlocked nations that saw fit to avoid the troubles of the coastal African states.

The fall of the western Sudan (West Africa) and the beginning of the slave trade did not mark the end of great state building in Africa. During the slave trade, and in spite of it, great nations and empires continued to be created. One of the most vivid examples is the nations of East and Central Africa.

The people and nations of Central Africa have no records

of their ancient and medieval history like the "Tarikh es Sudan" or the "Tarikh el Fettach" of the western Sudan (West Africa). The early travelers to these areas are mostly unknown. In spite of the forest as an obstacle to the formation of empires comparable to those of the western Sudan, notable kingdoms did rise in this part of Africa and some of them did achieve a high degree of civilization.

The Congo Valley became the gathering place of various branches of the people we know now as Bantu. When the history of Central Africa is finally written, it will be a history of invasions and migrations. According to one account, between two and three thousand years ago, a group of tribes began to move out of the region south or southwest of Lake Chad. Sometime during the fourteenth and fifteenth centuries, the center of Africa became crowded with pastoral tribes who needed more land for their large flocks and herds. This condition started another migration that lasted for more than a hundred years. Tribes with the prefix "Ba" to their names spread far to the west into the Congo Basin and southward through the central plains. The Bechuana and Basuto were among these tribes. Tribes with the prefix "Ama"—great warriors like the Ama-Xosa and Ama-Zulu—passed down the eastern side.

In the meantime, some of the more stable tribes in the Congo region were bringing notable kingdoms into being. The Kingdom of Loango extended from Cape Lopez (Libreville) to near the Congo; and the Kongo Empire was mentioned by the Portuguese as early as the fourteenth century. The Chief of Loango, Mani-Congo, extended his kingdom as far as the Kasai and Upper Zambesi Rivers. This kingdom had been in existence for centuries when the Portuguese arrived in the fifteenth century. They spoke admiringly of its capital, Sette-Camo, which they called San Salvador. The Kingdom of Kongo dates back to the fourteenth century. At the height of its power, it extended over modern Angola, as far east as the Kasai and Upper Zambesi Rivers.

Further inland, the Kingdom of Ansika was comprised of the people of the Beteke and Bayoka, whose artistic talents were very remarkable. Near the center of the Congo was the Bakuba Kingdom (or Bushongo), still noted for its unity, the excellence of its administration, its art, its craftsmanship, and the beauty of its fabrics.

South of the Congo Basin the whole Bechuana territory formed a vast state which actually ruled for a long time over the Basutos, the Zulus, the Hottentots, and the Bushmen, including in a single empire the greater part of the black population of southern and central Africa. This was the era of Bushongo grandeur; the people we now know as Bakubas.

Only the Bushongo culture kept its records and transmitted them almost intact to modern research. The Bakubas are an ancient people whose power and influence once extended over most of the Congo. Their history can be traced to the fifth century. For many centuries the Bakubas have had a highly organized social system, an impressive artistic tradition, and a secular form of government that expressed the will of the people through a democratic political system. Today, as for many generations in the past, the court of a Bakuba chief is ruled by a protocol as rigid and complicated as that of Versailles under Louis XIV.

At the top of the Bakuba hierarchy is the royal court composed of six dignitaries responsible for cabinetlike matters such as military affairs, justice, and administration. At one time there were in the royal entourage 143 other functionaries, including a master of the hunt, a master storyteller, and a keeper of oral traditions. In the sixteenth century, the Bakubas ruled over a great African empire. The memory of their glorious past is recalled in the tribe with historical exactitude. They can name the reigns of their kings for the past 235 years. The loyalty of the people to these rulers is expressed in a series of royal portrait-statues dating from the reign of Shamba Bolongongo, the greatest and best known of the Bakuba kings.

Shamba Bolongongo was a peaceful sovereign. He prohibited the use of the shongo, a throwing knife, the traditional weapon of the Bushongo. This wise African king used to say: "Kill neither man, woman, nor child. Are they not the children of Chembe (God), and have they not the right to live?" Shamba likewise brought to his people some of the agreeable pastimes that alleviate the tediousness of life. The reign of Shamba Bolongongo was really the "Golden Age" of the Bushongo people of the southern Congo. After abolishing the cruder aspects of African warfare, Shamba Bolongongo introduced raffia weaving and other arts of peace. According to the legends of the Bushongo people, their history as a state goes back fifteen centuries. Legends notwithstanding, their magnificent sculpture and other artistic accomplishments are unmistakable, the embodiment of a long and fruitful social experience reflecting the life of a people who have been associated with a higher form of culture for more than a thousand years.

In the chapter on "The Destruction of African Culture," Mr. Jackson has dealt with some of the main reasons that African history is so misunderstood and that so many students of the subject get confused while trying to make an assessment of the available information. There has been a deliberate destruction of African culture and the records relating to that culture. This destruction started with the first invaders of Africa. It continued through the period of slavery and the colonial system. It continues today on a much higher and more dangerous level. There are now attempts on the highest academic levels to divide African history and culture within Africa in such a manner that the best of it can be claimed for the Europeans, or at the very least, Asians. That is the main purpose of the Hamitic and the Semitic hypothesis in relationship to African history. It is also one of the main reasons so much attention is being paid to the Berbers and the Arabs in Africa. There is a school of thought supporting the thesis that, if the main bodies of African history, culture, and achievement have no European origin, they must, at least, have an Asiatic origin. The supporters of this thesis have forgotten several important facts about Africa, if they ever knew them at all: mainly, the evidence of high cultures that the first invaders of Africa found and to what extent these invaders destroyed a great deal of this culture. Every invader of Africa did Africa more harm than good. They destroyed the culture that they would later say never existed at all.

In this chapter, Mr. Jackson documents the events that led to the destruction of some of the great libraries in Africa that had old and priceless manuscripts relating to African history and culture. He further documents the tragedy of the destruction of millions of African men and women in the slave trade and shows the role that the Christian church willingly played in creating the rationale that attempted to justify this event.

His concluding chapter on "Africa Resurgent" recalls the need to look again at the nineteenth-century roots of the twentieth-century African resistance movements and the role that both Africans and Afro-Americans played in bringing this movement into being.

Until near the end of the nineteenth century the African Freedom struggle was a military struggle. This aspect of African history has been shamefully neglected. I do not believe the neglect is an accident. Africa's oppressors and Western historians are not ready to concede the fact that Africa has a fighting heritage. The Africans did fight back and they fought exceptionally well. This fight extended throughout the whole of the nineteenth century. This fight was led, in most cases, by African kings. The Europeans referred to them as chiefs in order to avoid equating them with European kings. They were kings in the truest sense of the word. Most of them could trace their lineage back to more than a thousand years. These revolutionary nationalist African kings are mostly unknown because the white interpreters of Africa still want the world to think that the African waited in darkness for other people to bring the light.

In West Africa the Ashanti Wars started early in the nineteenth century when the British tried to occupy the hinterland of the Gold Coast, now Ghana. There were eleven major wars in this conflict. The Ashanti won all of them except the last one. In these wars, Ashanti generals—and we should call them generals because they were more than equal to the British generals who failed to conquer them—stopped the inland encroachment of the British and commanded respect for the authority of their kings.

In 1844, the Fanti Kings of Ghana signed a Bond of agreement with the English. This Bond brought a short period of peace to the coastal areas of the country. In the 1860's, King Ghartey, the West African reformer, advocated democratic ideas in government at a time when the democratic institutions of Europe were showing signs of deterioration. King Ghartey ruled over the small coastal kingdom of Winnebah in pre-independent Ghana. He was the driving spirit behind the founding of the Fanti Confederation, one of the most important events in the history of West Africa.

There were two freedom struggles in pre-independent Ghana. One was led by the Ashanti in the hinterland and the other was led by the Fanti who lived along the coast. The Ashantis were warriors. The Fantis were petitioners and constitution makers. The Fanti Constitution, drawn up in conferences between 1865 and 1871, is one of the most important documents produced in Africa in the nineteenth century. In addition to being the constitution of the Fanti Confederation, it was a petition to the British for the independence of the Gold Coast.

In 1896 the British exiled the Ashanti king Prempeh and still was not able to completely take over the hinterland of the Gold Coast. Fanti nationalists, led by Casely Hayford, started the agitation for the return of King Prempeh and soon converted this agitation into a movement for the independence of the country.

The stubborn British still did not give up their desire to establish their authority in the interior of the country and avenged the many defeats that they had suffered at the hands of the Ashantis.

In 1900, the British returned to Kumasi, capital of Ashanti, and demanded the right to sit on the Golden Stool. Sir Frederick Hodgson, who made the demand on behalf of the British, displayed his complete ignorance of Ashanti folklore, history, and culture. The Ashanti people cherished the Golden Stool as their most sacred possession. To them it is the Ark of the Covenant. Ashanti kings are not permitted to sit on it. The demand for the Stool was an insult to the pride of the Ashanti people and it started the last Ashanti war. This war is known as the "Yaa Asantewa War," since Yaa Asantewa, the reigning Queen Mother of Ashanti, was the inspiring spirit and one of the leaders of this effort to save the Ashanti kingdom from British rule. After nearly a year of heroic struggle, Queen Yaa Asantewa was captured along with her chief insurgent leaders. At last, the British gained control over the hinterland of the Gold Coast. To accomplish this, they had to fight the Ashanti for nearly a hundred years.

In other parts of West Africa, resistance to European rule was still strong and persistent. While the drama of Ashanti and other tribal nations was unfolding in the Gold Coast, an Ibo slave rose above his humble origin in Nigeria and vied for commercial power in the market places of that nation. In the years before the British forced him into exile in 1885, he was twice a king and was justifiably called "The Merchant Prince of West Africa." His name was Ja Ja. The story of Ja Ja is woven through all of the competently written histories of Nigeria. His strong opposition to British rule in the 1880's makes him the father of Nigerian nationalism.

In the French colonies, the two main leaders of revolts were Behanzin Hossu Bowelle, of Dahomey, and Samory Touré, of Guinea. Behanzin was one of the most colorful and the last of the great kings of Dahomey. He was one of the most powerful of West Africans during the closing years of the nineteenth century. After many years of opposition to French rule in his country, he was defeated by a French mulatto, General Alfred Dodds. He was sent into exile and died in 1906.

Samory Touré, grandfather of Sékou Touré, President of Guinea, was the last of the great Mandingo warriors. Samory is the best known personality to emerge from the Mandingos in the years following the decline of their power and empire in the western Sudan. Samory defied the power of France for eighteen years and was often referred to by the French who opposed him as "The Black Napoleon of the Sudan." He was defeated and captured in 1898 and died on a small island in the Congo River in 1900.

In the Sudan and in East Africa, two men called Dervish Warriors, Mohammed Ahmed, known as the Mahdi, and Mohammed Ben Abdullah Hassen, known as the Mad Mullah of Somaliland, were thorns in the side of the British Empire. Mohammed Ahmed freed the Sudan of British rule before his death in 1885. The country stayed free for eleven years before it was reconquered. Mohammed Ben Abdullah Hassen started his campaign against the British in Somaliland in 1899 and was not defeated until 1921.

Southern Africa has furnished a more splendid array of

warrior kings than any other part of Africa. Chaka, the Zulu
king and war lord, is the most famous, the most maligned
and the most misinterpreted of all South African kings. By
any fair measurement, he was one of the greatest natural warriors of all times. He fought to consolidate South Africa and
to save it from European rule. When he died in 1828 he was
winning that fight.

Chaka's fight was continued with varying degrees of success and failure under the leadership of kings like Moshesh of
the Basutos; Khama of the Bamangwato; Dingan, Chaka's half-
brother and successor; Cetewayo, nephew and disciple of
Chaka; Lobengula, whose father, Maselikatze, built the second
Zulu Empire; and Bambata, who led the last Zulu uprising in
1906.

What I have been trying to say is this: For a period of
more than a hundred years, African warrior nationalists,
mostly kings, who had never worn a store-bought shoe or
heard of a military school, outmaneuvered and outgeneraled
some of the finest military minds of Europe. They planted the
seeds of African independence for another generation to harvest.

At the end of the nineteenth century, some of the personalities in the African and Afro-American Freedom Struggle met
and formed an alliance. Out of this meeting of men and ideas
the Pan-African concept was born. In Africa, the warrior
nationalists gave way to the new nationalists that were now
part of the small African educated elite. These men, stimulated by many Africans in the West such as W. E. B. DuBois
and Marcus Garvey, laid the basis for the African Freedom
Explosion. This was the preface to the "Resurgence of
Africa."

This book is about the history of Africa from the origin of
man to the present time. This is not just another book on
African history. It is, in my opinion, one of the best books

that has so far been written on this subject. Mr. Jackson de-
bunks most of the standard approaches and concepts relating
to African history. His book will cause many academic feathers to fly. In spite of this, I think this book, because of what
it reveals about Africa and its role in history, is of lasting value.

John Henrik Clarke
February, 1970

Chapter One

AFRICA AND THE ORIGIN OF MAN

Before discussing the origin of man, we must briefly survey the story of the world prior to the dawn of humanity. As recently as the middle of the seventeenth century, some of our best minds argued that our world was only about six thousand years old. Archbishop James Ussher, a scholarly Irish divine, in the year 1650 wrote a book entitled *Annals of the Ancient and New Testaments*, in which he declared that Earth was created in the year 4004 B.C. A few years later, Dr. John Lightfoot, Vice-Chancellor of Cambridge University, revealed the exact date and hour of this great event. The world was created, according to Dr. Lightfoot, on October 23, 4004 B.C., at 9 o'clock in the morning.

Today modern science presents for our consideration a much more imposing view. We are now told that the world is between four and five billion years of age. As the modern astronomers gaze into the heavens with their giant telescopes, they observe stars scattered through the vast reaches of space as numerous as the grains of sand on all of the seashores of the world. The planet Earth on which we dwell is a child of the sun, and the solar orb is a quite ordinary star in a great galactic system.

A widely held theory of the origin of the world was that of Sir James Jeans. He held that, as the sun floated through space billions of years ago, it was closely approached by a larger wandering star. The gravitational pull of the passing star raised tides on the sun of such disruptive force as to cause fragments of solar matter to shoot out into space, and these bits of sun-stuff then became the planets of the solar system.

This theory, though plausible, has in recent years fallen out of favor, and has been superseded by another promulgated by

Professor Raymond Lyttleton. Astronomers have discovered huge stars scattered throughout space that sometimes become unstable and explode like giant hydrogen bombs. These stars are called supernovae, and Lyttleton thinks that one of these celestial giants was a binary partner of our sun five billion years ago. This star was destroyed by a supernova explosion. Some of the debris of this great blowup was captured by the sun, and eventually it evolved into the several planets, of which our own Earth is one. (For an interesting discussion of this hypothesis, the reader might consult *The Modern Universe*, pp. 170–74, by Raymond A. Lyttleton.)

Earth began its career as a fiery ball of gas circling around the sun, but was gradually cooled by the intense cold of interstellar space until it became a solid. In its fiery youth our world was encircled by clouds of water in the form of steam, and as the globe cooled this gaseous mantle liquefied and formed the first ocean. As Earth lost heat it began to shrink, and its crust wrinkled like the surface of a dried apple, and in these deep valleys bodies of water collected. After many ages the world reached the stage of the origin of life.

The first life forms were little blobs of a jellylike substance called protoplasm. The earliest animals were little specks of protoplasm surrounding a microscopic nucleus, each such unit being known as a cell. The primitive one-celled animal, known as the protozoan, was the progenitor of all the many-celled types, the metazoa. The first metazoa were simple forms such as sea anemones and jellyfish. They were followed by wormlike animals which evolved into mollusks, echinoderms, crustaceans, and insects.

After many eons a new group of animals spread over the world. These more advanced types were the echinoderms (starfish, sea urchins, sea lilies, etc.). From these primitive echinoderms were evolved the *Chordata*, animals possessing a notochord—a gristly cord which in later species developed into vertebrae or joints, and became the first backbone. We are not suggesting that our remote ancestors were directly evolved from starfish. What most probably happened has been well stated by Professor A. S. Romer:

No one would believe that man or any other vertebrate descended from a starfish, but the evidence from the larvae strongly suggests that long ago, in the dawn of the world, there existed some type of small, bilaterally symmetrical animal of very simple structure possessing many of the features of the larval echinoderm or acorn worm but lacking the specializations of either starfish or vertebrate groups. From these forms, . . . came the echinoderms. But from these forms, too, seem to have risen types which retained their original bilateral symmetry and which gained specialized breathing organs in the form of gill slits, better possibilities of motility with the development of a comparatively powerful musculature and a notocord for its support, and better nervous control of activity through the development of a dorsal nerve cord. From this line, we believe, came the chordates, and finally, the true vertebrates [*Man and the Vertebrates*, Vol. I, pp. 16–17, by Alfred Sherwood Romer].

In the Devonian period of the Paleozoic era, about four hundred million years ago, the dominant type of animal life was the fish. In fact the Devonian era has been called the Age of Fishes. All the land vertebrates of later ages seem to have evolved from a group of fish known as the *Crossopterygii* (lobe-finned fish). These lobefins possessed lungs as well as gills. So, when overcrowding occurred in the water, some of these fish, using their fins as rudimentary feet, took to the land, and switched over from gill breathing to lung breathing.

A branch of lobe-finned fish gave rise to the amphibians (frogs, newts, etc.); and from these came the reptiles (snakes, lizards, crocodiles, etc.). A branch of the reptiles evolved into the birds. Another branch of the reptiles became the mammals, animals that nourish their offspring with milk. The most primitive mammals were egg-laying types such as the echidna (spiny anteater) and ornithorhynchus (duck-billed platypus). From the egg-laying mammals came the marsupials (pouched animals), a good example of such being the kangaroo. One of the many branches of the marsupials evolved into the lemurs, which in turn proliferated into monkeys, apes, and men.

The evolutionary process that culminated in man covers a vast expanse of time. The earliest forms of life have been traced back to one and a half billion years. Apes and men have a common ancestry, the first apes appearing about forty million years ago. Then about twenty-five million years ago man became differentiated from the common ape stem. The first true men appeared on the stage of the world only two million years ago, a very short time in the past from a geological viewpoint.

There were many evolutionists before Darwin but, with the publication of *The Origin of Species* in 1859, Darwin made the theory of evolution intellectually respectable. The bearing of evolution on the origin of humanity was barely noted in the concluding remarks of the aforementioned work. "Much light," said the author, "will be thrown on the origin of man and his history." (*The Origin of Species*, p. 373.) In 1871 Darwin's *Descent of Man* was issued, and in this book the Father of Natural Selection produced impressive evidence that man and the anthropoid apes could be traced to a common ancestor. Most of Darwin's contemporaries favored the continent of Asia as the birthplace of the human race, but Darwin suggested that Africa was most likely to have been the Cradle of Mankind. "We are naturally led to enquire," said he, "where was the birthplace of man. . . . In each great region of the world the living mammals are closely related to the extinct species of the same region. It is therefore probable that Africa was formerly inhabited by extinct apes closely allied to the gorilla and chimpanzee; and as these two species are now man's nearest allies, it is somewhat more probable that our early progenitors lived on the African continent than elsewhere." (*Descent of Man*, p. 520.)

Until well into the present century, the scientists studying prehistoric times looked mainly to Asia as man's original home. In the year 1921, this position was boldly challenged by the publication of *The Origin and Evolution of the Human Race* by Dr. Albert Churchward. Dr. Churchward was a distinguished medical man. He was a member of both the Royal Council of Physicians and the Royal Council of Surgeons; and besides this he was an anthropologist and an archaeologist. The earliest members of the human species appeared in Central Africa two million years ago, Churchward argued. From the Great Lakes region they spread over the entire continent. Certain groups of these early men wandered down the Nile Valley, settled in Egypt, and then spread out and colonized the entire world. The first migration was of primitive little men, known as Pygmies. Afterward came waves of Nilotic Negroes who also spread out over the world. As these early Africans wandered over the world, they differentiated into the various human subspecies that now inhabit the globe. Men who remained in the tropics and the equatorial regions retained their dark complexions; those who settled in temperate zones lost some of their pigmentation and developed a fairer skin.

Dr. Churchward's theories were not favorably received by his contemporaries. An age of two million years for the human race was quite preposterous, and the good doctor was asked to present some plausible evidence that the first member of our species was an African. As we shall see presently, Dr. Churchward's stand was eventually proved to be quite sound.

The town of Taung, Bechuanaland, South Africa, is the site of a limestone quarry operated by the Northern Lime Company. Late in 1924, a workman blasting rocks in the mine was startled by having the skull of an ape fly out of debris and land at his feet. This skull was passed on to the foreman of the quarry. After this relic was turned over to interested parties, it finally reached the hands of Professor Raymond Dart, an anatomist in Johannesburg. The professor noticed that, though the skull was that of an ape, the teeth approached the human type closer than those of any other ape, living or extinct. Dart immediately wrote a paper with the title, "The First South African Manlike Ape," which was published February 7, 1925. The great worth of this discovery, Dart asserted, was that "it exhibits an extinct race of apes intermediate between living anthropoids and man"; and he labeled the newly found fossil *Australopithecus africanus* (Southern Ape of Africa). Professor Dart's claims were examined by anthropologists in London, who could see no merit in his case. These experts held that the Taung skull was that of an ordinary ape, and of no importance to students of human evolution. Then the tide began to turn in the opposite direction. There was a medical doctor from Scotland living at Maquassi, a little town near the Karoo desert. His name was Robert Broom, and he had been professor of geology and zoology at Victoria College in Stellenbosch. Besides practicing medicine, Dr. Broom pursued research on the evolution of early types of mammals. When he read Dart's paper in 1925, he traveled to Johannesburg to take a look at the *Australopithecus* skull. An examination of the fossil convinced Broom that Dart was right. He regarded it as "practically the missing link, the most important fossil find ever made." The Taung ape-man was estimated to be two million years old. That made him four times as old as the Heidelberg man and five times the age of the Java ape-man.

Broom and Dart failed to convince the other experts that their claims were valid, so they decided to go out and look for more evidence. Dr. Broom gave up his medical practice and became curator of Vertebrate Paleontology and Physical

Anthropology at the Transvaal Museum in Pretoria. When time permitted, he and Dart visited the South African Desert to hunt for fossils. In early August, 1936, two of Dart's students called on Broom and told him they had found some small baboon skulls in caves at Sterkfontein. Dr. Broom visited the caves, which were in a limestone quarry managed by G. W. Barlow. The manager was asked to look out for fossil skulls, which Dr. Broom agreed to purchase. A few days later Barlow found part of a fossil skull, and Broom, after hours of digging, located most of the rest of it. The doctor found that he had unearthed another ape-man, which he appropriately named *Plesianthropus transvaalensis* (a being from the Transvaal closely allied to man).

On a visit to the quarry in 1938, Broom was greeted by Barlow, who said: "I have something nice for you this morning," as he handed the doctor the palate of a large fossil ape-man containing one molar. A teen-age schoolboy had found the fossil, and Broom went to look for him. The boy, Gert Terblanche, aged fifteen, was found at a school he attended, and Dr. Broom found the meeting most rewarding. In the doctor's own words, the youth "drew from his trouser pocket four of the most beautiful fossil teeth ever found in the world's history. Two of the four fitted on the palate Barlow had given to me. The other two had been weathered off." Broom bought the teeth from the student and was then told of the finding of another fossil which had been hidden. Dr. Broom then asked the principal to let Gert accompany him to the site of the hidden fossil, and was told that his request could be granted only on the condition that he first give the students a lecture on fossil men. The lecture was given, then the scientist and the schoolboy went to the hiding place of the fossil. It was a jaw containing some teeth, and was in a fine state of preservation. A search was made for the rest of the fossil, and Broom finally assembled most of the left side of the skull and the right lower jaw, with many teeth in good condition. This find was a new genus of the Australopithecines, with a bigger brain and jaw, and with teeth more humanoid. The new genus was called *Paranthropus robustus* (robust near-man). Since this fossil was found on a farm near Kromdraai, we might fittingly call it the Kromdraai Man.

Broom's field work was suspended during World War II, and was not resumed until 1947. In April, 1948, another fossil find was made, the skull of an adult female *Plesianthropus*. Another species of ape-man was discovered in October at Swartkrans. This was an outsized lower jaw of an Australopithecine with large teeth, so Broom named it *Paranthropus crassidens* (coarse-toothed near-man). In 1949 Dart found a fifth species, *Australopithecus Prometheus,* at Makapansgat. On the death of Dr. Broom at age eighty-four years in 1951, his work was taken over by his assistant, Dr. John T. Robinson. Over a period of several years Robinson uncovered fossils of another species, *Telanthropus capensis*, a species more advanced than any *Australopithecus* and hence more humanoid. All five Australopithecines so far discussed are members of a single genus, consisting of two species. The four earlier types are of the species *africanus*, the later, *robustus*. Yves Coppen, a paleontologist from France, unearthed a fossil skull in June, 1961, in the Republic of Chad. It was the sixth Australopithecine, and is believed to be older than its South African relatives. This fossil skull, assigned by some scientists to the Homo habilis group, has been named *Tchadanthropus uxoris*.

These South African ape-men were closer to man than the apes, but they were probably not direct ancestors of Homo sapiens. The search for the earliest men leads us to Olduvai Gorge, in Tanzania, East Africa.

The Olduvai story began in 1911 when Kattwinkel, a German entomologist, was in East Africa searching for rare insect specimens. He wandered into the Olduvai Gorge quite by accident and observed some fossil bones embedded in the wall of a steep cliff. The bones were taken to Berlin, where paleontologists recognized them as remains of Hipparion, an ancient three-toed horse. This intelligence convinced Professor Hans Reck, a geologist of the University of Berlin, that Olduvai might be a good place to prospect for fossils. Dr. Reck journeyed to the Gorge in 1913, and his subsequent findings were nothing less than spectacular. Fossils were found of animal species in the hundreds, several of them being unknown to science. One of Reck's finds was a skeleton of Homo sapiens which he believed to be one million years old; but later investigations showed this to be an error, and the fossil is now rated as being only twenty thousand years of age. At the outbreak of World War I in 1914, Reck's party was forced to suspend operations, and explorations were not resumed for seventeen years.

When a new expedition was formed to hunt for Stone Age artifacts at the Olduvai site in 1931, the moving spirit was a paleontologist, born in Africa, a young man named Louis Leakey. His parents were English missionaries, working among the Kikuyu of Kenya, and Louis was born there in a thatched hut. He grew up among the Kikuyu, played with the children of the tribe, and spoke their language. At the age of sixteen he left for England to study anthropology and archaeology. Five years later, in 1924, he returned to Kenya and explored Stone Age sites until 1929. Then he went to Berlin and asked Professor Reck to return with him for further work at Olduvai. Since Leakey occupies the post of curator of the Coryndon Museum, in Nairobi, Kenya, he has had to limit his work at the Gorge to a seven-week period each year. Prospecting in a chasm three hundred feet in depth and twenty-five miles in length has kept him busy over the years. Fortunately his wife, Mrs. Mary Leakey, is also a paleontologist and she has made some important discoveries of her own.

In the Olduvai Gorge there are five strata of rocks. In the lowest, many stone tools of a pre-Chellean design have been found. The stratum immediately above contains fossils and artifacts of a Chellean type. Altogether Leakey and his associates found twelve distinct stages of a hand axe culture. In the search for fossil men, Olduvai for many years proved disappointing. Leakey had better luck at Kanam and Kanjera in 1932, where he found fossil skulls of Homo sapiens, of uncertain age. In 1948, Mrs. Leakey located a fossil ape on Rusinga Island in Lake Victoria. This extinct primate lived about twenty million years ago in the Miocene epoch. He has been named *Proconsul africanus*, and may be in the direct ancestry of modern man. The first big discovery at Olduvai did not come until July 17, 1959, and this was another triumph for Mary Leakey. While Professor Leakey was inactivated by illness, his wife located a skull embedded in rocks eighty-three feet from the bottom of the Gorge. The fossil was in fragments and, after nineteen days of labor, was excavated and pieced together. The skull was hominid in type, somewhat flat on top, and crowned with a bony crest like that of a gorilla. The cranial capacity was about 650 cc. This ancient man was named *Zinjanthropus boisei* by Leakey. The "Zinj" part of the name is from the Arabic name for East Africa, and the "boisei" refers to the last name of Charles Boise, one of the financial sponsors of the Olduvai explorations. That *Zinjanthropus* was a man seems to be well established. We are informed by Mr. Silverberg that:

His brain was small and his teeth were big, but he walked upright, as was indicated by the structure of his skull and proved by the leg bones Leakey found on his 1960 expedition. He used tools, he made tools, and from his cheek structure, Leakey thinks he may have had the power of speech. *Zinjanthropus'* teeth were worn down, a human but not an ape-like characteristic. He must have used his crude stone tools to dig tough gritty roots from the ground for food. He was a strange being by our standards, with his flat, almost foreheadless head, topped by its odd crest. But he seems definitely to fit into the human family—perhaps a more direct relative of Homo sapiens, it would appear, than the Australopithecines of neighboring South Africa [*Man Before Adam: The Story of Man in Search of His Origins*, p. 178, by Robert Silverberg].

The next great discovery at Olduvai was again made by Mrs. Leakey in 1960. After noticing a tooth embedded in the side of the Gorge, Mrs. Leakey dug into the earth and uncovered several parts of a skeleton. Over the next three years six additional specimens were found. The new find was dubbed *Homo habilis* (man with ability). This ancient man had an erect carriage, was about four and one-half feet tall; his cranial capacity was about 700 cc; and his dentition was of a primitive human type. He possessed hands with opposable thumbs and capable of making tools, and his feet were definitely modern in structure. He flourished between one and two million years ago, and Leakey regards him as a direct ancestor of Homo sapiens.

In an orange grove, owned by Fred Wicker, at Fort Ternan, Kenya, Leakey came across a fossil ape, which was appropriately named *Kenyapithecus wickeri* (Wicker's Kenya ape). This primate is said to have lived twelve million years ago, and he certainly would not have been a desirable neighbor. An Associated Press dispatch dated Washington, May 15, 1968, was published in the *New York Times*, May 16, 1968, with the caption SCIENTIST FINDS HAMMER 12 MILLION YEARS OLD, from which we quote the following:

A National Geographic Society scientist has unearthed evidence that a bone smashing African ancestor of man used a crude stone hammer 12 million years ago.

This would be 10 million years earlier than previous estimates of the beginning of tool-making on earth.

The society said today that the evidence was found by Dr. Louis S. B. Leakey, British anthropologist, who has made a number of notable findings concerning prehistoric man.

The announcement said that Dr. Leakey, working at Fort Ternan in Kenya, had found evidence that the prehuman Kenyapithecus wickeri apparently hammered open animal skulls and bones with a crude stone hammer.

The above intelligence should create consternation in the anthropological fraternity, for it is axiomatic that a tool-making ape would be a man. According to F. A. Brooke:

> The differentiation between what constitutes Man and ape must be considered as having taken place at that point when an ape was able with his own hands to shape wood and stone in a very crude way, so that he could make them serve for a special purpose. Thus it may be said that the first man was the first ape that made a tool. . . . These apes or ape-men, must first of all have made use of sticks which already possessed a point or edge, and in time it must have gradually dawned upon one whose brain was slightly more capable than the rest that the points and edges of these sticks and stones could be improved upon by their being chipped or scraped by another stone. If such an individual succeeded in imparting this knowledge to others, these apes would have gained a slight superiority in finding their means of subsistence over their fellow apes, so that in this way they became true men [*The Science of Social Development*, p. 11, by F. A. Brooke].

Primitive man is thought to have passed through a series of Stone Ages as he traveled on the road to civilization. There was an Eolithic, or Dawn Stone Age; then a Paleolithic, or Old Stone Age; and finally a Neolithic, or New Stone Age. When certain early men learned to make implements of metal, the pace of progress was increased. There were ages of Copper and Bronze, but the true harbinger of civilization was the Iron Age.

Professor L. S. B. Leakey has surveyed many years of achievement in an article in *Tarikh*, 1966, Vol. I, No. 3, entitled: "Man in Africa: From the Earliest Beginnings to the

Coming of Metal." (Published for the Historical Society of Nigeria by Longmans. An American edition is issued by the Humanities Press.) An instructive summary of this article has been made by Basil Davidson, from which we cite some extracts:

It now appears the earliest African "first," the development of the basic stock which fathered the most remote ancestors of man and the apes, took place in the African Eocene, generally reckoned at between 60 and 40 million years ago. This order of primates then began to split into super-families: the ancestors of men and monkeys, for example, separated from those of the lemurs. Of these super-families the one that concerns ourselves was the hominoidea, consisting of the progenitors of men, apes and gibbons. Their oldest known fossils are from Egypt, where they lived in the Oligocene more than 30 million years ago. . . .

Next we have the Miocene, between 30 and 12 million years ago; and the Miocene marks the stage of the second African "first." Then it was that the hominoidea of Africa split into four new families: three of apes, gibbons and creatures who have disappeared and a fourth which was the hominidae; and the hominidae were the ancestors of all the types of "near men" and man who developed later. According to the evidence of Kenyapithecus wickeri, now widely accepted as representing a true member of the hominidae, this happened at least 14 million years ago.

Now we are down to almost recent times, a mere handful of million years before the present. The situation two million years ago was that Africa and Asia were the home of a number of types of "near man" while Africa was also the home of another type, Homo habilis, whom Leakey (but not all his colleagues) believes to have been the ancestor of Homo sapiens. This represents Africa's third "first"; that the ancestors of Homo sapiens split away from the rest of the hominidae in East Africa about two million years ago ["Mother Africa," by Basil Davidson, in *West Africa*, no. 2611, p. 791, June 17, 1967].

The African ancestry of the human race is now generally accepted as a fact. "It is quite probable," declares Professor Ashley Montagu, "that man's immediate ancestors as a group had already lost a considerable part of the hairy coat which is characteristic of all anthropoids, indeed, of all primates. What the skin color was we cannot be sure, but since the ancestors of man were almost certainly tropical animals of African origin, they were almost equally certainly black-skinned." (*Man: His First Million Years,* p. 42, by M. F. Ashley Montagu.)

Dr. Eric Higgs of Cambridge University has made a study of the migrations of ancient men, and claims that the first man of Europe came to that continent from central and east Africa about 250,000 years ago. Professor Chester Chard, of the University of Wisconsin, has studied the routes of early men who left Africa to colonize the rest of the world, and he has concluded that there were four prehistoric migration routes from Africa to Europe. Professor Leakey has been asked if he thinks any of the early Africans reached the New World, and his answer is as follows: "It is inconceivable that man, the most curious and mobile of all animals, would not have come to America when the elephants, the tapirs and deer came from Asia. . . . Man spread out from Africa to Asia to Europe. It is inconceivable that he would stay out of America. . . . At least people should go look for remains of man before they say he wasn't in America." (From an article, "The Man Dr. Leakey Dug Up," by Jeanne Reinert, *Science Digest,* Vol. 60, No. 5, November, 1966.)

After millions of years of evolution, an ape developed into the first man. Early man was a savage, and after more than a million years of social evolution, he finally reached a stage of culture known as civilization. The next question we have to discuss is how, when, and where did all this come about?

The philosopher Thomas Hobbes was of the opinion that in primitive society there was no law or order, but instead a

condition of a "war of all against all," and as a result that the
life of the savage was "solitary, poor, nasty, brutish, and
short." But this cannot be so, for in those circumstances the
human race would become extinct. In the food-gathering
stage our early ancestors possessed a social organization and
practiced mutual aid. In the literature of anthropology there
is considerable controversy concerning the nature of the
primitive human group, but we may safely say that it was not
the family as we know it today.

In the Old Testament of the Bible the first human group,
we are told, was a married couple, Adam and Eve. This pair
and their children were the first family, and the head of the
family was Adam. In other words it was a patriarchal family.
The idea of the primacy of the patriarchy, with its male head
and a subordinate position for women, was held to be the very
foundation of human society. This theory is no longer tenable,
for we know now that the patriarchal family was not the
primal human group. The first type of family was matriarchal,
since the role of the father in procreation was unknown. Even
today, among tribes in Central Australia and the inhabitants of
the Trobriand Islands, we find people possessing no knowledge of the nature of paternity. In such a society, the father,
even if he lives with the mother, is not considered the head of
the family. In fact, in Fiji, a father and his son were not considered to be related at all. The evidence at hand points to the
conclusion that the primordial human group consisted not of
a father, mother, and their descendants, but instead, of a
mother and her descendants in the female line, since no other
line of descent was then known. This system of female
descent is known among anthropologists as "Mother-right."
The pioneer American anthropologist, Lewis Henry Morgan,
was adopted as a member by one of the tribes of the Iroquois
Indians, and he lived with these people and studied their
customs. Morgan discovered that each tribe was divided into
several clans, each of which was based on common descent in

the female line, and that members of these groups were joined together for mutual protection, and that marriage within the group was forbidden. A member of one group would have to pick a mate from another group; in other words one must marry outside his or her own group. This type of matrimony is known as exogamy (marriage outside the group). Morgan found that among the Iroquois all maternal aunts were called "mother," and all paternal uncles "father"; and Morgan later learned that this system was duplicated in tribal societies widely scattered over the world. In Hawaii a custom was observed that gave a clue to this strange practice. There a number of men, members of one exogamous group, took as wives in common a number of women of another exogamous group. The offspring resulting from this group marriage were considered as their common children. A similar marriage system had been noted by Julius Caesar among the ancient Britons. Lewis Morgan concluded that from a primitive system of promiscuity there was an evolution that led successively to group-marriage, loose monogamy, and finally the patriarchal family. The researches of Howitt, Fison, Spencer, and Gillen in Australia were corroborative of Morgan's theory. To a lesser degree Morgan is sustained by Lord Avebury (Sir John Lubbock), Dr. Jane Harrison, Rivers, and Briffault. There is, however, a group of anthropologists who take an opposing viewpoint. Westermarck, Lang, Crawley, and Malinowski have stoutly defended the priority of the patriarchal family.

In primitive society, exogamy is closely connected with another institution called totemism: a complex of ideas and practices which is sometimes erroneously described as the worship of animals. But a totem is not a god, and hence is not an object of worship. According to Professor A. C. Haddon:

Totemism, as Dr. Frazer and I understand it, in its fully developed condition, implies the division of a people into several totem-kins (or, as they are usually termed, totem-clans), each of which has one or sometimes more than one totem. The totem is usually a species of plant or animal, occasionally a natural object or phenomenon, very rarely a manufactured object. Totemism also involves the rules of exogamy, forbidding marriage between the kins. It is essentially connected with the matriarchal stage of culture (mother-right), though it passes over into the patriarchal stage (father-right). The totems are regarded as kinfolk and protectors of the kinsmen, who respect them and abstain from killing and eating them. There is thus a recognition of mutual rights and obligations between the members of the kin and their totem. The totem is the crest or symbol of the kin [*The Making of Man: An Outline of Anthropology*, pp. 363–64, edited by V. F. Calverton].

Totemism is spread widely among primitive peoples in Australia, Africa, Asia, Polynesia, and the Americas. It is, in fact, a primitive theory of evolution; since the clan members believe themselves to be descended from the totem-species. "To be descended from a crocodile or blood-brother to the crow," asserts Professor Read, "or the same as a kangaroo, must be, we think, the grotesque notion of a lunatic. We never meet people who believe such a thing; it has no stronghold in our own breasts. . . . But every student of early institutions finds it necessary to give himself some intelligible account of its nature and sources." (*Man and His Superstitions*, p. 223, by Carveth Read.) The origin of totemism seems to be connected with the regulation of the food supply. When a primitive human group adopted as a staple food a particular species of animal or plant, that species became the group totem.

A higher stage in the evolution of totemism was reached when certain clans became oversized and began to split up so as to search for more adequate food sources. The several clans, each specializing in the production of a certain staple food, gave birth to a larger aggregation, known as the tribe. As the tribe increased in size, the subdivision was repeated, eventuating in two or more intermediate groups, called "phratries" ("brotherhoods"), each consisting of two or more clans. Each clan possessed its own totem-species, and engaged in ceremonies and rites to facilitate the increase of aforesaid species; and instead of dining on its own totem it interchanged it for food productions of the other clans. This prohibition of each clan eating its own totem helped to promote the tribal integrity. Since the members of the earliest clans were people claiming common descent in the female line, the rules of exogamy insured that husbands and wives would be members of different clans, hence enabling a man and his wife's relatives to consolidate their hunting lore. "The men lived with the clan into which they married." we learn from Professor Thomson, "and were obliged to surrender their products to the clan. Thus the practice of getting husbands from other clans enabled each to extend its diet by obtaining access to foods which it did not produce itself. The initial function of exogamy was to circulate the food supply." (*Aeschylus and Athens*, p. 17, by George Thomson.)

After countless thousands of years of social evolution, primitive man advanced from savagery to barbarism. The invention of pottery enhanced the art of cooking and greatly improved the diet. The domestication of cattle increased the food supply and extended human mobility. Milk became an important addition to the diet and was of special value to growing children. Men no longer had to depend entirely on food-gathering and the chase. Woolen clothing could now be manufactured, usually by the women of the tribe, and men could travel into cooler climates. During this period our ancestors learned to cultivate certain plants for food: first, garden plants; then such staples as wheat and barley in the river valleys of the Old World, and maize in the New World. The discovery of metal-working led to great improvements in the manufacture of tools and weapons. Copper and bronze implements were much superior to those made of stone, and the

advent of iron smelting enabled man to advance from barbarism to civilization. A plentiful food supply and improved
tools permitted people to settle permanently in villages, and
at the same time resulted in a more marked division of labor
between the sexes. Men became hunters and fighters and
tenders of livestock, and plowed and sowed in the fields; while
the women worked at cooking, weaving, spinning, truck
gardening, and the rearing of the children.

When animals were first domesticated, the herds were the
common property of the clan or tribe; and, among the first
agriculturists, land was also held in common. In due time
this system of collectivism was superseded by the institution of private property. This was a momentous change; and
in many parts of the world it led to the decline of female
egalitarianism, which was succeeded by a state of male dominance. As a well-known student of social evolution has
pointed out:

> Men who had acquired private property in cattle, slaves and
> weapons inevitably sought to transmit such possessions to their
> children. This was incompatible with the existence of the
> matrilineal clan. Mother-right meant that the children belonged
> to their mother's clan, not to their fathers, and that when a
> man died, his property, in order to remain in the clan, passed
> to his nearest clan relations—e.g., his brothers and sisters, or
> his sisters' children—but not to his own children. If the proud
> father wished to leave his property to his children, mother-
> right had to go. Man's ownership of cattle, slaves and weapons
> gave him the whip hand. So in due course . . . inheritance
> was shifted to the male line. . . . At the same time, in order to
> secure the legitimacy of children, the bond of marriage was
> tightened and chastity imposed as a duty on women—not on
> men. Thus, along with private property and slavery, arose the
> patriarchal family—the man with his house, his wife, his man-
> servant, his maidservant, his ox, his ass, and everything that was
> his [*Morals in World History*, p. 20, by Archibald Robertson].

These great changes in the foundations of society brought about a new outlook in primitive thought and religion. Robertson explains:

In matrilineal societies, the deity was naturally a mother-goddess. As the tribe became patriarchal a father-god became the rule. As the primitive food-gatherers and hunters had made totems of the plants and animals on which they lived, so in agricultural communities the mother-goddess was associated with the earth that bore the crop, and the father-god with the rain that fertilized the soil. As the chief had formerly been charged with the magical multiplication of the totem, so now he was responsible for the sex-ritual that made the rain fall and the crops grow; and as of old, when his powers failed he was killed in order that a successor with unimpaired vigor might discharge his duties. . . .

These birth pangs of civilization—the passage from food-gathering to food-production, from relative peace to chronic war, from primitive communism to private property and slavery, from mother-right to father-right, from magic to religion —made a deep imprint on folklore. Hesiod, the peasant poet of ancient Greece, sang of the golden age when Kronos was king and the earth bore fruit of herself, and the tribes of men lived without toil; and how Zeus in his anger hid the means of life and sent Pandora the temptress to bring labor and sorrow into the world; and how the golden age yielded place to the ages of silver, bronze and iron, and men wronged one another and filled the earth with violence and war. Similarly, the Hebrews, following some earlier Babylonian sources, fabled that the first man and woman lived happily on the fruit of trees until man, tempted by woman, ate of the tree of knowledge; that Jahveh, lest they should be as gods, cast them out of Eden, dooming man thenceforth to sweat for his bread, and woman to bear children in sorrow and to be subject to her husband; and that the age of innocence then gave place to the age of blood and violence, the first tiller of the ground being the first murderer. (Gen. II, 4-IV). Both myths connect social disharmony with agriculture and with the wrath of a jealous father-god; both regard work as a curse; and both, having arisen in a patriarchal society, put the blame for the whole business on woman [*Morals in World History*, pp. 21–22, by Archibald Robertson].

There has been much speculation on just how man passed from savagery through barbarism to civilization. A plausible scheme was suggested by Lewis Henry Morgan in his great book, *Ancient Society*, which shall be summarized as briefly as possible:

MORGAN'S CLASSIFICATION OF CULTURE STAGES

I. *Lower Status of Savagery:* From the infancy of the human race to the knowledge of the use of fire. These early men had acquired articulate speech, led an arboreal existence, and possessed a food-gathering economy. They had stone tools, first improvised and later manufactured.

II. *Middle Status of Savagery:* From the acquisition of a fish subsistence and a knowledge of the use of fire to the invention of the bow and arrow. The social organization was based on primitive group marriage and an incipient clan.

III. *Upper Status of Savagery:* From the invention of the bow and arrow to the invention of pottery.

IV. *Lower Status of Barbarism:* From the invention of the art of pottery to the domestication of animals in the Old World; and in the New World, to the cultivation of maize and other plants by irrigation, along with the use of adobe brick and stone.

V. *Middle Status of Barbarism:* From the domestication of animals in the Eastern Hemisphere, and in the Western from the cultivation of maize and plants by irrigation, with the use of adobe brick and stone, to the invention of the art of smelting iron ore.

VI. *Upper Status of Barbarism:* From the invention of the
   process of smelting iron ore, with the use of iron tools
   to the invention of a phonetic alphabet.
VII. *Status of Civilization:* From the invention of a phonetic
   alphabet, with the use of writing, to the present time.

When Lewis Morgan published *Ancient Society* in 1877,
he thought that civilization went back only five thousand
years. We have before us, as we wind up this chapter, a
remarkable book entitled *Maps of the Ancient Sea Kings*,
by Charles H. Hapgood, F.R.G.S. The subtitle of the book
is *Evidence of Advanced Civilization in the Ice Age.* This
work is scholarly and well documented. Among the conclusions reached by Professor Hapgood are the following:

> The idea of a simple linear development of society from the
> culture of Paleolithic (Old Stone Age) through the successive
> stages of the Neolithic (New Stone Age), Bronze, and Iron
> ages must be given up. . . . We shall now assume that some
> 20,000 or more years ago, while paleolithic peoples held out in
> Europe, more advanced cultures existed elsewhere on the earth,
> and that we have inherited a part of what they once possessed,
> passed down from people to people [*Maps of the Ancient Sea
> Kings,* pp. 193–94, by Charles H. Hapgood].

We have traced the birthplace of man back to the African
continent, and have presented evidence that this momentous
event occurred about two million years ago. There is also
an impressive body of evidence pointing to Africa as the home
of the world's first civilization. The discussion of this topic
will engage our attention in the next chapter.

ERA	Age and time in millions of years ago when it began	
QUATERNARY	RECENT	By 10,000 B.C. *Homo sapiens* was widespread on the African continent, and all other forms had disappeared.
	PLEISTOCENE	[UPPER PLEISTOCENE]. NEANDERTHAL MAN. Not a direct ancestor of modern man but more advanced than the Pithecanthropines. Probably still living at the same time as early modern men. *Homo sapiens* appears in Africa.
		[MIDDLE PLEISTOCENE]. PITHECANTHROPINES (more primitive than and not direct ancestors of modern men) living in Java, China, and Africa about half a million years ago. Earliest suggestions of *Homo sapiens*.
	2-3	[LOWER PLEISTOCENE]. ZINJANTHROPUS (probably not direct ancestor of man) and HOMO HABILIS (a direct ancestor of man?) lived in Africa in this period. First known stone tools made at this time (OLDOWAN culture). Probably made by Homo habilis.
TERTIARY	PLIOCENE 12	OREOPITHECUS lived in Italy in the early Pliocene (about 10 million years ago); his family probably started in the Miocene and is now extinct.
	MIOCENE	[UPPER (later) MIOCENE]. KENYAPITHECUS WICKERI, an early member of the HOMINIDAE, lived during this period. Ancestors of men therefore are now quite separate from those of apes.
	30	[LOWER (earlier) MIOCENE]. Super-family of HOMINOIDEA now split into four or five families. The HYLOBATIDAE (gibbons); OREOPITHECIDAE (now extinct); PONGIDAE (apes); PRECONSULIDAE (family of *Proconsul* who lived in Central Africa at this time—not everywhere accepted as being a separate family); the family of HOMINIDAE (man and his close relations) may have become separate by this time or even earlier. SIVAPITHECUS AFRICANUS may have been an early Hominid.
	OLIGOCENE	Oldest known members of the primate super-family of HOMINOIDEA (family of men, apes, and gibbons), lived in Egypt during the Oligocene. This super-family seems to have split up into at least three families before the end of the period.
	40	The order of primates was beginning to split up into a number of super-families during the early Oligocene. Ancestors of men and monkeys became separate from those of lemurs.
	EOCENE 60	The earliest known members of the order of primates, the family to which men, apes, monkeys, tarsiers, and lemurs belong, lived during this period Possibly primates had already begun to develop before the Eocene.
		Before the beginning of the Eocene, life had already existed on earth for hundreds of millions of years. Mammals, warm-blooded animals that give milk to their young, had appeared and were already beginning to develop into the orders of carnivores, grazing animals, etc., that we know today. Mammals had by this time become the dominant form of large land animal.

A Time Chart showing the geological periods, their approximate dates, and the ancestors of modern man who lived in them

Chapter Two

ETHIOPIA AND THE ORIGIN
OF CIVILIZATION

The search of any large library would reveal ponderous tomes treating the history of civilization; but strangely enough the authors of these voluminous works never tell us just what they mean by the word *civilization*. Of course, we can always consult a dictionary, where we are informed that: "Civilization is a state of being civilized." This is, no doubt, true, but it is not particularly enlightening; so we shall attempt to formulate a scientifically accurate definition of civilization. We may begin by saying that civilization is a form of culture. So, it is first necessary to define culture. Speaking precisely, culture is patterned behavior. In other words, culture may be described as the patterned behavior which the individual learns, either through instruction or imitation, from other members of his social group. Culture consists of all forms of human behavior except those found among the apes. Among the forms of behavior common to man and ape are the following:

1. Impulses toward mating and parenthood.
2. The impulses to play, hunt, and explore.
3. The tendencies to imitate and show off, to attack when angry, and to take flight when frightened.
4. The desire for companionship.

The above are classified properly as noncultural activities. The forms of behavior specifically restricted to man are truly cultural activities, and they are listed below:

1. The growing of crops.
2. Domestication of other animals.
3. Cooking.
4. Weaving of clothes.

5. The use of language, which may be defined as the expression of definite ideas by means of the larynx, lips, and tongue.

Now we are in a position to give an adequate definition of civilization; for civilization is nothing more or less than literate culture. A bare definition will not help much, but the following brief but brilliant explanation of the meaning of civilization, from the pen of a distinguished social anthropologist, is most illuminating:

> A society is civilized only if it contains scholars and scientists. The scholar consolidates and clarifies the knowledge which has already been acquired, and hands it on to the scientist, who, thus provided, proceeds to experiment, and thus to the increase of knowledge. Without the torch of learning, the scientist is reduced to groping in the dark, and without the scientist to use and test the results of his learning, the scholar sinks into a barren pedantry. Thus scholarship and science, in the widest sense of these terms, are the warp and woof of civilization. And the scientist, no less than the scholar, is dependent upon the written word; not only must he be able to use the learning of the scholar, but he must be able to record the results of his own investigations. Since, then, civilization depends upon scholarship and science, and these depend upon writing, civilization can only arise where the art of writing is known [*How Came Civilization?* pp. 3–4, by Lord Raglan].

The outstanding characteristic of civilized people is that they live in cities. But before men could build cities they must have possessed hard metal tools. For countless millennia before the age of metals, men used tools of wood and stone. After the stone ages, the archaeologists inform us there were three metal ages, in the following order: (1) Copper, (2) Bronze, and (3) Iron. According to Lowie, the Copper Age may be traced back to 4000 B.C., the Bronze Age started about 3000 B.C., and the Iron Age had its beginning about

2000 B.C. But it is doubtful if this scheme has any value; for Central Africa, Polynesia, Finland, northern Russia, southern India, Australia, North America, and Japan passed over the Copper and Bronze Ages, and made the transition directly from stone to iron. Bronze, even in cultures where iron was unknown, seems to have been a luxury restricted to aristocrats, kings, and priests; the common people had to get along with implements of stone. The Iron Age was instrumental in inaugurating the rise of civilization. The bearing of iron smelting on the origin of civilization is brilliantly presented by Lewis Henry Morgan as follows:

> When the barbarian, advancing step by step, had discovered the native metals and learned to melt them in the crucible and to cast them in moulds; when he had alloyed native copper with tin and produced bronze; and finally, when by a still greater effort of thought he had invented the furnace, and produced iron from the ore, nine-tenths of the battle for civilization was gained. Furnished with iron tools, capable of holding both an edge and a point, mankind were certain of attaining to civilization. The production of iron was the event of events in human experience, without a parallel, and without an equal, beside which all other inventions and discoveries were inconsiderable, or at least subordinate. Out of it came the metallic hammer and anvil, the axe and chisel, the plow with an iron point, the iron sword; in fine the basis of civilization, which may be said to rest upon this metal. The want of iron tools arrested the progress of man in barbarism. There they would have remained to the present hour, had they failed to bridge the chasm. It seems probable that the conception and process of smelting iron ore came but once to man. It would be a singular satisfaction could it be known to what tribe and family we are indebted for this knowledge, and with it for civilization [*Ancient Society*, p. 43, by Lewis Henry Morgan].

Evidence collected since the days of Morgan seems to point to central Africa as the place of origin of the Iron Age.

The following opinion is from the pen of an eminent American anthropologist, Professor Alexander F. Chamberlain:

> The question of the origin of the art of iron-smelting is now being treated in detail by ethnologists, and while general agreement has not been reached, the mass of evidence so far disclosed has convinced eminent men of science like Boas and Von Luschan that the smelting of iron was first discovered by the African Negroes, from whom, by way of Egypt and Asia Minor, this art made its way into Europe and the rest of the Old World ["The Contribution of the Negro to Human Civilization," *Journal of Race Development*, April, 1911, by Professor A. F. Chamberlain].

Professor Franz Boas, the Nestor of American anthropologists, was firmly convinced of the priority of Africa in iron culture. "Neither ancient Europe, nor ancient Western Asia, nor ancient China knew Iron," Boas declares, "and everything points to its introduction from Africa. At the time of the great African discoveries toward the end of the past century, the trade of the blacksmith was found all over Africa, from north to south and from east to west. With his simple bellows and a charcoal fire he reduced the ore that is found in many parts of the continent and forged implements of great usefulness and beauty." (Atlanta University Leaflet, No. 19.)

The Belgian anthropologist, Emil Torday, in Vol. XLIII of the *Journal of the Royal Anthropological Institute*, has noted that a piece of iron, possibly a tool, was found wedged in the masonry of the Great Pyramid of Egypt. Of this fact we feel quite certain. Our late friend, Mr. J. A. Rogers, member of the Paris Anthropological Society, when visiting Egypt some years ago, climbed to the top of the Great Pyramid and he observed this fragment of iron, lodged between two stone blocks of this great ancient structure. That iron tools were used by the ancient Egyptians in building the Great Pyramid is stated as a fact by Herodotus. In statements of fact we may safely rely on the judgment of the "Father of History."

"The writings of Herodotus (c. 480–425 B.C.)," asserts Professor Alfred C. Haddon, "are a veritable storehouse of information from the highest civilizations down to the veriest savagery, and his work has lost none of its freshness or value through the lapse of time. As a matter of fact, modern investigations, carried out in the areas treated of by him, more frequently confirm and amplify rather than refute his statements." (*History of Anthropology*, pp. 100–1, by Alfred C. Haddon.)

Some archaeologists believe that the civilization of Egypt is the oldest in the world, while others give that priority to western Asia or India. It has also been suggested that, since all these cultures possess certain points of similarity, all of them may have evolved from an older common civilization. This possibility has been conceded by men of outstanding scholarship. The following opinion was expressed by an eminent Orientalist:

"It would be wrong to say that the Egyptians borrowed from the Sumerians or the Sumerians from the Egyptians, but it may be submitted that the literati of both peoples borrowed their theological systems from some common but exceedingly ancient source. . . . The similarity between the two companies of gods is too close to be accidental." (*From Fetish to God in Ancient Egypt*, p. 155, by Sir E. A. Wallis Budge.)

A pioneer American Egyptologist advanced the following view:

In both Babylonia and Egypt the convenient and basic number (360), of fundamental importance in the division of the circle, and therefore in geography, astronomy and time-measurement, had its origin in the number of days in the year in the earliest known form of the calendar. While its use seems to be older in Egypt than in Babylonia, there is no way to determine with certainty that we owe it exclusively to either of these two countries. A common origin older than either is possible [*Time and Its Mysteries,* pp. 69–70, by Professor James Henry Breasted].

"It may be," to cite an English scholar, "as some indeed suspect, that the science which we see at the dawn of recorded history, was not science at its dawn, but represents the remnants of the science of some great and as yet untraced civilization. Where, however, is the seat of that civilization to be located?" (Brigadier-General J. W. S. Sewell, in *The Legacy of Egypt,* p. 15. Edited by S. R. K. Glanville, Oxford, 1942.)

A number of scholars, both ancient and modern, have come to the conclusion that the world's first civilization was created by a people known as the Ethiopians. The name "Ethiopian" we owe to the ancient Greeks. When the Greeks came in contact with the dusky inhabitants of Africa and Asia, they called them the "burnt-faces." The Greek word for burnt was *Ethios* and the word for face was *ops.* So *ethios* plus *ops* became Ethiopian. The Greeks reasoned that these people developed their dark complexion because they were closer to the sun than were the fairer inhabitants of Europe. According to a well-informed modern authority:

The fame of the Ethiopians was widespread in ancient history. Herodotus describes them as "the tallest, most beautiful and long-lived of the human races," and before Herodotus, Homer, in even more flattering language, described them as "the most just of men; the favorites of the gods." The annals of all the great early nations of Asia Minor are full of them. The Mosaic records allude to them frequently; but while they are described as the most powerful, the most just, and the most beautiful of the human race, they are constantly spoken of as black, and there seems to be no other conclusion to be drawn, than that at that remote period of history the leading race of the

Western world was a black race [*A Tropical Dependency*, p. 221, by Lady Lugard].

According to Homer and Herodotus, the inhabitants of the following territories were Ethiopians:

1. The Sudan.
2. Egypt.
3. Arabia.
4. Palestine.
5. Western Asia.
6. India.

(See *A History of Ethiopia*, Vol. I. pp. 1–2, by Sir E. A. Wallis Budge.)

The Ethiopians are currently thought of as being exclusively an African people, but the case was quite different in ancient times. An instructive discussion of this matter has been presented by a recognized modern authority on Ethiopian history, which we cite:

It seems certain that classical historians and geographers called the whole region from India to Egypt, both countries inclusive, by the name of Ethiopia, and in consequence they regarded all the dark-skinned and black peoples who inhabited it as Ethiopians. Mention is made of Eastern and Western Ethiopians, and it is probable that the Easterners were Asiatics and the Westerners Africans. In the present work which I have called "A History of Ethiopia," I have made no attempt to describe the history of that large portion of the earth's surface which the Greeks called Ethiopia, but only that comparatively small section of it which is today named, both by large numbers of Orientals and by Europeans generally, Abyssinia, and also of the country of Kush, which is now known as Nubia. . . .

The identification of Kush with Abyssinia under the name

of Ethiopia made by the translators of the Ethiopic version of the Bible in the 5th (or 6th) century, has, for many centuries been accepted by the Abyssinians. And to this day the Abyssinian, in reciting Psalm LXVIII (V. 31), says "Ethiopia shall make her hands reach unto God."

During the preparation of this work I have been driven to the conclusion that the Ethiopians whose manners and customs have been so fully described by Herodotus, Diodorus, Strabo, Pliny and others were not Abyssinians at all, but the natives of Upper Nubia and the Island of Meroe, and the Negroes and Negroid peoples who inhabited the hot, moist lands which extend from Southern Abyssinia to the Equator. . . . The hieroglyphic inscriptions of the VI, XII and XVIII Dynasties prove that caravans travelled from Egypt to the countries round about the Blue Nile, and to regions much further to the south, but there is no mention in them of any country which can be identified with Abyssinia proper. In fact, the Egyptian inscriptions cannot be said to yield any direct information about the real Abyssinia, or its peoples, and even the Nubian and Meroitic inscriptions throw very little light upon the history of the period in which they were written. From the cuneiform inscriptions we can expect no information about Abyssinia, though both the Assyrians and the Hebrews knew of the existence of the country of Kush, and that it lay to the south of Egypt [*A History of Ethiopia*, Vol. I, pp. vii and viii, by E. A. Wallis Budge].

Professor Thomas Henry Huxley thought that the Egyptians and the Dravidians of India could be traced back to a belt of dark-brown men stretching from India to Spain in ancient times. According to Wells, "this race of brunet-brown folk, spread even farther than India; they reached to the shores of the Pacific and they were everywhere . . . the beginners of what we call civilization. It is possible that these Brunet peoples are so to speak the basic peoples of our modern world." (*The Outline of History*, p. 139, by H. G. Wells, New York, 1940.)

This peculiar development of the Neolithic culture [adds Wells] which Elliot Smith called the Heliolithic (Sun-stone) culture included many or all of the following odd practices: (1) circumcision, (2) the queer custom of sending the father to bed when a child is born, known as couvade, (3) the practice of massage, (4) the making of Mummies, (5) Megalithic monuments (i.e., Stonehenge), (6) artificial deformation of the heads of the young by bandages, (7) tattooing, (8) religious association of the Sun and the Serpent, and (9) the use of the symbol known as the Swastika for good luck. . . . Where one occurs, most of the others occur. They link Brittany with Borneo and Peru. But this constellation of practices does not crop up in the primitive home of the Nordic or Mongolian peoples, nor does it extend southward much beyond Equatorial Africa.

For thousands of years from 15,000 to 1,000 B.C., such a heliolithic neolithic culture and its brownish possessors may have been oozing around the globe through the warmer regions of the world, drifting by canoes often across wide stretches of sea. . . . It migrated slowly age by age. It must have been spreading up the Pacific coast and across the island stepping stones, to America long after it had passed on into other developments in its areas of origin.

. . . The first civilizations in Egypt and the Euphrates-Tigris Valley probably developed directly out of this widespread culture [*The Outline of History*, pp. 141–43].

The theory of the Ethiopian origin of civilization has been discussed by many scholars, both ancient and modern. The French historian, Professor Charles Seignobos, in his scholarly *History of Ancient Civilization* argued that the first civilized inhabitants of the Nile and Tigris-Euphrates Valleys were a dark-skinned people with short hair and prominent lips; and they were called Kushites (Ethiopians) by some scholars, and Hamites by others. Africa is generally recognized as the original home of the Ethiopian culture, but there have been students of ancient history who thought that the Asiatic

Ethiopians possessed a better claim to priority in the history of civilization.

An English scholar and gentleman of the early nineteenth century wrote a ponderous two-volume work of amazing erudition, entitled *Anacalypsis*; and it is subtitled *An Attempt to Draw Aside the Veil of the Saitic Isis; or an Inquiry into the Origin of Languages, Nations and Religions.* The author of this unusual book was Godfrey Higgins, who was a Fellow of both the Royal Asiatic Society and the Royal Astronomical Society. The book was published in a limited edition in London, in 1836. Fortunately for students of the present day a new edition was issued by University Books of New Hyde Park, New York, in 1965. In Volume I, Book I, Chapter IV, of *Anacalypsis*, Higgins discusses "Two Ancient Ethiopias" and he says to the reader: "I shall, in the course of this work, produce a number of extraordinary facts, which will be quite sufficient to prove, that a black race, in very early times, had more influence of the affairs of the world than has been lately suspected; and I think I shall show, by some very striking circumstances yet existing, that the effects of this influence have not entirely passed away." (*Anacalypsis*, Vol. I, p. 51, by Godfrey Higgins.) Higgins's researches led him to the conclusion that the Asiatic Ethiopians of India were the founders of the world's most ancient civilization.

Another book on the Ethiopian origin of civilization was published by Harper & Bros. of New York in 1869. The title of this work was: *Pre-Historic Nations; or Inquiries concerning some of the Great Peoples and Civilizations of Antiquity, and their probable relation to a still older civilization of the Ethiopians or Cushites of Arabia*, by John D. Baldwin, Member of the American Oriental Society. Baldwin was well abreast of the scholarship of his day, and his book is still worth consulting. His study of Arab history led him to a conclusion, best expressed in his own words:

At the present time Arabia is inhabited by two distinct races, namely descendants of the old Adite, Kushite, or Ethiopian race, known under various appellations, and dwelling chiefly at the south, the east, and in the central parts of the country, but formerly supreme throughout the whole peninsula; and the Semitic Arabians—Mahomet's race—found chiefly in the Hejaz and at the north. In some districts of the country these races are more or less mixed, and since the rise of Mahometanism the language of the Semites, known to us as Arabic, has almost wholly superseded the old Ethiopian or Kushite tongue; but the two races are very unlike in many respects, and the distinction has always been recognized by writers on Arabian ethnology. To the Kushite race belongs the purest Arabian blood, and also that great and very ancient civilization whose ruins abound in almost every district of the country [*Pre-Historic Nations*, pp. 73–74, by John D. Baldwin].

That there was an Ethiopian element in ancient Arabia we have no doubt, although Baldwin offered no evidence that Arabia was the original home of the Ethiopians. A more objective opinion has been offered by Dr. Bertram Thomas, formerly Prime Minister to the Sultan of Muscat and Oman. He notes that:

Thousands of inscriptions have been collected in southwest Arabia. . . . They are in a character which resembles Ethiopic and is not related to the Arabic character which indeed, it antedates by a thousand years. . . . The languages of Ethiopia and of the southern kingdoms were, moreover kindred languages, and there was trade and other intercourse between these peoples . . . if indeed the two peoples were not of kindred origin, neither perhaps "Arab" in the familiar sense of the word [*The Arabs*, pp. 13–14, by Bertram Thomas].

In an appendix to the work just cited, the author discourses on the racial origins of the Arabs. Basing his conclusions on the researches of Sir Arthur Keith, who studied Arab skeletal remains, ancient and modern, Dr. Thomas states:

> The original inhabitants of Arabia . . . were not the familiar Arabs of our own time, but a very much darker people. A protonegroid belt of mankind stretched across the ancient world from Africa to Malaya. This belt, by environmental and other evolutionary processes, became in parts transformed, giving rise to the Hamitic peoples of Africa, to the Dravidian peoples of India, and to an intermediate dark people inhabiting the Arabian peninsula. In the course of time two big migrations of fair skinned peoples came from the north, one of them, the Mongoloids, to break through and transform the dark belt of man beyond India; the other, the Caucasoids, to drive a wedge between India and Africa [*The Arabs,* p. 339].

The ancient peoples of Mesopotamia are sometimes called the Chaldeans, but this is inaccurate and confusing. Before the Chaldean rule in Mesopotamia there were the flourishing empires of the Sumerians, Akkadians, Babylonians, and Assyrians. The earliest civilization of this region was established by the Sumerians. They are designated in the Assyrio-Babylonian inscriptions as the blackheads or black-faced people, and they are shown on the monuments as beardless and with shaven heads. This clearly distinguishes them from the Semitic Babylonians, who are depicted with beards and long hair. About four thousand years B.C. the Sumerians had attained a high level of civilization in southern Babylonia. They tilled the soil, practiced irrigation, erected cities, reared cattle, and invented a system of writing which they bequeathed to their Semitic successors. The Sumerians indubitably builded well, for none of the future cultures of Mesopotamia ever surpassed them in the various arts and sciences.

"Babylonian science," says Briffault, "was exactly as far advanced in the nebulous dawn of Sumerian culture as it was nearly four thousand years later when the Greeks came to gather up its crumbs. Not a single aspect or feature of Babylonian civilization shows in the course of the thousands of years of its supremacy the slightest indication of advance or development." (*Rational Evolution*, p. 49, by Robert Briffault.)

The Chaldean star-gazers made a creditable use of their Sumerian scientific heritage, for they cultivated a highly advanced system of mathematical astronomy. "There is said to be distinct evidence," Canon Rawlinson tells us, "that they observed the four satellites of Jupiter and strong reason to believe that they were acquainted likewise with the seven satellites of Saturn." (*The Five Great Monarchies of the Ancient Eastern World*, Vol. II, p. 577, by George Rawlinson.) Shortly before 500 B.C., the astronomer Naburiannu calculated the length of the solar year with great precision. His result was 365 days, 6 hours, 15 minutes, and 41 seconds. He made the year only 26 minutes and 55 seconds too long. Kidinnu, the last great Chaldean astronomer, who lived about 400 B.C., predicted eclipses so accurately that modern astronomers did not surpass him until about seventy-five years ago.

Tracing these Sumerians back to their origin is a problem that has engaged the attention of a number of scientists. Professor George A. Dorsey believed that the original Sumerians came from the Elamite Hills to the east of Mesopotamia. "If they lived today we should probably call them Arabs; but if they lived in Afghanistan, we should call them Afghans, perhaps they were prehistoric Mongols." (*The Story of Civilization*, p. 315, by George A. Dorsey.)

If the Sumerians were a colony of Elamites, as Dorsey suggests, then they were not very likely Mongoloids. More probably they were of an Ethiopic ethnic type. This seems to have been the opinion of Sir Harry Johnston. "The Elamites of Mesopotamia," according to Johnston, "appeared to have been a Negroid people with kinky hair, and to have transmitted this racial type to the Jews and Syrians. There is a curliness of the hair, together with a Negro eye and full lips in the portraiture of Assyria which conveys the idea of an evident Negro element in Babylonia." (*The Negro in the New World*, p. 27, by Harry H. Johnston.)

The opinions of Johnston are reinforced by archaeological finds. "The Assyrians themselves are shown," says Poole, "to have been of a very pure type of Semites, but in the Babylonians there is a sign of Kushite blood. . . . There is one portrait of an Elamite king on a vase found at Susa; he is painted black and thus belongs to the Kushite race." (Cited by Professor A. C. Haddon in his *History of Anthropology*, p. 6.)

The myths, legends, and tradition of the Sumerians point to the African Ethiopia as the original home of these people. (See Professor W. J. Perry's *The Growth of Civilization*, pp. 60–61.) The first Sumerian remains were unearthed by Hincks, Oppert, and Rawlinson in the middle of the nineteenth century. Sir Henry Rawlinson called these people Kushites; the name *Sumerian* we owe to a French Orientalist, Professor Julius Oppert. Rawlinson anticipated Perry by tracing the Sumerians back to Ethiopia and Egypt. The following extract is condensed from Sir Henry Rawlinson's "Essay on the Early History of Babylonia":

> Without pretending to trace up these early Babylonians to their original ethnic sources, there are certainly strong reasons for supposing them to have passed from Ethiopia to the Valley of the Euphrates shortly before the opening of the historic period:
>
> 1. The system of writing which they brought with them has the closest affinity with that of Egypt; in many cases indeed, there is an absolute identity between the two alphabets.
>
> 2. In the Biblical genealogies, Kush, (Ethiopia) and Mizraim (Egypt) are brothers, while from the former sprang Nimrod (Babylonia).

3. In regard to the language of the primitive Babylonians, the vocabulary is undoubtedly Kushite or Ethiopian, belonging to that stock of tongues which in the sequel were everywhere more or less mixed up with the Semitic languages, but of which we have probably the purest modern specimens in the Mahra of Southern Arabia and the Galla of Abyssinia.

4. All the traditions of Babylonia and Assyria point to a connection in very early times between Ethiopia, Southern Arabia and the cities on the Lower Euphrates [*The History of Herodotus*, Book I, Appendix, Essay VI, translated by George Rawlinson, with essays and notes by Sir Henry Rawlinson and Sir J. G. Wilkinson].

Dr. H. R. Hall, of the Department of Egyptian and Assyrian Antiquities, the British Museum, felt certain that the Sumerians were Dravidian migrants from India. His views, quoted below, are worthy of careful consideration:

The Sumerian culture springs into our view ready made. . . . We have no knowledge of the time when the Sumerians were savages; when we first meet with them in the fourth millennium B.C., they were already a civilized metal-using people, living in great and populous cities, possessing a complicated system of writing, and living under the government of firmly established civil and religious dynasties and hierarchies . . . the ethnic type of the Sumerians, so strongly marked in the statues and reliefs, was as different from those of the races which surrounded them as was their language from those of the Semites, Aryans or others; they were decidedly Indian in type. The face-type of the average Indian of today is no doubt much the same as that of his Dravidian race-ancestor thousands of years ago. . . . And it is to this Dravidian ethnic type of India that the ancient Sumerian bears most resemblance, so far as we can judge from his monuments. . . . And it is by no means improbable that the Sumerians were an Indian race which passed, certainly by land, perhaps also by sea, through Persia to the Valley of the Two Rivers. It was in the Indian home (perhaps the Indus Valley) that we suppose for them that their culture developed [*The Ancient History of the Near East*, pp. 172-74, by H. R. Hall].

Men of almost every shade of color can be found in modern India; but the early inhabitants of India were black. Their descendants survive in Central India today. They have Negroid features, dark skin, and woolly hair. The ancient Indians are described by Professor Lynn Thorndike as "short, black men with almost Negro noses." (*Short History of Civilization*, p. 227.) Dr. Will Durant pictures these early Hindus as "a dark-skinned, broad-nosed people whom, without knowing the origin of the word, we call Dravidians." (*Our Oriental Heritage*, p. 396.) The first great civilization of India was established by these Asiatic Ethiopians in the Indus Valley. They built large cities; the principal ones being Mohenjo Daro, Chanhu Daro, and Harappa. Their cities were well built: Mohenjo Daro was two square miles in area, with regularly laid out main and side streets, lined with attractive two-story brick houses. Bathrooms were common, and they were fitted out with runaway drains leading to brick sewers which were laid under the streets. This culture reached its peak about 3000 B.C. These people had domesticated cattle, sheep, and elephants; they cultivated wheat and cotton, possessed boats and wheeled carts, and were skillful workers in bronze and iron. They even discovered a process for making iron rustproof. There is still standing in India a pillar of stainless steel, and after three thousand years there is no sign of rust on its surface.

"The megalith builders in India," states Professor W. J. Perry, "made one great discovery. They found lying about on the surface in great quantities, in Hyderabad and elsewhere, iron of such a quality that it practically constituted a natural steel. In fact, it was of this iron that Damascus blades were made. . . . The craft of iron working was, in time, carried further east, so that we find the peoples of the East Indian Archipelago, which may be called Indonesia for short, working iron, in Borneo, Celebes, and elsewhere, they having in the case of Celebes, learned the craft from wonderful strangers who built megalithic monuments, and therefore belonged to the archaic civilization" [*The Growth of Civilization*, p. 108, by W. J. Perry]. The Indus Valley civilization was in a way unique. These people seem not to have had priest-kings like the Egyptians and Sumerians. Evidently there was no great centralization of power. The largest building unearthed in the ruins of Mohenjo Daro was not a temple or palace, but a public bath. The reader is advised to consult pages 659–66, of the second edition of Sir John Hammerton's *Wonders of the Past*, in which there is an instructive article, with fine illustrations, by S. G. Blaxland Stubbs, entitled "Wonder Cities of Most Ancient India."

The early Aryan literature of India [says Mr. Stubbs], the hymns of the Rigveda, which, it is commonly agreed, date from about 1000 B.C., speak of the people whom the proud Aryan invaders found in India as black-skinned barbarians, Dasas or slaves. But Aryan pride of race has received something of a shock from the archaeological investigations carried out by Sir John Marshall, and more recently by Dr. E. Mackay in the valley of the Indus. Here ample evidence has been found of a race whose complex civilization and high culture were equal, and in some respects superior to those of earlier Mesopotamia and Egypt.

The first civilization of Europe was established on the island of Crete. It is sometimes called the Minoan culture, after King Minos, an early legendary ruler of the island. The ancestors of the Cretans were natives of Africa, a branch of the western Ethiopians. They dwelt in the grasslands of North Africa before that area dried up and became a great desert. As the Saharan sands encroached on their homeland, they took to the sea, and in Crete and neighboring islands set up a maritime culture. According to Sir Arthur Evans, cultural influences were reaching Crete from beyond the Libyan Sea before the beginning of the Egyptian dynasties. Around 1700 B.C. this civilization reached its zenith. From their capital at Knossos, the Sea Kings of Crete ruled over a region which had become the cultural center of the eastern Mediterranean.

The seat of these kings was the Broad Palace of Minos, in Knossos. It was a huge building, five stories high, spread over an area of four acres. On the walls of its numerous rooms were beautiful frescoes and mosaics of high artistic merit. In this structure were bathrooms, with terra cotta baths, fitted with drains that were a revelation to the archaeologists who discovered them. These drains were constructed of faucet-jointed pipes superior to anything known in ancient Rome; and they were not surpassed in modern times until the middle of the nineteenth century. The Palace of Minos contained a throne room, a chapel, storerooms, living quarters, and amusement halls.

There were no walls around the city of Knossos, so the island must have enjoyed security from outside interference. Throughout Crete were attractive and comfortable homes, well-constructed ports, and fine, paved roads. The Minoan mariners were dominant in the Aegean Sea, and carried on a flourishing trade with Egypt, Sicily, and southern Italy. The people had considerable leisure time, so they engaged in music, dancing, theatricals, athletic contests, and other forms of entertainment. The social organization was based on the equality of the sexes, since women enjoyed the same rights and privileges as men. There was no powerful priesthood. The gods were worshiped in caves, or on hilltops, or at domestic shrines, but there were no temples. Around 1400 B.C., this splendid culture was laid in ruins by an invasion of semi-barbarous Greeks from the north. Upon the ruins of this Cretan culture the Greeks in later times built their own civilization. These Greeks were the first civilized white people.

This last statement may seem odd to the reader, but it is factual beyond all dispute. According to the late Professor Breasted, the Ethiopians, Egyptians, Sumerians, Dravidians, and Minoans were all members of a Great White Race; but this propaganda is quite groundless.

The position of the best modern scholarship was expressed by Joseph McCabe. "The accident of the predominance of white men in modern times," McCabe declared, "should not give us supercilious ideas about color, or persuade us to listen to superficial theories about the innate superiority of the white-skinned man. Four thousand years ago, when civilization was already one or two thousand years old, white men were just a bunch of semi-savages on the outskirts of the civilized world. If there had been anthropologists in Crete, Egypt and Babylonia, they would have pronounced the white race obviously inferior, and might have discoursed learnedly on the superior germ-plasm or glands of colored folks." (*Life Among the Many Peoples of the Earth*, p. 26, by Joseph McCabe.)

In another monograph Mr. McCabe is even more explicit on this issue: "It was neither Semites nor Aryans who first advanced from barbarism to civilization. It was a race, already civilized, which by some oversight doubtless had no representatives in the Ark. Six thousand years ago it had settled in four centers, Crete, Egypt, Mesopotamia, and Western India. . . . It was not a white but a dusky-skinned race." (*Lies and Bunk about Racial Superiority*, p. 5, by Joseph McCabe.) McCabe's position has been vigorously sustained by the anthropologist Lord Raglan. In the words of his Lordship:

> Assertions that people with black skins, for example, are less intelligent, less energetic, or more excitable than people with skins of other colors, are the result either of generalizations from inadequate data, or of wishful thinking. Differences in individual ability, most probably inherited, are found everywhere, but there is no evidence of racial abilities or disabilities.

Civilization is often thought of as associated with the possession of a white skin, and it is forgotten that the founders of
civilization were brown-skinned, many of whom were at a
fairly high stage of civilization at a time when the whites were
completely barbarous. . . . The whites were, it seems, incapable of civilizing themselves, but the Aryans in India, and the
Greeks, acquired culture from the Asiatics, and the Greeks
gradually transmitted it to the rest of Europe ["Anthropology
and the Future of Civilization," an article by Lord Raglan,
in *The Rationalist Annual*, 1946, pp. 39-40].

The ancient Egyptians, as we have already noted, were
considered by scholars of ancient Greece and Rome as Ethiopians. The African origin of the Egyptians and their culture
has been regarded as a theoretically sound proposition by
many modern scholars; and to name a few we mention Count
Volney, author of *The Ruins of Empires*, and a pioneer
orientalist; General Sir Henry Rawlinson, the "Father of
Assyriology"; Professor Arnold Herman Ludwig Heeren, an
historical scholar of great erudition; Gerald Massey, famous
as a social reformer, poet, philologist, and Egyptologist, and
author of *A Book of the Beginnings*, 2 vols., 1881; *The Natural Genesis*, 2 vols., 1883; and *Ancient Egypt*, 2 vols., 1907;
and last, but not least, Dr. Albert Churchward, distinguished
as a physician, surgeon, anthropologist, and archaeologist. His
principal books are *The Signs and Symbols of Primordial
Man*, 2nd edition, London, 1913; *The Origin and Evolution
of the Human Race*, London, 1921; and *The Origin and Evolution of Religion*, London, 1924. Since the Egyptian culture
will be surveyed in the next chapter, we do not propose to discuss it extensively at this point, but we are appending some ex-
cerpts from Heeren's *Historical Researches: African Nations*,
concerning the Ethiopian influence on Egypt:

The ancient civilization of Egypt spread, as we know from
south to north, and . . . there is seemingly no doubt that the

earliest center of civilization in Africa was the country watered by the Upper Nile. . . . The principal state of this Ethiopian country bore the well-known name of Meroe. . . . This is not the place, nor am I competent to discuss the arguments which form the ground of belief that the civilization of Meroe precedes that of Egypt. It is enough to say very briefly that on the site of the City of Meroe, there exist remains of temples and pyramids from which archaeologists have drawn the conclusion that the pyramids were a form of architecture native to Meroe, and only afterwards brought to perfection in Egypt. . . . The carvings of the monuments of Meroe show a people in possession of the arts and luxuries of civilization and having some knowledge of science. On the base of one of the monuments a zodiac has been found. . . . This remarkable spot is regarded by the ancients as the cradle of the arts of science, where hieroglyphic writing was discovered and where temples and pyramids had already sprung up while Egypt still remained ignorant of their existence [*Historical Researches: African Nations*, by A. H. L. Heeren, cited by William H. Ferris, in *The African Abroad*, Vol. I, pp. 492–93].

Colonel Alexandre Braghine, a contemporary archaeologist who has traveled widely over the world, is in general agreement with Professor Heeren:

The most interesting hypothesis concerning the origin of the Egyptians and their culture is the Ethiopian one. . . . Diodorus affirms that the ancient Egyptians took their hieratic writing, sculpture and some of their other knowledge from the Ethiopians. The Ethiopians themselves have a tradition supporting this statement. Theophrastes, in his biography of the famous magician Apollonius of Tyana, relates that the latter, after his education in India and Egypt, came to Ethiopia in order to enlarge his knowledge by learning from the Ethiopian mystagogues. The same Apollonius, according to Theophrastes, claimed that Pythagoras learned from Egyptian priests only what the latter themselves had learned from the Ethiopians. Very possibly the prehistoric Ethopian culture was superior to that of their neighbors [*The Shadow of Atlantis,* pp. 213–14, by Colonel Alexandre Braghine].

Colonel Braghine also believes that the ancient Ethiopians were in some way related to the lost continent of Atlantis. This is by no means a novel hypothesis, and we shall have something to say about it. The Greek historian, Proclus, tells of the visit of a certain Krantor to the Temple of Neith in Sais, a famous Egyptian city. The priests showed Krantor columns of hieroglyphs telling the story of Atlantis and its peoples. Proclus cited as another authority on the history of Atlantis, *The Ethiopian History* of an ancient writer named Marcellus. Skylax of Karyanda, a famous Carian navigator, told of how Phoenician mariners traded with the Ethiopians of the Island of Cerne, in the Atlantic Ocean. At a later time Diodorus Siculus specifically stated that western Ethiopia was inhabited by Atlanteans. The German scholar, Eugen Georg, a keen student of the Atlantis question, seems to think that the Atlanteans were Ethiopians, for he tells us, "The new age that began after the disappearance of Atlantis was marked at first by the world-wide dominance of Ethiopian representatives of the black race. They were supreme in Asia and Africa. . . . According to the occult tradition, Semitic peoples developed wherever the immigrating white colonists from the north were subjugated by the black ruling class, and intermixture occurred, as in oldest Egypt, Chaldea, Arabia and Phoenicia." (*The Adventure of Mankind,* pp. 121–22, by Eugen Georg.)

Professor Leo Frobenius held that there was an ancient Atlantean culture, but he did not believe there was actually an island in the Atlantic Ocean, known as Atlantis. Frobenius located Atlantis on the West Coast of Africa; for he unearthed ruins of palaces and beautiful statuary in Yorubaland, a territory between the Niger River and the Atlantic Ocean; and he heard among the Yorubans legends of an ancient royal city and its palace with walls of gold, which in the long ago had sunk beneath the waves. "Yoruba, with its channeled network of lakes on the coast and the reaches of the Niger; Yoruba whose peculiarities are not inadequately depicted in the Platonic account—this Yoruba, I assert is Atlantis, the home of Poseidon's posterity, the Sea God by them named Olokun; the land of peoples of whom Solon declared: 'They had even extended their lordship over Egypt and Tyrrhene!'" (*The Voice of Africa*, Vol. I, p. 345, by Leo Frobenius.) This learned Africanist also speculated that the ancient Yorubans had cultural links with the ancient Mayas of Central America. "I cannot finish," to cite his own words, "without devoting a word or two to a certain symptomatic conformity of the Western Atlantic civilization with its higher manifestations in America. Its cognate features are so striking that they cannot be overlooked, and as the region of Atlantic African culture is Yoruba, . . . it seems to be a present question, whether it might not be possible to bring the marvelous Maya monuments, whose dates have been deciphered by our eminent American archaeologists, into some prehistoric connection with those of Yoruba." (*The Voice of Africa,* Vol. I, p. 348.)

It has been suggested by the editor of the revised edition of Donnelly's *Atlantis* that thirteen thousand years ago, before the destruction of the Atlantean continent, "the West and Central African civilization must have been a magnificent spectacle." (*Atlantis: The Antediluvian World*, p. 223, by Ignatius Donnelly, edited by Egerton Sykes.) If the conclusions of Frobenius have any validity, ancient West Africa was Atlantis. "This tradition of the western situation of Ethiopia survived into the Middle Ages," Colonel Braghine notes, "at least we observe that one of the medieval maps calls the Southern Atlantic Oceanus Ethiopicus." (*The Shadow of Atlantis*, p. 214, by Colonel A. Braghine.) That this is a fact, we have no doubt, for on page 16 of *Africa's Gift to America*, the author has reproduced a copy of a map published in 1650, which shows the South Atlantic as "The Ethiopic Ocean." (We suggest that the interested reader consult *Africa's Gift to America*, by Joel A. Rogers.)

The ancient culture which we have discussed in this chapter has inspired a voluminous literature down through the ages. Perhaps the best modern study of this old civilization is contained in the works of Professor W. J. Perry, who has called it the "Archaic Civilization." The most important of Perry's works are: *The Megalithic Culture of Indonesia*, Manchester, 1918; *The Children of the Sun: A Study in the Early History of Civilization*, London and New York, 1923, second edition, 1926; *The Growth of Civilization*, London, 1924, second edition, 1926; and *The Primordial Ocean*, London, 1935.

Among the cultural elements associated with the archaic civilization, the following we believe to be the most important:

1. The practice of agriculture via irrigation.
2. The carving of stone images, and the use of stone for constructing pyramids, dolmens, rock-cut tombs, and stone circles.
3. Metal working.
4. Pottery making.
5. The practice of making mummies.
6. The worship of the Great Mother Goddess.
7. Rites of human sacrifice connected with agriculture and the cult of the Mother Goddess.
8. The worship of the heavenly bodies, such as stars, planets, the moon, and the sun.
9. A ruling class split into two divisions:
    a. A class connected with the sky-world, claiming kinship with the gods and practicing incestuous unions.
    b. Another class associated with the underworld.
10. The survival of the totemic complex.
11. The Dual Organization; operative in both the social structure and in political affairs.

12. The prevalence of mother-right, in which descent in the female line is connected with the succession of kings in the female line.

13. The presence of the institution of divine kingship, especially in Africa.

The institutions of totemism and exogamy were briefly discussed in our first chapter. Though the two systems are usually found together, the experts are inclined to believe that totemism is the older. It seems that, in the remote past, the clan organization was first evolved, that matrimonial classes developed later, and eventually the two systems effected a merger. The great authority on this ancient social organization is the late Sir J. G. Frazer. "If we exclude hypothesis and confine ourselves to facts," Frazer tells us, "we may say broadly that totemism is practiced by many savage and barbarous peoples, . . . who occupy the continents and islands of the tropics and the Southern Hemisphere, together with a large part of North America, and whose complexion shades off from coal black through dark brown to red. With the doubtful exception of a few Mongoloid tribes in Assam, no yellow and no white race is totemic." (*Totemism and Exogamy*, Vol. IV, p. 14, by Sir J. G. Frazer.)

The key feature of tribal society is the classificatory system of relationship, and the basic principle of this system is that kinship is reckoned between groups rather than between individuals. Under this system a man calls father, not only his actual father, but all men who according to tribal custom might have been his father. He names as his mother, not only his actual mother, but an entire group of women, any one of which might have been his mother under the tribal customs. He designates as his wife, not only his real wife, but also all of the women he might have married in agreement with the marital laws of the tribe. He gives the names of sons and daughters not only to his own children, but to the children of all of the women of the tribe which he might have married. This strange system of social kinship must have grown out of a widespread primitive practice of group marriage.

Such a system of group marriage would explain very simply [declares Frazer] why every man gives the name of wife to a whole group of women, and every woman gives the name of husband to a whole group of men, . . . why every man and every woman apply the names of father and mother to whole groups of men and women of whom it is physically impossible that more than two individuals can be their parents; why every man and every woman apply the name of brother and sister to whole groups of men and women with whom they need not have a drop of blood in common; and why, finally, every man and every woman claim as their sons and daughters whole groups of men and women whom they neither begat nor bare. In short, group marriage explains group relationship, and it is hard to see what else can do so [*Man, God and Immortality*, pp. 156–57, by Sir J. G. Frazer].

The classificatory system is based on the division of the tribe into two intermarrying groups, or matrimonial classes, as they are sometimes called. Besides the two-class system, some tribes have a four-class or eight-class system. The two-class system seems to be fundamental, whereas the four- and eight-class systems are derived from it. In the opinion of Sir J. G. Frazer, "The two-class system of exogamy or Dual Organization, as it is often called, suffices of itself to create the classificatory system of relationship, which appears not to have been materially affected by the subsequent adoption of the four-class and eight-class systems in certain tribes. This observation is important, because, while the classificatory system of relationship is found to be diffused over a great part of the world, the four-class and eight-class systems have hitherto been detected in Australia alone." (*Man, God and Immortality*, p. 159.) This system of matrimonial classes was a very ingenious organization. The purpose of such schemes seems to have been to restrict marriage between certain groups. The two-class system, for instance, prevents the marriage of brothers with sisters; the four-class system bars the marriage of parents with children; and the eight-class system prohibits the marriage of certain first cousins, the children of a brother and of a sister, respectively. The marriage of all other first cousins—the children of two brothers, or of two sisters—had already been forbidden by the two-class system.

The actual working of the classificatory system in practice is best illustrated by studying the organization of a tribe in which the system is operative. We choose for illustrative purposes the Kamilaroi tribe of southeast Australia. The tribe is divided into six clans, and the clans are grouped evenly into two phratries, or moieties, as follows:

PHRATRY A

Clans: 1. Emu 2. Bandicoot 3. Blacksnake

PHRATRY B

Clans: 4. Iguana 5. Kangaroo 6. Opossum

The matrimonial classes are eight in number, four of which are composed exclusively of males, and four of which are composed exclusively of females. The classes bear the following names:

MALE	FEMALE
1. Ippai	1. Ippata
2. Kumbo	2. Buta
3. Murri	3. Mata
4. Kubbi	4. Kapota

All Ippais of whatever totem are brothers to each other,

since they are theoretically descended from a common female ancestor. The same thing is true of all the Kumbos, Murris, and Kubbis, respectively. Similarly, all Ippatas of whatever clan are sisters to each other. The same is true of all the Butas, Matas, and Kapotas, respectively. Also all the Ippais and Ippatas are brothers and sisters to each other; and likewise with the Kumbos and Butas, the Murris and Matas, and the Kubbis and Kapotas, respectively. Each phratry is made of two divisions, as follows:

PHRATRY A	PHRATRY B
Division I	
Ippai	Kapota
Ippata	Kubbi
Division II	
Kumbo	Mata
Buta	Murri

A man in Phratry A, Division I, picks his wife from Division I of Phratry B. In other words an Ippai marries a Kapota. A woman in Division I of Phratry A, will marry a man from Division I of Phratry B. That is to say, an Ippata marries a Kubbi; and so on, as the table above shows.

Since descent is traced through the female line, the children are always members of the same clan as their mothers, but the children became members of a class different from that of either parent. This is shown in the following table:

MALE	FEMALE	MALE	FEMALE
Ippai marries Kapota.	Their children are Murri	and Mata.	
Kumbo marries Mata.	Their children are Kubbi	and Kapota.	
Murri marries Buta.	Their children are Ippai	and Ippata.	
Kubbi marries Ippata.	Their children are Kumbo	and Buta.	

It will be noticed that the child will be a member of the same phratry as its mother, but will belong to a different division. For example, an Ippai man (Phratry A, Division I) marries a Kapota woman (Phratry B, Division I). Their children will be Murri (male), and Mata (female). The children are members of Phratry B, Division II. With matrilineal descent, the children always belong to the same totem and phratry as their mother, but to the other division of the phratry.

The relationships between the totemic clans and the exogamous classes are shown in the following table:

CLANS   *MALE   FEMALE   MALE   FEMALE*

PHRATRY

A 1. Emu. All are   Kumbo and Buta or Ippai and Ippata.
   2. Bandicoot. All are ”   ”   ”   ”   ”   ”   ”   .
   3. Blacksnake. All are”   ”   ”   ”   ”   ”   ”   .

PHRATRY

B 1. Iguana. All are Murri and Mata or Kubbi and Kapota.
   2. Kangaroo. All are”   ”   ”   ”   ”   ”   ”   .
   3. Opossum. All are ”   ”   ”   ”   ”   ”   ”   .

We notice that one set of classes is common to all the clans of Phratry A, and the other set of classes is common to Phratry B. The three clans of each phratry are nothing more than subdivisions of an original clan; so that the six clans may be regarded as offshoots of two original clans. This circumstance would seem to confirm Sir J. G. Frazer's opinion that the classificatory system, in its fully developed form, is merely the logical outgrowth of the Dual Organization.

The totemic complex is of remote prehistoric origin and is found in more or less pristine purity only in Australia. In Africa, Asia, America, and the islands of the eastern seas, it now lingers on in a much modified or moribund condition. Dr. Churchward contends that totemism and exogamy had their birth in Africa. The migrants carried this culture complex into southern Asia, and from there it was carried to Australia, where, cut off from the rest of the world, the system proliferated and eventually became fossilized.

"What we have to deal with," say Baldwin Spencer and F. J. Gillen, in *The Native Tribes of Central Australia,* "is a great continental area, peopled most probably by men who entered from the north. . . . The class and Totem systems variously modified, which are now found in different tribes, can only be adequately accounted for on the hypotheses that when their ancestors reached the country they spread about in various directions, separated into local groups and developed along various lines, . . . each group retaining features in its customs and organizations such as can only be explained by supposing them to have had a common ancestry." (Cited by Dr. Churchward in *The Signs and Symbols of Primordial Man,* p. 46.)

The past history of these Australoids, to quote Churchward directly, "may be said to be bound up with these Totemic ceremonies, all of which are concerned with the doings of certain ancestors who lived in the past, back so far away that their origin has been totally forgotten, but, . . . are identical with the Nilotic Negro of the present day; the Australian Aborigines being an exodus from these early people." (*The Signs and Symbols of Primordial Man,* p. 46.)

Lest the reader regard this discussion of primitive social organization as digressive, let us say that this information, which we have attempted to transmit as clearly as we possibly could, will be of considerable value in understanding the great culture of ancient Egypt and its influence on world civilization; which it will be our task to elucidate in the following chapter.

Something must be said about the controversial question of the classification of races. The early scientific classifications of the varieties of the human species were geographical in nature. The celebrated naturalist, Linnaeus (1707–1778), for instance, listed four races, according to continent, namely: (1) European (white), (2) African (black), (3) Asiatic (yellow), and (4) American (red). Blumenbach, in 1775, added a fifth type, the Oceanic or brown race. In 1800 Cuvier announced the hypothesis that all ethnic types were traceable to Ham, Shem, and Japheth, the three sons of Noah. After that date, race classification developed into a contest. By 1873, Haeckel had found no less than twelve distinct races of mankind, and, to show the indefatigable nature of his researches, he annexed twenty-two more races a few years later, bringing the grand total of human types up to thirty-four. Deniker, in 1900, conceived of the human species existing in the form of six grand divisions, seventeen divisions, and twenty-nine races. And despite all this industry among the anthropologists, there is yet no agreement on the classification of races. Professor Franz Boas divided the human race into only two divisions. This classification by Boas is admirably explained by Professor Dorsey:

> Open your atlas to a map of the world. Look at the Indian Ocean: on the west, Africa; on the north, the three great southern peninsulas of Asia; on the east, a chain of great islands terminating in Australia. Wherever that Indian Ocean touches land, it finds dark-skinned people with strongly developed jaws, relatively long arms, and kinky or frizzly hair. Call that the Indian Ocean or Negroid division of the human race.
> Now look at the Pacific Ocean: on one side, the two Americas; on the other, Asia. (Geographically, Europe is a

tail to the Asiatic kite.) The Aboriginal population of the Americas and of Asia north of its southern peninsulas was a light-skinned people with straight hair, relatively short arms, and a face without prominent jaws. Call that the Pacific Ocean or Mongoloid division [*Why We Behave Like Human Beings,* pp. 44–45, by George A. Dorsey].

Professor Alfred L. Kroeber thought that the people of Europe had bleached out enough to merit classification as a distinct race. This would add a European or Caucasoid division to the Negroid and Mongoloid groups of the classification favored by Boas. This tri-racial scheme is now widely accepted; the best statement being given by Professor Barnes, as follows: "The yellow race is not only yellow in color, but also has a very round (brachycephalic) head, and very straight hair, round in cross section. The black race stands at the opposite extreme, with a very long (dolichocephalic) head, and curly hair, flat in cross section. Between these two extremes falls the white race, with an intermediate head form and wavy hair, elliptical in cross section." (*An Intellectual and Cultural History of the Western World,* pp. 21–22, by Harry Elmer Barnes.)

There has been considerable controversy concerning the proper racial classification of the original founders of civilization. Some authorities regard them as dark-whites of the Mediterranean branch of the Caucasoids, others consider them Negroids, and still other experts assign them to an intermediate mixed brown race. After discussing the civilizations of Egypt, Babylonia, and India, H. G. Wells designated them as a "triple system of white man civilizations." (*The Outline of History,* p. 175.) A diametrically opposite viewpoint is expressed by the German scholar, Eugen Georg, which we cite: "A splendid era of blacks seems to have preceded all the later races. . . . Blacks were the first to plow the mud of the Nile; they were the dark-skinned, curly haired Kushites. Blacks were the masters of Sumeria and Babylon before it became the 'country of the four tongues.' And in India, the kingdom of the Dravidian monarchs, the black and godless enemies existed until the period of written history." (*The Adventure of Mankind*, p. 44, by Eugen Georg. Translated from the German by Robert Bek-Gran.)

The late H. G. Wells noted that "Herodotus remarked upon a series of resemblances between the Colchians and the Egyptians." (*The Outline of History*, p. 184.) But Wells did not find it expedient actually to quote the "Father of History."

> There can be no doubt [Herodotus said] that the Colchians are an Egyptian race. Before I heard any mention of the fact from others, I had remarked it myself. . . . My own conjectures were founded, first, on the fact that they are black-skinned and have woolly hair, which certainly amounts to but little, since several other nations are so too; but further and more especially, on the circumstances that the Colchians, the Egyptians and the Ethiopians, are the only nations who have practiced circumcision from the earliest times. . . . I will add a further proof to the identity of the Egyptians and the Colchians. These two nations weave their linen in exactly the same way, and this is a way entirely unknown to the rest of the world; they also in their whole mode of life and in their language resemble one another [*The History of Herodotus*, Book II, pp. 114–15].

Ancient Colchis was on the northern shore of the Black Sea. This territory is now a part of the U.S.S.R., and is known as the Abkhazian Autonomous Soviet Socialist Republic; and it has such a large black population that it is called the "Black Soviet."

Chapter Three

EGYPT AND THE EVOLUTION OF CIVILIZATION

Several Egyptologists have theorized that the ancient Egyptians originally came from Asia. But no evidence has been adduced that would validate this opinion; and the only reason this thesis has been entertained is that it was fashionable to believe that no African people were capable of developing a great civilization. Mr. Geoffrey Parsons, in a scholarly historical work, refers to the culture of Egypt as "genuinely African in its origin and development." (*The Stream of History*, p. 154.)

The Edfu Text is an important source document on the early history of the Nile Valley. This famous inscription, found in the Temple of Horus at Edfu, gives an account of the origin of Egyptian civilization. According to this record, civilization was brought from the south by a band of invaders under the leadership of King Horus. This ruler, Horus, was later deified and became ultimately the Egyptian Christ. The followers of Horus were called "the Blacksmiths," because they possessed iron implements. This early culture has been traced back to Somaliland; although it may have originated in the Great Lakes region of Central Africa. In Somaliland there are ruins of buildings constructed with dressed stone, showing a close resemblance to the architecture of early Egypt. Professor Arthur G. Brodeur, in his *The Pageant of Civilization*, has conjectured that the ancestors of the South Egyptians came originally from this region; that they then entered the Nile Valley through Nubia, and brought with them a well-developed civilization. It is estimated that this migration must have occurred long before 5,000 B.C. That these ancient Africans possessed tools and weapons of iron should occasion

93

no surprise; for in the magazine, *Natural History*, Sept.–Oct., 1932, there is an article by the Italian explorer, Nino del Grande, entitled "Prehistoric Iron Smelting in Africa," in which the author tells of his discovery of an iron-smelting furnace in northern Rhodesia of an antiquity of from five thousand to six thousand years.

The Egyptian culture had attained a high level of development in very ancient times. "When the curtain goes up on the Nile Valley, at the dawn of history," Professor George A. Dorsey notes, "an astounding scene is disclosed, and one as far from primitive as the Café de la Paix. . . . The solid foundations of civilization had been laid; civilization was full-blown, as it were, and in full working order. Yet what mighty structures were to be erected on those foundations as the next three millenniums were ticked off on time's clock! And to be read in sequence and in detail as nowhere else on earth. Fifty-three centuries of unbroken history!" (*The Story of Civilization: Man's Own Show*, p. 297, by George A. Dorsey.)

Herodotus noticed that the Egyptian women went into the marketplace and engaged in trade, while their husbands stayed at home and sat at the loom; and that sons were not compelled to support their parents, but that daughters were obliged to do so, whether they chose to or not.

Diodorus Siculus, after reference to the matriarchal character of the Egyptian royal family, notes a similar state of affairs among the commoners. "Among private citizens," says that historian, "the husband by the terms of the marriage agreement, appertains to the wife, and it is stipulated between them that the man shall obey the woman in all things." (Cited by Dr. Robert Briffault, in *The Mothers*, 1-volume edition, p. 279.) These customs seemed strange to the Greeks, but they were normal features of African societies. This point is discussed by Briffault, as follows:

The social features of pre-patriarchal society have sometimes survived under conditions of advanced civilization. This happened notably in Egypt. Down to the time when a dynasty of Greek rulers sought to introduce foreign usages, the conservative society of the great African kingdom, which has contributed so largely to the material and intellectual culture of the Western world, never lost the lineaments of a matriarchal social order. . . .

The functions of royalty in ancient Egypt were regarded as being transmitted in the female line. While every Egyptian princess of the royal house was born a queen and bore the titles and dignities of the office from the day of her birth, a man only acquired them at his coronation, and could do so only by becoming the consort of a royal princess. . . . Those features of the constitution of Egyptian royalty are not singular. They are substantially identical with those obtaining in all other African kingdoms [*The Mothers*, pp. 274–75, by Robert Briffault].

According to Sir Gaston Maspero, the Egyptians made their first appearance on the stage of history about eight thousand to ten thousand years B.C. (See Maspero's *The Dawn of Civilization*, 2nd edition, p. 44.) This estimate should not be considered excessive. The ancient statue known as the Great Sphinx has been estimated by another French Egyptologist, Professor Pierre Hippolyte Boussac, to be at least ten thousand years old. There is an inscription of the Pharaoh Khufu, builder of the Great Pyramid, telling of how a temple adjoining the Sphinx, which had for generations been buried under the desert sands, was discovered by chance in his reign. This inscription, now in the Boulak Museum in Cairo, informs us that the Sphinx was much older than the Great Pyramid, and that the giant statue required repairs during the reign of Khufu. "In addition to the direct evidence for its prehistoric antiquity," Samuel Laing notes, "it is certain that, if such a monument had been erected by any of the historic kings, it would have been inscribed with hieroglyphics, and the fact recorded in Manetho's lists and contemporary records, whereas all tradition of its origin seems to have been lost in the night of ages." (*Human Origins*, p. 20, by Samuel Laing. See also *A Book of the Beginnings*, Vol. I, pp. 9–10, by Gerald Massey.)

The basis of Egyptian chronology is the lost *History of Egypt*, by Manetho. Ptolemy Philadelphus, King of Egypt in the third century B.C., commissioned Manetho, a learned Egyptian priest, of the Temple of Sebennytus, to write a history of Egypt from the earliest times up to his own day. Unfortunately the greater part of this history was lost in the destruction of the Alexandrian Library, but among the surviving fragments are Manetho's list of the kings of Egypt. This list divides the rulers of Egypt into thirty dynasties. Modern Egyptologists have grouped the dynasties into periods as follows: (1) The Old Kingdom (Dynasties I–VI), (2) The Middle Kingdom (Dynasties XI–XIV), (3) The Empire (Dynasties XVIII–XX), and (4) The Saite Age (Dynasty XXVI). In Dynasty XXVII the country was taken over by the Persians. Since that time Egypt has rarely been free from foreign domination. It will be noticed that there were interludes of chaos between the Old and Middle Kingdoms, between the Middle Kingdom and the Empire, and between the Empire and the Saite Age. In studying the history of Egypt we have a choice of two chronological schemes. There is a short chronology, compiled by Meyer and Breasted, and a long one by Petrie. Both lists are given below for comparison:

		Dates: -B.C.
Dynasties	*Petrie*	*Meyer and Breasted*
I	5500–5300	4186
IV	4780–4500	3430
VI	4275–4075	2920
XII	3580–3370	1995

XVIII	1587–1328	1580
XIX	1328–1202	1315
XX	1202–1102	1200
XXI	1102–952	1090
XXII	952–749	945
XXV	725–664	712
XXVI	664–525	663
XXVII	525–405	525
XXX	378–342	378

The first king of Dynasty I, was Aha Mena, or Menes; but before his time there were many petty kings ruling over small territories in Upper and Lower Egypt. One tribe in Lower Egypt had sixty kings before the reign of Menes. The tribal totem was the "Hornet"; and the king's crown was a low red cap with a high peak at the back. Further south was the "Reed" kingdom, whose regal headdress was a tall white crown. Still more distant to the south were two "Hawk" kingdoms.

All these kingdoms were in time united by marriage and conquest. The father of Menes, as ruler of the United Kingdom of the Reeds and Hawks of Upper Egypt, conquered the Hornets of Lower Egypt. Then Menes, when he ascended the throne, combined the red and white crowns into the famous double crown of United Egypt. Even in predynastic times the Egyptians had reached a high level of civilization. They imported gold, silver, copper, tin, lead, iron, hematite, emery, galena, turquoise, obsidian, serpentine, lapis lazuli, coral, and tortoise shell. With these materials they produced beautiful and useful works of art, which were to call forth the wonder and admiration of later ages.

Egypt's first Golden Age was initiated by an invasion from Ethiopia. According to Petrie: "A conqueror of Sudani features founded the Third Dynasty, and many entirely new ideas entered the country. This new movement culminated in the vast schemes of Khufu, one of history's most dominating personalities. With him the lines of Egyptian growth were established; and the course of events became the subject of the written record." ("Modern Discovery of the Unknown Past," by Sir Flinders Petrie, in *The Encyclopedia of Modern Knowledge*, p. 112, edited by Sir John Hammerton.) The great achievement of the reign of Khufu was the building of the Great Pyramid. The classic account of the building of the Great Pyramid was related by Herodotus, from which we quote the following:

> The Pyramid itself was twenty years in the building. It is a square 800 feet each way, . . . built entirely of polished stone, fitted together with the utmost care. The stones of which it is composed are none of them less than 30 feet in length. . . . After laying the stones for the base, they raised the remaining stones to their places by means of machines formed of short wooden planks. . . . There is an inscription in Egyptian characters on the pyramid which records the quantity of radishes, onions and garlic consumed by the laborers who constructed it; and I perfectly well remember that the interpreter who read the writing to me said that the money expended in this way was about 1,600 talents of silver. [A talent in ancient Egypt contained about 56 pounds of silver. So the modern equivalent of 1,600 talents would be the value of 89,000 pounds of silver.] If this then is a true record, what a vast sum must have been spent on the iron tools used in the work, and on the feeding and clothing of the laborers, considering the length of time the work lasted, which has already been stated, and the additional time—no small space, I imagine—which must have been occupied by the quarrying of the stones, their conveyance, and the formation of the underground apartments [*The History of Herodotus*, p. 125].

The French astronomer, Abbé Thomas Moreaux, Director of the Observatory of Bourges, wrote a book entitled *The Mysterious Science of the Pharaohs*. In this work the Abbé argues that the Great Pyramid was used as a vault for the preservation of scientific instruments, and of standard weights and measures, rather than as a tomb. In place of a sarcophagus there is a granite slab, which evidently served as a standard of measure. The length of this slab is one ten-millionth of the distance of either pole from the center of Earth. This invariable distance, only recently determined by modern scientists, is the basis of the metric system. The distance from each of the poles to the center of Earth is 3,949.79 miles. From this measurement we are enabled to calculate the circumference of Earth through the poles, which is 24,817.32 miles. Abbé Moreaux is convinced that this fact was known to the Egyptian astronomers six thousand years ago. The Chaldeans were able students of astronomy, but their best estimate of the circumference of Earth was twenty-four thousand miles.

It seems that the knowledge of mathematics and astronomy among the ancient Egyptians was considerably more extensive and exact than we had hitherto been led to suspect. The height of the Great Pyramid is one-billionth of the distance from Earth to the sun, a unit of measure not accurately established in modern times until 1874. Abbé Moreaux notes that this pyramid is oriented within one-twelfth of a degree, a remarkably accurate precision; and that the parallel of longitude passing through the pyramid traverses the most land and the least sea of any in the world—a fact which also applies to the parallel of latitude passing through the structure. In the north side of the Great Pyramid is the entrance to an underground tunnel, which is bored through 350 feet of solid rock, at an angle of 26 degrees 17 minutes to the horizon. Alpha Draconis, or Thuban, was the pole-star about 3440 B.C., and for several hundred years before and after that date. At its lower culmination, when 3 degrees 42 minutes from the pole, this star shone down the underground tunnel. The ascending passage runs off from the underground tunnel of the pyramid at the base-line level, and leads into the grand gallery. Both the ascending passage and the grand gallery are inclined to the horizon at an angle of 26 degrees 17 minutes—the same as that of the underground tunnel, but in the opposite direction. These passages seem to have served two purposes; first, they enabled the builders to orient the base and the lower layers of the masonry up to the king's chamber in a true north and south line; and secondly, the passages were so arranged that the grand gallery could serve as the equivalent of the equatorial telescope of a modern astronomical observatory.

The English astronomer, Richard A. Proctor, in his *Problems of the Pyramids*, presents convincing evidence tending to show that the Great Pyramid was used as an astronomical observatory. "The sun's annual course round the celestial sphere," says Proctor, "could be determined much more exactly than by any gnomon by observations made from the great gallery. The moon's monthly path and its changes could have been dealt with in the same effective way. The geometric paths, and thence the true paths of the planets, could be determined very accurately. The place of any visible star along the Zodiac could be most accurately determined." (Cited by Samuel Laing, in *Human Origins*, p. 56.) The triangular area of each of the four sides of the pyramid equals the square of the vertical height, a fact mentioned by Herodotus. The added lengths of the four sides of the square base bear to the vertical height the same proportion as that of the circumference of a circle to its radius. This involves the mathematical constant π (3.1416), so important in modern mathematics. The length of each side of the square base is equal to 365¼ sacred cubits, an equivalence of the length of the year in days. The two diagonals of the base contain 25,824 pyramid inches, a good approximation of the number of years in the precessional cycle. Professor Piazzi Smyth made very careful measurements of the Great Pyramid; and his results were summarized by Dr. Alfred Russel Wallace in an address before the British Association for the Advancement of Science, at Glasgow in 1876, as follows:

1. That the pyramid is truly square, the sides being equal and the angles right angles. 2. That the four sockets on which the first four stones of the corners rested are truly on the same level. 3. That the directions of the sides are accurately to the four cardinal points. 4. That the vertical height of the pyramid bears the same proportion to its circumference at the base as the radius of a circle does to its circumference.

Now all these measures, angles, and levels are accurate, not as an ordinary surveyor or builder could make them, but to such a degree as requires the best modern instruments and all the refinements of geodetical science to discover any error at all. In addition to this we have the wonderful perfection of the workmanship in the interior of the pyramid, the passages and chambers being lined with huge blocks of stone fitted with the utmost accuracy, while every part of the building exhibits the highest structural science [*British Association Report*, Glasgow Meeting, 1876, Part II, Notices and Abstracts, p. 117].

Sir Flinders Petrie began his archaeological career by journeying to Egypt in 1881. His first major undertaking was a study of the Great Pyramid, which kept him busy for nearly two years. The young scientist was overwhelmed by the amazing craftsmanship displayed by the pyramid builders. "The laying out of the base of the Great Pyramid of Khufu," Petrie asserts, "is a triumph of skill; its errors both in length and angles, could be covered by placing one's thumb on them." But in the inside of the structure he found some odd mistakes. "After having the casing made so finely, the builders made a hundred times the error in levelling of the king's chamber, so that they might have done it far better by just looking at the horizon. After having dressed the casing joints so beautifully, they left the face of the wall in the grand gallery rough chiselled." (Sir Flinders Petrie, cited by Robert

Silverberg in *Empires in the Dust*, p. 30.) Petrie's conclusion was that an architectural genius had planned and commenced the project, but had died before the job was completed; and that he had been succeeded by a man of lesser stature who was both careless and inept.

An unusual feature connected with the orientation of the pyramid has been studied by Colonel Braghine, and we give it in his own words:

> A detailed study of the structure will convince any investigator that the wealth of mathematical, geometrical and astronomical data concealed within it is not accidental, but has been produced intentionally after numerous and complex calculations, made by somebody possessing an astounding amount of knowledge. . . . Not the least interesting detail concerning the orientation of the pyramid is the following: the reflection of the sunrays from the sides of the pyramid indicates almost exactly the equinoxes and solstices and therefore, the sowing time. The northern side of the pyramid is lighted at sunrise for some moments during the period from the spring-equinox till the autumn-equinox. During the remainder of the year the southern side is lighted from sunrise till sunset. This phenomenon fixes the moment of the equinoxes within 12 hours. When the stone-facing was intact, this phenomenon of the missing shadows must have been still more pronounced and was noticed by the ancients. The Latin poet Ausonius writes:
>   "Quadrata cui in fastigio cono
>   Surgit et ipsa suas consumit puramis umbras."
> ["The pyramid itself swallows the shadow born on its summit."] This phenomenon has now been explained by Professor Pochan, who discovered that the northern and southern sides of the pyramid are not true planes, but dihedral angles of 179 degrees 50 minutes. Thus in plain speaking, the sides in question have been hollowed out to the extent of 94 centimeters, insuring a rapid disappearance of the shadow of the sunrise at the equinoxes [*The Shadow of Atlantis*, pp. 237–38].

The Pharaoh Khufu has been pictured by certain modern historians as a despot who employed slave labor to erect his colossal pyramid; but this opinion is most certainly erroneous; for slavery was practically unknown in ancient Egypt. "It seems that, on the whole," a modern authority observes, "slavery never attained the serious and infamous proportions that it had in Greece, or in Italy. The serfage, which probably continued throughout the history, prevented the requirements of slave labor on large estates. It was a mild and comparatively harmless obligation, which did not prevent ability from rising, and it saved the land from the ruin which slavery brings." (*Social Life in Ancient Egypt*, p. 25, by W. M. Flinders Petrie.)

The building of the Great Pyramid was a great and well-organized project. One hundred thousand men were employed three months at a time, in transporting the rocks to the construction site. This was during the season of the inundation, when there was no other work to be done. Ten years were needed to make the great causeway, over which the stones were hauled, and in the preparation of the site, and the leveling and hollowing out of the underground tunnel and chamber. The actual construction required an additional twenty years. Sir Flinders Petrie, basing his conclusions on data supplied by Herodotus, gives a vivid picture of how this vast engineering job was accomplished:

This time would imply that a gang of eight men (about as many as could work on one block) could move ten stones from the quarry across the Nile, up the causeways, and raised into place within three months. This would be quite possible with good organization. There are several causeways besides the main one, still visible on the desert, and they must have been closely packed by working gangs to get up the thousand blocks every day during the working season. Of course there were also highly-skilled masons necessary for the thirteen acres of finely jointed casing, and the internal parts; the barracks for these are still visible, and would hold, at the outside, 4,000 men, who would live there continuously. If half of them were engaged on the casing, each man would have to prepare accurately and fit in place one casing block every three weeks, or rather, a gang of three men doing a block in a week. This is also a reasonable result. Of course, the great blocks at the base would take far longer, and the small courses would be done in perhaps half the time for each stone. . . . Much nonsense has been written about the oppression of the people, their tears and groans. With the splendid organization evident in the work, the people must have been well managed, and there was no hardship, whatever, in carrying out the work. Each man might have been levied twice in his lifetime; he would be just as well off there as at home, for he could do nothing during the inundation. All that was necessary was to transport a couple of hundredweight of food with him, which he would eat there instead of home. The immense gain to the people was the education in combined work and technical training [*Social Life in Ancient Egypt*, pp. 25–27, by W. M. Flinders Petrie].

We are told by a well-known archaeologist that: "When the Greeks first began to come to Egypt, awed by its antiquity and overwhelmed by its multiplicity of gods, its castes and its ceremonies, what they really found was a nation of Fellahin ruled with a rod of iron by a society of Antiquaries." (*Progress and Catastrophe*, pp. 108–9, by Stanley Casson.) The priestly caste of Egypt may have been "a society of Antiquaries" in the seventh century B.C., when the first Greeks settled in the country, but that certainly was not the case in the days of the Old Kingdom. The priesthood of early Egypt comprised not only the sacerdotal officialdom, but also the entire learned and professional classes of the nation, including the civil service in its entirety. A colorful and accurate account of the achievements of these African savants is given to us by the brilliant author of *The*

Martyrdom of Man, from which work we are pleased to quote the following:

> Priests were the royal chroniclers and keepers of the records, the engravers of inscriptions, physicians of the sick and embalmers of the dead, lawyers and lawgivers, sculptors and musicians. Most of the skilled labor of the country was under their control. In their hands were the linen manufactories and the quarries between the cataracts. Even those posts in the Army which required a knowledge of arithmetic and penmanship were supplied by them: every general was attended by young priest scribes, with papyrus rolls in their hands and reed pencils behind their ears. The clergy preserved the monopoly of the arts which they had invented; the whole intellectual life of Egypt was in them. It was they who, with their nilometers, took the measure of the waters, and proclaimed good harvests to the people or bade them prepare for hungry days. It was they who studied the diseases of the country, compiled a pharmacopoeia, and invented the signs which are used in our prescriptions at the present day. . . . Their power was immense, but it was exercised with justice and discretion; they issued admirable laws, and taught the people to obey them by the example of their own humble, self-denying lives.
>
> Under the tutelage of these pious and enlightened men, the Egyptians became a prosperous and also a highly moral people. The monumental paintings reveal their whole life, but we read in them no brutal or licentious scenes. . . . The penalty for the murder of a slave was death; this law exists without parallel in the dark slavery annals both of ancient and modern times. . . . It is a sure criterion of the civilization of ancient Egypt that the soldiers did not carry arms except on duty, and that the private citizens did not carry them at all. Women were treated with much regard. . . . When a party was given the guests were received by the host and hostess, seated side by side in a large armchair. In the paintings their mutual affection is portrayed. Their fond manners, their gestures of endearment, the caresses which they lavish on their children, form sweet

and touching scenes of domestic life. . . . The civil laws were administered in such a manner that the poor could have recourse to them as well as the rich. The judges received large salaries that they might be placed above the temptation of bribery, and might never disgrace the image of Truth which they wore round their necks suspended on a golden chain [*The Martyrdom of Man*, pp. 12–14, by Winwood Rcade].

Before taking leave of the Pyramid Age, we must say something about Imhotep, the architect who designed the first pyramid. This truly great man, besides being an architect, was Vizier (Prime Minister) to King Zoser of the Third Dynasty (5345–5307 B.C.). In addition, he was an astronomer and magician, and held the post of Chief Physician to the Monarch. In later days he was deified and became the God of Medicine. Known to the Greeks as Imouthes, he was recognized as their own Aesculapius. "A temple was erected to him near the Serapeum at Memphis," we are informed by a pioneer American Egyptologist, "and at the present day every museum possesses a bronze statuette or two of this apotheosized wise man, the proverb-maker, physician and architect of Zoser. The priests who conducted the rebuilding of the temple of Edfu under the Ptolemies, claimed to be reproducing the structure formerly erected there after plans of Imhotep; and it may therefore well be that Zoser was the builder of a temple there." (*A History of Egypt*, p. 95, by James Henry Breasted.)

Egypt's first Golden Age ended in 4163 B.C., at the death of King Neterkere, the last ruler of the Sixth Dynasty. From 4163 to 3554 B.C. chaos reigned in the Nile Valley, and this intermediate period covers Dynasties VII through X. Very often several rulers claimed the throne at the same time. This era of confusion was ended by a nobleman from Thebes named Intef, who became the first king of the Eleventh Dynasty, which was the beginning of the Middle Kingdom. Intef I was succeeded by Intef II, who in turn was followed by five Mentuhoteps. Mentuhotep V was such a feeble monarch that he was toppled from his throne by a minister of state named Amenemhet I, who established the Twelfth Dynasty. This pharaoh was a man of outstanding ability, and we learn from an inscription of his age that "he restored that which he found ruined; that which a city had taken from its neighbor; while he caused city to know its boundary with city, establishing their landmarks like the heavens, distinguishing their waters according to what was in the writings, investigating according to that which was of old, because he so greatly loved justice." (Cited by Robert Silverberg in *Empires in the Dust*, p. 9.)

Under Sesostris I (3373–3327 B.C.) a period of expansion ensued, and the boundaries of Egypt were extended into Nubia. The armies of Amenemhet II invaded the Sinai Peninsula and, under Sesostris III, the conquest was extended into Syria. In the wake of the armies there followed the Egyptian merchants, and the country enjoyed the benefits of foreign commerce. In the year 3184 B.C. Amenemhet IV died, leaving no heirs to the throne. This created a problem, for in Egypt as well as many other African nations the kingship was inherited through the daughter of the monarch. In other words the new queen transmitted the regal prerogatives to her husband, who became the next pharaoh; that is to say that the kingly office passed from father to son-in-law. In order to preserve the royal succession within the family, the custom was adopted of having the oldest son of the king marry his oldest sister, through whom the right of rulership was transmitted. This made the son of the king also his son-in-law and gave him the right of succession to the throne. Now Amenemhet IV had followed the prescribed procedure by marrying his sister Sebeknefrure. Since this pharaoh died childless, the queen was privileged to select the next king, inasmuch as her new husband would by law inherit the throne.

Queen Sebeknefrure was expected to marry a member of

the Theban nobility and elevate him to the throne, but she had other ideas. Instead she married a commoner from Lower Egypt. This action brought on a civil war; for the Theban nobility refused to have a northerner from the Delta as their king. The civil strife that followed dragged on for about one hundred years. Kings of Dynasty XIII ruled from Thebes while a rival ruler of Dynasty XIV sat on the throne at Memphis. Both monarchs claimed the legal succession to Dynasty XII. The armies of both regimes fought each other up and down the Nile Valley, with neither side being able to put down the other. And while this senseless civil war was going on, the country was invaded by nomads from Asia, known as the Hyksos or "shepherd-kings." They first conquered Lower Egypt, then moved up the river and captured Thebes. These foreign invaders dominated Egypt during the Fifteenth, Sixteenth, and Seventeenth Dynasties; which covered a time span of about 150 years.

While these alien kings sat on the throne, certain Theban nobles traveled southward to Nubia and organized an underground liberation movement. The Hyksos were expelled from Thebes by an army led by Pharaoh Sekenenre, who ended his career on the field of battle. He was followed in the Theban kingship by Ahmose I, who ascended the throne 1709 B.C. This king led his army northward, liberated Memphis, and drove the "shepherd-kings" out of Egypt into the desert of Sinai. Thus began the Eighteenth Dynasty, which inaugurated the time of the New Kingdom. The new line of pharaohs erected palaces and temples at Thebes which were among the wonders of the world and were the heralds of a new Golden Age in the Nile Valley. Under Thutmose I (1662–1628) Egyptian imperial power reached its zenith. A fine summary of this achievement has been given by Professor Breasted, whom we quote:

Egypt had now become the controlling power in the far

reaching group of civilizations clustering in and about the eastern end of the Mediterranean, the center, perhaps the nucleus of the civilized world of that day. . . . Seated astride both the intercontinental and inter-oceanic highway, Egypt was building up and dominating the world of contiguous Africa and Eurasia. Traditional limits disappeared, the currents of life eddied no longer within the landmarks of tiny kingdoms, but pulsed from end to end of a great empire, embracing many kingdoms and tongues, from the Upper Nile to the Upper Euphrates. The wealth of Asiatic trade circulating through the eastern end of the Mediterranean, which once flowed down the Euphrates to Babylon, was thus diverted to the Nile Delta, long before united by canal with the Red Sea. All the world traded in the Delta Markets ["Zenith of Egyptian Power," by James Henry Breasted, in the *Cambridge Ancient History*, Vol. II, p. 88, edited by J. B. Bury *et al.*].

The true glory of the age emerged in the reign of Amenhotep III (1538–1501 B.C.). From Syria, timber was imported, and large seaworthy ships were built. With this fleet the Egyptians sailed down the East African coast and traded with the peoples of Punt, from whom they imported cargoes of ivory, ebony, ostrich feathers, spices, and gold. To the south they extended their sway over the Kushites of Nubia, and in the north they overcame a confederation of foes in a battle at Har-Megiddo (Armageddon). The domain of Amenhotep III extended from the confines of Nubia to the valley of the two rivers; and all the territories were so well organized and fairly governed as to greatly enhance their productive potential.

Thebes itself expanded into a great metropolis with walls nine miles in circumference. On the outskirts of the city were the elegant mansions of the nobility, some containing fifty or sixty rooms, and halls with the walls covered with colorful paintings, and embellished with costly inlaid furniture, beautiful vases, and attractively carved ornaments and utensils of ebony, bronze, and ivory. Along the great river, temples were built by the order of the king, and were linked together by avenues of sphinxes. Around the mansions and temples were tree-shaded boulevards and flower gardens; and the environing landscape was enhanced by a series of lakes. Since the vanquished Hyksos had introduced horses into Egypt, an improved system of transport was adopted: Bigger and better roads were constructed and Egyptian gentlemen traveled over the highways in horse-drawn chariots.

In the year 1501 B.C. the death of Amenhotep III brought to an end a brilliant reign of thirty-six years and five months. He was followed by his son, the boy Amenhotep IV. Queen Ti, mother of the youthful king, ruled as regent until her son reached his majority. The new monarch inaugurated a religious revolution which has made his name famous in the annals of history, and at the same time brought an ignominious end to the Golden Age established by his illustrious father. The young pharaoh quitted Thebes and built a new city, Tell el Amarna, for his capital. He disestablished the hundreds of gods of the Egyptian pantheon and worshiped only one god, Aton, whose symbol was the flaming disc of the sun; and he renamed himself Ikhnaton (devoted to Aton). Warnings from the nomarchs (provincial governors) that hostile armies were set to invade the nation were not heeded by the king, and the priests of the disallowed cults rose up in rebellion. So Ikhnaton, the "Heretic-king," died ingloriously, probably poisoned by enemies, and the Aton cult was abolished.

The youthful Tutankhamen, his son-in-law, ascended to the throne, moved back the capital to Thebes, and restored the old cults to their previous positions of power. The career of King Tut was cut short by his untimely death at the age of seventeen years. The throne was taken by a priest named Eye, whose reign was a disaster to the country; for during his brief rule nearly all the foreign territories annexed by the great kings of Dynasty XVIII were lost. Then a general from the north, Harmhab, seized the throne from the Usurper, Eye, and brought the period of political decline to an end.

Although the monotheistic Aton cult was crushed in Egypt, it did not perish altogether. For there was a young Egyptian priest named Moshe (Moses), who had received his theological education at Heliopolis, and who became a disciple of Ikhnaton. When Atonism was suppressed in Egypt, Moses led a group of "heretics" out of the country and into Palestine. Our authority for the statement that Moses was an Egyptian priest is the historian Manetho, whom we believe to be a reliable witness. The opinion of Manetho is endorsed by Strabo, who refers to: "Moses, who was one of the Egyptian priests, taught his followers that it was an egregious error to represent the Deity under the form of animals, as the Egyptians did, or in the shape of man, as was the practice of the Greeks and Africans. . . . It is for this reason, that, rejecting every species of images or idols, Moses wished the Deity to be worshipped without emblems, and according to his proper nature; and he accordingly ordered a temple worthy of him to be erected." (Strabo, *Geography*, *Book 16*, cited by C. F. Volney, in *The Ruins of Empires*, pp. 150–51.) As we know, Moses was not entirely successful, since many of his followers still worshiped the old gods.

But in vain did he proscribe the worship of the symbols which prevailed in lower Egypt and in Phoenicia [Volney observes] for his god was nevertheless an Egyptian god, invented by those priests of whom Moses had been the disciple. . . . In vain did Moses wish to blot from his religion everything which had relation to the stars; many traits call them to mind in spite of all he has done. The seven planetary luminaries of the great candlestick; the twelve stones, or signs in the Urim of the high priests; the feast of the two equinoxes (entrances and gates of the two hemispheres); the ceremony of the lamb (the celestial ram then in the fifteenth degree); . . . all remain as so many witnesses of the filiation of his ideas, and of their extraction from the common source [*The Ruins of Empires*, pp. 149–51, by C. F. Volney].*

The Nineteenth Dynasty began with the reign of Hormhab (1454–1395 B.C.), but the great ruler of this dynasty was Ramses II (1394–1328 B.C.). This pharaoh in a reign of sixty-six years conquered extensive territories in western Asia and built colossal temples in the Nile Valley. In Ethiopia, for example, this Ramses was worshiped as a god; for among the Kushites he erected six new temples, dedicated to Amen, Ra, and Ptah. In discussing these temples, Breasted tells us that "in all of them Rameses was more or less prominently worshipped, and in one his queen, Nefretiri, was the presiding divinity. Of his Nubian sanctuaries, the great rock-temple at Abu Simbel is the finest and deservedly the goal of modern travellers in Egypt." (*A History of Egypt*, pp. 373–75, by James Henry Breasted.) Ramses III (1230–1199 B.C.) of the Twentieth Dynasty was also a great ruler, and he was succeeded by eight kings all bearing the name Ramses, but none of them attained the status of greatness.

During the years 1075–714 B.C., known as the Third Intermediate period of Egyptian history, there were four dynasties, XXI, XXII, XXIII and XXIV—some of the rulers being of Libyan and Ethiopian extraction. Sheshonk I (926–905 B.C.), a Libyan, of the Twenty-Second Dynasty led an army into Palestine, captured Jerusalem, and looted King Solomon's temple.

Then in 761 B.C. the Ethiopian king, Piankhi, ascended the throne of Egypt, and rarely after that date was the Nile Valley ruled by Egyptian kings. Piankhi began his career as king of Nubia and, from his palace in the city of Napata, he watched with misgivings the tribute of gold, cattle, and

---

* For a more recent discussion of this question, the reader is referred to *The Signs and Symbols of Primordial Man*, pp. 235–40, by Albert Churchward; and to *Moses and Monotheism* by Sigmund Freud.

soldiers which his country was obligated to send to King Osorkon III, of Egypt. Finally he decided to end this unsatisfactory state of affairs and, gathering a large fleet and a mighty army, descended the river to lay siege to Hermopolis. The local ruler King Namlot surrendered the city to the Ethiopian conqueror, and turned over to him a great treasure trove; for from an inscription of Piankhi we read that "Hermopolis threw herself upon her belly and pleaded before the king. Messengers came forth and descended bearing everything beautiful to behold; gold, every splendid costly stone, clothing in a chest, and the diadem which was upon his head; the uraeus which inspireth fear of him, without ceasing during many days." On visiting Namlot's stables, Piankhi was distressed by the malnutrition visited on the horses during the siege of the city. "His majesty proceeded to the stable of the horses, and the quarters of the foals. When he saw that they had suffered hunger, he said: 'I swear as Ra loves me . . . it is more grievous in my heart that my horses have suffered hunger than any evil deed that thou hast done in the prosecution of thy desire.'" (Cited by James Henry Breasted, *A History of Egypt*, pp. 452–53.)

The conquering Kushite king continued down the river, and his next great prize was Memphis. Finally he captured Heliopolis, and was met there by King Osorkon III, of Bubastis, who yielded his regal powers to the Ethiopian monarch. After returning to Nepata, Piankhi had a granite stele erected in the temple of Amen, and on the four sides of this monument he describes his successful campaign in detail. This ancient record possesses intrinsic merit, and has been praised by a modern authority, as follows:

It displays literary skill, and an appreciation of dramatic situations which is notable, while the vivacious touches wound here and there quite relieve it of the arid tone usual in such hieroglyphic documents. The imagination endues the personages appearing here more easily with life than those of any other similar historical narrative of Egypt; and the humane Piankhi especially, the lover of horses, remains a *man* far removed from the conventional companion and equal of the gods who inevitably occupies the exalted throne of the pharaohs in all other such records [A *History of Egypt*, p. 456, by James Henry Breasted].

In the inscription referred to above by Breasted, King Piankhi tells of how he washed his face in a spring sacred to the Sun-god, Ra, at the Temple of Heliopolis. Then, to quote from the inscription:

He brought an offering on the sand-dune in Heliopolis to Ra at his rising, a great offering of white oxen, milk, incense, balsam, and all sorts of sweet smelling woods. Then he returned to the Temple of Ra; the superintendent of the Temple praised him highly: the speaker of the prayers spoke the prayer for the averting of enemies from the king. The king performed the ceremony in the Chamber of Purification, the putting on of the bands, the purifying with incense and the water of libations, the handing of flowers for the Hat Benben* of the god. He took the flowers, he ascended the steps to the great terrace to see Ra in the Hat Benben, he the king himself. When the prince was alone, he undid the bolt, he opened the doors and saw his father Ra in the Hat Benben, he saw the morning boat of Ra and the evening boat of Tum. He closed the doors, he put the seal on, and sealed it with the royal seal. He declared to the priests, "I have put on the seal, no other king shall go in thither." They threw themselves down before His Majesty and said, "May Horus, the darling of Heliopolis, exist, and remain and never pass away." And he went and entered into the Temple of Tum, and they brought the statue of Tum, the Creator, the lord of Heliopolis, and King Osorkon came to

* The Hat Benben referred to in Piankhi's inscription is a title given to the temple of the sun at Heliopolis, and means literally the "House of the Obelisk," for the Benben was a small stone obelisk or pyramid supposed to be an embodiment of the Sun-god Ra himself.

see his majesty* [extract from the "Inscription of King Piankhi," cited by Sir James George Frazer in *The Worship of Nature*, p. 563].

The Twenty-Fourth Dynasty consisted of only one king, Bocchoris, who according to Manetho reigned only six years (720–714 B.C.). The Twenty-Fifth Dynasty has been called the Kushite or Ethiopian Dynasty. It began in 714 B.C. when, to cite Herodotus: "Egypt was invaded by a vast army of Ethiopians, led by Sabacos, their king." (*History of Herodotus*, p. 129.) This king, better known as Shabaka (714–702 B.C.), successfully undertook the conquest of Lower Egypt and established Ethiopian supremacy in that region. Then he started an Asiatic campaign in which he waged war with the Assyrians. His army escaped defeat only because the Assyrian hordes were afflicted by a plague and were forced to retreat. This king was succeeded by Shabataka, who after a reign of twelve years was slain by Taharka, who seized the crown and set up his capital at Tanis. The reign of this pharaoh was marked by prosperity and cultural advance. The Egyptologist Weigall has referred to this period as "that astonishing epoch of nigger domination."

A temple erected at Karnak was one of the glories of ancient Egypt. "The temple built at Thebes," says Professor DuBois, "had a relief representing the four courts of the four quarters of the Nilotic world: Dedun, the great God of Ethiopia, represents the south; Sopd, the eastern desert; Sebek, the western desert; and Horus, the north." (*The World and Africa*, p. 137, by W. E. Burghardt DuBois.)

There is a tradition that Taharka led expeditions as far as

---

* Readers who would like to know more about King Piankhi are advised to consult the following: (1) "Sources for the Study of Ethiopian History," p. 32, by Professor William L. Hansberry, Howard University Studies in History, November, 1930; (2) *Personalities of Antiquity*, by Sir Arthur Weigall. This English Egyptologist devotes a chapter of his book to Piankhi and titles it "The Exploits of a Nigger King."

the Strait of Gibraltar. The country was faced with an invasion from Assyria, and Taharka fought the Assyrians until age forced him to turn over the reins of government to Tatutamen; but the new king could not contain the invading foe, and Ashurbanipal's Assyrian armies ascended the Nile and captured and looted the great city of Thebes. But the Assyrians could not hold on to Egypt, so they soon retreated to their own land. The next dynasty, the Twenty-Sixth, lasted from 663 to 527 B.C., and was the last line of native Egyptian kings to rule over the Nilotic dominions.

The last great African pharaoh to reign in Egypt was Ahmose II (569–525 B.C.), of Libyan ancestry. This king, whom the Greeks called Amasis, was a great statesman, but he could not save his country from foreign domination. The best soldiers of the Egyptian army had many years before deserted to the Ethiopian king at Meroe, and Amasis was forced to depend on Libyan and Greek mercenaries for defense against foreign invasion. Being a good diplomat, he managed to maintain peace in his realm, but after his death, early in 525 B.C., the kingship fell to Psamtik III, and after a few months the land of Egypt was overwhelmed by the armies of King Cambyses of Persia. Thus was ushered in Dynasty XXVII. Four puppet dynasties under Persian control followed, lasting until 332 B.C., when the Nile-land succumbed to Alexander the Great. His successors, the Ptolemies, ruled until 30 B.C., when Egypt became a Roman province.

From Menes to Amasis was almost five thousand years, and the record of Egyptian civilization under her native rulers was highly creditable. A summary of the achievements of this African culture has been so interestingly written by a contemporary German scholar that we take the liberty of reproducing it:

The insurgent Amasis stood at the end of Egypt's history, but at its beginnings lay the Nile mud, which came from the interior of Africa, spread itself over the annually-flooded river valley and proved to be an excellent fertilizer. And even in the Neolithic Age men were sowing wheat and barley there. These Neolithic children of the Nile were East Hamitic Africans, related to the present-day Galla, Somali and Masai in East Africa; the later Egyptians were their descendants. The language of the Egyptians was an East Hamitic dialect, as is spoken today by the natives between the Upper Nile and the Masai steppes. Egyptian skeletons, statues and countless pictures of Egyptians in their temples and monuments show the same racial characteristics as the Nubians and the Nilotic tribes, the brown-skinned hunters of the steppes and the savannah husbandmen of the Sudan. Therefore Egypt was a great kingdom created by Africans. . . . Of African inspiration are the pyramids, the golden burial chambers, the statues, plastic arts, temple friezes and other great Egyptian works of art. The Sphinx is an African monument, the hieroglyphs are an African script, and Ammon, Isis and Osiris are African gods. So great was the achievement of the Africans in the Nile Valley that all the great men of ancient Europe journeyed there—the philosophers Thales and Anaximander, the mathematician Pythagoras, the statesman Solon and an endless stream of historians and geographers whose works are all based on Herodotus' outstanding descriptions of Egypt, to which the second volume of his history is entirely devoted [*It Began in Babel*, p. 58, by Herbert Wendt].

Alexander the Great, shortly before his death, planned to build a new city on the Mediterranean coast of Egypt, but he never lived to see this city, which was actually built by one of his generals, named Ptolemy. The new city was named Alexandria, in memory of the Macedonian conqueror. The Alexandrian culture, which stemmed from the building of the city, was under the rule of Greek kings, but the civilization was more Oriental than Hellenic, for the Greeks were inferior to the Orientals, and even to the Romans, in material culture. Much of the lore of ancient Egypt was inherited and diffused by the Hellenistic Alexandrians of the Ptolemaic age. After the split-up of Alexander's empire, Ptolemy got Egypt as his share, and became the first king of the Ptolemaic Dynasty.

The city of Alexandria was built on a strip of land five or six miles long, and about two miles in width, between the Mediterranean Sea and Lake Mareotis. In the harbor of Alexandria was the Island of Pharos, and on this island was erected a lighthouse, one of the Seven Wonders of the World. It was built of marble and reared its pinnacle four hundred feet into the air, and on the summit was a light which could be seen thirty miles out at sea. This grand structure was erected at a cost of about $680,000; and in those days dollars were worth much more than they are at the present time. The walls of Alexandria were about fifteen miles in circumference, and underground cisterns were built to store a supply of fresh water sufficient to meet the needs of the entire population for one year. The city was laid out in modern fashion, with streets running north-south and east-west, and crossing at right angles to each other. Canobic Street ran from one end of the city to the other, from east to west, a distance of five to six miles; it was over one hundred feet wide, and was lined on both sides by a marble colonnade. Another boulevard, equally wide and stately, ran from north to south. These avenues were lined with noble palms and at night were illuminated with lamps.

The mansions, palaces, and public buildings were faced with white marble and polished granite. The glare of the sun was subdued by the use of veils and curtains of green silk, which could be seen everywhere. At the intersection of the two main boulevards was the magnificent tomb of Alexander the Great—in which rested the mummified remains of that monarch—surrounded by gardens, fountains, and obelisks. The glories of Alexandria were the Museum and the Library, institutions which outshone by far the superb palaces, temples, and theaters of the great city. In the establishment of the Museum, and the famous Library, which was an adjunct of the Museum, Ptolemy I had in view three objectives: (1) the perpetuation of extant knowledge, (2) the increase of such knowledge, and (3) the diffusion of knowledge.

On the abdication of Ptolemy I, his son Ptolemy II ascended the throne of Egypt (285 B.C.); and during his reign (285–247 B.C.), Alexandria entered its Golden Age. The coronation of Ptolemy II was an affair of great pomp and ceremony. The following splendid account of it is from the pen of Joseph McCabe:

> From morn to dusk of a mild November day a stupendous procession paraded broad, marble lined avenues. . . . Fourteen lions led a train of panthers, leopards, lynxes, and a rhinoceros. Nubian slaves carried 600 tusks of ivory, 2,000 blocks of ebony, and gold and silver vessels filled with gold dust. A large gold-and-ivory statue of Dionysus rode in a chariot at the head of a vintage pageant which included 24 chariots containing gaily-dressed Hindu ladies and drawn by elephants, and 80 chariots drawn by Asiatic antelopes, goats and wild asses. Hundreds of slaves carried strange birds in cages or on boughs of trees, and trays of perfume and spices, or led thousands of Indian dogs on the leash. Statues of Gods and kings rode in chariots of ivory and gold. In the royal box were a dozen of the Greek world's most famous scholars and poets; and doubtless they sat at the close in the specially built banquet hall, with marble columns shaped like palms, the choicest paintings in the world, hangings of Egyptian scarlet and Phoenician purple, and large gold vessels studded with diamonds and rubies. The coronation cost, it is said, 600,000 pounds; and the gold crowns presented to the young king and queen by the cities of the world were worth more than that in value [*The Golden Ages of History*, pp. 66–67, by Joseph McCabe].

The chief librarian of Ptolemy II was a man named Callimachus; and one of his projects was a collection of literature embracing the sacred books of the Ethiopians, Indians, Persians, Elamites, Babylonians, Assyrians, Romans, Phoenicians, Syrians, and Greeks. The chief librarian was ordered by the king to buy whatever books he could at the expense of the government. All books brought into Egypt by foreigners were taken to the Museum; correct copies of such works were made by a corps of transcribers; a copy was given to the owner and the original was placed in the Library. Sometimes large sums of money were paid for books. Ptolemy Euergetes obtained from a citizen of Athens the works of Sophocles, Euripides, and Aeschylus; and to the owner he returned transcripts of the books plus an indemnity of about $15,000. The Library boasted a large and fine collection of books, the total running to over 400,000 volumes.

The Museum was in fact a university, containing Faculties of astronomy, mathematics, literature, and medicine; and connected with the Museum were an astronomical observatory, a chemical laboratory, and an anatomical dissection room. The scientists and scholars of the Museum especially distinguished themselves in the fields of mathematics, astronomy, and geography. One of the shining lights of the Museum was the mathematician, Euclid, author of a "Geometry" still taught in our schools. Ptolemy I asked Euclid to simplify the study of geometry so that he could learn it without too much effort; and to this request Euclid replied: "In geometry there is no special path for kings." Also connected with the Museum was the mathematician Apollonius, author of treatises on conic sections; the famous mathematician and physicist, Archimedes; and Eratosthenes, who was both an astronomer and a geographer. Greatest among the astronomers were Hipparchus and Ptolemy. Another astronomer of note was Sosigenes, who revised the Egyptian calendar at the behest of Julius Caesar, and hence was the true author of the Julian calendar. At the Museum were also engineers and inventors, such as Ctesibius, who invented a single-cylinder fire engine;

while his pupil, Hero, improved this engine by constructing it with two cylinders. This same Hero invented the first steam engine, the forerunner of the modern steam turbine. As a center of scientific research the Museum flourished for one hundred years, then went into a decline.

The Library survived until it was burned by a Roman army led by Julius Caesar in 48 B.C. The Library was largely restored by the Romans, by importing books from other libraries, especially that of King Eumenes of Pergamum, whose library was presented to Queen Cleopatra by Mark Antony. This second Alexandrian Library was destroyed by fanatical Christian monks in 389 A.D. and was never re-built. The story of the destruction of the Library by the Arab invaders in the seventh century is false, since there was at that time no Library in Alexandria for them to destroy. By the time Alexandria's period of progress had come to an end the Romans had become the new custodians of civilization.

Among the great inventions of the Egyptians were the alphabet, paper, ink, and the pen. The first paper was made of thin strips of papyrus reeds pasted together; ink was made from vegetable gum and soot mixed with water. By dipping a pointed reed into the ink the Egyptian scribe wrote messages on the papyrus sheet. Writing was a basic invention, and its influence on the evolution of civilization was profound. "The invention of writing and of a convenient system of records on paper," says Breasted, "has had a greater influence in the uplifting of the human race than any other intellectual achievement in the career of man. It was more important than all the battles ever fought and all the constitutions ever devised." (*Ancient Times*, p. 45, by James Henry Breasted.)

Another great Egyptian invention is the calendar. The earliest Egyptians measured time by the moon; for the month, the interval between two new moons, was the unit of time measurement. The moon-month varies in length from 29 to 30 days, and the lunar calendar is cumbersome and inaccurate.

The lunar year of 354 days is 11 days shorter than the solar year; and such a calendar can be made to work only by intercalating an extra month at suitable intervals. The Egyptians met this difficulty by devising an accurate calendar. They noticed that the dog star, Sothis (Sirius), rose heliacally (before sunrise) on July 19th, at the beginning of the inundation (the annual overflow of the Nile). This gave them an improved calendar of 365 days in length. The 12 months of the Egyptian year were uniformly of 30 days each in duration, giving a total of 360 days; so 5 feast days were added at the end of the year to make the count come out right. Each 30-day month was divided into 3 weeks of 10 days each; and there were 3 seasons of the year; the Inundation, the Cultivation, and the Harvest, each season consisting of 4 months. The Egyptian astronomers soon discovered that the true length of the year was 365¼ days; hence the calendar could have been improved by adding an extra day every four years, but this was not done. Ptolemy Euergetes issued a decree in 238 B.C., in which it was commanded that every fourth year should be 366 days in length; but the Egyptians were opposed to the institution of leap year so they ignored the royal decree. This calendar, established in Egypt over six thousand years ago, has descended the stream of history to us. It was nearly ruined by certain Roman politicians who made awkward alterations in the length and names of the months, but for these deplorable changes the Egyptians were nowise responsible.

Since the lore of astronomy and the calendar were the basis of much of the mythology, ritual, and religion of ancient Egypt, which in turn has profoundly affected all the great religious systems of later days, we deem it proper to discuss certain aspects of these ancient African cults and creeds, and their effects on other cultures. Sun worship was dominant in the later phases of Egyptian culture, but it was preceded by stellar and lunar cults. The researches of Sir Wallis Budge and Sir Norman Lockyer have shown the priority of star worship in the Nile Valley. The pyramids of northern Egypt are oriented east and west; i.e., to the sun. In southern Egypt, the more ancient step pyramids face southeast; and, as Budge points out: "with such an amplitude that it could not have been a question of the sunlight entering the shrine, we are driven therefore to star-worship." ("On the Orientation of the Pyramids and Temples in the Sudan," by E. A. Wallis Budge, in Vol. 65, *Proceedings of the Royal Society*, London, 1899.) In fact some of the important temples of southern Egypt and Ethiopia were oriented to Alpha Centauri. Lockyer shows in his *The Dawn of Astronomy* that Canopus, a brilliant star of the southern hemisphere, figured prominently in the stellar worship of ancient Egypt. A good summary of Lockyer's data is given by Richard H. Allen, as follows:

> Lockyer tells us of a series of temples at Edfu, Philae, Amada, and Semneh, so oriented at their erection 6400 B.C., as to show Canopus heralding the sunrise at the autumnal equinox, when it was known as the symbol of Khons, or Khonsu,* the first southern star-god; and of other similar temples later. At least two of the great structures at Karnak, of 2100 and 1700 B.C., respectively pointed to its setting; as did another at Naga, and the temple of Khons at Thebes, built by Rameses III about 1300 B.C., afterwards restored and enlarged under the Ptolemies. It thus probably was the prominent object in the religion of Southern Egypt, where it represented the god of the waters [*Star Names and Their Meanings*, pp. 70–71, by Richard H. Allen].

In the pantheon of ancient Egypt, the moon-god Thoth held high rank; and on the monuments he is pictured as an ibis, with mingled black and white feathers, representing the dark and bright sides of the moon. The very name "Thoth"

* The star-god Khonsu later became a moon-god among the Ethiopians and Egyptians.

means "The Measurer," an appropriate epithet for the moon-god. So he is shown wearing the lunar crescent and disk, and holding a stylus and a notched palm branch; and he is also identified with Hermes Trismegistus, author of the sacred books, and the father of magic.

Egyptian sun-worship was a very complex affair; since the sun was known by several names, and its various attributes were differentiated, and made the objects of divine worship. "The Egyptians in the deification of the Sun," observes Mr. Olcott, "considered the luminary in its different aspects, separating the light from the heat of the Sun, and the orb from the rays. Egyptian sun worship was therefore polytheistic, and several distinct deities were worshipped as sun-gods. Thus, there were sun-gods representing the physical orb, the intellectual Sun, the Sun considered as the source of heat, and the source of light, the power of the Sun, the Sun in the firmament, and the Sun in his resting place." (*Sun Lore of All Ages*, pp. 150–51, by William Tyler Olcott.)

The greatest of the sun-gods of ancient Egypt, it seems, was Ra or Re, who was a personification of the physical sun; indeed Ra was just the ordinary everyday name for the sun. Ra was a member of a solar trinity, the other partners of the trio being Osiris and Horus. The sun-god Ra was usually represented as a man with the head of a hawk holding in one hand the regal scepter, and in the other the crux ansata (cross with a handle). On his head was a globe or disk, around which a uraeus, or asp, was coiled; the serpent being symbolic of the power over life and death. The figure of Ra and the disk on his head were generally painted red, since the god was particularly associated with the heat of the midday sun. Osiris, on the other hand, was emblematic of the setting sun. As a dweller among men, his form was that of the Apis Bull; as Judge of the Dead, he was pictured as a mummy, of sacred blue color, armed with the rod of authority and the crux ansata, and wearing the double crown of upper and lower

Egypt. His eldest son, Horus, was the rising sun, who slew the Dragon of Darkness with a spear (ray).

Another Egyptian sun-god, Amen or Ammon, was a personification of the sun after setting, and thus hidden from view. Amen was depicted as a man with the head and horns of a ram; and his figure was painted blue, the sacred color of the source of life. The word "ram" means "concealment" in the Egyptian language, and Amen as the sun-god was called, "the Concealed One," an appropriate title for the solar orb after it had disappeared in the west, and hence descended into the underworld. In Thebes, the cults of Amen and Ra were merged and the sun was there worshiped under the name Amen-Ra. Solarism reached its zenith in the reign of Akhnaton (Amenhotep IV); for this pharaoh forbade the worship of any god save the "great living disk of the Sun"; and he ordered the names of the other gods erased from the monuments and decreed the destruction of their images. This worship of the solar disk, under the name of Aton, came to an end with the death of the monarch, when the old gods again came back into their own. Among the minor Egyptian sun-gods were Ptah; an embodiment of the life-giving power of the sun, and Mandu, the personification of the power of the midday sun of summer. Even the rays of the sun were deified, under the names of Gom, Kons, and Moni; they were regarded as sons of the sun.

So far we have discussed star-gods, moon-gods, and sun-gods, but there were, in the Nilotic pantheon, other gods composite in nature; that is to say, they absorbed the traits and aspects of many other deities. A good example of this type of god is Osiris, the most popular divinity of ancient Egypt. As Professor Alexandre Moret explains:

Of all the gods called into being by the hopes and fears of men who dwelt in times of yore on the banks of the Nile, Osiris was the most popular. His appearance surprises us least of all, when the procession of Egyptian divinities pass before our eyes; this falcon is Horus; this goose Geb or Ammon; that crocodile is Sebek; yonder bull is Hapi, the Nile; and the hippopotamus is Ririt; the pair of lions is Shou and Tafnuit; the vulture and serpent are the goddesses of the South and the North. Stranger still are those divinities whose human bodies are surmounted by the heads of beasts; from the shoulders of Thoth arise the slender neck and the long bill of the ibis; Khnoum wears a ram's head with twisted horns; Sekhit has the terrifying muzzle of a lioness; and Bast carries the head of a cat with ears pricked up and gleaming eyes. By the side of these animals, fetishes and totems of the ancient tribes, raised to the rank of national divinities in more modern times, there appeared from the earliest days of United Egypt, a god whose worship became common to all the cities. Osiris in the beginning a multiform fetish, sometimes a tree, sometimes a bull, detaches himself from his totemic origins and at a very early date assumes a purely human form. Wherever shone forth the calm beauty of this face whose oval was prolonged by the false beard and tall white mitre, wherever was seen the melancholy outline of this body, draped in a shroud, the two fists crossed upon his breast and clasping the ox-herd's whip and the shepherd's crook, the Egyptians from every province recognized the "chief" of mankind, the "ruler of eternity," a god who by reason of his visible shape was nearly akin to man [*Kings and Gods of Egypt*, pp. 69–70, by Alexandre Moret].

Osiris was the son of the sky-goddess Nut, who was the wife of the sun-god Ra. The father of Osiris, however, was not Ra, but the earth-god Seb. When Ra discovered the unfaithfulness of his wife, he pronounced a curse upon her, predicting that the child would be born in no month and no year. But Nut had acquired another lover, namely the god Thoth. Thoth in the meantime had been playing a game of draughts with the moon, and had won from the lunar orb one seventy-second part of each day. The fractional parts were compounded into five whole days, and were added by

Thoth to the Egyptian year of 360 days. This was a mythological attempt to account for the five supplementary days
which were added to the Egyptian year in order to bring the
lunar and solar calendars into agreement; and since these extra
five days were regarded as entirely outside the year of twelve
months, the curse of the sun-god Ra did not rest on them.

Osiris was born on the first of the supplementary days; and
at his nativity a mysterious voice rang out announcing the
earthly advent of the "Lord of All." But Osiris was not an
only child; on the second supplementary day, Nut gave birth
to the elder Horus; likewise the sky-goddess became the
mother of Set on the third day; of the goddess Isis on the
fourth day; and of the goddess Nephthys on the fifth. In
due time Set married his sister Nephthys, and Osiris married
his sister Isis.

Osiris, it is said, forsook the realm of the gods and became
an earthly king; he found the Egyptians savages and conferred
on them the blessings of civilization; since the inhabitants of
the Nile-land had been cannibals before the earthly pilgrimage
of Osiris. Queen Isis found barley and wheat growing wild
on the banks of the great river, and King Osiris introduced
the cultivation of these grains among the people, who then
gave up cannibalism and accommodated themselves to a diet
of corn. Osiris was the original gatherer of fruit from trees;
he trained the creeping vines to twine themselves around poles,
and was the first to tread the grapes. The good king then
turned over the government of Egypt to his wife, Isis; while
he traveled over the world distributing the blessings of civilization and agriculture to all mankind. In lands where the
soil and climate did not permit the culture of the vine, Osiris
taught the people to brew beer from barley. On returning to
Egypt, the benevolent monarch, on account of the blessings
he had diffused among men, was recognized as a god, and thus
worshiped by a grateful people.

But Osiris had a wicked and jealous brother named Set;

and the evil Set, with seventy-two companions, plotted the death of Osiris. By craft, Set got the measure of his brother's body, and constructed a coffer of attractive design of exactly the same size; then at a banquet, when drinking and revelry were at their height, the wily Set brought in his coffer, and offered to make a present of it to anyone whose body would fit into it exactly. All present tried out the coffer, except Osiris, and none of them fitted into it. Then Osiris lay down in the coffer, which fitted him exactly. Immediately the conspirators slammed the lid of the coffer, fastened it with nails, and sealed it with molten lead. The coffer was then thrown into the Nile. According to Plutarch, all this occurred on the 17th day of the month of Athyr, when the sun entered the zodiacal sign of Scorpio (The Scorpion), and in the twenty-eighth year of the reign of Osiris.

The widowed Isis soon afterward went into exile in the papyrus swamps of the Delta; and here she gave birth to a son, the younger Horus. Meanwhile, the floating coffin of Osiris had drifted into the Mediterranean Sea, and was finally washed up on the coast of Phoenicia. Here a mysterious tree sprang up, and enclosed the chest in its trunk. The local king saw the tree, and so admired it that he had it cut down and fashioned into a pillar for his palace at Byblos. Isis wandered over the face of the earth seeking the body of her dead husband and eventually arrived at Byblos. After cutting open the tree-pillar and retrieving the coffer, Isis swathed the pillar in linen, poured ointment on it, and gave it to the King of Byblos. The sacred pillar was installed in a Temple of Isis, where it was afterward worshiped by the natives of Byblos. The body of Osiris was taken back to Egypt by Isis and there hidden in a secret place. But one night, while Set was hunting a boar by the light of the full moon, he by chance discovered the hidden chest. Proceeding then to open it, he took the body of Osiris, chopped it into fourteen pieces and scattered them all over the land of Egypt. Isis later searched for and found all of the parts except one, and she buried each fragment where she found it; and that is why so many cities of Egypt claimed possession of the grave of Osiris. The missing part of Osiris was the phallus; so Isis made an image of it for use in the religious festivals of the Egyptians. Such is the myth of Osiris as told by Plutarch in his treatise *On Isis and Osiris*, with some fragmentary data from the ancient Egyptian literature.

The story of Osiris has a happier ending in some of the native Egyptian versions which supplement the account by Plutarch. We are told that, when Isis had discovered the body and collected the fragments, she and her sister Nephthys sat down and wept. This lament was heard by the sun-god Ra who, moved by compassion, sent down from heaven the jackal-headed god Anubis. This divinity, with the help of Horus, Isis, Nephthys, and the ibis-headed Thoth, reassembled the body of Osiris from the numerous fragments; then the gods made a mummy of the corpse. Isis, who by good fortune was fitted out with wings, fanned the mummy with them. The breath of life returned to Osiris, and in consequence occurred his resurrection from the dead. He then betook himself to the other world to reign in perpetuity as King of the Dead. His son Horus, having grown to manhood, became a king and ruled on Earth; later he became the third person of the great Egyptian trinity of Osiris, Isis, and Horus. The resurrection of Osiris is pictured in a series of bas-reliefs on the walls of that god's temple at Denderah. First we see the dead god as a mummy lying on his bier; then he rises gradually from the bier; and finally we see him standing erect between the guardian wings of Isis, who is stationed behind him. In front of the risen god there is a male figure who holds up before his eyes a crux ansata, the symbol of eternal life.

Another representation of the momentous mystery is depicted in the Temple of Isis at Philae. In this sculpture we see the body of Osiris with stalks of corn growing out of it;

and nearby stands a priest pouring water on the cornstalks from a pitcher. Accompanying this scene is an inscription which reads: "This is the form of him whom one may not name, Osiris of the Mysteries, who springs from the returning waters." From the above, we gather that Osiris was a personification of the corn, which sprouts up out of the fields after they have been fertilized by the annual inundation of the Nile. In fact, Osiris was sometimes called the "crop," or the "harvest." So we may reasonably conclude that in one of his aspects this god was a personification of the corn which annually died and came to life again.

Besides being a corn-spirit, Osiris was, among other things, a tree-god. His tree aspect was probably the more primitive of the two, since tree-worship is thought to be an earlier form of religion than the worship of cereals. The church-father Firmicus Maternus wrote a book, *The Errors of the Profane Religions*, where a pagan religious ceremony is described, in which Osiris was featured as a tree-spirit. The worshipers of the god first chopped down a pine tree; then the center of the tree was hollowed out. From the excavated wood an image of Osiris was fashioned; and the image was buried like a corpse in the hollow of the pine. The enclosed image was kept for a year, then burned. In the Hall of Osiris at Denderah, there is a picture of a coffin, within which is shown the hawk-headed mummy of the god, and the coffin is portrayed as enclosed within the trunk of a tree. This scene tends to confirm the accuracy of the account of the ceremony given us by Firmicus Maternus.

Osiris was also a fertility-god. Phallic images of him were displayed in the temples and carried in processions.

As a god of vegetation [Frazer points out], Osiris was naturally conceived as a god of creative energy in general, since men at a certain stage of evolution fail to distinguish between the reproductive powers of animals and plants. Hence a striking feature of his worship was the coarse but expressive symbolism by which this aspect of his nature was presented to the eye not merely of the initiated but of the multitude. At his festival women used to go about the village singing songs in his praise and carrying obscene images of him which they set in motion by means of strings. The custom was probably a charm to ensure the growth of crops [*The Golden Bough,* abridged edition, p. 381, by James George Frazer].

A familiar role of Osiris was that of a god of the dead; among his titles were Ruler of the Dead, Lord of the Underworld, and Lord of Eternity. On the monuments he is shown occupying the judgment seat, armed with the staff of authority, and holding the crux ansata; while carved on his breast is a St. Andrew's cross; and the throne on which he sits is adorned with a pattern of squares in two colors, like a checkerboard, representing the good and evil which came before him for judgment.

Osiris also shone as a moon-god. He is said to have reigned in Egypt twenty-eight years. This is no doubt an allusion to the twenty-eight days of the lunar month. The rending of the body of Osiris into fourteen parts by Set and his evil companions refers to the waning of the moon, which was imagined to lose a portion of itself on each of the fourteen days of the second half of the lunar month. In the myth, Set finds the body of Osiris at the time of the full moon; the dismemberment of Osiris consequently began with the waning moon. That the god was sometimes identified with the moon we know from the fact that he was on occasion depicted as a mummy, wearing on his head a crescent moon in place of the usual crown. Plutarch in his *Isis and Osiris* discusses the theory that Osiris was the moon, and that Set, or Typhon, was the sun; "because the Moon," says he, "with her humid and generative light, is favorable to the propagation of animals and the growth of plants; while the sun with his fierce fire scorches and burns up all growing things, renders the greater part of the earth uninhabitable by reason of his blaze, and often overpowers the Moon herself."

Last, but not least, Osiris was a sun-god; and on this, most authorities on the history and religion of Egypt agree. An outstanding scholar renders the following verdict: "Mythologically, Osiris was the Sun after its disappearance in the west, where he was slain by the envious night, and yet destined to rise again the next morning." (*A Concise History of Religion,* Vol. I, p. 108, by F. J. Gould.) From this point of view Sir J. G. Frazer vigorously dissents; for he regards Osiris as a vegetation-god, and considers theories identifying that god with the sun as ill-founded. In his own words:

> The ground upon which some modern writers seem chiefly to rely for the identification of Osiris with the Sun, is that the story of his death fits better with the solar phenomena than with any other in nature. It may readily be admitted that the daily appearance and disappearance of the Sun might very naturally be expressed by a myth of his death and resurrection; and writers who regard Osiris as the Sun are careful to indicate that it is the diurnal, and not the annual, course of the Sun to which they understand the myth to apply. Thus Renouf, who identifies Osiris with the Sun, admitted the Egyptian Sun could not with any show of reason be described as dead in winter. But if his daily death was the theme of the legend, why was it celebrated by an annual ceremony? This fact alone seems fatal to the interpretation of the myth as descriptive of sunset and sunrise. Again, though the Sun may be said to die daily, in what sense can he be said to be torn in pieces? [*The Golden Bough,* p. 384, by James George Frazer].

The objections to identifying Osiris with the sun, urged by Frazer, have been ably criticized by the Right Honorable John M. Robertson. According to Robertson:

> Rightly intent on establishing a hitherto ill-developed principle of mythological interpretation, the cult of the vegetation

spirit, Dr. Frazer has unduly ignored the conjunction seen deductively to be inevitable and inductively to be normal between the concept of the vegetation-god and that of others, in particular the Sun-god. He becomes for once vigorously polemical in his attack on the thesis that Osiris was a sun-god, as if that were excluded once for all by proving him a vegetation-god. The answer is that he was both; and that such a synthesis was inevitable. . . . Mithra, who, so far as the records go, was primordially associated with the Sun, and was thereby named to the last, is mythically born on December 25th, clearly because of the winter solstice and the rising of the constellation of the virgin above the horizon. Dionysus and Adonis, Dr. Frazer shows, are vegetation gods. Yet they too are both born on December 25th, as was the Babe-Sun-God Horus, who was, however, exhibited as rising from a lotus plant. Now, why should the vegetation-God be born at the winter solstice save as having been identified with the Sun-god? [*Christianity and Mythology*, 2nd edition, p. 33, by John M. Robertson].

There is a considerable amount of literature on the Osirian cult of ancient Egypt. Among the best is *Adonis, Attis, Osiris: Studies in the History of Oriental Religion* by Sir James George Frazer, third edition, revised and enlarged, in two volumes bound in one; Part IV of *The Golden Bough: A Study in Magic and Religion* published by University Books, New Hyde Park, N. Y., 1961.

A smaller book, well worth reading, is *Osiris: A Study in Myths, Mysteries and Religion* by Harold P. Cooke. After a scholarly analysis of Osirianism, Cooke concludes: "The worship and rites of Osiris may have passed into Egypt, I think, from the neighboring state of Ethiopia." (*Osiris*, p. 154.) Cooke's opinion is quite plausible, for Osiris was indubitably a god of African origin.

This theory is sustained brilliantly by Sir E. A. Wallis Budge in *Osiris: The Egyptian Religion of the Resurrection.* In the introduction of the latest edition of this book we are told by a learned scholar, Dr. Jane Harrison, that: "We may say at once that we believe Dr. Budge triumphantly establishes his main thesis. Osiris is an African, though not necessarily a Nilotic god. Egyptian religion, in . . . its general Negroid coloring, is African through and through." Sir Wallis Budge possessed a profound knowledge of things Egyptian; and speaking of the ancient Egyptian people he declares: "Everything that we know of them proves that they possessed all the characteristics of the African race, and especially of that portion of it which lived in that great tract of country which extends from ocean to ocean, right across Africa, and is commonly known as the Sudan, i.e., the country *par excellence* of the Blacks." (*Osiris*, Vol. I, p. 174, by E. A. Wallis Budge. The Osirian mythology and religion are also discussed in *Traits of Divine Kingship in Africa* by the Reverend P. Hadfield.

Another phase of the myths, rites, and religious beliefs of the ancient Egyptians, which we must consider briefly, is that complex of astro-theology exemplified by the symbolism of the zodiac. The zodiac is an imaginary band encircling the celestial sphere; stretching eight degrees on each side of the ecliptic, the apparent path of the sun. The zodiac is divided in twelve sections, each corresponding to one month. The signs and constellations were originally the same but, due to the procession of the equinoxes, each sign moves westward into the next constellation in about 2,155 years. A sign therefore makes a complete circuit of the heavens in about 26,000 years. The constellations of the zodiac have the following names: Aries (the Ram or Lamb), Taurus (the Bull), Gemini (the Twins), Cancer (the Crab), Leo (the Lion), Virgo (the Virgin), Libra (the Balances), Scorpio (the Scorpion), Sagittarius (the Archer), Capricorn (the Goat), Aquarius (the Water-Carrier), and Pisces (the Fishes). These are the signs and constellations of the zodiac as standardized by the ancient

Greeks; but there were earlier zodiacs with other signs and symbols, which we shall discuss as we proceed.

The solar zodiac can be traced back to ancient Egypt, where it was known at a remote period of time; but the solar zodiac was preceded by a lunar zodiac, which was divided into twenty-seven or twenty-eight Lunar Mansions instead of twelve signs. "Although the Zodiac is now determined by the course in the heavens apparently pursued by the Sun in his annual journey through the sky," we are told by a noted astronomer, "it is very probable that it was originally determined by the path of the Moon, which follows very closely the path of the Sun, and which can be observed at the same time as the stars. The moon moves eastward among the stars at such a rate that it accomplishes a complete circuit of the sky in about 28 days." (*Astronomy*, p. 250, by Professor Arthur M. Harding.) Since the lunar month is between twenty-seven and twenty-eight days, the Lunar Mansions were sometimes twenty-seven in number, though twenty-eight was the usual figure. The Hindus had a Lunar Zodiac of twenty-seven mansions, whereas the Chinese and Arabs counted twenty-eight.

The symbolism of the zodiac is beautifully displayed in the myth of Hercules. "Of all the ancient divinities," Edward Carpenter observes, "perhaps Hercules is the one whose role as a Sun-god is most generally admitted. The helper of gods and men, a mighty traveller, and invoked everywhere as the Savior, his labors for the good of the world became ultimately defined and systematized as 12, and corresponding in number to the signs of the Zodiac." (*Pagan and Christian Creeds*, p. 48, by Edward Carpenter.) This myth of Hercules was known to the Sumerians, Phoenicians, and Greeks. Herodotus speculated on its origin and traced it back to the Egyptians. (See *The History of Herodotus*, pp. 96–97.) There is no god in the official Egyptian pantheon named Hercules, but

there was an ancient Greek tradition that Hercules was identical with the ancient Nilotic deity, Khonsu. Mr. George St.
Clair, after considering the principal gods of ancient Egypt,
directs our attention to "a little group of divinities standing
apart."

> These are Amen, Mut and Khonsu, often spoken of as the
> Triad of Thebes, or the Trinity of Ethiopia. . . . Budge tells
> us that the Theban triad had nothing whatever to do with the
> "Book of the Dead," and from this we may suspect that they
> were either gods newly come up or gods of foreign derivation.
> For some good reason the orthodox Egyptian of the old school
> kept them out of his sacred books. They were divinities of
> Thebes, and that city was hundreds of miles south of Heliopolis;
> they were the Trinity of Ethiopia and not of Egypt [*Creation
> Records Discovered in Egypt: Studies in the Book of the Dead,*
> p. 404, by George St. Clair].

In the myth of Hercules, the sun (of which Hercules is
the personification) begins his zodiacal journey in the constellation Leo, *the Lion.* So the first labor of Hercules was
the slaying of the Nemean lion. After killing the lion, the
hero flayed the beast and used its skin thereafter as a shield.
The skin of the lion has been compared to the tawny clouds
which the sun trails behind him as he fights his way through
the vapors which he eventually overcomes.

When the sun enters Virgo, the constellation of the *Hydra*
sets. The second labor of Hercules was the destruction of the
Lernean hydra. This monster had several heads, one of which
was immortal. As the hydra raised his heads one by one to
attack Hercules, the demi-god burned off the heads in turn.
He disposed of the immortal head by burying it beneath a
stone. "As the beast was possessed of many heads," writes
William Tyler Olcott, "so the storm-wind must continually
supply new clouds to vanquish the Sun; but the lighter vapor
and mist, the immortal head, is only conquered for a time.

The sun easily burns up the heavy clouds, the mortal heads, but only hides temporarily the immortal head which raises again and again to daunt him. In the fight Hercules was attended by his friend Iolus,—this name recalls that of Iole, signifying the violet tinted clouds, the attendants of the Sun in its serene moments." (*Sun Lore of All Ages*, pp. 72–73, by William Tyler Olcott.)

At the beginning of autumn, the sun enters Libra, and at this time of year the constellation of the *Centaur* rises above the horizon. In his third labor Hercules is entertained by a centaur. Later he slew a group of centaurs, fighting for a cask of wine. When the sun was in Libra, the constellation of the *Boar* rose in the evening sky. So after killing the centaurs, Hercules met the Erymanthian boar and disposed of him in mortal combat.

When the sun enters Scorpio, the constellation Cassiopeia, anciently known as the *Stag*, rises into view. The fourth labor of Hercules was the capture of a stag with golden horns and brazen feet.

As the sun passes into Sagittarius, three constellations, named for birds, rise. These three star-groups are called the *Vulture*, the *Swan*, and the *Eagle*. In his fifth labor Hercules kills three birds with arrows.

The constellation Capricorn is also known as the *Stable of Augeus*. The sixth labor of Hercules was the cleansing of the Augean stable.

When the Sun is in Aquarius, the Lyre, or celestial *vulture*, sets. Prometheus also sets, while the *Bull of Europa* is on the meridian. In the seventh labor, Hercules slays the vulture that had preyed on the liver of Prometheus; and also captured the wild bull which had laid waste the island of Crete.

While the sun is in Pisces, *Pegasus, the celestial horse*, rises. In his eighth labor Hercules carried off the horses of Diomede.

As the sun enters Aries, the *Ram* of the Golden Fleece,

the *Ship Argo* rises in the evening sky, and Andromeda sets. One of the stars of Andromeda is called her girdle. Hercules in the ninth labor sails in the Ship Argo to search for the Golden Fleece; he fought the Amazons and captured the girdle of Hippolyta, their queen, and rescued Hesione from a sea monster just as Perseus did Andromeda.

The sun passes into the *Bull*, or *ox*, as the *Pleiades* rise and *Orion* sets. The tenth labor of Hercules was to restore the seven kidnapped pleiades to their father, after killing their abductor, King Busiris (Orion); then he went to Spain and stole the oxen of Geryon.

When the sun goes into Gemini, Sirius, the *Dog-Star*, rises. In the eleventh labor Hercules conquered Cerberus, guardian Dog of Hades.

The sun enters Cancer as the constellations of the *River* and the *Centaur* set in the western sky. The constellation *Hercules* descends toward the west, followed by Draco, the *Dragon* of the Pole, guardian of the Golden Apples of the Hesperides. Hercules is represented in star atlases as crushing the head of the dragon with his foot. In his twelfth and last labor Hercules journeyed to the Hesperides to seek the Golden Apples; then he put on a robe dipped in the blood of a centaur slain by him at the crossing of a river. The robe mysteriously caught fire and Hercules perished in the flames. "In this death scene of the solar hero," says Olcott, "and in the glories of his funeral pyre, we have the most famous sunset scene that has ever been presented for our contemplation. All the wondrous coloring that adorns the western sky at set of Sun illuminates the canvas, and the reflection of the scene streams afar, lighting the waves of the Aegean and its clustering isles, and painting in enduring hues, a scene that all nations proclaim the sublimest that nature offers to man's vision." (*Sun Lore of All Ages*, p. 74, by William Tyler Olcott.)

In one of his major works Sir Wallis Budge makes the

incredible statement that: "The Egyptians borrowed their knowledge of the signs of the Zodiac, together with much else, from the Greeks, who had derived a great deal of their astronomical lore from the Babylonians." (*The Gods of the Egyptians*, Vol. II, p. 312.) This is putting the cart before the horse with a vengeance. A fitting rejoinder was made by Dr. Churchward, as follows:

> Why the knowledge of all this was old in Egypt before the Babylonians even existed or knew anything about it. . . . The Egyptians had worked out all the architecture of the heavens, and their priests had carried the same with them to all parts of the world—not only the Northern heavens but the Southern, as well. Probably they worked out the South before the North, and the Druids and the Mayas and the Incas knew it all from the priests of Egypt, the earliest probably thousands of years before the Babylonian nation existed. The Babylonians copied and obtained all their knowledge from the Egyptians, and we are surprised that Dr. Budge should write that they borrowed from the Greeks; they were old and degenerating in decay before the Greek nation was born! Well may he say that "it is a subject of conjecture at what period the Babylonians first divided the heavens into sections, etc.," because they never did; what they knew they borrowed either *direct from the Egyptians* or Sumerians—the latter obtained it from Egypt. It was the ancient Egyptians who mapped out the heavens into 12 divisions in the North, 12 divisions in the South, and 12 in the center, making 36 in all, and the 12 signs of the Zodiac. . . . It is very well to say that "whether the Babylonians were themselves the inventors of such origins—i.e. (the Zodiac), or whether they are to be attributed to the earlier non-Semitic Sumerian inhabitants of that country, cannot be said"—and when he states that "the Greeks borrowed the Zodiac from the Babylonians, and then the Greeks introduced it into Egypt, probably during the Ptolemaic period," it appears to us that Dr. Budge must have left that part of "the Gods of Egypt" to be written by one of his assistants,

who knew nothing about the history of the past [*The Signs and Symbols of Primordial Man*, pp. 212–13, by Dr. Albert Churchward].

Charles F. Dupuis, a French savant of the late eighteenth century, traced the origin of the solar zodiac back to ancient Egypt, and hence anticipated the conclusions of Dr. Albert Churchward by more than a century. And, presently, we shall see that modern research has revealed much evidence tending to support that viewpoint. In the *Open Court* magazine, August, 1906, there appeared a scholarly article entitled "Zodiacs of Different Nations," by Dr. Paul Carus. One illustration displays Egyptian and Greek zodiacs shown side by side in the photograph of a Late Roman Egyptian plaque. A list of the dual set of symbols is given below:

EGYPTIAN	GREEK
1. Cat	1. Ram
2. Jackal	2. Bull
3. Serpent	3. Twins
4. Scarab	4. Crab
5. Ass	5. Lion
6. Lion	6. Virgin
7. Goat	7. Scales
8. Cow	8. Scorpion
9. Falcon	9. Archer
10. Baboon	10. Goat
11. Ibis	11. Waterman
12. Crocodile	12. Fishes

The Egyptian Sphinx, a colossal statue, sacred to the sun-god Horus, was erected at least six thousand years ago. It has the body of a lion; emblematic, perhaps, of the entrance of the sun into the zodiacal sign of the Lion around 4000 B.C. The Temple of the Sphinx is constructed in the form of a cross, and symbolizes North, South, East, and West, or the cardinal points of the celestial sphere: the two solstices and the two equinoxes. It seems that there were originally only four signs of the zodiac, namely, the quarter· signs at the solstices and equinoxes. George St. Clair, an able student of astro-theological mythology has made some illuminating comments concerning the original four zodiacal signs, from which we quote the following:

> About 6000 years ago the Spring Sun would be entering Taurus; and the four quarter signs would be the Bull, the Lion, the Scorpion and the Waterman, though some of these signs might be otherwise named. In memory of that early arrangement—which in many ways left its mark—devices on rings were, for example, a scorpion, a lion, a hawk, and a cynocephalus ape. . . .
>
> From the four quarters we pass to the twelve signs. Between each two quarter signs two other signs were inserted. The planisphere of the Temple of Denderah shows four gods supporting the heavens at the four quarter points, corresponding to the Bull, the Lion, the Scorpion and the Waterman; and shows eight other divinities in pairs, one on either side of each pillar, making up the twelve [*Creation Records Discovered in Egypt*, pp. 136–37, by George St. Clair].

The four gods holding up the heavens were recognized in Egyptian mythology as the four children of the sun-god Horus, and their names were: Amset, Hapi, Tuamutef, and Gebhsennuf. These four amenthes, or Genii of Hades, were depicted as standing at the cardinal points of the celestial sphere and holding up the heavens. Each deity was identifiable by his particular features, as listed below:

> AMSET had the head of a MAN.
> HAPI possessed the head of an APE.
> TUAMUTEF was adorned by the head of a JACKAL.
> GEBHSENNUF wore on his shoulders the head of a HAWK.

These same sky gods are referred to in the "Bible" more than once (although the symbols are different), where they are called Cherubim. These celestial creatures were seen by Ezekiel in a vision which he had while in Babylon. "As for the likeness of their faces, they four had the face of a man, and the face of a lion, on the right side; and they four had the face of an ox on the left side; they four had the face of an eagle." (Ezekiel, I, 10).

In the Apocalypse we read about the "Four Beasts." In the "Book of Revelation," Chapter IV, Verse 7, we are told that: "The first beast was like a lion, and the second beast like a calf, and the third beast had a face as man, and the fourth beast was like a flying eagle." These "beasts" were the constellations, situated at the four cardinal points of the zodiac five thousand years ago. They were Taurus the Bull (Vernal Equinox), Leo the Lion (Summer Solstice), Scorpio the Scorpion (Autumnal Equinox), and Aquarius the Waterman (Winter Solstice). In the "Bible" the Eagle has been substituted for the Scorpion. We learn from the erudite Godfrey Higgins that: "The signs of the Zodiac, with the exception of the Scorpion, which was exchanged by Dan for the Eagle, were carried by the different tribes of the Israelites on their standards; and Taurus, Leo, Aquarius and Scorpio or the Eagle, the four signs of Reuben, Judah, Ephraim, and Dan, were placed at the four corners—the four cardinal points—of their encampment, evidently in allusion to the cardinal points of the sphere, the equinoxes and solstices, when the equinox was in Taurus." (*Anacalypsis*, Vol. II, p. 105, by Godfrey Higgins.)

The Egyptians, Chaldeans, and Greeks believed in certain star-gods called Decans. These decans were actually belts of stars extending across the sky, the risings of which followed each other by ten days. Dr. Wilhelm Gundel of Giessen, an authority on ancient astronomy, has produced a monumental work entitled *Dekane und Dekansternbilder* (*The Decans and Their Stars*). The book was published by J. J. Augustin at Gluckstadt and Hamburg, in Germany in 1936. It has not been translated into English, but it was reviewed in *Nature*, the scientific journal, by a famous naturalist, and since this review contains information both interesting and important we are pleased to quote from the same, as follows:

> When the year (of 360 days) had been divided into its 12 months and put under the zodiacal signs, each of the 12 was again divided into 3 parts, of 10 days each; and these 36 "decans" had their 36 gods, or rulers, or dynasts, watchers of the hours ("horoscopes"), servants or messengers of the greater gods, or of Horus himself in his holy name spelled with 36 letters; each had his own "face," which chance to be (in Egypt) the face of a bull or an ibis, or of an eagle, or of a man. These were the angels and archangels, the demons and archi-demons, of Hellenistic writers. Each had his own name; in mummy-cases and papyri in obscure and fragmentary works like Hermes Trismegistus, or the Testimonium Salomonis, in Celsus and Firmicus, in the traditionary learning of men like Kircher, Salmasius or Scaliger, we find the names of Chont-har, Chont-Chre, Siket, and the 33 others in all kinds of variants and corruptions. Egyptian they were in the beginning, but the true form and meaning of many are long lost ["The Science of Astrology," a book review, by Professor D'Arcy Wentworth Thompson, in *Nature*, Oct. 23, 1937].

After tracing the zodiacal symbols back to ancient Egypt, we might still wonder why these star signs were, in the main, named after animals.

> The impression we receive [to cite an authority] is that Sun-worship, and indeed the whole cosmic system of which it is typical was secondary in Egypt, imposing itself on a substratum of Totemism. In any case, . . . one thing is clear, namely, that nine-tenths of the mythology of ancient Egypt is cosmic in ori-

gin, and that it was grafted on to a totemic system with which it had originally no connection. Thus to Horus, a Falcon Totem in origin, was attached the whole of the mass of myth which centered around the Sun, while to Thoth, originally an Ibis Totem in the north-eastern Delta, accrued all the legend connected with the Moon [Professor T. Eric Peet, in *The Cambridge Ancient History*, Vol. I, p. 331, edited by Bury *et al.*].

In other words, the stellar symbolism of the zodiac was based on a still more ancient totemic symbolism. When the agriculturists of the Archaic Civilization of Africa were faced with the problem of determining the proper seasons for planting their crops by observing the motions of the stars, they projected the animal symbols of the totemic hunters into the skies, to become the Signs of the Zodiac.

The zodiacal symbolism which we have been discussing is closely connected with the rites and ceremonies of great religious systems, both ancient and modern. For instance in Egypt three thousand years ago, the birthday of the Sun-god was celebrated in the temples on the 25th of December; it was the first day to lengthen obviously after December 21st, the day of the winter solstice. At the midnight hour, on the very first minute of the 25th of December, the birth of the sun was commemorated. At that time the sun was in the zodiacal sign Capricorn, which was known as the Stable of Augeus; so the infant Sun-god was said to have been born in a stable. Shining brightly on the meridian was Sirius (the Star from the East); while rising in the east was Virgo (the Virgin), the line of the horizon passing through her center. To the right of Sirius was Orion, the great hunter, with three stars in his belt. These stars lie in a straight line and point toward Sirius; and in ancient times they were known as the Three Kings. We meet them in the Gospels as the Three Wise Men, or Magi. In the zodiac on the interior of the dome of the Temple of Denderah, the constellation Virgo was pictured as a woman with a spike of corn in one hand; and on the adjacent margin the Virgin is annotated by a figure of Isis with Horus in her arms.

> But it is well known as a matter of history [Edward Carpenter observes] that the worship of Isis and Horus descended in the early Christian centuries to Alexandria, where it took the form of the worship of the Virgin Mary and the infant Savior, and so passed into the European ceremonial. We have therefore the Virgin Mary connected by linear succession and descent with that zodiacal cluster in the sky! . . . A curious confirmation of the same astronomical connection is afforded by the Roman Catholic Calendar. For if this be consulted it will be found that the festival of the Assumption of the Virgin is placed on the 15th day of August, while the festival of the Birth of the Virgin is dated the 8th of September. . . . At the present day the zodiacal signs (owing to precession) have shifted some distance from the constellations of the same name. But at the time when the zodiac was constituted and these names were given, the first date obviously would signalize the actual disappearance of the cluster Virgo in the Sun's rays— i.e., the Assumption of the Virgin into the glory of the God— while the second date would signalize the reappearance of the constellation, or the Birth of the Virgin. The Church of Notre Dame of Paris is supposed to be on the original site of a Temple of Isis; and it is said (but I have not been able to verify this myself) that one of the side entrances—that, namely on the left in entering from the north (cloister) side—is figured with the signs of the Zodiac, except that the sign Virgo is replaced by the figure of the Madonna and Child [*Pagan and Christian Creeds*, pp. 32–33, by Edward Carpenter].

At the winter solstice (Christmas), the sun is at its southernmost position in the celestial sphere. After that date it begins to travel northward along the ecliptic; and at the vernal equinox (Easter), it passes over the celestial equator. This passing over of the sun from the south to the north of the equator was the origin of the festival of the Passover. When the sun reached the equinoctial point and crossed, or passed over, the equator three thousand years ago, it was situated in Aries, the Ram or Lamb; so the Lamb became the symbol of the god. Here we have a clue to the origin of the passover Lamb, which has been widely regarded as a type of the crucified Christ. If the reader should consult such books as *The World's Sixteen Crucified Saviors* by Kersey Graves, and *Bible Myths and Their Parallels in Other Religions* by T. W. Doane, he would find that several pagan sun-gods were said to have been crucified. The meaning of this solar crucifixion has been explained in a scholarly manner by L. Gordon Rylands:

> For in an astronomical chart, the Sun is apparently crucified upon the intersecting lines of the equator and the ecliptic at the moment of his descent into the lower hemisphere, the hemisphere of darkness and death; and it is so again at the moment of his resurrection into the hemisphere of light and life; while the period of transit is three days. . . . At the time when the myth of the death of the Sun-god originated, the Sun being in the constellation Aries at the Spring Equinox, was identified with the Ram. That is the Lamb which had been "slain from the foundation of the world." The custom of dressing the paschal lamb in the shape of a cross is referable to the same myth [*The Beginnings of Gnostic Christianity*, p. 217, by L. Gordon Rylands].

Limitations of space preclude a more extensive discussion of the symbols, myths, and rites of the ancient Egyptian religion. For the reader who would like to know more about such subjects, we recommend *The Secret Societies of All Ages and Countries* by Charles William Heckethorn.

The great merchants and mariners of the ancient world were the Phoenicians, who adopted much of the culture of ancient Egypt and were instrumental in the spread of its elements to other nations, various and remote. We first hear of them dwelling on the shores of the Persian Gulf, and we are told that they later colonized the land of Canaan at the eastern end of the Mediterranean. These people called themselves Canaanites; the name Phoenicians was bestowed upon them by the Greeks. These ancient mariners were manufacturers of a famous dye known as "royal purple," which the Greeks called "Phoenix," and as a result they were nicknamed Phoenikes or Phoenicians. We know almost nothing of the early history of these people. "The historical colonization of Africa by Alien peoples," we are told by a modern African scholar, "begins with the exploits of the Phoenicians in Mauretania. . . . The Phoenicians were a Semitic people who, originally, appear to have resembled the Jews in race and language." (*African Glory*, p. 15, by Professor J. C. deGraft-Johnson.)

We think the professor is a bit too dogmatic, for there is a tradition that the ancestors of the Phoenicians originally came from the land of Punt, in East Africa. Though these people adopted a Semitic language, we know that they were considered Ethiopians by the ancient Greeks. Here the opinions of a philosophical American historian are germane: "Who, now, were those Phoenicians . . . whose ships sailed every sea, whose merchants bargained in every port? The historian is abashed before any question of origins; he must confess that he knows next to nothing about either the early or the late history of this ubiquitous, yet elusive, people. We do not know whence they came, nor when, we are not certain that they were Semites." (*Our Oriental Heritage*, pp. 291–92, by Dr. Will Durant.)

On the eastern Mediterranean coast the Phoenicians carried on their industrial and commercial operations from the famous cities of Byblos, Aradus, Sidon, and Tyre. The port of Byblos was exporting timber to Egypt as far back as the 3rd dynasty, when forty ships laden with the famous Cedars of Lebanon sailed up the Nile. We learn from a stone tablet, dating from the reign of the Pharaoh Snefru, that: "We brought 40 ships

laden with cedar trunks. We built ships of cedarwood. . . .
We made the doors of the king's palace of cedarwood."
(Cited by Robert Silverberg in *Empires in the Dust*, p. 112.)
In later days when their homeland was overwhelmed by in-
vaders, the Phoenicians established many colonies, among
them being Carthage, Utica, and Bizerte on the North Afri-
can shore, and at Gades (Cadiz) in Spain, and Palermo in
Sicily.

Carthage, a city-state, the most celebrated of the Phoenician
colonies, was established on the North African coast in the
year 814 B.C. Carthage was one of the great cities of the
ancient world, and it is one of the tragedies of history that,
after the three Punic Wars, waged by the Romans, Carthage
was finally destroyed. After losing Sicily to Rome in 242 B.C.,
the Carthaginians were faced with a rebellion of their Libyan
vassals at home. To forestall Roman aid to the rebels, Carthage had to surrender the island of Sardinia to the Romans.

The Libyans were subdued by Carthaginian arms, under
the generalship of Hamilcar Barca in 238 B.C. Hamilcar had
a dream of restoring the ancient glories of Carthage, and of
recapturing Sicily and Sardinia. So the second Punic War
was waged in Europe and Africa, with Hannibal, a son of
Hamilcar, leading the Carthaginians, and Cornelius Scipio
heading the armies of Rome. A series of blunders on the part
of Hannibal brought about the final debacle of the Carthaginians at the Battle of Zama, in 202 B.C. The Roman peace
terms were harsh. Carthage was compelled to pay, over a
period of fifty years, an indemnity of 10,000 talents of silver,
about $20,000,000 in modern currency. All the ships of war
and elephants of Carthage were confiscated by the Romans;
and the establishment of new colonies or involvement in
foreign wars was forbidden, unless approved by Rome. The
great African city-state, despite all these trials and tribula-
tions, made a good recovery, and might have survived and
prospered; but in the year 150 B.C., the armies of King

Masinissa of Numidia, an African ally of Rome, invaded Carthaginian territory. The Carthaginians counter-attacked, and a war was on. The Romans, led by the evil-minded Cato, a member of the Roman Senate, who was out to crush Carthage under any pretext, declared war on Carthage. This war, started by Rome in 149 B.C., under the perfidious claim that an old treaty had been violated, raged for three years. In 146 B.C., the city of Carthage was captured by the Romans and was completely destroyed by fire. This wanton destruction of the great African city by the Romans must be regarded as one of the great crimes of history. For the Carthaginians, and their Phoenician forebears, were culturally and intellectually superior to the Romans. We all have heard about the Library at Alexandria, but how many know about the great Library of Carthage? In the words of Professor Hapgood: "They [the Romans] burned the great city of Carthage, their ancient enemy and their incalculable superior in everything relating to science. The library of Carthage is said to have contained about 500,000 volumes, and these no doubt dealt with the history and the sciences of Phoenicia as a whole." (*Maps of the Ancient Sea Kings,* p. 196, by Charles H. Hapgood.)

The ships of the Phoenicians traded with ports on the shores of the Indian Ocean, the Mediterranean, the Black Sea, and the Atlantic Ocean. The Phoenician seafarers and traders worked tin mines in Cornwall and traded with the ancient Britons; and their ships circumnavigated Africa and crossed the Atlantic Ocean to America. The Phoenicians have been credited by certain scholars with the invention of the alphabet, but this claim must be disallowed. It has been shown by the researches of the French Egyptologist, Prisse d'Avennes, that we owe our alphabet to the Egyptians. The Phoenicians adopted the Egyptian alphabet and simplified, and then diffused, it among other nations. "It is sufficiently proved," observes one scholar, "by the papyrus in the Bibliotheque Nationale, Paris, actually the oldest book in the world. It consists of eighteen pages written in black ink with a bold round character, the prototype of the letters copied by the Greeks from the Phoenicians and transmitted through the Latins to us." (*Lost Civilizations*, p. 15, by Charles J. Finger.)

Gerald Massey in his learned work, *A Book of the Beginnings*, argued persuasively that civilization first arose in the interior of the African continent and then, after passing through Egypt, was in due time diffused over the rest of the globe. We have no evidence that the ancient Egyptians ever sent any colonists to the British Isles, yet Mr. Massey shows that there was a definite Egyptian cultural influence among the ancient Britons. In *A Book of the Beginnings* is a long list of English words, still in use today, that seem to be of ancient Egyptian origin. Massey's book is long out of print, but a short selection from his list of Egypto-English words has been reproduced by Lillian Eichler in *The Customs of Mankind*, from which we cite a few examples:

ENGLISH	*EGYPTIAN*
Abode (habitation)	Abut (abode)
Attack	Atakh
Autumn (the season)	Atum (the red autumnal sun)
Canoe	Khenna (a boat)
Count (a title)	Kannt (a title)
Cow	Kaui (cow)
Foot	Fut (a measure)
Hag (witch)	Hek (magic)
Kick	Khekh (to repulse)
Mamma (the mother)	Mama (to bear)
Married	Mer-T (attached)
Mayor	Mer (he who rules)
Ray (of sunlight)	Ra (the sun)
Suit (to satisfy)	Suta (to please)
Write	Ruit (to engrave)
Youth	Uth (youth)

"Whether this great similarity between English and Egyptian words is coincidence," Miss Eichler comments, "or whether at some remote time there was a pro-Hamitic language which branched off into the Aryan group, is not definitely known. It is a tempting problem for speculation." (*The Customs of Mankind*, p. 133, by Lillian Eichler.)

Many of the problems and puzzles of history could be cleared up if we could only get over the absurd propaganda that Africa for some strange and mysterious reason has for ages been cut off from the rest of the world. If this were so, how is it that the great nations of both ancient and modern times have worshiped black gods, and embraced religious systems of African origin? "At Corinth there was a black Venus," we learn from the extensive researches of Mr. Godfrey Higgins, and that learned author continues:

> "In my search into the origin of the ancient Druids I continually found at last, that my labors terminated with something black. . . . Osiris and his Bull were black; all the Gods and Goddesses of Greece were black; at least this was the case with Jupiter, Bacchus, Hercules, Apollo, Ammon. The Goddesses Venus, Isis, Hecate, Diana, Juno, Metis, Ceres, Cybele, are black." (*Anacalypsis*, Vol. I, pp. 137–38, by Godfrey Higgins.)

Among the Christian nations of Europe, even into modern times, we notice a similar tendency, and we follow Mr. Higgins in his observations:

> In all the Romish countries of Europe, in France, Germany, Italy, etc., the God Christ, as well as his mother, are described in their old pictures and statues to be black. The infant God in the arms of his black mother, his eyes and drapery white, is himself perfectly black. If the reader doubt my word, he may go to the cathedral at Moulins—to the famous chapel of the Virgin at Loretto—to the church of the Annunciata—the

church of St. Lazaro, or the Church of St. Stephen at Genoa
—to St. Francisco at Pisa—to the Church at Brixen, in the
Tyrol, and to that at Padua—to the church of St. Theodore,
at Munich . . . to a church and to the Cathedral at Augsburg,
where are a black virgin and child as large as life—to Rome,
to the Borghese Chapel Maria Maggiore—to the Pantheon—
to a small chapel of St. Peter's, on the right hand side on entering, near the door; and, in fact, to almost innumerable other
churches, in countries professing the Romish religion. There
is scarcely an old church in Italy where some remains of the
worship of the BLACK VIRGIN and BLACK CHILD are not to be
met with. Very often the black figures have given way to
white ones, and in these cases the black ones, as being held
sacred, were put into retired places in the churches, but were
not destroyed, but are yet to be found there [*Anacalypsis,*
Vol. I, p. 138, by Godfrey Higgins].

We now have evidence of cultural influences from Egypt
and other parts of Africa having reached the New World at
least three thousand years ago. This material will be discussed
in our chapter on "Africa and the Discovery of America."

It may be of interest to the reader to know that the ancient Egyptians did not call themselves "Egyptians"; the name was invented by the Greeks. The first Greek visitors to Egypt, in the seventh century B.C., were greatly impressed by the Temple of Ptah, at Memphis. They regarded it as the grandest structure in the Nile Valley and they afterward referred to this ancient land as Hekaptah (The Land of the Temple of Ptah). In the Greek language Hekaptah became Aiguptos; and under the Roman rule the name was Latinized into Aegyptus, from whence we get the name Egypt. The ancient inhabitants of this African land called their country Khem, or Kam, or Ham, which literally meant "the black land"; and they called themselves Khemi, or Kamites, or Hamites, meaning "the black people." (For further information along these lines, see *The Wisdom of the Egyptians* by Brian Brown.)

There is an interesting discourse on this question in Gerald Massey's *A Book of the Beginnings;* and since this work is now rare and almost impossible to obtain, we shall quote from it briefly as follows:

"Egypt is often called Kam, the black land, and Kam does signify black; the name probably applied to the earliest inhabitants whose type is the Kam or Ham of the Hebrew writers." (*A Book of the Beginnings*, Vol. I, p. 4, by Gerald Massey.)

"It will be maintained in this book that the oldest mythology, religion, symbols, language had their birthplace in Africa, that the primitive race of Kam came thence, and the civilization attained in Egypt, emanated from that country and spread over the world. The most reasonable view on the evolutionary theory . . . is that the black race is the most ancient, and that Africa is the primordial home." (*Ibid.*, p. 18.)

"The Hebrew scriptures, among their other fragments of ancient lore, are very emphatic in deriving the line of Mizraim from Ham or Kam, the black type coupled with Kush, another form of the black. They give no countenance to the theory of Asiatic origin for the Egyptians. In the Biblical account of the generations of Noah, Mizraim is the son of Ham, i.e., of Kam, the black race." (*Ibid.*, p. 33.)

Note: THE ORIGIN OF THE ZODIAC; THE OPINIONS
OF COUNT VOLNEY

Should it be asked at what epoch this system [the zodiacal symbolism], took its birth, we shall answer on the testimony of the monuments of astronomy itself, that its principles appear with certainty to have been established about 17,000 years ago. And if it be asked to what people it is to be attributed, we shall answer that the same monuments, supported by unanimous traditions, attribute it to the first tribes of Egypt; and when reason finds in that country all the circumstances which could lead to such a system; when it finds there a zone of sky, bordering on the tropic, equally free from the rains of the equator and the fogs of the north; when it finds there a central point of the sphere of the ancients, a salubrious climate, a great, but manageable river, a soil fertile without art or labor, inundated without morbid exhalations, and placed between two seas which communicate with the richest countries, it conceives that the inhabitant of the Nile, addicted to agriculture, from the nature of his soil, to geometry from the annual necessity of measuring his lands, to commerce from the facility of communications, to astronomy from the state of his sky, always open to observation, must have been the first to pass from the savage to the social state; and consequently to attain the physical and moral sciences necessary to civilized life.

It was then, on the borders of the Upper Nile, among a black race of men, that was organized the complicated system of the worship of the stars, considered in relation to the productions of the earth and the labors of agriculture; and this first worship characterized by their adoration under their own forms and natural attributes, was a simple proceeding of the human mind. . . .

As soon as this agricultural people began to observe the stars with attention, they found it necessary to individualize or group them; and to assign to each a proper name. . . . A great difficulty must have presented itself. . . . First the heavenly bodies, similar in form, offered no distinguishing characteristics by which to denominate them; and secondly, the language in its infancy and poverty had no expressions for so many new and metaphysical ideas. Necessity, the usual stimulus of genius, surmounted everything. Having remarked that in annual revolution, the renewal and periodical appearance of terrestrial productions were constantly associated with the rising and setting of certain stars, and to their position as relative to the sun, . . . the mind by a natural operation connected in thought the terrestrial and celestial objects, which were connected in fact; and applying to them a common sign, it gave to the stars and their groups, the names of the terrestrial objects to which they answered.

Thus the Ethiopian of Thebes named the stars of inundation or Aquarius, those stars under which the Nile began to overflow; stars of the ox or bull, those under which they began to plow; stars of the lion, those under which that animal, driven from the desert by thirst, appeared on the banks of the Nile; stars of the sheaf, or of the harvest virgin, those of the reaping season; stars of the lamb, stars of the two kids, those under which these precious animals were brought forth. . . .

Thus the same Ethiopian having observed that the return of the inundation always corresponded with the rising of a beautiful star which appeared towards the source of the Nile, and seemed to warn the husbandman against the coming waters, he compared this action to that of the animal who, by his barking, gives notice of danger, and he called this star the dog, the barker (Sirius). In the same manner he named the stars of the crab, those where the sun, having arrived at the tropic, retreated by a slow retrograde motion like the crab or cancer. He named stars of the wild goat or Capricorn, those where the sun, having reached the highest point in his annuary tract . . . imitates the goat, who delights to climb to the summit of the rocks. He named the stars of the balance, or Libra, those where the days and nights being equal, seemed in equilibrium, like that instrument; and stars of the Scorpion, those where certain periodical winds bring vapors, burning like the venom of the scorpion. In the same manner he called by the name of rings and serpents the figured traces of the orbits of the stars and the planets, and such was the general mode of naming all the stars and even the planets, taken by groups or as individuals, according to their relations with husbandry and terrestrial objects, and according to the analogies which each nation found between them and the objects of its particular soil and climate [*The Ruins of Empires*, pp. 120–23, by C. F. Volney].

Chapter Four

AFRICA AND THE CIVILIZING OF EUROPE: THE EMPIRE OF THE MOORS

Most of North Africa is covered by the desolate sands of the Sahara Desert; but this region has not always been a desert. In prehistoric times this area was quite fertile, and was the home of a fairly advanced culture. A pioneer in the study of this region was Professor Leo Frobenius. In exploring many caverns in North Africa, Frobenius found numerous frescoes, ceramics, statues, and ideograms. Some of the paintings found in these caves are of considerable artistic merit. Among them are pictures of extinct birds and other animals. The paintings show elephants and buffaloes of a larger size than our contemporary species, and thus give us an idea of their great antiquity.

Another great discovery of the North African past was made in 1933 by a young French army officer, Lieutenant Brenans. This soldier was on a mission that led him to the Tassili-n-Ajjer Plateau in the Central Sahara; and, while preparing to spend the night in a cave, he noticed a drawing of a giraffe on a wall. After scraping off a film of dust encrusting the figure, Lieutenant Brenans found himself gazing at a fine painting done in colors by some prehistoric artist. The next morning, neighboring caves and rocks were examined; and many other drawings, dating back to a remote past, were discovered. Brenans made sketches of the ancient drawings and sent them to Paris.

The response was most gratifying; for an expedition was organized in Paris, which set out for the Sahara. Among the leading scientists in the party were Professors Gauthier, Reygasse, and Perret, and last, but not least, a young anthropologist, Henri Lhote. After six weeks of exploring, the professors returned to France, leaving Brenans and Lhote to continue the work. The rock paintings of Tassili-n-Ajjer showed that eight thousand to nine thousand years ago the Sahara region was not a desert, but a fertile territory of grasslands, forests, and rivers, inhabited by antelopes, giraffes, elephants, crocodiles, hippopotami and rhinoceroses. The human inhabitants seem to have been hunters and pastoral people.

During World War II, Brenans died, and Lhote continued the work on his own. Fortunately, in 1955 the National Research Center of France provided funds to hire a team of artists and photographers to assist Lhote in his explorations; and in 1957 the young scientist was able to return to Paris with a large number of fine reproductions of the Saharan drawings. On some of the rocks were as many as sixteen layers of drawings. This could only mean that the area sheltered human inhabitants over a period of thousands of years. The drawings show that hunting tribes were succeeded by herders accompanied by their flocks of cattle. In many paintings are scenes of primitive rituals of a magical or religious nature.

The archaeological exploration of the African continent is still in its infancy, and the future indubitably has many marvels and wonders to reveal. Herodotus, as he traveled widely in Asia and Africa in the fifth century, B.C., noticed that in Africa there were four easily recognizable groups of people—two of native origin and two of foreign derivation. The two native groups were the Ethiopians and the Libyans, and the two foreign peoples were the Phoenicians and the Greeks. The Libyans spoke a Hamitic type of language similar to that of the Egyptians, which is not surprising, since both peoples were members of the African Ethiopian group. The word Hamite is often used ambiguously. Anyone who speaks a Hamitic language or dialect is a Hamite, and there is no necessary racial connotation involved. But certainly the idea, widely entertained, that the ancient Hamites of Africa were of Caucasoid origin is demonstrably untenable. The late Sir Harry Johnston, who was considered an authority on the Hamites, defined them as: "That Negroid race which was the main stock of the ancient Egyptian, and is represented at the present day by the Somali, the Galla and some of the blood of Abyssinia and of Nubia, and perhaps by the peoples of the Sahara Desert." (*The Uganda Protectorate*, Vol. II, p. 473, by Harry H. Johnston.)

These Libyans are referred to in ancient records often by the names of their various tribes, such as Atalantans, Getulians, Maurusians, Nasamonians, and Tehennu. Herodotus has an interesting account of how a group of young men of the Nasamonian tribe crossed the Sahara Desert and made contact with Pygmies dwelling on the banks of the Niger River. The Father of History first tells us that "the Nasamonians are a Libyan race"; and then he continues his story as follows:

They said there had grown up among them some wild young men, the sons of certain chiefs, when they came to man's estate, indulged in all manner of extravagancies, and among other things drew lots for five of their number to go and explore the desert parts of Libya, and try if they could not penetrate further than any had done previously. The coast of Libya along the sea which washes it to the north, throughout its entire length from Egypt to Cape Soloeis, which is its furtherest point, is inhabited by Libyans of many distinct tribes who possess the whole tract except certain portions which belong to the Phoenicians and the Greeks. Above the coast line and the country inhabited by the maritime tribes, Libya is full of wild beasts; while beyond the wild beast region there is a tract which is wholly sand, very scant of water, and utterly and entirely a desert. The young men therefore, despatched on this errand by their comrades with a plentiful supply of water and provisions, travelled at first through the inhabited region, passing which they came to the wild beast tract, whence they finally entered upon the desert, which they proceeded to cross in a direction from east to west. After journeying for many

days over a wide extent of sand, they came at last to a plain
where they observed trees growing; approaching them, and
seeing fruit on them, they proceeded to gather it. While they
were thus engaged, there came upon them some dwarfish men,
under the middle height, who seized them and carried them
off. The Nasamonians could not understand a word of the language, nor had they any acquaintance with the language of
the Nasamonians. They were led across extensive marshes and
finally came to a town, where all the men were of the height
of their conductors, and black complexioned. A great river
flowed by the town, running from west to east and containing
crocodiles [*The History of Herodotus,* Book II, pp. 91–92].

After the destruction of the old city of Carthage in 146
B.C., the Romans established a group of five provinces in
North Africa, which territory was called Africa Romana.
The ancient Libyan inhabitants of this region, originally a
branch of the western Ethiopians, became intermixed with
the Phoenician, Greek, and Roman immigrants. The modern
obsessions of racial and religious prejudice were unknown in
the ancient world, and the various ethnic groups intermarried
freely. The Romans called the indigenous dwellers of North
Africa Barbari (barbarians), from whence we get the name
"Berber." So in medieval and even modern times the North
Africans have generally been known as Berbers. The Romans
dubbed these Africans "barbarians," not because of any cultural inferiority, but merely because they had certain social
customs that were different from those of the Romans. The
Libyans or Berbers possessed a matriarchal type of social organization, which was common to all African societies, but
which seemed quite odd and strange to the Romans of Europe.

The Roman imperialists were able to conquer Carthage
only because they were aided by the rulers of Numidia and
Mauritania and by the citizens of the Phoenician colony of
Utica. The tragic result of this misguided policy of the Afri-

can brothers of the Carthaginians is well told by Professor J. C. deGraft-Johnson, as follows:

> The Numidian and Mauritanian kings and chiefs allied themselves to the Romans because they desired home rule or self-government, and for that reason they wanted the power of Carthage destroyed, as Carthaginian influence was already making itself felt in their internal and external affairs. But no sooner had the Numidian kings and chiefs assisted Rome to destroy Carthage than Rome picked a quarrel with them and annexed their country. The Mauritanian kings, who occupied part of modern Morocco and Algeria, had hoped to exercise self-determination and enjoy full self-government, but this was not to be. Within the hundred-odd years from the fall of Carthage in 146 B.C. to 42 B.C., Rome incorporated or absorbed into her Empire the regions equivalent to western Tripolitania, Tunisia, and all the coastal regions of Algeria and Morocco. Rome also annexed the old Greek colonies in Cyrenaica, and in 30 B.C. added the newly acquired territory of Egypt to the Cyrenaican possessions in order to form a Roman province [*African Glory*, p. 25, by J. C. deGraft-Johnson].

Julius Caesar, in the first century B.C., decided, after having a strange dream while encamped near the ruins of Carthage, that a new Carthage should be built on the site of the old city. He died before the plan could be carried out, and it was left to Augustus Caesar actually to undertake the project. The story of the genesis of the new city of Carthage has been so well narrated by Dr. DeGraft-Johnson, that we give it in his own words:

> When he was encamped near the ruins of Carthage in 46 B.C., Julius Caesar had a dream. He dreamt that he saw a great army of men and that he heard their bitter weeping. When he awoke he scribbled words on his tablets that led to the rebuilding of the doomed city. I say "doomed" city because the

ancients believed that there was a curse on the city of Carthage.
Not long after Julius Caesar had planned the rebuilding of the
ruined city of Carthage, he lay dead in the Forum in Rome,
with twenty-three gaping wounds in his sides. Caesar, because
he had dared to plan the rebuilding of a cursed city, had himself been destroyed, so at least some of the ancients thought.
The curse was still working, they remarked under their breaths.
Upon Caesar Augustus, however, devolved the unpleasant duty
of ignoring the curse and, in accordance with established religious convention, carrying out the dead Julius Caesar's written
instructions.

Carthage was rebuilt in the finest Roman architectural style.
The builders worked under military discipline, and soon the
temples, palaces, baths, theatres, high houses, and market-places
sprang up on the old sites. A new Forum was erected, the
villas and lovely gardens of the Carthaginian suburb of Megara
reappeared. . . . Utica and Carthage were joined by a splendid
road in the true Roman style and blockhouses were built at
intervals along the route in order to protect the caravans against
robbers. Other forts and cities soon made their appearance,
and with the rebuilding of Carthage the prosperity of North
Africa increased tremendously. . . . Julius and Augustus
Caesar had in part atoned for the sins of the past [*African
Glory*, pp. 27–29].

After the end of the Hellenistic culture of Alexandria, the
Romans became the new custodians of civilization. But the
Roman system of society was not built to last; for in intellectual acumen the Romans were greatly inferior to the
Greeks. In the fields of pure science and abstract thought the
Romans made a sorry showing. Contrariwise, in the industrial
arts, and in the applied sciences, their contributions to culture
were of considerable merit. The defects of the Roman system, however, overshadowed its virtues, and in due time led
to its disintegration. The main shortcomings of Roman civilization were slavery, militarism, and a bad fiscal system; and
these vices gradually led the Empire into the debacle of the

Dark Ages in Europe. The Roman ruling class attempted to postpone the impending crisis by disestablishing the old pagan cults and making Christianity the state religion, but this was of no avail. The barbarians began to overrun the western Roman Empire in the early part of the fifth century C.E. (Christian Era); and by the end of the century Roman civilization was in ruins. The Empire possessed a dual government, with an Emperor of the West ruling from Rome, and an Emperor of the East with his throne in Constantinople. In the year 476 A.C. (After Christ), the last Roman ruler of the West was toppled from his throne, and what remained of the Roman imperial power was transferred to the Byzantine, or Eastern Roman Empire. A vivid account of this transfer of power was penned by an eminent authority on medieval history:

> In the summer of 477 A.D., a band of ambassadors, who claimed to speak the will of the decayed body which still called itself the Roman Senate, appeared before the judgment seat of the Emperor Zeno, the ruler of Constantinople and the Eastern Empire. They came to announce to him that the army of the West had slain the patrician Orestes, and deposed from his throne the son of Orestes, the boy-emperor Romulus. But they did not then proceed to inform Zeno that another Caesar had been duly elected to replace their late sovereign. Embassies with such news had been common of late years, but this particular deputation, unlike any other which had yet visited the Bosphorus, came to announce to the Eastern emperor that his own mighty name sufficed for the protection of both East and West. They laid at his feet the diadem and purple robe of Romulus, and professed to transfer their homage and loyalty, to his august person [*The Dark Ages,* p. 1, by Sir Charles Oman].

By the end of the fifth century, Europe had begun the long night of the Dark Ages, which lasted five hundred years (500–1000 A.C.). The blame for the fall of Rome has generally been attributed to the barbarians, but they cannot fairly be held entirely responsible for the disaster. "The Dark Ages," declares Professor James Thompson, "were at least as much due to the corruption of the church as to the decay of Roman civilization or the barbarian invasions." (*Economic and Social History of the Middle Ages,* p. 74, by James Westfall Thompson.) Among the barbarians who invaded the Roman Empire were a Teutonic tribe called the Vandals. We first hear of them as dwelling near the shores of the Baltic Sea. They later moved southward by way of the Upper Danube into Gaul, and then into northern Spain, where they settled down for awhile. In fact, in 411 A.C. they attained official status as subjects of the Roman Empire and were ceded grants of land from that body. The Vandals, however, were soon evicted from their holdings by an invasion of the Visigoths. The Vandals retreated to southern Spain, where their tenure was quite insecure, since they were in danger of being overwhelmed by the still oncoming Visigoths. But luck was with them; in their hour of need and peril, Count Boniface, a Roman Legate in North Africa invited them to come over and settle in Africa Romana. Why, we ask, was this generous offer made to the Vandals, and what was the result of it? We give the graphic details in the words of Dr. J. C. deGraft-Johnson:

When Count Boniface, Roman Legate in Africa, sent an invitation to the Vandals to come over in order to assist him to govern the five provinces of North Africa, he opened up a new chapter in African history. Why did Count Boniface choose to betray Rome and to rebel against its imperial might? The explanation is that, having been summoned to Rome, he received reports before he set out that the Empress Placidia was resolved on his ruin. He therefore sought to protect himself as best he could, and in the end turned traitor. Count Boniface's wife was a Vandal, and it was only natural that he should have sought help from that quarter. We do not know what other reasons Boniface had for inviting the Vandals to

Africa, but the invitation was sent, in spite of the eloquent protests of St. Augustine, Bishop of Hippo. . . . Count Boniface's invitation therefore was very welcome, and the Vandals there and then took the serious decision to leave Spain forever. . . . This tremendous invasion found Africa unprepared. Count Boniface realized his mistake when it was too late, and the irony of the situation was that he found no city in which to seek refuge except Augustine's city of Hippo. Boniface held out in Hippo for fourteen months, but he had to surrender to the Vandals in the end. . . . The city fell in 430 and with its fall began the rule of the Vandals in Africa [*African Glory*, pp. 53–54].

Genseric, King of the Vandals, was recognized as a Vassal ruler by the Roman government in 435. His rule extended over certain provinces of Africa Romana, but Carthage was specifically excluded from his domain. For a while the son of Genseric was held as a hostage by the Romans; and, after securing release of his son, the king treacherously invaded and conquered Carthage in the year 439. The African subjects of the Vandal monarch were harshly treated: He seized the wealthiest African nobles and made them slaves to his sons and to his most important followers. The best African land was confiscated and parceled out among the Vandals; while the African people were left with land of inferior quality and were afflicted with exorbitant taxes. It has been truly reported of them that: "They found Africa flourishing and they left it desolate, with its great buildings thrown down, its people reduced to slavery, and the Church of Africa—so important in those early days of Christianity—practically non-existent." (Cited by Dr. DeGraft-Johnson in *African Glory*, p. 56.)

The Vandal tyranny in North Africa was ended in 533, when Emperor Justinian of the Byzantine (Eastern Roman) Empire decided on the reconquest of Africa Romana. The Byzantine forces under General Belisarius defeated the army of King Gelimer of the Vandals, and the African provinces were again brought under Roman rule. The city of Carthage enjoyed marked prosperity under Byzantine rule, but the African people in general did not fare so well; in fact, they were little better off than they had been in the days of the Vandal occupation. The condition of Byzantine Carthage was described by a contemporary writer, the Monk Salvian, as follows:

> Where are there more abundant treasures than with the Africans? Where can we find more prosperous commerce— shops better stocked? The Prophet Ezekiel said of Tyre: "Thou has filled thy treasury with gold and silver by the extent of thy commerce; but I say of Africa that her commerce enriched her so much that not only were her treasuries filled, but she seemed able to fill those of the whole universe. . . ." Carthage, the Rome of Africa, held in her bosom all the treasures of the State; here was the seat of government and of all the institutes of the State; here there were schools for the liberal arts, audiences for philosophers, chairs for professors of all languages and for every branch of law [cited by Dr. DeGraft-Johnson in *African Glory*, p. 57].

The fate of the masses of the African people is best described in the words of the Byzantine historian Procopius, the official secretary of General Belisarius, who declared that:

> Justinian, after the defeat of the Vandals, took no trouble to ensure the complete occupation of the country. He failed to realize that the best guarantee of authority resides in the goodwill of the subject, but made haste to recall his general, Belisarius, whom he unjustly suspected of aspiring to the Imperial Crown, while he himself, administering the African provinces from a distance, pillaged and sucked them dry at his pleasure. He sent agents to estimate the value of the soil, instituted new and heavy taxes, himself claimed all the best lands, forbade the Arians to practice their religion, and ruled the army very harshly, continually putting off the dispatch of reinforcements. This policy led to troubles which were bound to

end in disaster [Procopius, *History of the Wars,* cited by Dr. DeGraft-Johnson in *African Glory,* p. 56].

In the latter part of the sixth century, shortly after the death of the Emperor Justinian, a child was born in Arabia and, upon reaching man's estate, established a new system of religion, which profoundly affected the course of human history. The story of the great Arab-Moorish civilization begins with the birth of Mohammed in the year 571 C.E. It is claimed by his followers that his birth was heralded by a spectacular display of miracles. Mohammed himself, however, seems never to have suspected that there was anything unusual about either his birth or his career until he was about thirty years of age, when he began to hear strange voices. While he was in a cave on Mount Hara, engaged in religious meditation, the angel Gabriel appeared before him, proclaiming him as Mohammed, the prophet of God. It is said that Gabriel brought Mohammed the Koran page by page, as they met clandestinely in the desert.

In Mecca, Mohammed was so unpopular that he was forced to flee to Medina, where he was received with open arms in the year 622 C.E. This year, known as the Hejira (Flight), was the beginning of the Mohammedan era. The doctrine of the Arabian prophet spread like wildfire; for a period of drought had desolated the Arabian peninsula shortly before the advent of Mohammed, and the tribes were restless, and hence ready to listen to a new prophet. The essence of Mohammedanism is very simple: "There is no god but God [Allah], and Mohammed is the prophet of God." This very simplicity appealed to many. Large numbers of Jews and Christians were converted because Mohammed also recognized Moses and Jesus as prophets of God. Islam appealed to all classes of people. The doctrines of equality and brotherhood were cherished by the oppressed; the policy of conquest met with the approval of the desert tribes; the city dwellers were pleased by Mohammed's encouragement of commerce; and the superstitious were flattered by ceremony and ritualism.

Mohammed brooked no opposition, challenging all dissenters to mortal combat, and saying boldly: "I, the last of the prophets, am sent with the sword. Let those who promulgate my faith enter into no argument or discussion, but slay all who refuse obedience to the law. Whoever fights for the true faith, whether he fall or conquer, will assuredly receive a glorious reward." The head of the Mohammedan religion bears the title of "caliph," a word meaning "Successor" or "Representative of Mohammed"; and on the death of the Prophet of Islam, his father-in-law, Abu Bekr, was elected caliph. This caused a split among the faithful, for there were many who thought that the office should have gone to Mohammed's brother-in-law, Ali. The partisans of Abu Bekr justified their stand by claiming that the office should be filled by election; whereas the advocates of Ali argued that the succession was by rights hereditary. The first group is known as the Sunnites, and is dominant in Arabia, Africa, Turkey, and Turkestan; the second sect, known as the Shiites, prevails in Persia and India. Despite their differences, the successors of Mohammed vigorously pursued a policy of conquest. Six years after the death of the prophet, Asia Minor and Mesopotamia had been captured by the armies of Islam; and the fall of Persia and India was to follow soon afterward. A century later the Moslem dominions stretched from Spain through North Africa, across Asia to China. The first great line of Caliphs in the East were called the Omayyads, being descendants of Omar, the St. Paul of Islam; they were followed by the Abbasids, descendants of Mohammed's uncle, Abbas; while in Egypt the Fatimite Caliphate was established, the Fatimites being descended from Mohammed's daughter, Fatima. After losing power in the East, the Omayyads established their dynasty in Spain and North Africa.

The Islamic conquests, following the death of Mohammed in 632, were remarkable for their rapidity of accomplishment. Within two years of the death of the prophet, the army of the Emperor Heraclius of Byzantium went down to defeat at the hands of Caliph Abu Bekr and his Saracen hordes at the Battle of the Yarkmuk, a tributary of the Jordan River; and as a result the cities of Damascus, Jerusalem, Antioch, and Palmyra passed into the hands of the Arabs. Three years later, 637 A.C., a Persian army under the generalship of Rustam, after a three-day battle at Kadessia, was routed by the Arabs, and Persia became a Moslem province. The first invasion of Africa occurred in 640, when Amru the Conqueror led his Arab army into Egypt, and by the year 642 Egypt was another province of the expanding Moslem domains. In North Africa the Islamic armies met stiff opposition, but by 672 they had overrun Tunisia, having in 671 founded the city of Kairouan, in order to safeguard their lines of communication with Egypt. The resistance of the African people to the Arab conquest has been lucidly related by a contemporary African scholar, whom we quote:

In 669 Oqbar-ben-Nafi over-ran Fezzan and was appointed governor of Ifriquah, now the modern Tunis. Dinar Bu'l Muhajr was appointed to succeed Oqbar-ben-Nafi and carried the conquest of North Africa westward as far as Glemsan, on the borders of modern Morocco. In 681, Oqbar-ben-Nafi was sent back as governor and he continued the conquest still further westward and on to the Atlantic seaboard. Oqbar-ben-Nafi's second term of office as governor lasted for only a year, for the indigenous inhabitants of North Africa, finding the rapacity and greed of the Arabs equal only to those of the Romans, Greeks, and Vandals, decided to rise up against Arab rule. The North Africans rallied under the banner of one Kuseila and defeated and killed Oqbar-ben-Nafi in 682. Kuseila ruled as King of Mauritania for five years, but in 688 he was defeated and killed by fresh Arab forces. His position as leader of Afri-

can resistance was quickly taken up by another relative—a
woman named Dahia-al-Kahina. Under her leadership the Africans fought back valiantly and drove the Arab army into
Tripolitania. The Arab general Hassin-bin-Numan, was successful in capturing Carthage in 698. But his victory was short-
lived, for Kahina, rallying the African forces once more, drove
Hassan from the city. . . . Kahina was finally defeated and
slain by Hassin-bin-Numan in 705, and with her death came the
end of one of the most resolute attempts to keep Africa for
the Africans [*African Glory*, pp. 66–67, by J. C. deGraft-
Johnson].

The Arab conquest of North Africa was completed in
708, when Musa-ibn-Nusair subdued all of Morocco except
Ceuta, which was under the rule of the Byzantine governor,
Count Julian. But Ceuta did not hold out long, for Count
Julian was on bad terms with Roderick, King of the Visigoths
in Spain, and decided to help the Arab general and his Moorish
allies to invade the Iberian peninsula. Julian had sent his
daughter to visit the court of King Roderick at Toledo in
Spain. The Visigoth monarch took advantage of Count
Julian's daughter, Florinda; and Julian decided as a measure
of revenge to aid and abet an African invasion of Spain. So
Count Julian visited Musa, the governor of North Africa, and
offered him the hand of friendship. The Count told the Arab
leader of the great wealth and natural beauty of Spain, of
its vines, olives, pastures, and rivers, and of its fine cities and
palaces, not to mention the extensive treasures of the Visigoths. The country was poorly defended, and Julian suggested
that Musa should invade it; and promised to cooperate in
this project by lending boats to the invaders.

In the year 710, Musa borrowed four ships from Count
Julian and sent a force of five hundred men under the com-
mand of Tarif, an officer in his army, to make a raid on the
Andalusian coast. The army landed at a place later renamed
Tarifa in honor of Tarif. (It was at the port of Tarifa that

the Moors later levied a certain tax, which, taking its name from the town, became known as the tariff.) Tarif and his small detachment plundered Algericas and other towns and returned to Africa with their boats loaded with spoils. The success of this venture encouraged Musa, who then decided on a more extensive foray into Spain. In 711, when Musa learned that King Roderick was busy in the north of his country trying to put down an uprising of the Basques, he decided that the time was ripe for an invasion of the Visigothic realm. So an army of twelve thousand Africans was recruited and placed under the leadership of the Moorish general, Tarik. General Tarik and his army landed on an isthmus between an escarpment, then called Mons Calpe, and the continent of Europe. (After that, Mons Calpe was renamed Gebel Tarik—The Hill of Tarik—or, as we now call it, Gibraltar.) Tarik's African army captured several Spanish towns near Gibraltar, among them, Heraclea. Then he advanced northward into Andalusia. King Roderick learned of the invasion and raised a large army for defense. The two armies met in battle near Xeres not far from the Gaudalete River.

There is an old legend concerning Roderick, which is so engrossing and fantastic that we deem it proper to convey it to the reader as concisely as possible. According to this tale, at a time before the Moorish invasion of Spain, while King Roderick was seated on his throne in Toledo, two elderly men walked into his audience chamber. They were clad in white robes of antique design, wearing girdles adorned with the signs of the zodiac, and from which hung a large number of keys. Then, addressing the monarch, the old men said: "Know, O King, that in days of yore, when Hercules had set up his pillars at the ocean strait, he erected a strong tower near to this ancient city of Toledo, and shut up within it a magical spell, secured by a ponderous iron gate with locks of steel; and he ordained that every new king should set a fresh lock to the portal, and foretold woe and destruction to him who should seek to unravel the mystery of the tower. Now, we and our ancestors have kept the door of the tower from the days of Hercules even to this hour; and, though there have been kings who have sought to discover the secret, their end has ever been death or sore amazement. None ever penetrated beyond the threshold. Now, O King, we come to beg thee to affix thy lock upon the enchanted tower, as all the kings before thee have done." After delivering this quaint discourse, the aged pair departed from the presence of the king. Roderick naturally was highly desirous of finding out the secret of the tower, and announced to his court that he intended visiting the tower and that he planned to search out its secret. His bishops and counselors warned him against such a move, and told him that no one had ever entered the tower and lived to tell of it; and that even the great Julius Caesar had not dared to try an entrance into this stronghold. These admonishers of the king even conveyed to him a warning in poetic form, which reads as follows:

> Nor shall it ever ope, old records say,
> Save to a king, the last of all his line,
> What time his empire totters to decay,
> And treason digs, beneath, her fatal mine,
> And high above, impends avenging wrath Divine.

But this did not deter King Roderick, who, surrounded by his cavaliers, one day approached the tower, which stood on a lofty rock, hemmed in by cliffs and precipices. The walls of this tower were of marble and jasper, inlaid with designs which sparkled in the rays of the sun. The entrance was by way of a passage cut through stone, and was closed by a massive iron gate covered with rusty locks dating back to the days of Hercules; and on each side of the gate stood the two ancients who had visited the audience chamber of the king. For the better part of a day, the two elderly watchmen, aided by the cavaliers of the king, turned keys in the rusted locks, until just before sunset the gate was opened and the royal party entered the tower. Inside the gate was a hall, on the other side of which was a door, guarded by a gigantic bronze figure of terrible aspect, which continuously swung a large mace which smote the ground in the vicinity with powerful blows. On the breast of this bronze monster, King Roderick saw the words: "I do my duty"; so the king appealed to the animated image to let him pass, since he planned no sacrilege, but only wished to solve the mystery of the tower. The figure then became still, with uplifted mace, and allowed the king and his companions to pass through the door into the second room. Then they found themselves in a chamber encrusted with precious stones, in the midst of which was a table which had been installed therein by Hercules; on the table was a casket, upon which was engraved an inscription, which read: "In this coffer is the mystery of the Tower. The hand of none but a king can open it; but let him beware, for wonderful things will be disclosed to him, which must happen before his death."

The king opened the coffer, and on the inside was a piece of parchment folded between two plates of copper. On the parchment were pictures of fierce warriors on horseback armed with bows and scimitars and above them was the slogan: "Behold rash man, those who shall hurl thee from thy throne and subdue thy kingdom." As the king and his courtiers gazed at the figures on the parchment, they suddenly heard the sounds of battle and the figures of the horsemen began to move, and before them arose a vision of war:

They beheld before them a great field of battle, where Christians and Moors were engaged in deadly conflict. They heard the rush and tramping of steeds, the blast of trump and clarion, the clash of cymbal, and the stormy din of a thousand drums. There was the flash of swords and maces and battle axes, with the whistling of arrows and the hurling of darts and lances. The Christians quailed before the foe. The infidels pressed upon them and put them to utter rout; the standard of the Cross was cast down, the banner of Spain was trodden under foot; the air resounded with shouts of triumph, with yells of fury, and with the groans of dying men. Amidst the flying squadrons King Roderick beheld a crowned warrior, whose back was turned towards him, but whose armor and device were his own, and who was mounted on a white steed that resembled his own war-horse Orelia. In the confusion of the fight, the warrior was dismounted, and was no longer seen to be, and Orelia galloped wildly through the field of battle without a rider [*The Conquest of Spain*, Bohn's edition, pp. 378 ff., by Washington Irving; cited by Stanley Lane-Poole, in *The Story of the Moors in Spain*, pp. 18–19].

As the vision of the future disaster came to an end, the king and his attendants fled from the tower in a state of fright. By this time the great bronze image had disappeared and the two old men were lying dead at the entrance to the tower. The tower itself then became enveloped in flames and every stone of it was consumed by fire.

When King Roderick went forth to join battle with the Moors, he led a large army that outnumbered his foe six to one, and he wore a suit of ornate armor and was protected by a magnificent canopy. But the Africans did not quail, for as General Tarik led them into battle, he shouted: "Men, before you is the enemy and the sea is at your backs. By Allah, there is no escape for you save in valor and resolution." This electrified the Moorish army and they yelled in reply: "We will follow thee, O Tarik," as they charged into the ranks of the enemy. The battle lasted a whole week, but finally the African invaders broke through the Spanish lines, and King Roderick and his army were routed, the king himself being killed in the battle. "The conflict was a bloody one," as Dr. DeGraft-Johnson truly states, "but Tarik was victorious and soon he became the master of Spain. The conquest of Spain was an African conquest. They were Mohammedan Africans, not Arabs, who laid low the Gothic kingdom of Spain." (*African Glory*, pp. 69–70.)

After overrunning the Iberian Peninsula, the Moorish invaders pushed on through to France, where they were repulsed with heavy losses at Poitiers by the Franks under Charles Martel. After this setback, they retired into Spain and there laid the foundations of a new civilization. The country was incalculably enriched by their labors: They, for instance, introduced the silk industry into Spain. In the field of agriculture they were highly skilled, and introduced rice, sugar cane, dates, ginger, cotton, lemons, and strawberries into the country. Ibn-al-Awam and Abu Zacaria wrote learned works on agriculture and husbandry. A translation of a treatise on agriculture by Ibn-al-Awam (twelfth century) was published in Spain as late as 1802 for the instruction of Spanish farmers. Ibn Khaldun, another Moorish expert on agriculture, wrote a valuable treatise on farming, and worked out a theory of prices and the nature of capital.

Besides being scientific agriculturists, the Moors were engineers of no mean ability. The Caliph Abd-er-Rahman III had an aqueduct constructed, which conveyed water from the mountains to Cordova through lead pipes. Modern Spain retains only a fragment of the fine irrigation system built by Moorish engineers, who also erected large underground silos for the storage of grain in case of emergency.

The mineral wealth of the land was not neglected; for gold, silver, copper, quicksilver, tin, lead, iron, and alum were mined on a large scale. Up to the twelfth century the maritime commerce of the Saracens on the Mediterranean was greater than that of the Christians; hundreds of ships were engaged in it, and this widespread trade naturally stimulated manufacturing. The sword blades of Toledo were the most excellent and beautiful in all Europe, and a factory near

Cordova had an output of twelve thousand shields per year. Murcia became famous for the manufacture of all kinds of brass and iron instruments; the tanneries of Cordova and Morocco were the best in the world; Almeria produced sashes famed far and wide for the bright colors and fine texture; carpets were made in Teulala; and bright-hued woolens came from Baza and Granada. The Moors also produced fine glass and pottery vases, mosaics, and jewelry.

Cordova in the tenth century was very much like a modern city; the streets were well paved and there were raised sidewalks for pedestrians. At night, one could walk for ten miles by the light of lamps, flanked by an uninterrupted extent of buildings; and this was hundreds of years before there was a paved street in Paris or a street lamp in London. The population of the city was over 1,000,000; and there were 200,000 homes, 800 public schools, many colleges and universities, 10,000 palaces of the wealthy, besides many royal palaces, surrounded by beautiful gardens. There were 5,000 mills in Cordova at a time when there was not even one in the rest of Europe; and there were 900 public baths, besides a large number of private ones, at a time when the rest of Europe considered bathing as extremely wicked, and to be avoided as much as possible. Cordova was also graced by a system of over 4,000 public markets.

Toledo, Seville, and Granada were rivals of Cordova in respect to magnificence. Education was universal in Moslem Spain, being given to the most humble, while in Christian Europe 99 percent of the people were illiterate and even kings could neither read nor write. The Moorish rulers lived in sumptuous palaces, while the monarchs of Germany, France, and England dwelt in big barns, with no windows and no chimneys, and with only a hole in the roof for the exit of smoke.

About the middle of the tenth century, a small group of Germans conducted a monk to the court of Abd-er-Rahman

III, Caliph of Cordova. The monk delivered a letter to the Caliph, which had been sent to him by Emperor Otto the Great, of the Holy Roman Empire. The wonders of Cordova, and the scenic beauty of its suburbs and the Andalusian countryside, must have made the German travelers rub their eyes in bewilderment; for they surely thought that they had been bewitched and transported by some enchanter to fairyland. A vivid reconstruction of the splendors of Moorish Spain, as seen by the monk and his companions, has been preserved for us by a recognized authority on the history of the period:

> The Germans would find Andalusia in those days a real garden of song and flowers and gaiety. It had tens of thousands of prosperous villages, and the Germans would for the first time in their lives see peaches, pomegranates, strawberries, apricots, lemons, almonds, dates, oranges and sugar-cane growing; while at the hostels they would find coffee, spinach, asparagus, the daintiest cooking, and all the spices of the East. Not an acre of ground was left untilled, and tunnels cut through mountains, aqueducts, dams and reservoirs provided ample irrigation wherever it was needed. The land bore a larger population than it does today—probably larger than that of Germany, France, England and Italy put together at that time—and an immeasurably happier and more prosperous population.

> In Cordova, the old packed Cordova, they would find a city of 250,000 houses and 1,000,000 people when no city in Europe outside Moorish Spain had a population of 30,000. Its massive walls had a circuit of fourteen miles and had seven large iron gates faced with brass. Its streets were paved—so soundly, indeed, that in some of them you tread the same stones today, just as you cross the Guadalquivir on the same noble bridge— drained by large sewers, flushed with water from the many fountains which sparkled in the sun, and lit by lamps at night. It had 80,455 shops besides 4,300 markets, and in these you could buy amber from the Baltic, Russian furs, Chinese tea,

Indian spices, African ebony, and ivory, and such native products in leather, metal, silk, glass and pottery as could not be found elsewhere. It had 900 public baths—we are told that a poor Arab would go without bread rather than soap—and more than 1,000 mosques, the largest of which is still one of the architectural wonders of the world in spite of later Spanish disfigurement. Its low scarlet and gold roof, supported by 1,000 columns of marble, jasper and porphyry, was lit by thousands of brass and silver lamps which burned perfumed oil, the largest being thirty-eight feet in circumference containing 46,000 silver plates for reflecting the light. The exquisite prayer chamber (Mihrab), the unique pulpit, and the Caliph's private section with floors of silver and gold plated doors completed this wonderful monument of opulence and art. . . .

Some five miles along the broad road which led to it from the city, they would enter the most wonderful garden or park in the world. Engineers, who had a skill that was unequalled until modern times, so directed its water-supply that there were lakes, cascades and superb fountains on every side while every flower and shrub that would grow in Andalusia had been brought from the ends of the earth. At the farther side of it were the 400 white mansions of officials, visiting merchants, and distinguished travellers, and above the waving palms and dark cypresses and slender white manarets one saw, on the lower slope of the Sierra, framed by a higher slope which was entirely planted with roses, the white-marble palace of Al Zahra. . . . From first to last it seems to have cost more than 30,000,000 pounds ($120,000,000) in our money; and the Spaniards have not left a stone upon a stone of it.

Silk awnings shut the sun from the broad marble courtyard, and the monk would surely cross himself when he entered the great hall. Its eight large doors were of scented wood and were decorated with gold, jewels, ivory and ebony. The central dome and ceiling were supported by columns of alabaster and rock-crystal, their capitals studded with pearls and rubies. The walls were coated with onyx and mosaics, and the ceiling and the interior of the dome were plated with gold and silver. The tapestries, curtains and carpets, and the robes and gems in which the Caliph sat, on a throne of solid gold encrusted with jewels, may be left to the imagination [*The Golden Ages of History*, pp. 152–55, by Joseph McCabe].

Other cities in Spain were scarcely less wonderful than Cordova. Sheik Ash-shakandi, a celebrated Moorish scholar of the early thirteenth century, although a citizen of Cordova, was widely traveled in both Spain and Morocco, and he has written with unstinted praise of the glories of several other great cities of the Moorish Empire. Almeria, for instance, was a prosperous seaport, and was the home of a shipyard in which fine boats were manufactured. The sheik tells us that it was "the greatest mart in Andalusia"—and he further informs us that: "Christians of all nations came to its port to buy and sell, and they had factories established in it, where they loaded their vessels with such goods as they wanted, owing to which, and to its being a very opulent and large city, filled with passengers and merchants, the produce of the tithe imposed upon the goods, and paid by the Christian merchants amounted to very considerable sums, and exceeded that collected in any other seaport."

Almeria was famous for its fine silk factories, which specialized in the production of damasks and brocades and of tissues of silver and gold. Thousands of artisans were employed in each sector of this extensive silk trade. This city also excelled in the quality of glass and pottery that its factories turned out and was noted for the excellence of its productions in the field of hardware. Vessels from the Orient brought to its docks the very best goods of China and India. To quote Ash-shakandi again: "Almeria is an opulent and magnificent city, whose fame has spread far and wide. God has endowed its inhabitants with various gifts, such as a temperate climate and abundance of fruits; they are handsome, well-made, good natured, very hospitable, very much attached to their friends, and are above all things very refined in their manners, and very elegant in their dress. Its coast is the finest in all the Mediterranean as well as the safest and the most frequented." The citizens of Almeria were rated as the wealthiest in all Andalusia, and could boast of building a large factory town without diminishing its natural beauty and charm. Among its features were numerous public baths and the presence of a picturesque river; and we are told that, winding over the landscape for forty miles, the course of the river "contributed no little to the ornament of the city and its environs," since along its banks were "orchards, gardens and groves, where singing birds delight with their harmony the ears of the traveller."

All over the Arab-Moorish world a brisk intellectual life flourished; for the caliphs of both the East and the West were, for the most part, enlightened patrons of learning. They maintained immense libraries and offered fortunes for new manuscripts. In the year 970 A.D. Caliph Al Hakem of Cordova filled an entire palace with books collected from all parts of the known world, and the classified shelves of the library were adorned with 600,000 volumes, all carefully catalogued and in order. The Caliph Al-Mamun of Baghdad is said to have imported hundreds of camel loads of books into the great metropolis of the East. He made a treaty with Emperor Michael III of Byzantium in which it was stipulated that an entire library in Constantinople should be given to him. In this library was a rare literary treasure, the treatise of Ptolemy on the mathematical construction of the heavens. The caliph, himself an astronomer, had the work translated into Arabic under the title of *The Almagest*.

The Caliph Harun al-Rashid founded the University of Baghdad, at which the most celebrated professor was Joshua Ben Nun, a Jew; and there Greek classics were translated into Arabic. Harun was a patron of the Medical College of Djondesabour, in Southern Persia; and graduates in medicine had to pass an examination given by the faculty of that school, or by that of the University of Baghdad, before entering upon the practice of the healing art.

The Caliph Al-Mamun appointed a Christian scholar to the presidency of a college in Damascus. This shows the spirit of toleration then prevalent in the Baghdad caliphate. The Saracens adopted the decimal system of numerical notation from the Hindus, and this was improved by Mohammed Ben Musa, who, in the ninth century, introduced zero as a mathematical quantity. This same Mohammed Ben Musa wrote the first systematic treatise on algebra, devised a formula for the solution of quadratic equations, and was the author of a *Treatise on Spherical Trigonometry*. Omar Khayyám, now remembered for his poetry, was better known to his contemporaries as a mathematician and an astronomer.

There were many experts in the physical sciences. The Caliph Al-Mamun (ninth century), determined the obliquity of the ecliptic, and calculated the size of Earth by sending out an expedition which measured the length of a degree of latitude on the shore of the Red Sea. The tenth and eleventh centuries brought forth two great physicists: Al Hazen, a famous optician, and Ali Ibn-Isa, a noted oculist. Most of our school histories teach us that the prevalent belief, before the circumnavigation of the globe by Magellan in 1519, was that the world was flat. This popular view is entirely false, for the Moors in their schools taught geography from globes long before Magellan was born. For example, El Idrisi, a Moorish scientist, wrote a book on geography about the middle of the twelfth century. In that work there appears the following passage: "What results from the opinion of philosophers, learned men, and those skilled in observation of the heavenly bodies, is that the world is round as a sphere, of which the waters are adherent and maintained upon its surface by natural equilibrium. It is surrounded by air, and all created bodies are stable on its surfaces, the earth drawing to itself

all that is heavy in the same way as a magnet attracts iron."
(Cited by Lady Lugard in *A Tropical Dependency*, pp. 37–
38.) The unusual industry and ability of the medieval Moslem
scientists and scholars may well be illustrated by a consideration of the achievements of Avicenna of Bokhara (980–1037),
who was a philosopher, physician, and geologist; and was
the author of many scientific and philosophical treatises. The
following titles of his best-known works are representative
of the broad scope of his knowledge: (1) *The Utility and
Advantage of Science*; (2) *Health and Remedies*; (3) *Canons
of Physic*; (4) *Astronomical Observations*; (5) *Mathematical
Theorems*; (6) *The Arabic Language*; (7) *The Origin of
the Soul and the Resurrection of the Body*; (8) *An Abridgment of Euclid*; (9) *Physics and Metaphysics*; and (10) *An
Encyclopedia of Human Knowledge*, in twenty volumes.
The high state of development of science and scholarship in
Moorish Spain has been summarized by a modern historian,
as follows:

> While in the tenth and eleventh centuries all Europe could
> show scarcely a single public library and could boast of only
> two universities that were worthy of the name, there were in
> Spain at that same time more than seventy public libraries of
> which the one in Cordova alone contained six hundred thou-
> sand manuscripts. In addition, the country possessed seventeen
> famous universities, among which those at Cordova, Seville,
> Granada, Malaga, Jaen, Valencia, Almeria and Toledo were
> especially outstanding.
>   . . . Astronomy, physics, chemistry, mathematics, geometry,
> philology, geography, reached in Spain the highest stage at
> that time known anywhere. . . . Artists and scholars united
> in special associations for the pursuit of their studies. There
> were regular congresses of all branches of science where the
> latest achievements of research were announced and discussed,
> which naturally contributed greatly to the spread of scientific
> thought [*Nationalism and Culture*, p. 412, by Rudolph Rocker].

The Omayyad dynasty survived in Spain until 1031, but it was obviously in a state of decline by the year 1000. Abd-er-Rahman III, one of the greatest of the Moorish monarchs, reigned for fifty years (911–961) and both stabilized and expanded the territories of his dominions. In Europe, we are informed by the chronicler of the king: "The Moslems subdued the country of the Franks beyond the utmost limits reached during the reigns of his predecessors. The Christian nations beyond the Pyrenees extended to him the hand of submission, and their kings sent costly presents to conciliate his favor. Even the kings of Rome, Constantinople, Germany, Slavonia and other distant parts, sent ambassadors asking for peace and suspension of hostilities, and offering to agree to any conditions which he should dictate."

Abd-er-Rahman, not wishing to risk the presence of hostile regimes in West Africa, invaded that region and annexed considerable territory which he added to his own extensive realms. Under the scepter of this ruler, the western caliphate extended from the Pyrenees to the borders of the Sudan, and this dual government, with courts in both Spain and Morocco, became known as The Empire of the Two Shores. We are assured by a contemporary report that: "Never was the Mohammedan Empire more prosperous than during his reign. Commerce and agriculture flourished; the sciences and arts received a new impulse, and the revenue was increased tenfold." It was in the days of Abd-er-Rahman that cotton manufacture was introduced into Europe. The Moors at this time also established the art of printing calicoes from wooden blocks. From the contemporary annals we get the impression that Abd-er-Rahman was mild of disposition, and an enlightened patron of progress. "His meekness, his generosity, and his love of justice became proverbial. . . . He was fond of science, and the patron of the learned, with whom he loved to converse, spending those hours that he stole from the arduous labors of the administration in literary meetings, to which all the eminent poets and learned men of his court were admitted." (*A Tropical Dependency*, p. 51, by Lady Lugard.)

In the year 1048, the Emir Yahia of Morocco visited Mecca. Here he met a religious reformer, Ibn Yasin, whom he persuaded to return home with him to teach his doctrines to the Moors. Ibn Yasin with a few followers set his headquarters on an island in the Senegal River in West Africa. The new movement proved to be popular, and the leader named his disciples Morabites (Champions of the Faith), which in time was changed to Almoravides. A crusade was urged by Ibn Yasin, the purpose of which was to "maintain the truth, to repress injustice, and to abolish all taxes not based on law." The leadership of the Almoravides, which started in Upper Senegal, was assumed by the Emir Yahia. After consolidating his position in southwestern Morocco, Yahia died in 1056, and was succeeded by his brother Abu Bekr, who led his armies to further victories. Abu Bekr retired to southern Morocco and turned over the northern part of the country to his cousin Yusuf Tachefin, who soon became the master of northwest Africa.

In the year 1062 Yusuf laid the foundation of the town of Morocco with his own hands [we learn from a recognized modern authority], and not long afterwards declared the independence of the northern kingdom of which was to become the capital. . . . By the year 1082 he had long been the supreme ruler of that portion of the world. His court had begun to attract the learning and civilization which civil war was driving out of Spain. . . . It was to this court and to this man that Al Mutammed of Seville came in 1083 to ask for help against the Christians. . . . When therefore he consented to cross over to Spain, and in the course of time drove back the Christians and established once more a supreme Sultan upon the throne of Andalusia, his conquest and the dynasty which he founded must be regarded as an African conquest and an African dynasty [*A Tropical Dependency*, pp. 55–56, by Lady Lugard].

When Yusuf I crossed over to Europe, he was in command of an army of 15,000 men, armed mainly with swords and poinards; but his shock troops were a 6,000-strong detachment of Senegalese cavalrymen mounted on white Arabian horses, said to be as fleet as the wind. Once in Spain, Yusuf was met by the chief rulers of Spain: the kings of Almeria, Badajoz, Granada, and Seville. The Moorish army, only 10,000 men in all, joined the African forces of Yusuf and marched northward to join battle with King Alphonso VI, who headed a Christian army of 70,000. The opposing armies battled each other at Zalakah in October, 1086, and first the Christian hosts seemed to be winning. Al Mutammed, leading the Moslems, had three horses killed under him and, though wounded, kept his men in line until Yusuf came up with reinforcements and attacked the Christians from the rear. The outcome of this famous conflict has been so well described by J. A. Rogers that we cite it here:

> Throughout all the day the battle raged savagely. The Moorish soldiers who had fled at the first Christian attack, returned, giving fresh ardor to the combat. Night was coming. Yusuf, who in spite of his seventy-nine years, had everywhere been in the thickest of the fight, felt with the instinct of the born general, that the decisive moment had come. Three thousand of his invincible black horsemen on their white chargers had been kept fresh in reserve. Now he unleashed them. With blood-curdling yells they swept down on the Christians, passing through their ranks with fearful carnage. The white hosts, panic-stricken, wavered, broke and fled. The rout became a massacre. Alfonso, stabbed in the thigh by a black horseman, ran away with 150 of his men [*World's Great Men of Color*, Vol. I, p. 121, by J. A. Rogers].

After the conquest of Spain, Yusuf I returned to his palace in Morocco City, hoping to enjoy the pursuits of peace; but before long messages from his generals in Spain informed him that the Christians were again on the march, and that the kings of Andalusia were too lazy and cowardly to fight them. Yusuf ordered his generals to invade these petty kingdoms and put their towns and cities under military governors. This policy was implemented, and finally, with the fall of Seville, order was restored, and the King of Seville was taken prisoner and sent to Africa, where he died in 1095. Yusuf died in 1106, at the ripe old age of ninety-nine. His son succeeded him on the throne of the Empire of the Two Shores. The Sultan of Morocco and Spain continued to rule with dual courts, one in Africa, the other in Europe, until the overthrow of the African dominion in 1142, followed by the fall of the Spanish dominion, in 1145. The last Almoravide king died in 1147, we are informed by the North African historian Ibn Khaldun. During the whole era of the Almoravides, as under the previous dynasty of the Omayyads, there was a brisk intercourse in commodities and ideas between the empire of the Moors and the kingdoms of the Sudan.

In the early part of the twelfth century another religious reformer, calling himself the Mahdi, appeared in Morocco. He named his followers Almohades (Unitarians). After the conquest of Morocco in 1147, when the last Almoravide king was dethroned and executed, the Almohades seized the reins of government, and then invaded Europe. By 1150 they had defeated the Christian armies of Spain and placed an Almohade sovereign on the throne of Moorish Spain; and thus for the second time a purely African dynasty ruled over the most civilized portion of the Iberian peninsula.

Under a great line of Almohade kings the splendor of Moorish Spain was not only maintained but enhanced; for they erected the Castle of Gibraltar in 1160 and began the

1. Aries.

2. Taurus.

3. Gemini.

4. Cancer

5. Leo.

6. Virgo.

7. Libra.

8. Scorpio.

9. Sagittarius.

10. Capricornus.

11. Aquarius.

12. Pisces.

The Great Pyramid and the Sphinx.

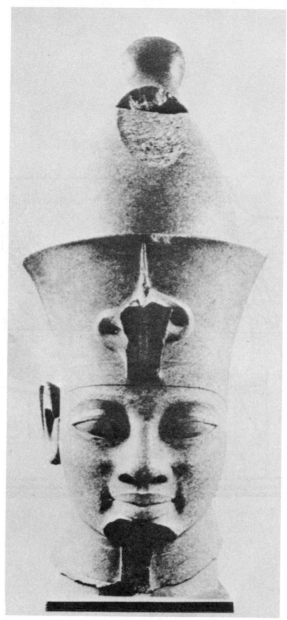

Colossal head of Tahutmes III.

Akhnaten and Nefertiti with their three daughters.

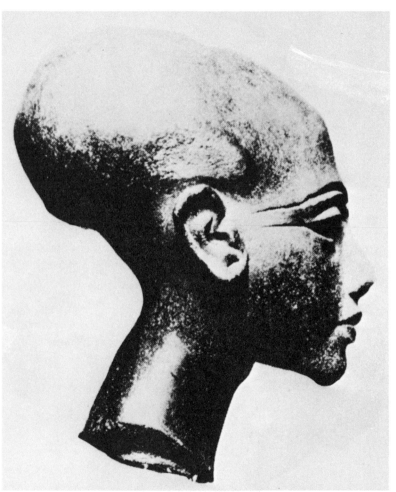

A daughter of Akhnaten.

Akhnaten carrying scepters and wearing a bracelet inscribed with Aten's name. The emaciated features have been exaggerated to emphasize his inhuman and therefore godlike quality.

Akhnaten and his family worshiping Aten. Note how rays from the disc terminate in hands. The hands near the eyes of Akhnaten and Nefertiti bear the symbol of life.

Akhnaten and Nefertiti.

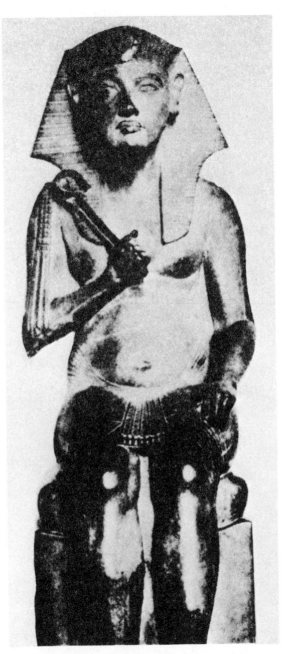

Akhnaten.

King Taharka of the 25th Dynasty, known as the Kushite (Ethiopian) Dynasty. This dynasty consisted of three rulers and lasted fifty years. Shabaka ruled twelve years, 712–700 B.C. Shabataka ruled twelve years, 700–688 B.C. Taharka ruled twenty-five years, 688–663 B.C.

Herodotus at Aswan (also spelled Assuan, a name meaning "the market"). At this place Egyptian and Ethiopian traders met and exchanged merchandise.

Fort St. Jago, 1724–25 (by Mølster)

Carved statue in wood of King Shamba Bolongongo, said to have been made in his lifetime.

Translation of the above in part: "The Great King, Monomotapa.
Very powerful and rich in gold. Several kings are tributary to him.
His territory comprises lower Ethiopia. . . . His empire is very large
and has a circuit of 2,400 miles. His court is at Zimboae [Zymbabwe].
There are women in his guard. . . . He has a great number of them
in his army, and they give great help to the men. He also has a great
number of elephants. His subjects are black, brave, and swift runners,
and he has very fast horses. Idolaters, sorcerers, adulterers, and thieves
are severely punished."

The Black Madonna from Nuria, Spain. She is called "The Queen of the Pyrenees."

A great stone head. Relic of the Olmec Culture of Ancient Mexico. The Olmec Culture has been traced back to 1000 B.C.

building of the great Mosque of Seville in 1183. The Geralda of Seville was originally an astronomical observatory constructed in 1196 under the supervision of the mathematician Geber. The Almoravides had established a Spanish court at Seville. The Almohades set up an African court in the City of Morocco; and Ibn Said in the thirteenth century describes Morocco as the "Baghdad of the West," and says that under the early Almohade rulers the city enjoyed its greatest prosperity. "Both dynasties had two courts, one in Africa and one in Spain. Thus, whatever was the prosperity or greatness of one part of their empire, it was shared by the other and under the Almohades there was a shifting towards the African center." (*A Tropical Dependency*, p. 60, by Lady Lugard.)

In the early part of the thirteenth century, the Moorish power in Spain began to decline. Unfortunately the Moslems, due to religious and political differences, began to split into factions and wage war among themselves. At the same time the Christians of Europe, having absorbed the science and culture of Moors, which enabled them to bring to an end the long night of the Dark Ages, began to form a united front in order to drive the Moors back into Africa. The dominions of the Almohades were slowly but surely captured by the Christian armies, and after almost a century of brilliant achievement the Almohade dynasty was ended when their last reigning sovereign was deprived of his throne in the year 1230. Moslem Spain declared independence under the rule of Ibn Hud, the founder of the Huddite dynasty. The Christian forces, in the meantime, conquered one great city after another, taking Valencia in 1238, Cordova in 1239, and Seville in 1260.

In Africa internal dissension was rife. The province of Ifrikiah (Barbary) declared itself an independent state under the rule of a sultan of the Hafside dynasty. In 1269 the throne of Morocco passed into the hands of the Merinite dynasty, who made Fez their capital city. Before the end of the thirteenth century the Empire of the Two Shores had disintegrated completely. In Spain the Huddites lost out to a Hafside monarch named Ibn Ahmar, who built the celebrated Alhambra palace, and ruled over whatever territory he could hold onto in and around Granada. In Africa the Hafside dynasty of Barbary and the Merinite dynasty of Morocco were almost continually at war with each other. The Moors introduced the manufacture of gunpowder into Europe; later the Christian Europeans used this weapon against them. After several centuries of brilliance the lucky star of Islam began to set. The Sarcacens never recovered from the conquests of the Seljuk Turks in the eleventh century and the Mongols in the thirteenth century. The Mongols under Hulagu Khan captured and sacked Baghdad in 1258. They also destroyed the great irrigation system of Mesopotamia, dating from ancient times, and thus turned a large area of fertile land into a desert. The disintegration of the caliphate of Cordova dates from the year 1031, when the internal troubles of the Moslems had made it impossible for them to maintain an adequate defense against their Christian enemies.

By 1492 the Moors had lost all Spain except the kingdom of Granada. The Christians, although not free from internal disputes, were finally united by the marriage of Ferdinand and Isabella, which joined in peace the formerly hostile royal houses of Aragon and Castile. The united Christian forces surrounded the city of Granada and blockaded it for eight months. The Moorish king, Abu Abdallah (also known as Boabdil), finally surrendered. The Moors lingered in Spain for a little more than a century; but by 1610, through expulsion and migration, a million, among them many Jews, had returned to northern and western Africa.

The word "Moor" literally means "Black," so the Moorish people were the Black people. Some anthropologists assign them to an arbitrary Brown race, and others label them as

Dark-Whites. The late Joseph McCabe once observed that perhaps an African anthropologist would call the same people Pale-Blacks. In medieval times the name of Moor was not restricted to the inhabitants of Morocco, but it was customary to refer to all Africans as Moors. The highly ambiguous word "Negro" had not yet been invented. We know from contemporary records which have come down to us from the era of medieval Moorish supremacy that the Moors did not consider themselves as white men. An interesting discussion of this point may be found in one of the many valuable works of Professor J. B. S. Haldane, as follows:

We are so accustomed to hearing of the superiority of Europeans that it is perhaps worth quoting from the Moorish writer Said of Toledo, who wrote at the time when Toledo was in Moorish hands. Describing the people who lived north of the Pyrenees, he said: "They are of cold temperament and never reach maturity. They are of great stature and of a white color. But they lack all sharpness of wit and penetration of intellect." We must remember that seven hundred years ago such a point of view had at least an empirical justification, for at that time trigonometry was being studied in Toledo, while in Europe a man was regarded as learned if he had got as far as the fifth proposition of the First Book of Euclid [*Heredity and Politics,* pp. 138–39, by J. B. S. Haldane].

Even the Arabs, who were always a minority in the so-called Arab culture of the Middle Ages, regarded a dark complexion as a badge of honor. One of the most learned of modern historians, Professor Arnold Toynbee, has noted that: "The primitive Arabs who were the ruling element of the Ommayad Caliphate called themselves 'the swarthy people,' with a connotation of racial superiority, and their Persian and Turkish subjects 'the ruddy people,' with a connotation of racial inferiority, that is to say, they drew the distinction that we draw between blonds and brunets, but reversed the value." (*A Study of History*, Vol. I, p. 226, by Arnold J. Toynbee.) The curious idea that a great white race has been responsible for all the great civilizations of the past is nothing more than a crude superstition propagated mainly by European-oriented racist historians; and we think that the memory of courageous dissenters from this theory should be held in honor and respect.

The superior germ-stuff of the great white race is completely discredited [Joseph McCabe argued] by the fact that our ancestors remained in the wings, pure barbarians, during the two thousand years when the dark men of the Mediterranean race were constructing civilization, and that our white race, first in the Greeks and then in the Teutons, devastated civilization for centuries. Until about 700 B.C. the philosophers of the world would have said that white men seemed incapable of civilization. . . . None of our modern sophistry redeems the squalor of Europe from the fifth to the eleventh century. And it was again the dark-skinned men of the south who restored civilization. By the year 1,000 Europe was reduced to a condition which, if we were not Europeans, we should frankly call barbarism, yet at that time the Arabs had a splendid civilization in Spain, Sicily, Syria, Egypt, and Persia, and it linked on to those of India and China. We write manuals of the history of Europe or of the Middle Ages, and we confine ourselves to a small squalid area (Russia and Prussia were not yet civilized and Spain was Moorish) and ignore the brilliant civilization that ran from Portugal to the China Sea [*The New Science and the Story of Evolution*, pp. 292–98, by Joseph McCabe].

The expulsion of the Moors from Spain was a serious setback to modern civilization. The true greatness of the Moorish culture is not generally known even to the educated classes of the Western world. One of the best studies of the contributions of the Moors to world history is *The Story of the Moors in Spain* by Stanley Lane-Poole, published in London and New York in 1886. This valuable work is now out of print and hard to obtain even from dealers in rare books; so for the benefit and enlightenment of the reader we give the gist of this fine study in the words of its distinguished author:

The history of Spain offers us a melancholy contrast. Twelve hundred years ago, Tarik the Moor added the land of the Visigoths to the long catalogue of kingdoms subdued by the Moslems. For nearly eight centuries, under her Mohammedan rulers, Spain set to all Europe a shining example of a civilized and enlightened state. Her fertile provinces, rendered doubly prolific by the industry and engineering skill of her conquerors, bore fruit an hundred-fold. Cities innumerable sprang up in the rich valleys of Guadelquivir and the Guadiana, whose names, and names only, still commemorate the vanished glories of their past. Art, literature, and science prospered, as they then prospered nowhere else in Europe. Students flocked from France and Germany and England to drink from the fountain of learning which flowed only in the cities of the Moors. The surgeons and doctors of Andalusia were in the van of science: women were encouraged to devote themselves to serious study, and the lady doctor was not unknown among the people of Cordova. Mathematics, astronomy and botany, history, philosophy and jurisprudence were to be mastered in Spain and Spain alone. The practical work of the field, the scientific methods of irrigation, the arts of fortification and shipbuilding, the highest and most elaborate products of the loom, the graver and the hammer, the potter's wheel and the mason's trowel, were brought to perfection by the Spanish Moors. In the practice of war no less than in the arts of peace they long stood supreme. Their fleets disputed the command of the Mediterranean with the Fatimites, while their armies carried fire and sword through the Christian marches. The Cid himself, the national hero, long fought on the Moorish side, and in all save education was more than half a Moor. Whatsoever makes a kingdom great and prosperous, whatsoever tends to refinement and civilization, was found in Moslem Spain.

In 1492 the last bulwark of the Moors gave way before the crusade of Ferdinand and Isabella, and with Granada fell all Spain's greatness. For a brief while, indeed, the reflection of the Moorish splendor cast a borrowed light on the history of the land which it had once warmed with its sunny radiance. The great Epoch of Isabella, Charles V, and Philip II, of Columbus, Cortes, and Pizarro, shed a last halo about the dying moments of a mighty state. Then followed the abomination of desolation, the rule of the Inquisition, and the blackness of darkness in which Spain has been plunged ever since. In the land where science was once supreme, the Spanish doctors became noted for nothing but their ignorance and incapacity, and the discoveries of Newton and Harvey were condemned as pernicious to the faith. Where once seventy public libraries had fed the minds of scholars, and half a million books had been gathered at Cordova for the benefit of the world, such indifference to learning afterwards prevailed, that the new capital, Madrid, possessed no public library in the eighteenth century, and even the manuscripts of the Escurial were denied in our own days to the first scholarly historian of the Moors, though himself a Spaniard. The sixteen thousand looms of Seville soon dwindled to a fifth of their ancient number; the arts and industries of Toledo and Almeria faded into insignificance; the very baths—public buildings of equal ornament and use—were destroyed because cleanliness savored too strongly of rank infidelity. The land, deprived of the skillful irrigation of the Moors, grew impoverished and neglected; the richest and most fertile valleys languished and were deserted; most of the populous cities which had filled every district of Andalusia fell into ruinous decay; and beggars, friars and bandits took the place of scholars, merchants and knights. So low fell Spain when she had driven away the Moors. Such is the melancholy contrast offered by her history [*The Story of the Moors in Spain*, pp. vii–ix, by Stanley Lane-Poole].

The tragic consequences of the destruction of the Moorish culture are so finely described by Mr. Lane-Poole in the concluding passage of his great work that we append it here as a fitting conclusion to this chapter:

> For centuries Spain had been the center of civilization, the seat of arts and sciences, of learning, and every form of refined enlightenment. No other country in Europe had so far approached the cultivated dominion of the Moors. . . . The Moors were banished; for a while Christian Spain shone, like the moon, with a borrowed light; then came the eclipse, and in that darkness Spain has grovelled ever since. The true memorial of the Moors is seen in desolate tracts of utter barrenness, where once the Moslem grew luxuriant vines and olives and yellow ears of corn; in a stupid, ignorant population where once wit and learning flourished; in the general stagnation and degradation of a people which has hopelessly fallen in the scale of nations, and has deserved its humiliation [*The Story of the Moors in Spain*, p. 280].

Valuable knowledge of the past may be gleaned from historical novels and adventure stories. A good example of a work of the latter type is a book entitled: *A Moor of Spain* by Richard Parker, a Puffin Story Book, published by Penguin Books. This fine tale of adventure is set in the last days of the Moorish Empire in Spain, shortly before Columbus set sail in his quest for the Indies. The hero of the story is a bright Moorish lad, age fourteen years, named Zati. The narrative, though written in fictional form, is historically accurate, and gives a good picture of what life was like in Spain in the latter part of the fifteenth century, when the Moors and Jews were being driven out of the country. A good example of how this situation appeared to the eyes of an intelligent Moorish lad is, to quote from Mr. Parker's story, as follows:

> The king and queen of Christian Spain, Ferdinand and Isabella, had begun to make war on our Moorish kingdom. We were Moslems—"infidels" they called us—and they wanted to drive us all out of Spain, or, what would have been worse in our eyes, conquer and rule us in their own uncivilized way. I knew the story as well as I knew my prayers, perhaps better, for my mother, as I have said, was devout and with her devoutness went a shining pride in the way our people, hundreds of years before, had driven our faith half-way across the world, conquering, civilizing, making all clean and beautiful as we went. Once, she said, we had ruled all Spain. Then the tide had turned. The white barbarians, as we called the Christians, had massed against us and driven us slowly back. This war, said my mother, was not a new one, it was the same war continued. It had been going on since the days of the Prophet [*A Moor of Spain*, p. 10].

Later in this adventure story there is a dialogue between

the Moorish boy Zati, and the Spanish historian Hernando del Pulgar. The scholar had taken a liking to the lad and did not want to see him fall into the clutches of the Inquisition. "When I have shaken off this little fever," Pulgar says to the boy, "we'll go back to our beloved Seville. Then I can finish my chronicle up to the end of the war, and die in peace."

"Don't talk about dying," Zati replied.

"Nonsense," retorted Pulgar. "Why not? I've left you a few thousand maravedis in my will. Take the money and leave Spain as soon as you can."

"Leave Spain?" answered the lad. "Where would I go then?"

"Anywhere, so long as you go," was the rejoinder of the scholar. "Spain will be no place for Moors in a few years' time. I'm something of a prophet and you can take my word for it that you'll be best out of it. Already there is an order being drafted to eject all the Jews from the country. Do you think the Moors will be allowed to stay long after them?"

"But I'm a good Christian," young Zati protested.

"You are not a true Christian at all," said Pulgar. "But even if you were it would not save you now. Winning this war has given the *white* Spaniards such an idea of their own strength that they'll be having the country swept clean of any other color or race. It won't matter that the Jews have all the money and business and the Moors all the brains: they'll go just the same. You'll see." (*A Moor of Spain*, p. 108, by Richard Parker.)

Chapter Five

THE GOLDEN AGE
OF WEST AFRICA

The history of West Africa dates back to a remote antiquity. An African scholar, Abdurrahman Es-Sadi, who was born in Timbuktu in 1596, wrote the *Tarikh-es-Sudan* (*History of the Sudan*). In this work the author claims that there was a town on the banks of the Niger River near where Gao is now situated, which was flourishing in the days of the eighteenth dynasty of ancient Egypt. The *Tarikh* was translated from Arabic to French by Professor Houdas of the Oriental School of Languages. So far as we know, there has been no English translation of this important work. Lady Lugard, who made a scholarly study of the ancient history of the western Sudan in the early part of the present century, seems to have obtained a good knowledge of the best sources and authorities dealing with that period of history; so we consider it proper to cite some of her reflections on the *Tarikh-es-Sudan.*

> The ancient capital of the Songhay Empire stood where Gao now stands upon the Eastern Niger, and was generally called Kaougha or Kaukau by the ancients. . . . The "Tarikh" tells us that, according to tradition, it was from this town that Pharaoh obtained the magicians who helped him in the controversy which is related in the Twentieth Sourate of the Koran as having taken place between him and Moses. Barth, travelling through this neighborhood in the middle of the nineteenth century, also heard at Burrum, a little town near Gao, that it had once been a residence of the Pharaohs [*A Tropical Dependency*, p. 157].

Another West African city that has laid claim to an antiquity that connects it with ancient Egypt is Jenne.

The most westerly manifestation of the influence of ancient Egypt in the Soudan [to quote again her Ladyship] is placed by the talented author of "Timbuctoo the Mysterious" in this town of Jenne, where, when he visited it at the end of the nineteenth century, he found to his amazement, "a colony of Ancient Egypt" in the heart of the Sudan. He describes the architecture of Jenne as "neither Arabic nor Byzantine, Greek nor Roman, still less Gothic nor Western." "At last," he says, "I recall these majestically solid forms, and the memory is wafted to me from the other extremity of Africa. . . . It is in the ruins of ancient Egypt, in the Valley of the Nile, that I have seen this art before" [*A Tropical Dependency*, p. 161].

The talented author of *Timbuctoo the Mysterious* was Major Felix Dubois, a noted French authority on West African history.

Another place in West Africa that can boast of an ancient past, according to Lady Lugard, is Borgu.

We have seen in the "Tarikh-es-Sudan" that Gao was celebrated in ancient times as a town of magicians, whence the Pharaoh on occasion summoned help. Borgu and its neighborhood to the south of Gao is to this day celebrated for the pursuit of magic, and the whole coast of West Africa is permeated with a belief in witchcraft and charms. Doubtless when Egyptian records speak of the south, they frequently mean Ethiopia and Meroe. But that the name of Ethiopia was extended in some instances as far west as the Atlantic is made quite clear by ancient writers. Strabo expressly says so [*A Tropical Dependency*, p. 229].

Archaeological investigations of the future will in all probability bring to light some of the lost history of West Africa. The ancient Ethiopian city-state of Meroe was conquered in the fourth century of the Christian era by another group of Ethiopians, whose capital city was located at Axum in Abyssinia. Meroe became one of the lost cities of Africa.

Between the fall of Meroe and the appearance of written records concerning West Africa, there is a gap of nearly four hundred years; and when written documents become available they are generally surrounded by an aura of mythology. The earliest account in Arabic of the West African peoples was written in 738 by Wahb ibn Munabbeh. According to this eighth century Arab chronicler, among the descendants of the sons of Kush, who was the son of Ham and the grandson of Noah, were the peoples of the Sudan, who were the Qaran (perhaps the Goran, who live east of Lake Chad), the Zaghawa (who still dwell in western Darfur and Wadai), the Habesha (Abyssinians), the Qibt (the Copts), and the Barbar (the Berbers).

Two centuries later we get a similar story from the great geographer, Al Masudi of Baghdad, who published, in 947, a famous book entitled: *Meadows of Gold and Mines of Gems*. In this work, we are told that: "When the descendants of Noah spread across the earth, the sons of Kush, the son of Canaan, travelled toward the west and crossed the Nile. There they separated. Some of them, the Nubians and the Beja and the Zanj, turned to the rightward, between the east and the west; but the others, very numerous, marched toward the setting sun." (Cited by Basil Davidson, in *The Lost Cities of Africa*, p. 54.) In commenting on this passage, Mr. Davidson says: "Somewhere behind the legend of migration from the valley of the Nile there may lie a large core of historic truth." (*The Lost Cities of Africa*, p. 54.)

Lady Lugard expressed a similar opinion on this matter, many years ago, and she had the good fortune to have her view confirmed by a meeting with Zebehr Pasha, at Gibraltar in 1886. The narrative is best given in her own words:

> In corroboration of the view that the trade and influence of Meroe may have extended farther west than has as yet been ascertained by modern exploration, I may mention a fact told

me by Zebehr Pasha. . . . It was that, having occasion to act as the military ally of a certain native king Tekkima, whose territory lay somewhere south and west of the spot marked upon modern maps as Dem Suleiman or Dem Zebehr—that is, presumably about 8 degrees N. and 25 degrees E., he was informed that he had to fight against magicians, who habitually came out of the earth, fought, and then disappeared. A careful system of scouting disclosed to him the fact that they came from underground, and when, after cutting off their retreat and conquering them, he insisted upon being shown their place of habitation, he found it to be deeply buried in the sand, a wonderful system of temples, "far finer," to use the words in which he described it, "than modern eyes have seen in the mosques of Cairo and Constantinople." It was, he said, such work of massive stone as was done only by the great races of old. Through this underground city of stone there ran a stream, and by the stream his native antagonists lived in common straw native huts. "Were your people, then," he asked them, "a nation of stonecutters?" And they said, "Oh, no! This is not the work of our forefathers but our forefathers found it here, and we have lived for many generations in these huts" [*A Tropical Dependency*, p. 225, by Lady Lugard].

The Golden Age of West Africa, which we propose to discuss in this chapter, covers a time span from the beginning of the eighth century to the end of the eighteenth century. This period of history, in Africa, deals with the records of four great Trading Empires, namely: Ghana (700–1200), the first great empire of the Medieval Sudan; Mali (1200–1500), which absorbed the empire of Ghana and expanded it westward; Songhay (1350–1600), which slowly but surely took over the empire of Mali; and Kanem-Bornu, which evolved separately further eastward in the Sudan.

The Ghanaian Empire of the Medieval era originated in the western Sudan, in a region northeast of the Senegal River and northwest of the Niger River. At the apex of its political power it ruled over lands stretching westward to the Atlantic Ocean; eastward it extended to the great southward bend of the Niger; southward it expanded to a point near the headwaters of the Niger; and on the north the Empire of Ghana faded into the sandy wastes of the Sahara Desert. In its heyday the Ghanaian Empire covered a realm that would include parts of the modern nations of Guinea, Senegal, Mali, and Mauritania. The founders of Ghana were a people known as the Soninkes. They were a group of tribes related by a common ancestry; and each tribe was made up of a number of clans. Among the most important clans of the Soninke were those who were called the Sisse, Drame, Sylla, and Kante. The various clans embodied a system of division of labor that was instrumental in regulating the various functions of government. For example, the Sisse was the clan of the ruling class; for from it was chosen the sovereign, the principal political officials, and the governors of provinces. The Kante clan provided the artisans who engaged in metal-working, such as blacksmiths, goldsmiths, silversmiths, etc. Other clans specialized in such activities as agriculture, fishing, animal husbandry, and the manufacture of clothing.

We learn from Soninke traditions that the Ghana Empire had its beginning about the year 300 of the Christian era. The first ruling dynasty seems to have been Berber invaders from North Africa. These interlopers remained in power until about 700 A.C., when a leader of the Sisse clan of the Soninkes organized a revolution which ousted the Berbers. The Soninke rulers built up an empire by subduing neighboring tribes. This was comparatively easy, since the Ghanaians had fine weapons and tools of iron, and their neighbors did not. Besides iron, Ghana possessed another source of wealth that made it a power to be reckoned with, namely a seemingly inexhaustible supply of gold. The first Arab invaders in northern Africa in the eighth century learned from their Moorish converts of the existence in the Sudan of a great nation whose wealth was based on a gold supply of fabulous extent. The Arabs, chiefly through efforts of their Moorish allies, had easily taken over the Iberian peninsula; and they thought it would be a good idea to cross the desert and invade Ghana. The lure of gold was a powerful attraction; so the invasion got under way, but it came to naught. The invading party was decisively defeated by the armed forces of Ghana; so the Arabs called off the program of invasion and settled down in towns of the western Sahara and the Sudan and decided to become traders.

The Empire of Ghana started out as a kingdom, then annexed other kingdoms, and, like many other kingdoms of the past, evolved into an empire. The people of this original kingdom called their native land Ouagadou; so it is of some interest to learn the origin of the name Ghana. The Soninkes spoke the Mande language, and in that tongue Ghana meant "warrior king," and was adopted as one of the titles of the King of Ouagadou. Another title of the king was Kaya Magha ("king of gold"), in allusion to the vast gold treasures of the country. As the fame of the Soninke warrior kings, or Ghanas, spread over North Africa, the people there referred to both the king and the nation over which he ruled as "Ghana."

The ruler of Ghana was regarded as the patriarch, or father, of the Soninke people; and besides this he was commander-in-chief of the army, head of the state religion, chief dispenser of justice, and supreme overseer of the nation. On the death of the monarch, his successor was not his own son, but the son of his sister. The Soninkes, like most African peoples, possessed a matriarchal system of social organization, and hence adhered to the matrilineal principle of succession, which even to this day is a prominent feature of West African society.

The inhabitants of Ghana enjoyed great prosperity in the tenth and eleventh centuries. An efficient standing army discouraged invaders and kept the peace internally, and the rich lands of the realm produced ample crops of cotton, millet,

and sorghum. But the chief source of the wealth of the empire was not agriculture, but trade. The caravan routes that
traversed Ghana did a brisk business, bringing into the country various commodities that were in demand, including a
large variety of food products. These goods were traded for
objects of local manufacture such as metal artifacts, cotton
cloth, and high-grade leather goods. (The famous Morocco
leather of the Middle Ages was imported by the Moors from
the West Africans who actually made the product.)

But in Ghana there were two items that overshadowed all
others as potential staples of trade, and these were salt and
gold. In Ghana there were neither salt nor gold mines, but
it happened that the Ghanaians were situated at a crossroads
vantage point where they could control the flow of these
highly desirable substances. The people of the western Sudan
south of the desert had much gold, but they had to import
salt from the northern Sahara, whereas the people north of
the desert possessed an abundance of salt but lacked gold.
A trade between the two areas developed and the citizens
of Ghana, by acting as middlemen, found it very lucrative.
Starting from the north, the trade route commenced at Sijil-
masa, then ran south to salt mines near the village of Taghaza,
and from there across the desert to Ghana, and to the goldmining regions further south. Gold became so plentiful that
it had to be regulated by royal action. A decree was issued
that all gold in nugget form become the property of the emperor, and the people were restricted to the use of gold dust.
A Moorish writer of the eleventh century, El Bekri of Cordova, in writing about the gold situation in Ghana, remarked
that: "Without this precaution, gold would become so plentiful that it would practically lose its value." The imperial
treasury of gold nuggets at the royal palace in Kumbi, the
capital city of Ghana, must have been of incalculable value.
One nugget was so large that it was used as a hitching post
for the ruler's favorite horse. The prize nugget of the royal

collection was a lump of gold weighing thirty pounds. The gold which was imported into Ghana came from a place named Wangara. The exact location of Wangara is still unsettled, since the old gold traders did not want anyone to know the source of their wealth. El Edrisi (or Idrisi), a Moorish geographer, writing in the twelfth century, tells about the gold country of Wangara. His description of the region is worth reproducing, but his location of it is certainly false. According to Edrisi:

> From the town of Ghana to the frontier of Wangara is an eight days' journey. This latter country is renowned for the quantity and quality of the gold which it produces. It forms an island of about 300 miles in length by 150 in breadth, which the Nile surrounds on all sides and at all seasons. Towards the month of August, when the heat is extreme, and the Nile overflows its bed, the island or the greater part of the island, is inundated for a regular time. When the flood decreases, natives from all parts of the Sudan assemble and come to the country to seek for gold during the fall of the water. Each gathers the quantity of gold great or small which God has allotted to him, no one being entirely deprived of the fruit of his labor. When the waters of the river have returned to their bed everyone sells the gold he has found. The greater part is bought by the inhabitants of Wargelan, and some by those of the extreme west of Africa, where the gold is taken to the mints, coined into dinars, and put into circulation for the purchase of merchandise. . . . In Wangara there are flourishing towns and famous fortresses. Its inhabitants are rich. They possess gold in abundance, and receive productions which are brought to them from the most distant countries of the world [cited by Lady Lugard in *A Tropical Dependency*, pp. 111–12].

Lady Lugard rightly concluded that the Wangara country could not have been anywhere near the Nile. Her conjecture —that the location was on the banks of the Niger—is just a guess, and we may safely dismiss it as a statement of fact.

Modern scholarly opinion favors the environs of the Senegal River as the true location of the Wangara gold fields. The ancient gold deposits of Bambouk and Bure, near the Senegal River, are believed to have been the sites of the Wangara gold mines. The merchants of Ghana were shrewd traders, and the government saw to it that exports and imports were duly taxed. A tax of one dinar of gold was levied on every donkey-load of salt that entered the country, and two dinars of gold were levied on each donkey-load of salt leaving the country.

The North African merchants who wished to trade in gold first journeyed to Ghana, and the jobbers of that country would lead them with their salt and other merchandise to the river banks of the gold country. Then the trading was conducted through a system known as dumb barter or silent trade. When the merchants arrived at the trading site, they would beat on drums to signal the opening of the market. The traders piled up the salt and other goods in rows—each merchant marking his pile with identifying insignia. Then the caravan would retreat one-half-day's trip from the trading place. While the merchants were absent, the gold miners would come in boats loaded with gold. A pile of gold would be placed near every pile of merchandise, and then the miners would retire a half-day's journey. When the merchants returned, if they found the gold supply correct, they would gather in the gold, and beat their drums to let the gold miners know that the deal was satisfactory and they should come and pick up the merchandise. If not enough gold was left in the first instance, the traders left the precious metal untouched until the miners brought what they thought was the right amount. In the end each group would return separately to the trading spot, to gather up their respective commodities, each pleased with the result of the exchange.

The Wangara gold miners were able to keep secret the exact location of their mines; but the location of the salt mines was known to one and all. Salt came mainly from the great salt mines at Taghaza, a town way out in the desert regions. The caravans from the north obtained their supplies of salt from the mines at Taghaza to carry it southward to be exchanged for the gold of Wangara. Right in the path of this caravan route was Kumbi, the capital city of Ghana; and this city became a great trading emporium. Gold dust was the usual medium of exchange, but salt was so valuable that it also was used for exchange purposes. The famous Moorish traveler Ibn Batuta visited the Sudan in the middle of the fourteenth century and noticed that salt was used as a medium of exchange, in the same manner as gold and silver, and that people who owned slabs of salt cut them up into pieces which they used as money.

Merchants from all directions converged on the markets of Kumbi bringing in an extensive variety of goods. Wheat was the main import from the north; sheep, cattle, and honey came in from the south; whereas dried fruits, raisins, and other food products were drawn in from all points of the compass. The merchants did a thriving business in such locally produced goods as leather, and tassels made of pure golden thread, and a popular cloth known as chigguyiya. There was also a brisk demand for imports, such as robes from Morocco, and red and blue blouses from Moorish Spain. Among the exports were gum arabic, which was bought for use in the manufacture of silk in Spain. There was a good market for cowrie shells, which were used for currency, and for such items as ivory, pearls, and copper.

Besides the establishments of the merchants, there were the numerous shops of the various craftsmen dotting the markets. Blacksmiths turned out iron tools and weapons; gold, silver, and coppersmiths engaged in the production of fine jewelry. Besides these were the shops of the potters, sandalmakers, and the weavers of cloth. And, sad to relate, there was also a trade in slaves. Since Ghana was a trading empire, the tariffs and other taxes levied by the state brought in a splendid revenue. The traders, on whom the prosperity of the country chiefly depended, were well taxed, but the imposts were not onerous, and the traders did not complain too much, for they made good profits, and an efficient governmental organization maintained peace and prosperity throughout the land.

Kumbi, the capital of Ghana, was a twin city, composed of two towns about six miles apart connected by a long boulevard. Eventually the spaces between the two towns became so filled with dwellings that the two towns merged into one big city. One town, El-Ghaba (The Forest), contained a sacred grove of trees used for religious purposes by the Ghanaians. Also in El-Ghaba were the royal palace and a mosque for the use of visiting Moslem officials. The other town was populated by Moslem merchants from the north, whose religious needs were served by no less than one dozen mosques.

By the middle of the eleventh century the Empire of Ghana had reached its zenith; then a few years later it began a sudden decline that led on to destruction. The neighbors of Ghana envied its wealth, and began to make raids on the fringes of the empire. A strong government and a large and efficient army managed to keep the empire intact during the first half of the eleventh century. About this time occurred the rise of the Almoravides, a Moslem religious sect. They were bent on the conquest of Ghana, since that empire, though it housed a large Moslem population, was basically a pagan state. The official religion of Ghana was the worship of the serpent-spirit Ouagadou-Bida.

In the year 1062, the Almoravide hordes under the leadership of Abu Bekr began an invasion of Ghana; but the task was not an easy one, since they did not reach the gates of Kumbi until 1067. For ten years, first under the Emperor Bassi and finally under his successor Tunka Menin, the people of Ghana put up a magnificent resistance; but the city fell to the invaders in 1077. The Almoravide conquerors compelled the Ghanaians to submit to Islam and to pay them tribute and taxes; and those who resisted were massacred. When Abu Bekr died in 1087, the Almoravide organization in the Sudan disintegrated. Surviving members of the Soninke ruling class tried to restore the Empire of Ghana, but they met with no success. The kingdoms of Mali, Songhay, and Tekrur had been parts of the Ghanaian dominions, and these states now declared themselves independent. A branch of the Soninkes established a kingdom further south with its capital at the city of Susu. The outstanding ruler of the Susus, King Sumanguru, captured Kumbi and made it part of his realm in 1203. But the new kingdom was not to last long. In 1235 the Susu army was defeated by hosts of invaders from the new kingdom of Mali. Kumbi held out for five years, and then was captured and destroyed by invaders from Mali. This was the death knell of the once great empire of Ghana.

The new state of Mali was established by the Mandinka (or Mandingo) people, whose capital city, Kangaba, was located on the Niger River, about 250 miles south of Kumbi. The first great ruler of Mali was King Sundiata, who ascended the throne in the year 1230. This monarch expanded his kingdom into an empire. The capital was moved from Kangaba to Niani; and the king strove to build up a political organization that would guarantee peace and prosperity throughout his realms. He gained control of the salt and gold trade that had in times past been monopolized by Ghana; and of equal, if not more, importance, he promulgated a great program of agricultural expansion. He turned many of his soldiers into farmers. The rich soil was planted with cotton, peanuts, grains, and a variety of other crops. The soldier-farmers were also trained in the raising of poultry and cattle. With an adequate food supply assured, the foundations of the empire were greatly strengthened.

Mali was the first great Moslem state in the Sudan, unlike

Ghana, whose rulers never embraced Islam. Sundiata, on his death in 1255, was succeeded by one of his sons, named Wali. This ruler adopted the title of Mansa, which means emperor or sultan, and this title was transmitted to his successors. Mansa Wali was an able, but not a great, ruler; and, after the end of his earthly career in 1270, the country was governed for many years by monarchs of mediocre stature; but there was a turn of the tide in 1307, when Mansa Musa I ascended the throne. In a reign of twenty-five years, he made his empire illustrious, not only in Africa, but in the Middle East and Europe as well. He was a man of many talents and interests, being an ardent patron of the sciences and the arts, and also a sincere devotee of the Moslem faith. Though a devout adherent to Islam, he was not a religious fanatic, and he adopted a policy of toleration toward his pagan subjects. One day when the Mansa was holding court in Niani, an Egyptian merchant and a Moorish trader were in the crowd gathered in the palace courtyard. The Egyptian said to the Moroccan: "Is it true, as they say, that Mansa Musa is a generous and virtuous prince?" The Moor answered: "I have come to Mali often. Mansa Musa is indeed a good ruler and a devout Moslem."

The Egyptian then asked: "Has he believed in that religion long?"

"He and his ancestors have been followers of Mohammed for perhaps three centuries," was the reply of the gentleman from Morocco, who then told the Egyptian: "Mansa Musa is loved by all his people."

"Are they all Moslems too?" was the query of the merchant from Egypt.

"The men who run the government are Moslems," was the explanation of the Moorish trader. "But they are few compared to the many people who are still pagans. I understand this troubles Mansa Musa. Too many of his people worship many gods, including the sun, moon, and stars. He would like to have all his subjects worship the one God the Moslems call Allah."

On one occasion Mansa Musa sent a representative to the goldminers of Wangara, who were pagans, for the purpose of converting them to the Moslem faith. On the return of the special messenger, the monarch eagerly awaited his reply; and this is what he heard: "Your Majesty, this is not the time to pursue the Wangara people of the south. They have refused to accept our faith. The miners of Wangara even threatened to stop producing gold if they were forced to become Moslems. It would not be wise to try to force them. The Wangara are skilled at forest fighting. They use poisoned arrows. The tsetse fly that brings the deadly sleeping sickness could destroy our army."

This message did not please Mansa Musa. He had hoped to bring the Wangara goldminers into the Islamic fold; but he had a genuine respect for the rights of all the people, and deemed it right and proper to follow the advice of his courier.

The greatest event of the reign of Mansa Musa was his famous pilgrimage to Mecca, which occurred in 1324. Of all pilgrimages to Mecca, this one was beyond all doubt the most spectacular. After months of preparation, the royal pilgrimage, 60,000 strong, started the long trek to Mecca. To finance this journey, 80 camels were loaded each with 300 pounds of gold dust. All necessities and accessories for such a journey had been provided for—including a highly efficient commissary department, staffed by excellent cooks who prepared elaborate meals which were served to the multitude at each halting-place.

When Mansa Musa and his entourage reached Cairo, in July, 1324, the Sultan of Egypt responded with a grand celebration. After visiting the holy cities of Mecca and Medina in Arabia, the Mansa and his party returned to Cairo. Gold and other valuable gifts were distributed with a lavish hand. There was a slump in the gold market in Cairo, brought about by a sharp increase in supplies of the precious metal, due to generous gifts to prominent citizens of Cairo by Musa. An official of the Egyptian government reported that the Cairo gold market required twelve years to return to normalcy. The Mellestine monarch was such a free spender that he finally ran out of gold in Cairo, and found it necessary to borrow enough money from certain merchants of that city to finance the return trip of his pilgrimage back home; and, he being a good credit risk, the debt was liquidated in due time.

During the visit to the holy cities of Arabia, Mansa Musa was introduced to Es-Saheli, a Moorish poet and architect from Granada. They became friends, and the Mansa one day said to Es-Saheli: "I would like you to return to Mali with me. We need men with your talents."

The Moor smiled, and replied: "Your Majesty, I shall be honored to return with you, and to help in any way I am able."

The elaborate pilgrimage was talked about for years, and gained widespread prestige for Mansa Musa. In the fourteenth century, cartographers of Europe published maps showing the location of Mali and calling attention to the wealth of its sovereign. In an atlas prepared for King Charles V of France, there is a drawing depicting Mansa Musa wearing regal robes and a kingly crown, and holding a scepter in one hand and a nugget of gold in the other.

Under Musa I, the Mali Empire embraced an area just about equal to that of western Europe. Under the direct rule of the Mansa were provinces governed by ferbers; and the chief municipalities were headed by inspectors, known as mocrifs. Law and order prevailed in the provinces, and merchants with their caravans traveled freely, having no fear of banditry. There were also certain vassal kingdoms not directly under imperial control. During the regime of Musa I, from thirteen to twenty-four of these semi-independent kingdoms were in alliance with the empire. A standing army of one hundred thousand men was maintained, of which ten percent were cavalrymen, mounted on camels and horses. While Mansa Musa was away on his pilgrimage in 1325, the Malian army, under the command of Sagaman-dir, captured the city of Gao, on the middle Niger. This place was the capital of the kingdom of Songhay, and this territory hence became a vassal state of Mali. On the return trip from his hajj (pilgrimage), Musa visited the captured city of Gao, and received the allegiance of the Songhay ruler, King Assibai. Musa, as a measure of insuring the loyalty of the new kingdom to his rule, carried back to Niani as guest-hostages, two sons of the Songhay king: the princes Ali Kolon and Sulayman Nar. Some years later, after the death of Musa, these princes escaped from Niani, returned to Gao, and founded a dynasty that challenged the supremacy of Mali.

Everything in Mali seemed to be abundant. The food supply existed in plentitude, and was of such variety as to assure a balanced diet to all. Large cotton crops were grown, and ample supplies of cotton cloth were manufactured. From the baobab tree, which grew wild, there were derived a meal for making bread, a red dye, and a liquid possessing medicinal properties. In cities, towns, and villages, throughout the land, the various craftsmen plied their respective skills. Besides weavers, dyers, and tanners, there were blacksmiths, goldsmiths, silversmiths, and coppersmiths, but the lifeblood of the empire was trade; and taxes were the paramount source of income for the government. Trade and commerce were brisk, and the tax collectors of the Mansa performed their duties with admirable efficiency. In addition to the salt mines of Taghaza and the gold mines of Wangara, the Malians tapped another source of wealth: the copper mines of Takedda, which were situated about 250 miles east of Gao. It is said that Mansa Musa regarded the Takedda copper mines as his prime source of revenue. Foreign merchants who traded in Mali marveled at the prosperity of the region and noticed that even the common people were not oppressed by poverty.

Besides Niani, there were other great cities in Mali, noted not only for commercial activities, but also for culture and scholarship. Among these were Walata, Gao, and Timbuktu. Timbuktu, on the banks of the Niger, at the point of the Great Bend of that river, was between Gao and Niani. It reached its days of greatness after the empire of Mali was superseded by that of Songhay. As a center of both commerce and culture, Timbuktu had no superior in the western Sudan. Another city in the western part of the Sudan, also famous for both commerce and scholarship, was Jenne. This place was an independent city state, which never submitted to the rule of Mali.

When Musa I died in 1332, he was succeeded by his son Maghan. Mansa Maghan was neither as wise nor able as his father, and during his reign Mali went into a decline. First, the city of Timbuktu was lost to enemy forces. An army of the Mossi people who lived near the Volta River attacked the city early in the reign of Maghan. The Mandinka garrison, defending the city, was overpowered, and Timbuktu was captured and burned. Secondly, Mansa Maghan was not alert enough to prevent the escape of the two Songhay princes whom his father had been holding as hostages. The escaped princes returned to Gao, where they established a new Songhay dynasty. Maghan died after a four-year reign, and was succeeded by his uncle, Sulayman—a brother of Mansa Musa I. Mansa Sulayman was a sovereign of high competence, and he ably presided over the destinies of Mali until his death in 1359.

The great age of Mali was now at an end; for the later rulers were undistinguished men, under whom the empire disintegrated. About the year 1475, the Songhay Empire, with its capital at Gao, rose to supremacy in the west Sudan, as Mali continued to decline. In 1481 Portuguese sailors landed on the Atlantic coast of Mali. The Mali government attempted to hire these Portuguese as mercenaries to fight the rising power of Songhay, but the proposed alliance was never effected. Mali lingered on for nearly two centuries, but its day of greatness had passed into history, and it finally expired from innocuous desuetude.

From times stretching into the dim and distant past, the Songhay people have dwelled alongside the banks of the Middle Niger. The earliest traditions of these tribes tell of two groups of people, who were known as "masters of the soil" and "masters of the water." Other tribes later moved into the area and intermingled with the indigenous dwellers, and this mixture of groups in time became the Songhay nation. The traditional accounts of these early days are not consistent. A judicial appraisal of these traditions has been made by a talented student of African affairs, which we deem it appropriate to cite:

Tradition says that these migrants included the Sorko, a fisherfolk coming from the east (perhaps from Lake Chad by way of the Benue River), and the Gow, who were hunters; and these two appear among the founders of the Songhay nation. Their most important settlement was at Koukya, or Gounguia; almost certainly this was near the falls of Labbezenga in the Dendi country, lying on the northwestern frontiers of what is now Nigeria.

Another tradition says that a group of Berber migrants arrived at Koukya, perhaps in the seventh century A.D., being connected with the Lemta of Libya; and established themselves as chiefs of the Songhay people. Disturbed by this, the Sorko people are said to have migrated upstream and founded the settlement and later city of Gao, and even to have pushed on westward as far as Mopti in the lake region above Timbuktu. The "Berber" kings of Koukya later followed them; in A.D. 1010 Dia (or Za) Kossoi took Gao from the Sorko and established the Songhay capital there, and it is from them that the state and later empire of Gao may be said to have begun. One need take neither the dates nor the traditions too seriously. All that comes out as relatively sure is that the Songhay empire of Gao had its organized beginnings in the region of Dendi; that its civilization was the product of native initiative stimulated by migrant incursion; and that, with others, it took its rise in early centuries after the western Sudan had fully entered its Iron Age [*The Lost Cities of Africa*, pp. 99–100, by Basil Davidson].

We have told of the escape of the Songhay princes, Ali Kolon and Sulayman Nar, from their captivity in Mali. Ali Kolon, as legitimate heir to the Songhay throne, followed the last ruler of the Dia dynasty, and established a new line of monarchs, called the "Sunni," which means "replacement." During the greater part of the fourteenth century and first half of the fifteenth century, the Sunni dynasty of Songhay gradually extended its sway of the territory of the declining empire of Mali. When in the year 1464, Sunni Ali the Great succeeded to the Songhay throne, an age of great achievements began. The new age was heralded by the capture of Timbuktu, a center of both commerce and culture. It was a place where the river people and the nomads of the desert met for trading purposes; and it was also the seat of the celebrated University of Sankore, which attracted scholars and students from many near and distant lands.

Another great metropolis coveted by Songhay rulers was Jenne, a city established in the thirteenth century by the Soninkes of Ghana. This city was situated in the backwaters of the Benue River (a tributary of the Niger), about three hundred miles southwest of Timbuktu. The Mali had made ninety-nine attempts to capture Jenne during the days of their supremacy in the western Sudan, and finally gave up. But Sunni Ali of Songhay was able to add that city to his expanding domains. After bringing Timbuktu into the fold, he decided that Jenne should be next on his agenda of conquest. The capitulation of Jenne was no pushover, for the siege of the city lasted for seven years, seven months, and seven days. "At the end of the siege, the town," we learn, "yielded by honorable capitulation. No injury of any kind•was done to its inhabitants, and the seven days which are added to the period of the siege were consumed, it is said, by festivities on the occasion of the marriage of Sunni Ali with the widow of the ruler of the town who had died during the siege." (*A Tropical Dependency*, p. 174, by Lady Lugard.) The exact date of the fall of Jenne is not known, but it is believed to have occurred in the year 1473.

Jenne was a valuable prize to the Songhay, since it was a prosperous trading center, containing buildings of attractive design, and surrounded by great scenic beauty. It was also the home of advanced culture, being the seat of a noted university, which employed a staff of thousands of teachers who gave courses of lectures and conducted researches on a variety of subjects. Their medical school trained physicians and surgeons of great skill. Among the difficult surgical operations performed successfully by doctors in Jenne was the removal of cataracts from the human eye.

Sunni Ali the Great incorporated much of the territory of the old Mali Empire into his own realm, and before his death in 1492 he had become one of the most famous rulers of his day. In North Africa he was regarded as the greatest sovereign south of the Sahara, and in the annals of Europe we find him mentioned as Sunni Heli, King of Timbuktu, whose empire extended to the coast of the Atlantic Ocean. The son of Sunni Ali inherited the throne and, though nominally a Moslem, he was, like his late father, a pagan at heart. Some of his Moslem subjects attempted to convert him to what they regarded as the true faith, but the new sovereign rejected these overtures, taking the position that his personal religious convictions were none of the business of his subjects. The Moslem group staged a revolution, dethroned the incumbent ruler, and elevated Askia Mohammed I, a devout Moslem, to the supreme leadership of the Songhay Empire.

The first sovereign of the Askia dynasty enjoyed much popularity among his Moslem subjects. He relished the society of lawyers, doctors, and students of the Islamic persuasion. He sought their advice and counsel, and bestowed honors upon them. Like every good Moslem, he was eager to make the pilgrimage to Mecca and Medina; and, in the year 1495, he proceeded to do so, accompanied by an army of 1,000 infantry and a cavalry detachment of 500 horsemen. Some 300,000 pieces of gold were allotted for the financing of this trip. One third of the amount was used to cover the costs of travel; another third was distributed as alms in the holy cities of Arabia, and for the support of an inn in Mecca for the housing of Sudanese pilgrims; and the last third was expended in the purchase of merchandise. While in Egypt, Askia Mohammed was honored in a special ceremony by the Caliph of Cairo, who appointed him as his personal representative in the Songhay Empire.

Since many neighboring countries were inhabited by pagans, Askia Mohammed considered it his duty as a Moslem potentate to launch a series of jihads (holy wars), in order to bring these infidels into the fold. For example, he annexed the territory of the Mossi, on his southern border, and seized a large number of Mossi children, whom he reared as Moslems and trained for service in his army. In or near the year 1513, the Askia led the armed forces of Songhay into the Hausa States, a complex of kingdoms between Lake Chad and the Niger River. In time all the Hausa States except Kano capitulated. After a siege of one year, the king of Kano sued for peace; and Askia Mohammed displayed the magnanimity of his character by allowing the defeated monarch to retain his throne. As a further gesture of good will, he gave one of his daughters in marriage to the king of Kano. After consolidating his Hausa conquests, the Askia subdued the nomad Tauregs of

Air, and settled a Songhay colony in that region. The military record of the Askia was not crowned with complete success, for one kingdom proved itself invincible. Kebbi, a small kingdom, wedged between the Hausa states and the Niger River, was ruled by King Kanta. This ruler, protected by the strong walls of his capital city, was able to maintain the independence of his nation.

Askia Mohammed must be credited with the creation of a strongly centralized government in the Songhay Empire. The governors of the several provinces were the personal appointees of the sovereign; and a council of ministers was instituted, and was directly responsible to the crown. The most important ministerial posts were the Chief Tax Collector; the Chief of the Navy; the Chiefs of Forests, Woodcutters, and Fishermen; and, last but not least, the Treasurer. The Songhay Empire under Askia Mohammed not only enjoyed a high level of material culture, but was also the home of an intellectual achievement of no mean order. In the principal cities of West Africa, such as Gao, Jenne, and Timbuktu, universities and other educational institutions were established, and their level of scholarship was of a high caliber. In the schools, colleges, and universities of the Songhay Empire, courses were given in astronomy, mathematics, ethnography, medicine, hygiene, philosophy, logic, prosody, diction, elocution, rhetoric, and music. Professor Ahmed Baba, of the faculty of the University of Sankore, in Timbuktu, was a scholar of vast erudition. He was the author of more than forty books, which treated of such diverse fields of study as astronomy, ethnography, biography, and theology; and he owned a fine library of 1,600 volumes.

When the Askia Mohammed ended his career on Earth on March 2, 1538, at the age of ninety-seven, he was followed on the throne by his sons, and under their misrule the empire began to fall apart. Daoud, the last son of Askia Mohammed to rule the empire, maintained a stable government from 1549 to 1582. But the great days of Songhay power were now fast approaching an end. In 1585 the salt mines of Taghaza passed into the hands of the sultan of Morocco. This was a disaster to the Songhay Empire, and they were too disorganized to prevent it. Five years later Songhay was invaded by a Moorish army led by Judar Pasha, a Spaniard, captured by the Moors in infancy, and reared in the precincts of the royal palace. This army numbered only five thousand men, but about half of them were armed with firearms imported from England. The superior numbers of the Songhay army were no match for the gunpowder of the Moors. In 1591, both Gao and Timbuktu fell to the invaders from the north. The Moorish forces settled down as an army of occupation and quartered themselves in the Songhay cities for another century and a half. This period completed the decline and fall of the Songhay Empire. "From that moment on," we hear from a contemporary Sudanese scholar, "everything changed. Danger took the place of security; poverty of wealth. Peace gave way to distress, disasters and violence." At the beginning of the seventeenth century, the Golden Age of the western Sudan had reached its nadir.

After the passing of the Songhay Empire, West Sudanic culture moved eastward to the Central Sudan, to Kanem-Bornu and the Hausa States; but none of these nations ever rose to the levels attained by Ghana, Mali, and Songhay in their Golden Age. The kingdoms of Kanem and Bornu, in the vicinity of Lake Chad, were originally separate states, but they later merged to form the Kanem-Bornu Empire. Like Ghana, Mali, and Songhay, the beginnings of Kanem-Bornu are rooted in a remote past. There are no written records, to which we can refer, until the early part of the ninth century. About that time a small group of states were clustered about Lake Chad, the most important being those of the Zagawa and Kanuri peoples. The early state of Kanem-Bornu, in territories stretching both east and west of Lake Chad, was first ruled by kings of the Sefuwa family, and this dynasty managed to survive for about one thousand years. The first king of this line, who ascended the throne about 850, was pagan, and so were his successors until 1086, when a Sefuwa monarch named Ibn Abd al-Jelil embraced Islam and adopted it as the official religion of the state; and all future rulers of Kanem-Bornu of the Sefuwa dynasty, which lasted another eight hundred years, were professing Moslems. The penetration of Islam into the Medieval Sudan was not an unmixed blessing. A judicial appraisal of this question is given in a recent authoritative work dealing with West African history, as follows:

The appearance of Islam in the Western Sudan was important for more than religious reasons. It opened many West African states to the influence of Muslims from North Africa and Egypt, and from still further afield, who introduced the arts of writing and scholarship. It insured good trading relations between the Western Sudan and the lands beyond the Sahara, so that contact between Kanem-Bornu and Egypt, Tunisia and Tripoli became valuable and constant. These were clear gains. On the other side it also opened the way for many bitter conflicts between those who accepted Islam and those who did not. Later history has much to say of these religious conflicts.

The actual size of the empire of Kanem-Bornu varied with time and fortune, as did all these systems. Its central or metropolitan people were the Kanuri, just as the Mandinka were the metropolitan people of Mali and the Songhay the metropolitan people of the empire of that name. . . .

But whether large or small, according to the stress and shift of events, the success of the empire of Kanem can be compared to that of ancient Ghana, while it was perhaps even greater than the empires of Mali and Songhay, if only because it lasted longer. What the Kanuri and their allies and subjects were able to do, over a very long period and in a region of great importance, was to bring the advantages of a single system of law and order to a great many different peoples. And it was through this large empire that West Africa kept in regular touch with vital centers of civilization beyond the Sahara, especially Egypt. It was through Kanem that the goods of Egypt and other northern lands, horses and fine metalware, salt and copper came into West Africa by way of the Eastern Sahara; and it was often through Kanem that the goods of West Africa, notably Kola and ivory, were taken in exchange to those northern lands. In this respect the markets of Bornu and Kanem were sometimes as important as the markets of Hausaland, or as those of the central and western regions of the Western Sudan [*A History of West Africa to the Nineteenth Century*, pp. 84–86, by Basil Davidson, with F. K. Buah, and the advice of J. F. Ade Ajayi].

For a comprehensive account of Kanem-Bornu history, the reader is advised to consult the book cited above. For a good short biography of Mai Idris (1580–1617), one of the great rulers of Kanem-Bornu, see *Great Rulers of the African Past* by Lavinia Dobler and William A. Brown.

The Hausa States, situated in the region now known as northern Nigeria, may justly claim a remote past history, but most of it is based on ancient traditions. More or less authentic records carry us back less than one thousand years. The Kano Chronicle, a collection of traditions of the Hausas, informs us that the first king, or "sarki" of Kano, was Bogoda, whose reign began in 999. There were originally seven Hausa states, namely: Biram, Daura, Gabir, Kano, Katsina, Rano, and Zaria. These states never formed an empire, nor were they ever brought under the rule of a centralized government; each unit was independent. Since they sometimes cooperated with each other for the attainment of common objectives, we may designate them as a confederation of independent states.

The nucleus of each of these states was a city or town, in which was located the seat of the government. The prosperity of these cities was based on agriculture and trade, for the local farmers traded their products for goods manufactured by the craftsmen in their shops located in the cities. These cities in time became foci of international trade, since they were patronized by traders from other parts of the Sudan, and from Guinea, North Africa, and Egypt.

There was sometimes conflict between city dwellers and the inhabitants of the rural areas. According to the Kano Chronicle, the ruler of Kano in the year 1290 was Sarki Shekkarau. Some of the counselors of the king came to him one day and reported that a spirit of rebellion seemed to be in the air throughout the surrounding countryside; and they suggested that repressive measures be taken. Shekkarau did not agree with his counselors: He thought that such problems could be settled amicably; so he agreed to meet delegates representing his discontented subjects. The delegation came to the royal palace at Kano and addressed their complaints to the king. They made an eloquent plea for local autonomy in respect to their customs and religious beliefs, declaring that: "If the lands of a ruler are wide, then he should be patient. But if his lands are not wide, he will certainly not be able to gain possession of the whole countryside by impatience." Sarki Shekkarau agreed that their arguments were meritorious, and, in the words of the Kano Chronicle, "he left them their power and their own religious customs."

By the end of the fourteenth century, Kano and Katsina had become the great commercial emporia of the Hausas. After 1400, most of the Hausa rulers were Moslems, and there was a wider contact with other Moslem states, such as Songhay and Kanem, which brought new ideas and practices into the region. Under monarchs like King Mohammed Rumfa of Kano (1465–99), palaces were constructed, armies organized, and a labor force conscripted. In due time Kano became a thriving center of trade and industry, and even forged ahead of Timbuktu and Gao. The city of Kano manufactured cotton goods for the entire western Sudan. By the advent of the nineteenth century, Kano might have become to West Africa what Manchester was to England; but unpredictable tides of history decided otherwise.

The Hausa States were an important link, commercially, between the other states of the Sudan and the Mediterranean coast. For instance, the Yoruba people sent their trade goods through Hausaland to North Africa, and received their North African imports by way of the same channels. The prosperity of the Hausa States courted invasion from outside. They came under Songhay rule for a short time, but soon regained their freedom. Kano was in vassalage to Kanem for a part of the fifteenth century, but as a rule the Hausa States remained independent until the end of the eighteenth century.

Although the Golden Age of West Africa was over by the end of the sixteenth century, there were some parts of the western Sudan that managed to survive and prosper well into the nineteenth century. Between the years 1823 and 1830, among English explorers who visited West Africa, were Dixon Denham and Hugh Clapperton. They expected to find a land peopled by untutored savages; but what they did find was quite different. Winwood Reade, who explored the Niger region later in the same century, has left to us a bright picture of what the earlier explorers experienced:

> Denham and Clapperton, who first reached the lands of Hausa and Bornu, were astonished to find among the Negroes magnificent courts; regiments of cavalry, the horses caparisoned in silk for gala days and clad in coats of mail for war; long trains of camels laden with salt and natron and corn and cloth and cowrie shells—which form the currency—and Kola nuts, which the Arabs call the coffee of the Negroes. They attended with wonder the gigantic fairs at which the cotton goods of Manchester, the red cloth of Saxony, double-barrelled guns, razors, tea and sugar, Nuremberg ware and writing paper were

exhibited for sale. They also found merchants who offered to cash their bills upon houses at Tripoli, and scholars acquainted with Avicenna, Averroes, and the Greek philosophers [*The Martyrdom of Man*, p. 230, by Winwood Reade].

We have had occasion to cite frequently a scholarly work, entitled *A Tropical Dependency: An Outline of the Ancient History of the Western Sudan with an Account of the Modern Settlement of Northern Nigeria*, by Lady Flora Shaw Lugard. The author of this book calls the Sudan "Negroland"; however, even a cursory reading of the text shows that the people who founded the great nations of the Sudan were not Negroes; at least this is the opinion of Flora Shaw Lugard, and she is by no means alone in adhering to this viewpoint. Mrs. Lugard, in discussing the Fulah (Fulani), traces their origin to the neighborhood of the sources of the Senegal River, and then refers to them as "a partly white race." After that, her Ladyship proceeds as follows:

> The movement of this remarkable people in Africa within historic time has unquestionably been from west to east, but this does not preclude the theory of some more remote eastern origin which may have preceded their African immigration. Whether Phoenician, Egyptian, Indian, or simply Arab, they are evidently a race distinct from the Negroid and other black types by which they have been surrounded, and notwithstanding the marked effects produced on some portions of their people by intermarriage with Negro women, they have kept the distinctive qualifications of their race through a known period of two thousand years. The Fulah of today is as distinct from the pure Negro as was the first Fulah of whom we have record. How long they may have existed in Africa before any record of them was made it is with our present knowledge impossible to say. The Hausa and the Songhay are other races which, though black, are absolutely distinct from the pure Negro type [*A Tropical Dependency*, p. 22].

In the *West African Review*, for September, 1951, there

was an article entitled "The Negro Enigma," by Professor M. D. W. Jeffreys. So as not to risk any distortion of his opinions, we cite extracts from that article in his own words:

The Black Belt, anthropologically speaking, is that area on the earth's surface that comprises the dark-skinned races. . . . The black belt extends from Africa via India, to Melanesia and Australia. In this great arc the position of the Negro is the enigma. At the two ends, or horns, are people who are Negroes, but in the center there are none. The center is occupied by a dark-skinned race, the Hindu, but he offers no difficulty. He belongs to the same race as the European, namely the Caucasian. . . . The Caucasian comes from an old human stock—a stock that is today called modern man. . . . The Swanscombe skull found in Great Britain is dated 250,000 years, and is our stock, not Negro. The skeletal remains dug up by the Leakeys in East Africa are us, not Negro. Boskop Man found in the Cape, is dated 50,000 years, and falls into our group, not that of the Negro. There are no Negro skulls of any antiquity. . . . The two Grimaldi skulls, one of a woman, the other of a boy are not Negro skulls. . . . So the enigma deepens: all the evidence points to the Negro being a comparatively recent race and here is the old Caucasian race in a continuous stretch from Britain to India. . . . Now in Africa there is continuous evidence, unlike anywhere else on the globe, of man's uninterrupted occupation of the earth for close on a million years. Africa is thus today accepted by many scientists as the cradle of the human species. Thus, in Africa from the Old Stone Age to Modern times, Modern Man is the tool maker. Nowhere is the Negro, unlike the Bushman, associated with these stone-age cultures.

Let us now turn to the scholarly production of a contemporary authority. We have in mind *It Began in Babel: The Story of the Birth and Development of Races and Peoples* by Herbert Wendt, translated from the German by James Kirkup. In this interesting work the author has a ten-page dis-

cussion on the topic: Where did the Negroes come from?
"Even in the wisest and most detailed anthropological and
ethnological works," we are told, "no answer will be found
to this question, though there are all kinds of hypotheses,
suppositions and questionable indications." (*It Began in Babel*,
p. 368.) First Mr. Wendt takes a look at southern Asia and
Oceania and concludes that they could not have been the
original home of the Negroes. Then he moves on to Africa,
and we are assured that: "The African Negroes are of even
more 'Negroid' type than the dark races in Asia and the South
Seas. Their skin color is generally darker, their hair woolier,
their lips more prominent—in short their whole appearance
is more 'Negro-like' than that of a Tamil or a Papuan. Accordingly they must be the pure, original Negroes, and the
black race must have had its birth in Africa. But apart from
one or two exceptions, there is no proof of this. All primitive
Africans, ignoring Neanderthal or even older human types,
belong broadly speaking to European humanity. . . . Then
if there are no primeval Negroes in the dark continent, how
did the Negroes come to Africa?" (*Ibid.*, pp. 368–69.)

Mr. Wendt finally concludes that the word "race" has lost
its meaning in Africa, and we should speak instead of "cultural group." "It is enough to say here," he concludes, "that
there is after all no 'real Negro Civilization,' but that Africa
is a mirror reflecting the most varied human cultures—just
like Eurasia and America." (*Ibid.*, p. 377.)

We do not wish to prolong this discussion unduly but, in
contrast to the opinions cited above, it is only fair to consider
the conclusions of Sir Harry Johnston, who has been widely
acclaimed as an outstanding authority on Africa and its peoples. "Whether the African Negro was the first human colo-
nizer of Africa," Johnston writes, "or was preceded by a
more brutish or more generalized type, such as the Galley-
Hill man, is not yet known to us. But from the little we
possess in the way of fossil human remains and other evidence

it seems probable that every region of Africa, even Algeria and Egypt, once possessed a Negro population. . . .In Egypt a dwarfish type of Negro seems to have inhabited the Nile delta some 10,000 years ago; and big black Negroes formed the population of Upper Nubia and Dongola as late as about 4,000 years ago." (*A History of the Colonization of Africa*, p. 5, by Sir Harry H. Johnston.)

Though holding that Negroid peoples can be traced to a very remote antiquity in Africa, Sir Harry Johnston felt certain that some part of southern Asia, possibly India, was the original home of this particular branch of the human species.

There is a strong underlying Negroid element in the mass of the Indian population [Sir Harry declares] and in the Southernmost part of the great peninsula there are forest tribes of dark skin and strikingly Negro physiognomy, with frizzled or wooly hair. . . . In the more eastern among the Malay Islands—especially in Buru, Jilolo and Timor—the interior tribes are of obvious Negro stock. Still more marked is this in the case of New Guinea, and most of all in the Bismarck Archipelago and northern Solomon Islands. In these last the resemblance of the natives to the average Negro of Africa is most striking, although the distance is something like 8,000 miles. Negro affinities extend east of the Solomon Archipelago to Fiji and Hawaii, and south to New Caledonia, Tasmania and even New Zealand. On the other hand, Africa for many thousand years has been obviously the chief domain of the Negro [*A History of the Colonization of Africa*, p. 3].

The attentive reader will have noticed that, if Johnston is correct in the conclusions enunciated above, then the opinions defended by Jeffreys and Wendt must lack all credence; and vice versa. In order to discuss any debatable or controversial question, we must clearly define the subject matter under discussion. If this is not done, then any such discourse will end up in a morass of utter sophistry, and will have no valid meaning. It is pointless to discuss the question of where did the Negro come from, or to pontificate on the Negro Enigma, if we do not, first of all, define the term "Negro." This has never been done; or if it has, we are not aware of it.

The late Sir Grafton Elliot Smith was a well-known anthropologist. Among his many published works was one with the title of *The Ancient Egyptians and the Origin of Civilization*. In this little book, he undertakes the solution of the question of the racial origins of the Egyptian people. He starts off as follows:

"Not a few writers, like the traveler Volney in the eighteenth century, have expressed the belief that the ancient Egyptians were Negroes, or at any rate strongly Negroid. In recent times even a writer so discriminating as Ripley* usually is, has given his adhesion to this view, which I consider to be the most serious blot on his most valuable and interesting memoir, *The People of Europe*." (*The Ancient Egyptians and the Origin of Civilization*, p. 37, by G. Elliot Smith.)

"Within recent years," we are further told by Dr. Smith, "many scholars have advocated the view that there is a large element of Negro in the composition of the Proto-Egyptian population, and Ripley, apparently as the result of a misunderstanding of Sergi's views, boldly states that the Egyptians and the whole Mediterranean race are descendants of Negroes!" (*Ibid.*, p. 79.)

Sir Elliot Smith admits that the ancient Egyptians were not members of the white race, and he is equally certain that they were not classifiable in the black race. The Egyptians, according to Professor Smith, should be listed under the designation of the brown race. "There can be no doubt that in respect of many features," he allows, "the brown and the black races present many points of similarity. . . . That there is no close

* The late Professor William Z. Ripley of Harvard University; the correct title of the book referred to is *The Races of Europe*.

affinity between the two races is shown by an analysis and comparison of the intimate structure of the bodies of representative individuals. In the texture of bone, the architecture of the skull, the nature of the asymmetry of the body and the character of the variations—in these and many other respects there is evidence of the profound gap that separates the Negro from the rest of mankind, including the Egyptian." (*Ibid.*, pp. 79–80.)

If there is a "profound gap" separating the Negro from the rest of the human race, one would expect Sir Elliot Smith to adduce some evidence tending to validate his theory; but this he does not even attempt to do.

The fact is that the stereotype of the so-called Negro race corresponds to no reality in the objective world. The German anthropologist, Ratzel, in his *History of Mankind* noted the fact "that the hideous Negro-type, which the fancy of observers once saw all over Africa, is really to be seen only as a sign in front of tobacco-shops, has on closer inspection evaporated from almost all parts of Africa." (*The History of Mankind*, 2nd edition, Vol. II, p. 313, by Friedrich Ratzel.)

In our own United States anyone reputed to have an African ancestry, however remote, is supposed to be a Negro. Let's carry this thesis to its logical conclusion. Since there is overwhelming evidence that the Cradle of Mankind was in Africa, then everybody must be considered a Negro. According to the theory of evolution, to carry the argument a step further, we all have a common ancestry with the apes; therefore, we are all apes. If the reader thinks this is an exercise in leg pulling, we should like to offer the following example.

Soon after the United States became involved in World War II, an open-air political meeting was held in the Harlem section of New York City. In the crowd attending the affair was a gentleman who was in New York on a visit, and next to him stood a member of the staff of the local Y.M.C.A. The two men began to converse with each other, and the visitor asked the Y.M.C.A. clerk to point out to him the celebrities seated on the platform from which the meeting was being conducted.

The Y.M.C.A. man addressed the out-of-towner, as he pointed to political bigwigs on the platform, as follows:

"Sir! Reading from left to right you will notice a short, stout dark complected man; that is Mayor LaGuardia. Seated next to him you see another man of dark complexion; and he is Commissioner Newbold Morris. They may look like colored men from here, but they are, in fact, both white men.

"Now, on the other side of the platform you observe the presence of two men of very fair complexion. The one at which I am pointing is Congressman A. C. Powell, Jr.; and the individual seated immediately to his right is Mr. Walter White, the Secretary of the N.A.A.C.P. Though these two gents look like white men, they are actually Negroes."

Any word that can be used so ambiguously as "Negro" should be discarded, since for descriptive purposes it is totally devoid of meaning; but getting rid of this word is not going to be easy. That branch of the human race which may be described as black or dark brown is customarily labeled "Negroid," a word which means "Negro-like." If "Negro" is disallowed, then "Negroid" will soon follow it into oblivion; for if "the Negro" is a mythical concept, how can anything be likened to a nonexistent entity. The question naturally suggests itself that, if we get rid of the word "Negro," what will we put in its place? This is a fair question, and we have a suggestion to present. In ancient times black men were called "Ethiopians." Why cannot we today, following the usage of modern anthropology, refer to members of the Black Race as "Ethiopoids," rather than "Negroids"?

Lord Bertrand Russell, the eminent philosopher and mathematician, stated some years ago that many great men of the past, listed in our history textbooks as white men, were, if the truth were known, in reality, colored men. Offhand we think of Spinoza, one of the great metaphysicians of all time. In that deservedly popular book, *The Story of Philosophy*, a chapter is devoted to the exposition of the philosophical system of Spinoza. The author of that work, Dr. Will Durant, gives a description of Spinoza as recorded by a contemporary biographer. "To the portraits of Spinoza which have come down to us," Dr. Durant declares, "we may add a word of description from Colerus." In the words of Colerus: "He was of a middle size. He had good features in his face, the skin somewhat black, the hair dark and curly, the eyebrows long and black, so that one might easily know by his looks that he was descended from Portuguese Jews." (*The Story of Philosophy*, p. 173, by Will Durant.)

Chapter Six

AFRICA AND THE DISCOVERY
OF AMERICA

The idea that ancient America was entirely cut off from the rest of the world can no longer be entertained. American scientists and scholars have strived to maintain this position; but it has now become untenable. The late Professor Paul Radin was an authority on Amerindian cultures, and he was admittedly baffled when he tried to trace the Mayan civilization to its source:

> Their culture seems to have arisen suddenly and to have disappeared in as mysterious a fashion. . . . As early as the year 100 B.C. the hieroglyphic system had already been fully developed. . . . Where and when this hieroglyphic system developed, of that we have not the remotest idea. The earliest hieroglyphic date is found on a little statuette and it is not until two hundred years later that we find monuments with inscriptions and dates. Then without warning or preparation we find enormous mounds with elaborate temples built upon them, public squares, stelae and altars. No excavations have ever revealed to us any civilization of a simpler nature from which this elaborate culture could possibly have been developed [*The Story of the American Indian*, pp. 76–77, by Paul Radin].

A solution to the riddle of the origin of early American civilizations was attempted by Professor Leo Wiener, of Harvard University. After many years of research, he published a three-volume work: *Africa and the Discovery of America.* This was followed by another scholarly production: *Mayan and Mexican Origins*, which was published by the author in 1926. These books were not kindly received in academic circles. One of Wiener's Harvard colleagues, Professor Herbert J. Spinden, of the Peabody Museum, regarded the entire project as an example of misdirected energy. In an essay on "The Prosaic vs. the Romantic School in Anthropology," Spinden discusses Wiener's hypothesis as follows:

> Professor Wiener solves the riddle of old American civilizations with an Arabico-Mandingo lexicon and derives everything of importance in the New World from the highly civilized coasts of Gambia and Sierra Leone. From brightest Africa came the principal American food plants, the Mayan calendar and the Mexican religion. . . . The full splendor of his disarticulation is demonstrated in several books. One, freshly off the press, has 110 colored plates and 16 plates in black and white, a veritable monument to misguided enthusiasm. . . . It may be added that Professor Wiener swarms his Negroes across the Atlantic in no less than fifty voyages before Columbus [*Culture: The Diffusion Controversy*, by G. Elliot Smith, Bronislaw Malinowski, Herbert J. Spinden, and Alexander Goldenweiser].

It is a fact that the first Spanish and Portuguese explorers found colonies of black men on the eastern coasts of South and Central America, and in Yucatan and Nicaragua. Father Roman, one of the earliest Catholic missionaries to arrive in the New World, records that a tribe of black men came from the south and landed in Haiti, and that they were armed with darts of guanin (an alloy of gold, silver, and copper), and were called the Black Guaninis.

> These might have been the Negroes of Quareca, mentioned by Peter Martyr d'Angleria, or some other American Negro nation [asserts Peter DeRoo], the like of which there were many, as we may see in Rafinesque's "Account of the Ancient Black Nations of America." Such are the Charruas of Brazil, the black Carabees of St. Vincent, in the Gulf of Mexico, the Jamassi of Florida, the dark complexioned Californians, who

are perhaps the dark men mentioned in the Quiche traditions and by some old Spanish adventurers. Such, again, is the tribe of which Balboa saw some representatives in his passage of the Isthmus of Darien in the year 1513. It would seem from the expressions made use of by Gomara, that these were Negroes [*History of America Before Columbus*, pp. 306–7, by Peter DeRoo].

In a short scholarly monograph, entitled *African Explorers of the New World*, Harold G. Lawrence asserts:

That Africans voyaged across the Atlantic before the era of Christopher Columbus is no recent belief. Scholars have long speculated that a great seafaring nation which sent its ships to the Americas once existed on Africa's west coast. . . . We can now positively state that the Mandingoes of the Mali and Songhay Empires, and possibly other Africans, crossed the Atlantic to carry on trade with the Western Hemisphere Indians, and further succeeded in establishing colonies throughout the Americas [*African Explorers of the New World*, p. 2].

The Arab historian Abulfeda (1273–1332) describes the world as spherical in shape, and tells of ships that had circumnavigated the globe. An African scholar, Al Omari, in a work published in Cairo about 1342, tells of mariners of the Mali Empire crossing the Atlantic Ocean to the New World during the reign of Mansa Musa I. We are informed by Basil Davidson that, "Omari in the tenth chapter of his 'Masalik al Absar,' reproduces a story which suggests that Atlantic voyages were made by mariners of West Africa in the times of the Emperor Kankan Musa of Mali; and which roundly states that the predecessor of Kankan Musa embarked on the Atlantic with 'two thousand ships,' and sailed westward and disappeared." (*The Lost Cities of Africa*, p. 74, by Basil Davidson.) Al Omari claims that he obtained his information from Ibn Amir Hajib, and quotes him as follows:

"And I asked the Sultan Musa how it was that power had come to his hands and he replied: 'We come of a house where royalty is transferred by heritage. The monarch who preceded me would not believe that it was impossible to discover the limits of the neighboring sea. He wished to know. He persisted in his plan. He caused the equipping of two hundred ships and filled them with men, and another such number that were filled with gold, water and food for two years. He said to the commanders: "Do not return until you have reached the end of the ocean, or when you have exhausted your food and water."

" 'They went away, and their absence was long: none came back, and their absence continued. Then a single ship returned. We asked its captain of their adventures and their news. He replied: "Sultan, we sailed for a long while until we met with what seemed to be a river with a strong current flowing in the open sea. My ship was last. The others sailed on, but as each of them came to that place they did not come back, nor did they reappear; and I do not know what became of them. As for me, I turned where I was and did not enter that current' " [cited by Basil Davidson in *The Lost Cities of Africa*, pp. 74–75].

Basil Davidson regards Al Omari's narrative as "a tall story perhaps," but we think he is being unduly skeptical. We now have evidences of African contacts with America going back at least three thousand years; and the researches of Professor Leo Wiener have convinced us, beyond all doubt, that people of the Mali Empire sent trading expeditions to America and made cultural contributions to the New World in pre-Columbian times. In a final chapter of conclusions, Professor Wiener gives us the gist of his three-volume work on Africa and the discovery of America. We cite briefly some of his conclusions, as follows:

The presence of Negroes with their trading masters in America before Columbus is proved by the representation of

Negroes in American sculpture and design, by the occurrence of a black nation at Darien early in the XVI century, but more specifically by Columbus' emphatic reference to Negro traders from Guinea, who trafficed in a gold alloy, guanin, of precisely the same composition and bearing the same name, as frequently referred to by early writers in Africa. . . .

There were several foci from which the Negro traders spread in the two Americas. The eastern part of South America, where the Caraibs are mentioned, seems to have been reached by them from the West Indies. Another stream, possibly from the same focus, radiated to the North along roads marked by the presence of mounds, and reached as far as Canada. The chief cultural influence was exerted by a Negro colony in Mexico, most likely from Teotihuacan and Tuxtla, who may have been instrumental in establishing the City of Mexico. From here their influence pervaded the neighboring tribes, and ultimately, directly or indirectly reached Peru. That the Negro civilization was carried chiefly by the trader is proved not only by Columbus' specific reference, but also by the presence of the African merchant, the *tangoman*, as *tiangizman* in Mexico, hence Aztec *tiangiz* "market," and by the universality of the blue and white shell-money from Canada to LaPlata, and the use of shells in the Peru-Guatemala trade. . . . The African penetration in religion and civic life and customs was thorough and to judge the survival of the Arabic words in a Malinke or Soninke form in America, especially among the Caraibs and Aztecs, proceeded almost exclusively from the Mandingoes, either the ancestors of the present Malinkes, or a tribe in which the Sonike language had not yet completely separated from its Malinke affinities [*Africa and the Discovery of America*, Vol. III, pp. 365–66].

In the year 1861 an important book was published in New York City. Its title was *History of the Intellectual Development of Europe*. The author of this work, Dr. John William Draper, was a scientist and scholar of considerable reputation.

In one passage of this study of European cultures, the author digressed from his main theme and mused philosophically on the sad plight of certain natives of what was then called the Dark Continent. He pictures the benighted inhabitants of the West Coast of Africa as gazing out upon the mighty Atlantic Ocean, vaguely wondering what lay on the other side of it; but not clever enough to build boats and embark on a voyage of exploration. This book of Draper's proved quite popular, and in 1876 the publishers issued a revised edition. One improvement in this revision of the original work was that Professor Draper left out the passage about the purblind African gazing at the sea, wondering what lay beyond, etc. What caused the distinguished author of the *History of the Intellectual Development of Europe* to drop the aforesaid passage, we cannot say with certainty; but we have an idea that, sometime between 1861 and 1876, Dr. Draper learned that evidence had been adduced showing that Africans had indubitably reached the New World in pre-Columbian times. Apparently, not willing to admit the making of erroneous statements, the author just quietly dropped the dubious passage, when he undertook the revision of the book.

The reader of this dissertation has in all probability heard about the huge stone heads, displaying an African type of physiognomy, which have been unearthed in Mexico by several archaeological parties. The first of these stone heads to come to the attention of the outside world was found in the wilds of Veracruz. It was seen by a Mr. J. M. Melgar, who published a report of it in 1869. This *cabeza colosal*, as the Mexicans called it, was half buried, but enough of it was visible for an occasional observant traveler to notice its "Ethiopian features" and the presence of a headdress resembling a football helmet. Early in 1938, Dr. Matthew W. Stirling, Director of the Bureau of American Ethnology, a branch of the Smithsonian Institution of Washington, D. C., visited the Veracruz

forests and took a look at the colossal head. The old monument was located near the village of Tres Zapotes, and after
a preliminary observation Dr. Stirling decided that the area
looked promising as a site for archaeological exploration. He
then returned to Washington and organized an expedition,
sponsored jointly by the Smithsonian Institution and the National Geographic Society. The expedition, later in the same
year, betook itself to Tres Zapotes and began excavating the
great stone head. The head turned out to be a solid block of
basalt, six feet in height, and eighteen feet in circumference,
with its base attached to a platform of crudely hewn stones.
A member of Dr. Stirling's staff noted the African features
of the stone face and thought that the headdress resembled
the training headgear of a pugilist, and then gave the *cabeza
colosal* the nickname "Joe Louis." In exploring the surrounding areas, the expedition found a stone containing a date.
They were able to decipher a series of dots and bars, of the
same type as used by the Mayas of Yucatan in recording dates
in their calendar. The translation of the date into the termi-
nology of our calendar was found to be November 4, 291
B.C.—the oldest date, up to that time, that had yet been
found in the New World.

In 1939, Dr. Stirling moved his party to LaVenta, on an
island near the coast of the Gulf of Mexico, in the State of
Tabasco. A stone head had been spotted at this site by an
expedition from Tulane University in 1925, but it had not
been excavated. Stirling's group in looking for one head had
the good luck of finding five. One head had a circumference
of twenty-two feet, and each was estimated to weigh twenty
or more tons; and they all showed a close resemblance to the
cabeza colosal of Tres Zapotes.

Another expedition was organized in 1946 by Dr. Stirling.
The site chosen for exploration was the San Lorenzo plateau,
located in the southeastern part of Veracruz. Again gigantic
stone heads were uncovered; this time there were five of them.

One of the lot was a super-giant head, estimated to weigh thirty tons, with a mouth over three feet wide and eyes that measured almost two feet across. It was appropriately dubbed "El Rey" ("The King").

In the spring of 1967, another archaeological party began work at the San Lorenzo site. This group, led by Dr. Michael Coe of Yale University, enjoyed a successful season marked by rewarding finds, such as another huge basalt head, with the typical African facial features. (A reproduction of this particular stone head was featured on the cover of *Science Digest* for September, 1967.) These relics dug up by expeditions led by Stirling, Coe, and other archaeologists were all remains of the ancient Olmec culture. This early civilization flourished in Veracruz, Tabasco, and Chiapas; and it was the principal source of the later Maya, Aztec, Toltec, and Zapotec cultures. There is an interesting and instructive article concerning the Olmec culture, from which we cite the following:

> The first Olmec artifact to attract archeologists turned up in a plowed field in 1902 not far from the Bay of Campeche in the Gulf of Mexico. Sculpted in pale green jadette was a beautifully carved fat, bald-headed Indian priest about eight inches high. Undecipherable glyphs were incised on its stomach. Also on its stomach was a Mayan date. The date corresponded to 98 B.C., well before any known Maya civilization and in the wrong area of Mexico for Maya.
>
> The long-count calendar, attributable at that time to the Maya, is a more accurate calendar than the one we use today. It begins, for unknown reasons, in the year 3113 B.C. Closely correlated to astronomical observations, it can be read precisely for any day and year in the intermediate period and transcribed into a date in terms of our calendar. It is a masterpiece of mathematical and astronomical knowledge, and it was the Olmecs not the Maya who developed it ["Secrets of the People of the Jaguar," an article by Jeanne Reinert, in *Science Digest*, pp. 8–9, September, 1967].

(The Olmecs are sometimes called the People of the Jaguar because in their numerous works of art the jaguar motif is outstanding; and it is believed that the jaguar was worshiped as a god by the Olmecs.)

In his authoritative work *The Aztec: Man and Tribe*, Victor Wolfgang von Hagen devotes a chapter to the pre-Aztec cultures of Mexico. His sketch of the Olmecs is a model of concise description:

> In Aztec mytho-history, the Olmecs were known as "the people who live in the direction of the rising sun" and a glyph history of them shows that their paradisiacal "wealth" consisted of rubber, pitch, jade, chocolate and bird feathers. We do not know what they called themselves. "Olmec" derives from *olli* (rubber); their symbol, often seen, is that of the tree of life, the "weeping wood." They traded rubber and they presumably made the rubber balls used for the game called *tlachtli*. A talented and mysterious people, they appeared as early as 1000 B.C. along the Isthmus of Tehuantepec (where the waist of Mexico is slender and level between the two oceans), but they were particularly centered about the Coatzacoalcos River basin on the Gulf Coast. . . . Only in recent times have the great Olmec stone heads been unearthed by Dr. Matthew Stirling. At Tres Zapotes he found one colossal head, seven feet high, flat-nosed and sensually thick-lipped. The carving is sensitive and realistic; the style is found among no other people and once seen will never be forgotten or confused with any other. . . . Only now are Olmec structural complexes coming into focus. They had temple-cities, erected stone stelae to mark the flight of time or to commemorate important events; the stepped pyramid, the courtyard, the *tlachtli* ball game, were all cultural features in general use [*The Aztec: Man and Tribe*, pp. 31–32, by Victor Wolfgang von Hagen, Revised Edition].

Among the pioneer archaeologists to study the Mayan remains in Yucatan was Professor Augustus LePlongeon. In

1885 he published a book with the title *Maya Archaeology*; and in this study he recorded the tradition of an ancient Olmec culture, which had preceded that of the Toltecs, and the belief that these ancient people had come from the east in ships in order to settle in the New World. Had LePlongeon had an open mind he would have concluded that these immigrants had come from Africa; but since he knew little of the African past, he surmised that their original home was the lost continent of Atlantis.

Columbus has been hailed as the discoverer of America; but Columbus himself never succumbed to any such delusion. According to Harold G. Lawrence:

> Proof of this is evidenced by the fact that Columbus was informed by some men, when he stopped at the Cape Verde Islands off the coast of Africa, that Negroes had been known to set out into the Atlantic from the Guinea coast in canoes loaded with merchandise and steering toward the west. The same Christopher Columbus was further informed by the Indians of Hispaniola when he arrived in the West Indies that they had been able to obtain gold from black men who had come from across the sea from the south and southeast. . . . It must also be added that Amerigo Vespucci on his voyage to the Americas witnessed these same black men out in the Atlantic returning to Africa [*African Explorers of the New World*, p. 6, by Harold G. Lawrence].

Professor Leo Wiener in 1926 announced that he had been able to trace the presence of Africans in the Americas only as far back as the ninth century. Now we know that they were in the Western Hemisphere at least three thousand years ago; and as new discoveries are made by the archaeologists, we confidently expect this dating to be pushed back to times far more remote. Evidence pointing to this conclusion has been garnered by Colonel Braghine, and is best expressed in his own words:

Hitherto, ethnologists imagined that Negroes appeared in the New World only during our own epoch, when they were imported as slaves; but the most recent researches demonstrate that they first came to America in a period very remote. . . . I have seen a statuette of a Negro in the archaeological collection of Mr. Ernesto Franco in Quito [Ecuador]: according to the opinion of local archaeologists, this statuette is at least 20,000 years old.

The autochthonous black races in America were either gradually mixed with the Indian ones, or became extinct, but in a very remote time Negroes, or Negroids, were numerous in the New World. . . .

Once I had the opportunity of living for about a month in Oyapoc, a locality in a lonely situation among the equatorial forests of French Guiana. There I saw representatives of the local Negro tribe of Saramaccas, which lives all by itself and is ruled by its own chiefs. The Saramaccas are divided into several clans and each clan possesses a sort of a coat of arms tattooed on the faces of its members. The opinions of scientists concerning the origin of the Saramaccas vary: Whilst some consider these Negroes to be an autochthonous American tribe, others think that the Saramaccas are none else than the progeny of ancient slaves imported into South America, who deserted from their masters in the forests of Guiana. The Saramacca tongue resembles the dialect of the African Gold Coast which is situated directly opposite the Guiana shores. My own view is that the latter hypothesis is wrong: clearly it would be very difficult to transport into slavery an entire tribe, and still more difficult for that tribe to escape together with its wives and children. The complement of the slaves' group was always entirely casual, so that each group of slaves was composed of the representatives of various tribes. Furthermore, the Saramaccas of today are a very kind-hearted people, friendly to the whites, which would not have been the case if their ancestors had been slaves, subjected to the bestial cruelty of the planters. So I am inclined to believe that the Saramaccas are the last Aboriginal Negro tribe preserved in America. The most surprising thing about this tribe is its knowledge of sorcery methods, inherited, perhaps, from an unknown and peculiar culture which flourished on the globe in a very remote epoch [*The Shadow of Atlantis*, pp. 40–41, by Colonel Alexandre Braghine].

A Peruvian scientist decided in 1952 to investigate the truth or falsity of an old tradition stemming from the period of the Spanish Conquest of the Incan Empire. This legend told of colossal stone figures of men and beasts seen by the conquistadors on a certain mountain plateau. The investigator, Daniel Ruzo, climbed up to the Marcahausi plateau, in the Western Cordilleras, and hopefully began his search. The plateau was attainable only by one pass, and this was indubitably made by men who were expert workers in stone. A road had been constructed to the plateau; and alongside the road was a wall containing embrasures from which rocks could be propelled at potential invaders. In addition, small forts and observation posts were built overlooking the road. Mr. Ruzo was amazed by what he saw on this lonely plateau. He found a large system of irrigation canals, some of which descended underground; two dams, in a good state of preservation, and twelve artificial storage lakes. Tombstones were observed, which had been carved in the form of fish, rabbits, toads, and rats. Remains of Incan and pre-Incan culture were discovered; the most ancient of which seemed to be of African origin. Mr. Ruzo, seeing images of animals on a slab of stone, made some photographs of them. Later, when examining the film, he noticed the figure of a man in the pictures. This was puzzling, for the scientist had not noted the presence of the man on the stone slab sculpture. An interesting report of Ruzo's amazing discoveries is contained in a recent edition of *On the Track of Discovery* by the Russian scientific writer, Rudolph Bershadsky. He, in speaking of Ruzo's bewilderment in not being able to see the image of the man on the slab, gives the following explanation of just what had happened:

He could not understand how he had not noticed it before until he realized that when he took the photographs he did not scrutinize the slab carefully because he had done so earlier *under different illumination*. The explanation was that the figure of the man could be seen only at a definite time of the day; the sculptor who made it knew that secret.

Ruzo wasted no time examining all the other slabs and cliffs in the plateau at different times of the day and from different angles. What he saw made him gasp with astonishment. Some of the cliffs had been artistically worked and represented mammoth sculptures: for example a head of a Negro (it was made long before Columbus discovered America, that is to say, long before the first Negro known to historians was brought to the American continent), camels (that likewise were unknown in America), elephants, cows and horses, i.e., animals that were not known to the inhabitants of America when Europeans discovered the New World [*On the Track of Discovery*, Series 2, p. 157].

The reader has probably heard about the remains of the ancient Mound Builders, who long ago dwelt in the eastern half of the United States. There is a considerable literature on the cultures of the Mound area; and by far the best account of these ancient Americans is given in a recent study by Robert Silverberg, entitled *Mound Builders of Ancient America*. It seems that the Mound Builders flourished from about 1000 B.C. to around 1000 A.C., although the period after the middle of the sixth century of our era seems to have been one of decline. Numerous culture complexes sprang up in the Mound area—among the outstanding being the Crystal River complex in Florida, and the Adena and Hopewell groups of Ohio. The researches of Edward V. McMichael, of the West Virginia Geological and Economic Survey, have led him to conclude that the Olmec culture of Mexico had contacts with the Mound Builders of the United States. McMichael's views are summarized by Mr. Silverberg, who writes:

Flat-topped platform mounds are characteristic of the southern United States, but the obvious origin of the style was in Mexico. McMichael thinks that the Hopewells experimented with platform mounds after learning about them in Florida— and their Floridian tutors, the Crystal River people, were in direct contact with the Mexican civilization centered about Veracruz. . . . McMichael feels that traders or even colonists traveled in large canoes across the Gulf of Mexico from Northern Veracruz, to the northwest coast of Florida, and that the ideas that took root at Crystal River were passed along to the Hopewells before A.D. 1 [*Mound Builders of Ancient America,* pp. 286–87, by Robert Silverberg].

We may recall from our discussion of Egyptian mythology in Chapter III that the four sons of Horus were represented as standing at the four cardinal points of the celestial sphere and holding up the heavens; and that their names were Amset, Hapi, Tuamutef, and Gebhsennuf. The same symbolism was prevalent in pre-Columbian America. In discussing the ancient Mayan religious rites, Dr. Paul Radin points out the importance of the four gods of the cardinal points: "The earth was held in place by four deities, the four cardinal points. With each cardinal point was associated a definite color. It is difficult to over-estimate the significance of these deities. Indian ceremonialism is almost unthinkable without them." (*The Story of the American Indian,* p. 66, by Paul Radin.) These gods were known as the four Bacabs. Their symbolic colors were yellow, white, black, and red, and their names were respectively Kan, Muluc, Ix, and Cauac. This symbolism, almost identical in form, prevailed among the Aztecs, where these compass-point divinities were known as the four Sky-bearers. An accurate description of this scheme is given by Lewis Spence, as follows:

The Mexicans divided the universe into 4 regions, governed by 4 gods who were supposed to uphold the skies at the 4 directions of the compass. These compass-directions were associated with various colors, red, white, black, yellow. . . . These sky-bearers were supposed to be spirits or gods of the stars. . . . They were usually symbolized by insects, particularly scorpions, spiders and bees. They were also associated with the only 4 days on which the calendar could begin, ACATL, TECPATL, CALLI AND TOCHTLI [*The Religion of Ancient Mexico*, p. 48, by Lewis Spence].

Dr. Churchward claims that this four-god complex may be traced directly back to the four sons of Horus of the Egyptian pantheon. The same symbolism is found in West Africa. "The people of Bavili, Bini and Yorba, West Africa," says Churchward, "have the same under the names of:

1. IBARA.
2. EDI.
3. OYEKUN.
4. OZ-BE.

and build these names, with the name of Ifi, the Son of God —i.e. Horus—into the walls of their houses." (*The Signs and Symbols of Primordial Man*, p. 320, by Albert Churchward.)

It is necessary to say something about the strange calendrical system of ancient America, since it was ultimately of Olmec origin, and contained African elements. The construction of a very accurate calendar complex must be credited to the ancient Maya. This system of time measurement was passed on to the Zapotecs and Aztecs, where we find it operational in a somewhat simplified form. The Mayan calendar, like that of the Aztecs of Mexico and the Incas of Peru, was originally based on the lunar year. Starting with a lunar year of 12 months of 30 days each, the Mayan astronomers later introduced a sacred calendar called the Tzolkin. It was made up of 13 months, each consisting of 20 days, making a total of 260 days for the entire year. This Tzolkin Calendar, which was called the Tonalmatl by the Aztecs, was made up of a series of 20-day signs combined with the numbers 1 to 13; and, in the words of Professor Herbert J. Spinden: "These two series revolve upon each other like two wheels, one with thirteen and the other with twenty cogs. The smaller wheel of numbers makes twenty revolutions while the larger wheel of days is making thirteen revolutions, and after this the number-cog and the name-cog with which the experiment began, are again in combination. Thus a day with the same number and the same name recurs every 13 × 20 or 260 days."

The Maya people possessed another calendar, called the Haab, consisting of 18 months of 20 days each, giving a total of 360 days. To this were added five days called Uayeb, which corrected the year to its true length of 365 days. "The actual year is about 365 days 6 hours long," Robert Silverberg notes, "and the Mayas, aware of this, periodically adjusted their calendar to account for this, just as we do with leap years. But the Maya calendar was even more precise than ours, by a matter of some seconds a year." (*Lost Cities and Vanished Civilizations*, pp. 120–21, by Robert Silverberg.) These two calendars, the Tzolkin and the Haab, were combined to form a third calendar, called the Calendar-Round.

Now the Calendar-Round [as Professor Radin explains] is arrived at by remembering that the day-numbers associated with the day-names entering into the ritual year of 260 days can run the whole gamut of thirteen changes. As a result a particular day with a particular number can occupy a particular month-position every 13 × 4 or 52 years, that is 18,980 days. This period the Mayas called the Calendar-Round and it is of vast importance both among the Maya and the Aztecs in connection with their astronomy and their whole ceremonial life [*The Story of the American Indian*, p. 74, by Paul Radin].

The Mayan calendar-makers were not satisfied with the Tzolkin, the Haab, and the Calendar-Round; they showed their profound knowledge of astronomy by constructing a Venus Calendar. This calendar, based on the phases of the planet Venus, which has a year of 584 days, was divided into four parts, consisting of 236 days (morning star), 90 days (superior conjunction), 250 days (evening star), and 90 days (inferior conjunction)—which is mathematically accurate. The equivalence in length of eight solar years of 365 days each, and five Venus years of 584 days each, was recognized and accurately calculated; and we have reason to believe that a discrepancy of eight-hundredths (0.08) of a day between the mean Venus year and the true Venus year was corrected by a marginal subtraction of two days after a period of twenty-five revolutions of that planet.

The Zapotecs used a ritual calendar of 260 days, which was probably derived from the Maya; and in addition they connected it with the astronomical symbolism of their sky-gods, with reference to the four cardinal points. "In one of the old codices," says Dr. Radin, "they are represented as follows. The first, the east, is a figure wearing as a helmet-mask an alligator's head; he is a good and fruitful deity. The second, the north, has as his mask a death's head; he signifies drought and death. The third, the west, wears the head of an unknown animal. The fourth figure, the south, wears the vulture's head. There is a fifth figure representing the center. His colors are those of the gods of the night-heaven and twilight and the symbols accompanying him refer to war." (*The Story of the American Indian*, p. 158, by Paul Radin.) These Zapotec sky-bearers described in the above citation resemble the four Bacabs of the Maya.

Opposite page 266 in Volume III of *Africa and the Discovery of America*, is a copy of a Maya drawing labeled *Plate of the Bacabs*. Professor Leo Wiener compares this "Plate" to an Arabic talisman known as the gadwal. Gadwal seems to mean, among other things, a vertical column, a zodiacal table, or talismanic signs written in columns. Says the professor:

> To us the most interesting gadwal is the one which is the basis of the "Plate of the Bacabs" in Central America. Like that one, it consists of a central circle with four radiating demi-diagonals of a square surrounding it. . . . The form is identical in a general way with the American "plate," but the American "plate" belongs to one of the more complicated Gadwals. . . . We have no means of ascertaining whether the Mandingoes possessed the gadwal from which the American "plate" and its like were produced, since nothing of documentary antiquity has come down to us, but we have still ample documentary evidence to prove that the American "plate" has gone through a Mandingo redaction. In the first place, the central square contains the Mandingo tutelary god with his attributes and appurtenances. The numerical calculation based on 20 and 13, which is the essence of the American calendars, is surely built on African models. . . . For astrological purposes there was in use a division of the Zodiac into thirteen parts, such has been found on three calabashes in Western Africa, and it is a curious fact that a similar division into thirteen is recorded only among the Kirghizes and in America. . . . Precisely such gadwals have been found in the region of the Mandingoes, and these have glyphs that bear an amazing resemblance to the Central American glyphs, especially those of the Tuxtla statuette, where we find similar signs encysted in squares and parallelograms. Unfortunately we possess only the three photographs of the African inscriptions which Desplagnes has reproduced. Most of the columns in two of these begin with the forms of animals, the spider and lizard, which are also scattered throughout the columns. The spider is identical in form with the one given on Mound-builders' gorgets, where the cross in the center indicates that it is related to the *tonalamatl* of the Mexicans and the maya calendar. In Africa the spider is connected with an enormous number of tales, and among the Hausas the rainbow is called *bakan gizzo*, literally,

"the spider's bow," which indicates the relation which the divinities that came down from heaven bear to the spider. . . . In some places in Africa the scorpion has taken the place of the spider. . . . As the spider is connected with the rainbow, it connects heaven with earth, and the spirits of heaven, the stars, the constellations, are thus brought in contact with the spider; whence it is only natural that the gadwal, which deals with astrology or astronomy, should be connected with the spider. For this reason, the spider of the Mound-builders has in its middle the cross, which is the simplest representation of the fourfold division of the gadwal. This ornamentation is in constant use in the Western Sudan. It forms the central design of circular objects, is done in square patterns with looped ends exactly as in bird gadwals in Mound-builders' gorgets. . . . In the Mound-builders' gorgets we not only have the spider with its gadwal, but the looped-end gadwal with a cross in the middle, all placed within a circle, is the most striking object found in the mounds. That we have in these cases a development and simplification of the gadwal with the Mandingo *dasiri*, the tutelar god and rain giver, who lives upon a tree, is brought out in a number of cases, where each side of the square has the representation of a bird's head [*Africa and the Discovery of America*, Vol. III, pp. 269–73, by Leo Wiener].

After careful study of much other evidence of African influence in pre-Columbian America, Professor Wiener expressed the following conclusion:

The identity of the spiritual civilizations, down to the minutest details in the Sudan and in Mexico and elsewhere in America, leads to the assumption that other cultural elements, identical in both continents and frequently bearing the same names, are of African origin. This is preeminently the case with cotton, which in Africa has a religious purification significance, and the presence of which in America before Columbus outside its religious use in connection with burials cannot be proved from documentary evidence [*Ibid.*, p. 369].

Among the greatest of all globe-trotters was Ibn Batuta (fourteenth century), a native of Morocco, who traveled over a period of thirty years. He visited Russia, Egypt, Palestine, Syria, Asia Minor, China, Byzantium, India, the Malay Peninsula, Borneo, Sumatra, Java, the Sudan, and Arabia. He journeyed far enough north in Russia to see the Midnight Sun, made four pilgrimages to Mecca, visited Constantinople, crossed Africa from the Atlantic Ocean to the Red Sea twice, traveled through the perilous passes of the Hindu Kush Mountains; and finally he wrote the most fascinating of all books of travel.

Ibn Batuta, who was born in 1303, started on his career of extensive travel in his youth. By the year 1349 he was back in Fez, the capital of Morocco under the Merinite Dynasty, where he decided to settle down and take a respite from his wanderings. The reigning monarch at that time was Abu el Hacen. Ibn Batuta regarded the administration of the sovereign and conditions of living in the kingdom as worthy of praise. His sentiments at that time are conveyed to us by a modern commentator, as follows:

For reasons which he sets forth at length, his judgment was convinced that the noble country over which its sovereign ruled was the best country and the best administered of all those that he had visited. Here he found the conditions of life better than in any other country. Food was more plentiful, varied and cheap; life and property were more secure, law was milder, justice was more assured, charity more fully organized, religion more truly maintained, and literature, science and art more honored than in any other center of civilization. He mentions, in regard to the organized charities of the country, that free hospitals were constructed and endowed in every town of the kingdom. As regards the endowment of science and literature, he describes the great College of Fez as having "no parallel in the known world for size, beauty and magnificence." He speaks of the deep interest taken by the sovereign

in all that related to science and literature, the very considerable
literary achievements of the sovereign himself, and of the
generous protection which he gave to all persons who were
devoted to the study of science [Lady Lugard, in *A Tropical
Dependency*, pp. 74–75].

At the court of King Abu el Hacen there was much talk
of the glories of the Empire of Mali, on the other side of the
great desert. Being a born traveler, Ibn Batuta decided to
pay a visit to Mali; so on February 18, 1352, he crossed the
border of Morocco and headed south for Mali. This journey,
which occupied upwards of eighteen months of time, was
terminated in December of 1353, when he returned to Morocco.

The Moorish traveler crossed the frontier of Mali at the
city of Walata, which had been the capital of the old kingdom
of Ghana. Though the climate of Walata was exceedingly
hot, Batuta was favorably impressed by his visit to that city.
There was an abundance of foodstuffs, and the citizens were
attractively attired in clothing, imported chiefly from Egypt.
Another pleasing feature of the city of Walata was the outstanding beauty of its women, whom Ibn Batuta regarded
as decidedly superior to the men. Some of their customs
seemed to the visitor to be somewhat odd, especially the habit
of tracing kinship in the female line through a maternal uncle,
and of inheritance passing not from father to son, but from
father to the son of a sister. This practice was quite common
in the Sudan, but Batuta records that the only other place
he had come across these customs was among the inhabitants
of Malabar in India.

From Walata to Niani, the capital of Mali, was a journey
of twenty days. The country was well supplied with trees,
and along the highway villages were numerous. Traveling was
safe, good food was plentiful, and among the trees bearing
fruits the traveler noticed those "resembling plums, apples,

peaches and apricots, but not quite like them." Anything needed for a journey could be purchased at the roadside villages.

Ibn Batuta reached Niani in time to attend the ceremony of the ending of the fast of Ramadan. The main feature of this celebration was the presenting of arms to the Sultan. Squires presented to the ruler arms described as "magnificent." They were, in the words of Batuta, "swords ornamented in gold, with scabbards of the precious metal; spears of gold and silver; quivers made of gold and clubs made of crystal." This was followed by dramatic performances, with fencing, dancing, gymnastics, and the recitation of comic poetry included, which the Moorish visitor rated as very fine.

Lady Lugard devotes an entire chapter to the adventures of Ibn Batuta in Mali. One feature of these adventures that arrested the attention of Lady Lugard was the fact that some of the customs of Mali in the fourteenth century were almost identical with those of the contemporary Aztecs of Mexico. In her words:

> Poets wearing masks and dressed like birds were allowed to speak their opinion to the monarch. Ibn Batuta states that this practice was of great antiquity, long anterior to the introduction of Islam amongst these people. The description which he gives in some detail can hardly fail to recall similar practices inherited from the Tezcucans by the Aztecs, who in nearly the same latitude on the American continent were at this very moment, in the middle of the fourteenth century, making good their position upon the Mexican plateau. . . . They had other customs which correspond to those of the Sudanese. The Aztec crown was transmitted, like that of Mali, in collateral descent, though in both kingdoms exceptions to the rule occurred. The practice of keeping the sons of subject princes as a sort of honorable hostage at the court of the monarch was perhaps too general to be worthy of special note, though it was also common to the two people. The more

terrible custom of propitiating the gods with human sacrifice which was so extensively practiced by the Aztecs, was, it will be remembered, only the other day brought to an end under British rule in Benin, and is probably still practiced in less accessible portions of the pagan belt. . . . The custom of wearing the heads of animals as a head-dress, which was also common to the Aztecs, was preserved amongst the pagans of the West African coast at the time of the first occupation of the Gold Coast by the Portuguese in 1481 [*A Tropical Dependency*, pp. 137–39, by Lady Lugard].

The common features of certain African and Amerindian mores in the fourteenth century seemed to Lady Lugard to be odd coincidences; and she certainly would have dismissed as absurd the idea of any actual contact between the two peoples dwelling on opposite sides of the Atlantic Ocean. But truth is sometimes stranger than fancy; for we now know that the ancestors of the Mandinka people were sending traders, and perhaps colonists, to America, many centuries before the time of Columbus.

The idea that Africans were in the New World three thousand years ago is hard for many people to believe, even among the educated classes; for old stereotypes die hard. But there is no lack of evidence in this respect. J. A. Rogers, in *Africa's Gift to America*, cites Latin-American scholars on the African influence in America. For example, C. C. Marquez is quoted as saying: "The Negro type is seen in the most ancient Mexican sculpture. . . . Negroes figure frequently in the most remote traditions." From the Mexican historian, Riva-Palacio, we have the following: "It is indisputable that in very ancient times the Negro race occupied our territory [Mexico]. . . . The Mexicans recall a Negro god, Ixtilton, which means 'black-face.'" And also we have the testimony of Nicolas Leon, who declares that: "The almost extinction of the original Negroes during the time of the Spanish conquest and the memories of them in the most ancient traditions induce us to believe that the Negroes were the first inhabitants of Mexico."

The presence of an African substratum in the religious systems of ancient America is undeniable. It has been noticed by that careful observer, Colonel Braghine, that: "Some statues of the Indian gods in Central America possess typical Negro features and certain prehistoric statues there undoubtedly represent Negroes. We have for instance, such statues in Teotihaucan, in Palenque, and a gigantic Negro's head carved in granite near the Mexican volcano of Taxila." (*The Shadow of Atlantis*, p. 40.)

This African religious influence had a profound effect on the Mayan people; and their descendants still cherish the old traditions, even to the present day. We choose the Maya for illustrative purposes, since they were among the greatest of the Amerindian cultures, and we are able to draw upon the expert testimony of a field archaeologist of high authority. We refer to A. Hyatt Verrill, of the Museum of the American Indian, Heye Foundation, of New York City. Mr. Verrill has a thorough knowledge of the customs and languages of the Indians of Latin America. He has traveled and lived among the descendants of the ancient Maya for many years, and his account of their religious rites is of special value; and from his engrossing study of American Indian civilizations, we quote the following:

> The great cities of the Mayan Empire were deserted, many were completely lost and hidden in the rank jungle and forest growths of the tropics, and the existing Indians had little more than vague traditions and legends regarding their origin and their past. Yet they worshipped their old gods, using the ancient temples for their ceremonials wherein the Chilams or priests performed the rites. . . . Even today, many of the Indians of Central and South America secretly venerate or worship the gods of their forefathers. The Mayan tribes are no exception, although often the ancient Mayan deities and rites and the

Christian rituals and saints are almost inextricably confused.

In the little church at Esquipultas, Guatemala, is the image of the Black Christ to which thousands of Indians journey annually from all parts of Central America, and even from Mexico and South America. The spot has become a shrine or Mecca for the Indians, and for hundreds, even thousands of miles, they travel to the obscure Guatemalan village carrying with them all of their possessions in order to have them sanctified at the famous church. To all outward intents and purposes they are Christians making a pilgrimage to a Christian church in order to worship before a figure of Christ. No doubt many if not most of them actually are sincere in believing this to be the case. But, as a matter of fact, the underlying cause, the real urge that leads them to the spot is the ineradicable faith in their ancient gods and religion. The very fact that the image is black has a symbolic significance which can be traced directly to the ancient religions and mythologies . . . and, delving deeper into the details of the annual pilgrimage and the shrine, we find evidences of the observance of the Mayan religion numerous. The Indians who care for the church and the image are of the Mayan priest clan or caste. Many of the ceremonies, rites and festivals of the pilgrims are obviously of ancient Mayan origin, and the little *santos* or images which the devout Indians bring to the church to be sanctified, and which serve as their own household gods, are figures of the ancient Indian deities. Moreover, among many of the Indians, the Black Christ is referred to in private as Ekchuah or as Hunabku (the former, the Mayan god of merchants, husbandmen and travellers; the latter, the *God-father* or supreme deity of the Mayas), often prefixed with the Spanish Cristo (Christ), as Cristo Ekchuah or as Cristo Hunabku. [*Old Civilizations of the New World*, pp. 143–46, by A. Hyatt Verrill].

There is an extensive literature dealing with the lost continent of Atlantis; and the source of all this is a story told by Plato. We are not here concerned with whether Atlantis actually existed or not; but Plato's account should be noticed for certain information which it conveys on the antiquity of civilization both in the Old and New Worlds. An illuminating discussion of this matter is contained in Rudolph Bershadsky's article on Atlantis. He writes as follows:

Crito, in whose name Plato tells the narrative, says that when he was a boy he heard of the flourishing country of Atlantis from his nonagenarian grandfather, who had, in his turn, heard about it from his friend Solon, the famous Athenian lawgiver. Solon got the story from an Egyptian priest, who had access to ancient temple chronicles, having met him during his wanderings in Egypt. The story had made a rather long journey, but in spite of that it has an authentic ring about it. There is nothing to indicate that it was the product of somebody's fancy. It contains details that Plato's sources could not have invented. . . .

Over the past few years archaeological excavations have brought to light that the Hellenic culture was preceded by an Aegean culture and mighty states. The ancient Greeks knew nothing of this. Yet Plato begins his story about Atlantis with a description of powerful states that preceded the Hellenes. He even gives the lay-out of the capital of Atlantis which duplicates the lay-out of Tenochtitlan, the Aztec capital (and now the site of Mexico City). The entire story, as told by Plato, is woven of similar coincidences. There are other astonishing coincidences; the chronology of the ancient Egyptians and Assyrians is the same as that of the ancient Mayas in America. Can we assume that they knew about each other? We have no grounds for that. But even if we make this assumption, it will not explain why they selected the same date from which to begin their count of time. Our only other conjecture is that the concurrence of the calendar of three different peoples is due to some staggering event known to them, an event that to them could only have seemed to mark the end (or beginning) of the world. That is probably why it was retained in the memory of these peoples for thousands of years. . . . The Egyptians and Assyrians give the exact date: 11542 B.C. This is approximately the date the chronology of the Mayas also begins [*On the Track of Discovery*, pp. 174–76].

The year 11542 B.C. seems to have been important in the annals of ancient astronomy; and much light was focused on this point by Professor Julius Oppert in a paper read at a scientific meeting in Brussels in 1868. The title of this discourse was "La Chronologie Biblique fixee par les Inscriptions Cuneiformes." The paper was published in Paris in the same year, 1868.

There is no English translation of this paper, but its key points were summarized by Ignatius Donnelly in his famous book *Atlantis*, published in 1882. From his account we cite the following passage:

> M. Oppert read a paper at the Brussels Congress to show, from the Astronomical observations of the Egyptians and Assyrians, that 11,542 before our era man existed on the earth at such a stage of civilization as to be able to take note of astronomical phenomena, and to calculate with considerable accuracy the length of the year. The Egyptians, says he, calculated by cycles of 1,460 years—zodiacal cycles, as they were called. Their year consisted of 365 days, which caused them to lose one day in every 4 solar years, and, consequently, they would attain their original starting point again only after 1,460 years (365 × 4). Therefore, the zodiacal cycle ending in the year 139 of our era commenced in the year 1322 B.C. On the other hand, the Assyrian cycle was 1805 years, or 22,325 lunations. An Assyrian cycle began 712 B.C. The Chaldeans state that between the Deluge and their first historic dynasty there was a period of 39,180 years. Now, what means this number? It stands for 12 Egyptian zodiacal cycles plus 12 Assyrian lunar cycles.
>
> $$\left. \begin{array}{l} 12 \times 1460 = 17,520 \\ 12 \times 1805 = 21,660 \end{array} \right\} = 39,180$$

These two modes of calculating time are in agreement with

each other, and were known simultaneously to one people, the Chaldeans. Let us now build up the series of both cycles, starting from our era, and the result will be as follows:

ZODIACAL CYCLE	LUNAR CYCLE
1,460	1,805
1,322	712
—	—
2,782	2,517
4,242	4,322
5,702	6,127
7,162	7,932
8,622	9,737
10,082	11,542
11,542	

At the year 11,542 B.C. the two cycles came together, and consequently they had in that year their common origin in one and the same astronomical observation [*Atlantis*, pp. 26–27, by Ignatius Donnelly].

If these dates seem excessive, we can check them from a reliable source. When Herodotus was in Egypt in the fifth century B.C., he visited the Temple of Amen-Ra in Thebes. The scholarly priests of that establishment gave the Father of History a summary of the dynastic history of Egypt from the official records. In the words of Herodotus: "The priests said that Menes was the first king of Egypt. . . . Next, they read me from a papyrus, the names of 330 monarchs, who they said were his successors upon the throne." (*The History of Herodotus*, p. 113.) When Herodotus studied the data given to him by the priests, he counted 341 generations of Egyptian royalty, and gives the following estimate of the time span involved: "Now 300 generations of men make 10,000 years, 3 generations filling up the century; and the remaining 41 generations make 1,340 years. Thus the whole number of years is 11,340." (*Ibid.*, p. 131.)

If ancient civilizations in Africa, Asia, and America show certain traits pointing to a common origin in times remote in the past, then civilization is much older than many modern authorities are willing to admit. It is our opinion, and we have presented some of the data in Chapters II and III of this work, that all the early civilizations were of African Ethiopian origin. If these ancient Kushites could found such cultures as those of Egypt and Sumer, there is no reason that they could not have sailed across the Atlantic and planted the seeds of the first civilization in the New World.

When the history of the Negroland comes to be written in detail [declares Lady Lugard], it may be found that the kingdoms lying towards the eastern end of the Sudan were the home of races who inspired, rather than of races who received, the traditions of civilization associated for us with the name of ancient Egypt. For they cover on either side of the Upper Nile, between the latitudes of 10 degrees and 17 degrees, territories in which are found monuments more ancient than the oldest Egyptian monuments. If this should prove to be the case, and the civilized world be forced to recognize in a black people the fount of its original enlightenment, it may happen that we shall have to revise entirely our view of the black races, and regard those who now exist as the decadent representatives of an almost forgotten era, rather than as the embryonic possibility of an era yet to come [*A Tropical Dependency*, pp. 17–18, by Lady Lugard].

In Chapter VI, we cited Basil Davidson as referring to Mansa Musa's claim of Mariners of the Mali Empire embarking on voyages to the New World as "a tall story perhaps." We are now pleased to inform the reader that Mr. Davidson has changed his mind.

In the magazine *West Africa*, for Saturday, June 7, 1969, there is an article by Basil Davidson, with the title "Africans Before Columbus?" We are told by Mr. Davidson that:

> Columbus and other early European arrivals in the Americas came back with quite a bit of evidence, suggestive but inconclusive, that black peoples from Africa had already reached those shores. Various writers have pointed, from time to time, over the past twenty years and more, to the likely West African origins of these black explorers, notably of that "tribe of Almamys" who were said to have settled in Honduras.

"And then, of course," to cite Davidson again, "there is the famous conversation of 1324–5 on trans-Atlantic voyaging between the Emperor, Mansa Musa of Mali (c. 1312–37) and a Cairene scholar called Ibn Amir Hajib (recorded in turn by al-Omari, a few years later, in his *Masalik ab Absar fi Mamalik al Amsar*)."

The account of the conversation between Mansa Musa and Ibn Amir Hajib is given by Mr. Davidson as follows:

> "I asked the Sultan Musa how it was that power came into his hands. 'We are,' he told me, 'from a house that transmits power by heritage. The ruler who preceded me [probably Mansa Muhammad] would not believe that it was impossible to discover the limits of the neighboring sea [i.e. the Mali empires' western and south-western sea, the Atlantic]. He wanted to find out and persisted in his plan.

"He had two hundred ships equipped and filled with men and others in the same number filled with gold, water and supplies in sufficient quantity to last for years. He told those who commanded them: Return only when you have reached the extremity of the ocean, or when you have exhausted your food and water. They went away; their absence was long before any of them returned. Finally, a single ship reappeared. We asked the captain about their adventures.

" 'Prince,' he replied, 'we sailed for a long time, up to the moment when we encountered in mid-ocean something like a river with a violent current. My ship was last. The others sailed on, and gradually as each of them entered this place, they disappeared and did not come back. We did not know what had happened to them. As for me, I returned to where I was and did not enter that current.

" 'But the Emperor [Muhammad] did not want to believe him. He equipped two thousand vessels, a thousand for himself, and a thousand for water and supplies. He conferred power on me [Mansa Musa] and left with his companions on the ocean. This was the last time that I saw him and the others, and I remained absolute master of the empire.' "

"Now it seems very probable indeed," Basil Davidson comments, "that Musa said this to Ibn Hajib who told al-Omari, a careful annalist whose information about Mali rested on other eye-witness accounts by Egyptian scholars who had sojourned there. . . ."

Continuing his speculation on the topic, Davidson observes:

Those who believe that the sailors of Mali did in fact reach the Americas have other evidence to adduce. They point out that ships sailing west from Senegal would pass the Cape Verdes a little north of latitude 10 degrees North, and that in doing so they would sail into the steady westward-flowing Equatorial current, and thence into the Antilles Current as far as the Gulf of Mexico. They also recall that Columbus on his third voyage had information from the Cape Verde Islands that "canoes had been found which start from the coast of Guinea and navigate to the west with merchandise."

The view that Mansa Muhammad's expeditions were a figment of Mansa Musa's imagination, or that, if they really did take place, they altogether failed to reach the Americas, has thus to overlook a great many bits of and pieces of evidence to the contrary. This evidence has been largely set aside by historians, one cannot help feeling, because of some inherent preconception about the inability of Africans to navigate at sea. . . . Medieval Mali was no mere outpost of the civilised world of those times: on the contrary, it was in touch with the eastern world of Islam through many travellers and learned men, and the eastern world of Islam was very familiar with the sea. Travelling was very much in the spirit of West Africa, then as later; and if by land, why not by sea as well [*West Africa*, No. 2714, Saturday, June 7, 1969].

Chapter Seven

MARINERS AND MERCHANTS
OF THE EASTERN COAST

The Phoenicians were the most celebrated mariners and merchants of the ancient world, but they certainly were not the earliest. Professor Charles H. Hapgood of Keene State College, University of New Hampshire, has made a study of ancient maps, which he traces back to a civilized people who lived about twenty thousand years ago. In his recent book *Maps of the Ancient Sea Kings,* he has reproduced copies of these maps, along with a discussion of their origin and meaning. In Chapter VIII of that work, entitled "A Civilization That Vanished," he draws certain conclusions that are best stated in his own words:

> The evidence presented by the ancient maps appears to suggest the existence in remote times, before the rise of any of the known cultures, of a true civilization, of a comparatively advanced sort, which either was localized in one area but had worldwide commerce, or was, in a real sense, a *worldwide* culture. This culture, at least in some respects, may well have been more advanced than the civilizations of Egypt, Babylonia, Greece, and Rome. In astronomy, nautical science, mapmaking and possibly ship-building it was perhaps more advanced than any state of culture before the 18th century of the Christian Era [*Maps of the Ancient Sea Kings,* p. 193, by Charles H. Hapgood].

Professor Hapgood does not conjecture, in what people, or in what part of the world, this ancient culture had its genesis. These problems, he seems to think, will probably be cleared up by future discoveries. Many scholars of the past have suspected the existence of a remote primitive civilization, anterior to all those of recorded history. As an example, there come to mind the opinions of Professor A. H. L. Heeren, a German historical scholar of the nineteenth century, who gave favorable consideration to the Ethiopian theory of the origin of civilization:

From the remotest times to the present, the Ethiopians have been one of the most celebrated, and yet the most mysterious of nations. In the earliest traditions of nearly all the more civilized nations of antiquity, the name of this distant people is found. The annals of the Egyptian priests were full of them; the nations of Inner Asia, on the Euphrates and Tigris, have interwoven the fictions of the Ethiopians with their own traditions of the wars and conquests of their heroes; and, at a period equally remote, they glimmer in Greek mythology. When the Greeks scarcely knew Italy and Sicily by name, the Ethiopians were celebrated in the verses of their poets; and when the faint gleam of tradition and fable gives way to the clear light of history, the lustre of the Ethiopians is not diminished. They still continue to be the objects of curiosity and admiration, and the pen of cautious, clear-sighted historians often places them in the highest rank of knowledge and civilization [*Historical Researches: African Nations*, cited by John D. Baldwin in *Pre-Historic Nations*, p. 62].

In very ancient times, before the emergence of Phoenicia as a sea power, there was an extensive maritime trade carried on between cities on the coasts of the Persian and Arabian Gulfs and other cities on the East African coast as far south as Delagoa Bay, and perhaps even to the southern coast of the continent. There were also trade connections between East Africa and the west coast of India, southward to Ceylon, and further east to China. There was a well-established sea trade between India, China, and Africa dating back to the days of the earliest Egyptian dynasties. The Ethiopian ports for this Indo-Chinese commerce were Adule and Azab, both situated on the Red Sea coast. We learn from a nautical handbook, written in the first century of the Christian era, by Arrian, with the title *Periplus Maris Erythraee* (*Periplus of the Erythean Sea*), that: "Before merchants sailed from Egypt to India, Arabia Felix was the staple (or market), both for Egyptian and Indian goods, just as Alexandria now is for the commodities of Egypt and foreign merchandise." In commenting on this passage, Lady Lugard tells us that:

> The Indians nowhere appear as navigators; the Arabians always do. It seems to be demonstrated that they possessed the navigation of the Indian Ocean, not only in our own medieval times, but certainly through the period of the Ptolemies, and probably much earlier. That they communicated with Ethiopia in early ages is not a matter of doubt. Africa contributed largely in gold and probably also in Frankincense—which was obtained in the regions now known as Somaliland—to the ancient commerce of the Indian Ocean. Considering the position occupied by Arabia in that Commerce, it is not surprising to find that the ports through which the trade entered Ethiopia were Asab and Adule, both situated within the Straits of Babel-Mandeb on the western shore of the Red Sea. Roads from these two points led to Axum, in the interior, on the western side of the Abyssinian mountains, a town of which the colossal remains still testify to its ancient greatness. From Axum, which had its temples and was itself a great center of trade, the road led northwestward through the State of Meroe to the town of the same name. The town of Meroe was a great center, whence roads spread in many directions [*A Tropical Dependency*, pp. 222–23, by Lady Lugard].

The ancient Kushites of the Nile Valley, which we have discussed in an earlier chapter, had their capital city at Napata. Later they established a new capital further south at Meroe. That city was near the caravan routes along the Atbara River, which led into the highlands of Abyssinia, and finally to the western parts of the Indian Ocean, via which the

Kushites carried on a long-established trade. Meroe was a center for the smelting and manufacture of iron, which had a ready market in the Indian Ocean commerce.

In the first millennium prior to the beginning of the Christian era, invaders from southern Arabia established a kingdom in northern Ethiopia, with its capital at Axum. The Axumites cut the caravan routes between Kush and the ports of the Indian Ocean. A series of wars followed and finally Kush was defeated soon after the three-hundredth year of the Christian Era. The Axumites gained the ascendancy, and Meroe declined and finally became one of the dead cities of an extinct culture.

A third or fourth century Himyarite inscription from South Arabia refers to an alliance with Gadarat, king of the Habashan (Abyssinians). These Habashan, the founders of Axum, were mentioned in Egyptian inscriptions of the 18th dynasty (1709–1395 B.C.), in connection with the trade between Egypt and the land of Punt. "And although the legend that takes the rise of the Lion of Judah back to Solomon and his love for the Queen of Sheba is of course a pious forgery," declares a contemporary commentator, "there is more than a little truth in its symbolic essence: northwestern Ethiopia, the land of Habashat, was part of the world of Punt and frankincense in that venerable time when the ships of Hiram, King of Tyre, plied up and down the Red Sea and brought the wealth of Ophir into Israel." (*The Lost Cities of Africa,* p. 216, by Basil Davidson.)

The Ethiopian culture, stemming from Axum, flourished for a while, but it did not have the staying power of the old Kushites of Meroe. In the fourth century the rulers of Axum were converted to Christianity. From a cultural standpoint this was unfortunate, for it eventually isolated them from the outside world. Upon the rise of Islam the Red Sea ports were closed to all but the ships of Moslem nations. From the sixth to fourteenth century the Christian Ethiopians were engaged in almost continual warfare with the Muslims of the north and the pagans of the south; and during those centuries Ethiopia was conspicuous by its absence from the annals of history. After emerging from this dark age era, Axum had joined the many lost cities of the past, and the Amharic people of the Tigre and the central mountains had risen to a position of dominance. There was an early invasion of Ethiopia some hundreds of years B.C., by a people from the southern part of Arabia, who spoke a Semitic language. One of their inscriptions, found at Yeha, a place near Axum, dates about the fourth century B.C., and is contained in the dedication of an altar to the pagan goddesses Nauran and Ishtar. From this evidence some historians have concluded that the Ethiopian culture was entirely of Semitic origin, but this, as Basil Davidson argues, is not the case, for: "The Habashan, as Egyptian inscriptions of a much earlier date have shown, were already in the land. Not Semites themselves, these early Abyssinians survived Semitic invasion, took much from it, and gradually built their own strange and strangely distinguished civilization of Axum. Here was one more example of an invaded people surviving the invaders, absorbing their culture, and producing another culture of their own." (*The Lost Cities of Africa*, p. 218, by Basil Davidson.)

There is an old legend declaring that, in the tenth century B.C., an Ethiopian king on his deathbed appointed his daughter Makeda to succeed him on the throne; and that the aforesaid daughter became the monarch of the Ethiopian dominions under the title of the Queen of Sheba. The source of this folklore may be traced back to Ethiopic manuscripts of the fourteenth century of the Christian Era. They were acquired by the British Museum, and an English translation of this work, *The Kebra Nagast (Glories of the Kings of Ethiopia)*, was made by Sir E. A. Wallis Budge and was published in London in 1923. According to this account, when King Solomon was building his Temple, he contacted merchants in foreign lands to come to Jerusalem to bring him certain materials which were needed for that project. Among these traders was an Ethiopian merchant named Tamrin, from whom Solomon purchased gold, marble, and exotic woods. When the Ethiopian merchant returned home, Solomon sent with him valuable presents for the Queen of Sheba. In giving his impression of King Solomon, Tamrin, in an audience with the queen, asserted: "When he speaks, Your Majesty, it is with gentleness and humility. He pardons those who commit wrong; the wisdom and fear of God govern his house and his kingdom; proverbs are in his mouth; his voice is as delicious as honey; his beauty excelleth that of other men; and everything about him is surprising."

The Queen of Sheba was so impressed by the report of the merchant that she organized a large caravan, visited the court of King Solomon, and gave him many presents of great value. A romance developed between the royal pair, which eventuated in the birth of a son to the queen, which was named Menelik.

Solomon recognized Menelik as his first-born son [we learn from a contemporary student], and decreeing that only Menelik's male heirs were to rule Ethiopia, he sent back with him as his servants all the first-born sons of his own officers and counselors. Today, Emperor Haile Selassie claims direct lineage from Menelik, and one of his principal titles is "Conquering Lion of the Tribe of Judah." The black Jews of Ethiopia, the Falashas, who practice an archaic type of Judaism, claim descent from the first-born sons, as do several noble Ethiopian families. The Imperial Coat of Arms of Christian Ethiopia consists of a combination of the Christian Cross and the Jewish Star of David [*The Splendour of Africa*, pp. 14–15, by Don Carl Steffen].

Among the outstanding features of the material culture of Ethiopia were: (1) hillside terracing, (2) the practice of building forts on the summits of high hills, and (3) the presence of monuments displaying phallic symbols. All these traits have been attributed to non-African sources; but their widespread prevalence in the African continent makes such an assumption unnecessary. The ancient Ethiopian culture radiated out from Africa, and not vice versa. The Christian Bible is often cited on questions of history, sometimes ambiguously; but on the question of the African genesis of the primitive Ethiopians, the Good Book is quite clear; for we read that: "Kush begat Nimrod: he began to be a mighty one in the earth. . . . And the beginning of his kingdom was Babel, and Erech, and Akkad, and Kalneh, in the land of Shinar." (Genesis X, 8–10.) Baron Bunsen, a noted German scholar in 1854, in the third volume of his *Philosophy of Universal History*, declared that Nimrod, the legendary father of the Babylonians, was in no way related to Kush (Ethiopia). It is true that they had come into Babylonia from Africa; and so, having come from the land of Kush, were called Kushites; but the expression was purely geographical; for from a racial standpoint they had no kinship with either the Egyptians or the Ethiopians. This conclusion was contested by General Sir Henry Rawlinson, on archaeological and philological grounds. His findings are well presented by his celebrated brother, Canon George Rawlinson of Canterbury, as follows:

A laborious study of the primitive language of Chaldea led him [Sir Henry Rawlinson] to the conviction that the dominant race in Babylonia at the earliest time to which the monuments reached back was Kushite. He found the vocabulary of the primitive race to be decidedly Kushite or Ethiopian, and he was able to interpret the inscriptions chiefly by the aid which was furnished to him from published works on the Galla (Abyssinian) and the Mahra (South Arabian) dialects. He noted, moreover, a considerable resemblance in the system of writing which the primitive race employed, and that which was established from a very remote date in Egypt. Both were pictorial; both to a certain extent symbolic; both in some instances used identically the same symbols. Again, he found words in use among the primitive Babylonians and their neighbors and kinsmen, the Susianians, which seemed to be identical with ancient Egyptian or Ethiopic roots. The root *hyk* or *hak*, which Manetho interprets as *king* and which is found in the well-known *Hyksos* or *Shepherd Kings*, appeared in Babylonian and Susianian royal names under the form of *Khak*, and as the *terminal* element—which is its position also in royal Ethiopic names. The name *Tirkak* is common to the royal lists of Susiana and Ethiopia, as that of Nimrod is to the royal lists of Babylon and Egypt. The sun-god is called *Ra* in Egyptian and *Ra* was the Kushite name of the supreme god of the Babylonians. . . . The author of Genesis unites together as members of the same ethnic family the Egyptians, the Ethiopians, the Southern Arabians, and the primitive inhabitants of Babylon. Modern ethnology finds, in the localities indicated, a number of languages, partly ancient, partly modern, which have common characteristics, and which evidently constitute one group. Egyptian, ancient and modern, Ethiopic, as represented by the Galla, Agau, etc., southern Arabian (Himyaric and Mahra), and ancient Babylonian, are discovered to be cognate tongues, varieties of one original form of speech [*The Origin of Nations*, pp. 212–14, by George Rawlinson].

In the middle of the sixth century, a few years before the birth of Mohammed, a religious conflict broke out in Yemen. It was a war between Christians and Jews. The Yemenite ruler, King Dhu Nowas, professed the Jewish faith. The Jewish power was dominant, and the king had ordered the burning of the Christian Church at Zhafar, and the desecration of the bones of St. Paul of Zhafar, the patron saint of the Christians of Yemen. The Christians met a crushing defeat when twenty thousand of them were trapped in a cave, which was transformed into a furnace, and the multitude of Christians perished in the flames. The surviving Christians of Yemen appealed to the Byzantine Emperor Justinian for assistance;

and this monarch through the patriarch of Alexandria enlisted the aid of the Abyssinian Negus. A fleet of one hundred and fifty ships sailed from Adulis in Annesley Bay, manned by an army of seventy thousand men, under the leadership of General Abraha Al-Arsham. The Ethiopian forces were victorious and Yemen was conquered. An Arab prince visited the king of Persia and sought his aid against the African invaders. The Persian monarch emptied all the jails of his kingdom and enlisted the able-bodied convicts into an army which was turned over to the prince for service in Arabia. This army drove out the Abyssinians, but they later returned and recaptured Yemen. Then the Persian ruler, King Chosroes, mobilized his regular army against the invaders, ordering his soldiers to slay all men with black skins and curly hair. The Africans were driven out again and Yemen became a province of the Persian kingdom.

The Ethiopians of Abyssinia held their own until the rise of Islam cut them off from the outside world; then their culture suffered a disastrous decline. In the words of the historian Edward Gibbon: "Encompassed on all sides by the enemies of their religion, the Ethiopians slept near a thousand years, forgetful of the world, by whom they were forgotten." (*The Decline and Fall of the Roman Empire*, Vol. II, p. 517, by Edward Gibbon.)

In the year 912 A.C., mariners of Oman, in the south of Arabia, sailed southward in the Indian Ocean to trade with the Zanj of the East African coast. A passenger in one of their boats was Al Masudi of Baghdad, one of the great historians of his age. Over four hundred years later Ibn Khaldun referred to him as "the model of all historians and the authority upon which they rely for the critical estimate of many facts which form the subject of their labors." These Zanj, as the Arabs called the dwellers of the East African shore, were the "black people" who lived beyond Ethiopia. Though the word "Zanj" is attributed to the Arabs, it may have been Persian in origin; for it was first used in a Persian inscription of 293 B.C. which tells of certain dealings between King Narseh of Persia and an African "King of the Zhand." The name still lives today in Zanzibar (Coast of the Zanj), and in the use of the word "Zanj" to describe Africans of dusky hue among Arabic-speaking peoples. The various tribes of these East African black men, we learn from Al Masudi, dwelled in a country about 2,500 miles in length along the Indian Ocean; stretching from the Horn of Africa to Mozambique. The territory is described as divided by valleys, mountains, and deserts, and as having a large population of wild elephants. The ships of the Arab traders went as far south as Sofala, which Masudi describes as "the most distant frontier of the territory that is reached by the ships of Oman and Siraf."

The Arab merchants, as far as we know, never went further south than Sofala (which was located in Mozambique near the modern town of Biera); but they had trade connections with peoples beyond Sofala, from whom they bought gold and ivory; and this territory was called the land of the Waq Waq. It has been suggested that the land of Waq Waq may have been Natal and its inhabitants were probably Bushmen; or again this Waq Waq land may have been the island of Madagascar.

Al Masudi refers to a kingdom in the land of Sofala known as Waqlimi, and although the exact location is not given he seems to be speaking of the territory now known as Rhodesia.

These Zanj of the Waqlimi [asserts Basil Davidson, in commenting on Masudi's account] are those who built their capital in the far south in the land of Sofala, "which produces gold in abundance and other marvels." He does not say exactly where, though it was evidently not in the same place as the Arab trading station of Sofala itself; but Ibn Said, writing on hearsay two hundred years later, puts this capital at Sinna. This was certainly the Sena of later Portuguese discovery, lying about one hundred fifty miles up the Zambesi River from the sea. Edrisi, at about the same time, has Sinna as a town "on the borders of the land of Sofala," and we may reasonably take it that the capital of these southern Zanj, in Masudi's time, was on the lower reaches of the Zambesi [*The Lost Cities of Africa*, p.154, by Basil Davidson].

This capital city was already ancient in the time of Masudi, and we learn from him that, after establishing the city, the people "elected a king whom they called Waqlimi"; and we are also told that this name "was that of their kings from time immemorial." The Zanj are described as being of a jet black complexion. They were skilled workers in metal, especially gold and iron, and they rated iron above gold in value. They employed oxen as beasts of burden, since in their country there were no horses, mules, or camels. The staple foods of their diet were sorghum, and a plant known as *kalari*, which was extracted from the earth like a truffle. They also ate bananas, honey, and meat, and owned many islands devoted to the cultivation of the coconut. "All this suggests a long-settled people or group of peoples," a modern student comments, "who lived by mixed agriculture, cultivating grain and grazing cattle, and by trade; and who understood the smelting and manufacture of metals. It is indeed a clear and convincing account of the early Iron Age culture of east and southeast Africa which archaeology would begin to uncover a thousand years later." (Basil Davidson, in *The Lost Cities of Africa*, pp. 155–56.)

A good example of cultural continuity in Africa may be shown by comparing Masudi's narrative of the customs of the Zanj of southeast Africa in his day with those of the contemporary Shilluk of the southern part of the Sudan. According to Al Masudi, the Zanj had no established religion of the dogmatic type, for: "Everyone worships what he pleases, a plant, an animal, a metal." Their religion was a type of nature-worship, with which was connected the institution of Divine Kingship. For Waqlimi, which was the kingly title, "means Son of the Great God: they call him thus because they have chosen their king to govern them with equity. As soon as he exercises a tyrannical power and departs from the rules of justice, they kill him and exclude his posterity from royal succession, because they say that in acting thus he has ceased to be the son of the great god—that is, the king of heaven and earth."

Now let us move forward one thousand years in time and consider the Shilluk, a black people who live in villages on the west bank of the White Nile, and who even today are called Zanj by the Arabic-speaking dwellers in the Sudan. These people specialize in the rearing of cattle, but they also cultivate grain on a small scale, and maintain a group of blacksmiths. Their kingship is elective, and the monarch is endowed with divine attributes. Professor Evans-Pritchard, who has an expert knowledge of Shilluk mores, tells us that all Shilluk kings "are believed to be descended from Nyikang, the leader of the Shilluk in their heroic age, who led them to their present homeland, conquering it from its inhabitants and dividing it among the lineages of his followers; and Nyikang, or, as we should say, the spirit of Nyikang is believed to be in every king or to have passed from king to king down the line of his successors. Nyikang is thus a mythological personification of the divine kingship which itself symbolizes the national structure. . . . We can only understand the place of the kingship in Shilluk society when we realize that it is not the individual at any time reigning who is king, but Nyikang who is the medium between man and God, and is believed in some way to participate in God as he does in the king."

As the Zanj of southeast Africa in the tenth century in certain circumstances killed their kings, so do the modern Shilluk. "Our authorities," states Evans-Pritchard, "say that the Shilluk believe that should the king become physically weak the whole people might suffer, and further, that if a king becomes sick or senile he should be killed to avoid some grave national misfortune, such as defeat in war, epidemic or famine. The king must be killed to save the kingship and with it the whole Shilluk people."

Another parallel between the tenth-century southern Zanj and the twentieth-century Shilluk of the Upper Nile is that in both cases the kingly office was elective, since the prerogatives of the kingship were the possessions of the whole people and were in nowise restricted to a royal clan.

The close parallels noted above do not prove any direct contact between two different peoples separated by a millennium of time. But they do suggest a common source in times more remote; for this divine kingship was a part of the Archaic Civilization which was discussed in Chapter II. The ancient Kushites of the Nile Valley had a custom of slaying their divine kings on occasion; but this practice was abolished by one wily monarch who objected to being killed. This king, Arnq-Amen, or Ergamenes, of Ethiopia, had attended the University of Alexandria, in Egypt, where he improved his mind by the study of Greek philosophy. After ascending the throne he was one day ordered by the priests of Amen to submit to being sacrificed for the good of the nation. This king had no intention of committing suicide, and, summoning the priests to his Golden Chapel, he laughed satirically as he marched in at the head of his guards and put all the priests to the sword.

Al Masudi was a voluminous writer. Unfortunately most of his works have perished, but one important production of his pen has survived. This is his *Meadows of Gold and Mines of Gems*. A complete French translation in nine volumes was published in Paris in 1864. There is an abridged English translation by Aloys Sprenger, published in London in 1841. Masudi has an interesting description of how the Arabs of

Oman acted as middlemen in the ivory trade that flourished in the tenth century between East Africa and India and China. He states that the tusks of ivory from the country of the Zanj "go generally to Oman, and from there are sent on to China and India. . . . In China the kings and their military and civilian officers use carrying-chairs of ivory; no official or person of rank would dare to visit the king in an iron chair, and ivory alone is used for this purpose. . . . Ivory is much prized in India: there it is made into handles for the daggers known as *harari*, or *harri* in the singular, as well as for the hilts of curved swords. . . . But the biggest use of ivory is in the manufacture of chessmen and other gaming pieces." (Cited by Basil Davidson in *The African Past: Chronicles from Antiquity to Modern Times*, p. 109.)

Besides the Zanj of Africa, Masudi writes of another Zanj Empire in Asia, centered in Indo-China and spreading out into Indonesia and Malaysia. "India is a vast country," says Masudi, "having many seas and mountains and borders upon the Empire of ex-zanij, which is the kingdom of the Maharaj, the king of the islands, whose dominions form the frontier between India and China, and are considered as part of India." He refers to the "splendor and high civilization" of the Asiatic Zanj, and observes that, "the Maharaj is lord of the sixth sea," and "king of the islands from which drugs and spices are exported"; and that "the population and the number of the troops of his kingdom cannot be counted; and the islands under his sceptre are so numerous that the fastest sailing vessel is not able to go round them in two years." (*Meadows of Gold and Mines of Gems*, Sprenger's translation; cited by John D. Baldwin in *Pre-Historic Nations*, p. 263.) Baldwin adds the following comment on the above quotations from Masudi: "The people of this great island empire, he tells us, were black."

These Asiatic black men were in fact the Khmers, who were the dominant people in southeastern Asia for six hundred years. The center of this culture was in Cambodia, and it flourished from about 800 A.C. to 1432; although the history of these Khmers may be traced back to an earlier period.

> The Khmers began to develop their civilization about 2,000 years ago [we learn from a modern investigator] under the influence of traders from India and later from China. A Chinese traveller of the third century A.D. reported, "The men are all ugly and black. Their hair is curly. They go naked and barefoot." A later account of the Khmer region, which the Chinese called Funan, said, . . . "The people of Funan make rings and bracelets of gold and vessels of silver." In the middle of the sixth century, Funan merged with another Khmer kingdom inland known as Chenla to form a larger nation that called itself Kambujadesa—in its westernized form, Cambodia [*Lost Cities and Vanished Civilizations*, p. 137, by Robert Silverberg].

There was a brisk trade between the peoples of East Africa and India during the twelfth century, especially in iron. The iron was mined in Africa and exported to India and Indonesia. This intelligence has been bequeathed to us by Abu Adullah Mohammed el Idrisi (born 1100, died 1166), a Moorish historian who dwelled at Palermo as a member of the court of King Roger II of Sicily. He wrote a book with the title *Kitab Rujar* (*Book of Roger*), and it contains much valuable information on the countries bordering on the Indian Ocean. Special mention is made of the export of iron from southeast Africa to the Zabaj Islands (Java and Divah). In the words of Idrisi:

> The inhabitants of the Zabaj Islands and other residents of the surrounding islands go there (the land of Sofala) and, exporting it [the iron] from there, supply it to all the lands of India and to its various islands. They sell it at a good price, because in India most of the trade and exchange is in iron. Nevertheless, although iron is found in the islands of India, and

there are also mines of it there, in the land of Sofala it is found in the largest quantities, most superior in quality and most malleable.

But the Indians are very good at making various compounds of mixtures of substances with the help of which they melt the malleable iron; it then turns into Indian iron, and is called after India. There [in India], there are workshops where swords are manufactured, and their craftsmen make excellent ones surpassing those made by other peoples. . . . No iron is comparable to the Indian one in sharpness. This is a well known fact, and no one can deny its superiority [Idrisi's *India and the Neighboring Territories*, translated from the Arabic by Dr. Maqbul Ahmad; cited by Basil Davidson in *The African Past*, pp. 111–12].

The "Indian iron" referred to by Idrisi was the famous wootz steel, produced in India from iron imported from southeast Africa. The celebrated Damascus blades of the Middle Ages were made from this steel.

When the first explorers from Portugal sailed up the east coast of Africa on the way to India they were dazzled by a series of seaport cities, such as Malindi, Mombasa, Sofala, Kilwa, and Zanzibar. Kilwa seems to have been the greatest of these trading cities. In the year 1331, the famous Moorish traveler Ibn Batuta traveled down the East African coast. Of all the towns and cities of that region that he visited, he was most favorably impressed by Kilwa. His impressions are so interesting that we transcribe them in his own words:

Then I set off by sea from the town of Mogadishu for the land of the Swahili and the town of Kilwa, which is in the land of Zanj. We arrived at Mombasa, a large island two days' journey from the land of the Swahili. The Island is quite separate from the mainland. It grows bananas, lemons and oranges. . . . The people do not engage in agriculture, but import grain from the Swahili. The greater part of their diet is bananas and fish. . . .

We spent a night on the island [of Mombasa] and then set sail for Kilwa, the principal town on the coast, the greater part of whose inhabitants are Zanj of very black complexion. . . .

Kilwa is one of the most beautiful and well-constructed towns in the world. The whole of it is elegantly built [*East African Coast, Select Documents*, p. 31; translated from the Arabic text by G. S. P. Freeman-Grenville].

The fair city of Kilwa flourished for another two centuries and then was destroyed by invaders from Europe; and of this we will have more to say in a later chapter. As that very able Africanist, Basil Davidson, notes:

Today only a shabby village stands there. Yet beyond the village can still be found the walls and towers of ruined palaces and large houses and mosques, which is what the Moslems call their churches. A great palace has been dug out of the bushes that covered it for hundreds of years. It is a strange and beautiful ruin on a cliff over the Indian Ocean. Many other ruins stand nearby. But the strangest thing about Kilwa and the towns nearby is that there is little to be found about them in the newer history books. Even when the cities are described, they are said to be not African, but the work of people from Arabia and Persia. History books saying this are out of date, and they are wrong. People who have studied these cities on the East Coast say that the cities were an important part of Africa's life between the years 1000 and 1700. And these cities were African, or to be more exact, Swahili. This is the name of the people of the coast of Kenya and Tanganyika and the Island of Zanzibar [*A Guide to African History*, pp. 30–32, by Basil Davidson].

These great cities evolved from trading villages established over two thousand years ago. This we know from *The Periplus*, an Egypto-Greek guidebook on the maritime trade along the Indian Ocean shores at the beginning of the Christian Era. Merchants, mainly from southern Arabia, settled on the

East African coast and intermarried with African coast people. These trading posts in time became great mercantile cities, trading with such distant lands as India and China. To refer to this culture as "Arab" is a misnomer; the few original Arabs were soon absorbed into the African population.

> Just as the Hausas invaded the west coast of Africa and caused their language to be almost a lingua franca in that part of the continent [we learn from Mr. Wells], so did the Arabs invade the east coast and produce a hybrid race with the Africans. These people are known as the Swahilis or "coast people," and their language has become a lingua franca not only on the east coast but as far inland as Uganda. There are very few pure Arabs in East Africa, and the name Arab denotes caste rather than race. The Swahili is a black man, and his language is as useful in East Africa as the Malay language is in Malaysia [*Introducing Africa*, p. 13, by Carveth Wells].

In the tenth century, gold from the mines of southern Rhodesia and Mozambique was transported to the cities on the coast and from them exported to the lands of the Far East. Over a period of centuries the merchants of Kilwa gained control of the gold trade and, acting as brokers in the foreign export-import transactions, they became extremely wealthy; and Kilwa developed into a very fine city. There were many other trading cities which became powerful city-states and even reached imperial status. About the year 1400, one African city sent a giraffe to the emperor of China; and the Chinese ruler was so pleased with the gift that a few years later he sent back costly presents to his African friends, transported by a fleet of many ships manned by thousands of sailors.

Most of these great trading cities of the East African coast were later destroyed by Portuguese vandals in the early sixteenth century. Among those that survived is Zanzibar.

After the ending of the Civil War in the United States, a lame duck carpetbagger was dispatched as consul to a small republic in South America. At the termination of this appointment he was named consul to Zanzibar. The politician gave a party before leaving Washington for his new assignment. He told his friends that the Sultan of Zanzibar maintained a harem of very attractive young ladies, and that his journey to that exotic land was certain to be rewarding. About six months later the consul was back in Washington, looking very much depressed; and, when his friends asked about how things were in Zanzibar, he answered: "Zanzibar! Zanzibar! Where in Hell is Zanzibar? I've been cruising all over creation looking for the place, but I'll be darned if I ever found Zanzibar!" Zanzibar, an island famous for its spices is about 400 miles south of the equator, and about 20 miles off the coast of Tanzania. The great export specialty of Zanzibar is cloves. In 1940, from 14 million clove trees, a crop of 15,000 tons of cloves resulted. About 80 percent of the cloves of the world come from Zanzibar. But anyone planning to visit Zanzibar needs a rugged constitution. This we gather from the statement of an old resident of the city, who tells us: "There are worse places than Zanzibar, but not much worse. The place is so windy that passengers on landing are blown up the beach right into the Africa Hotel, which serves whiskey with lizards in it. You'll be sorry if you visit Zanzibar, but you will be equally sorry if you do not. The Island has a railroad that goes to a place called Boobooboo. It is of very narrow gauge, and has eight engines; one for every mile." (Cited by Carveth Wells in *Introducing Africa*, p. 158.)

NOTE: We have no present plans for visiting Zanzibar, but if business or pleasure ever brings us to the place, we plan to board the train for Triple-Boo; it should be worth visiting.

Chapter Eight

ZIMBABWE, MONOMOTAPA, AND OTHER KINGDOMS OF THE INTERIOR

In 1871, Karl Mauch, a German explorer, came across the ruins of Zimbabwe, located on the high plateau of Mashonaland. Among the ruins were blocks of granite so accurately carved that they were fitted together without the use of cement. Some of the walls are thirty-five feet high and sixteen feet in thickness at the base. Among the most imposing structures in the ruins are two buildings, one called the "acropolis," and another, the "temple." Excavations showed that some of the extensive ruins apparently dated back to prehistoric times, while others were comparatively recent. The conclusion was drawn by the pioneer European explorers that this lost city was of non-African origin. Mauch was joined by Hall and Bent, both English archaeologists, in identifying Zimbabwe with the Biblical Ophir, from whence King Solomon and his friend King Hiram of Tyre, in the middle of the tenth century B.C., imported gold, gem-stones, ivory, and valuable works of art.

Other scholars joined the guessing game and traced the founding of Great Zimbabwe to the Egyptians, Cretans, Phoenicians, Etruscans, Sabeans, Persians, Sumerians, and Indians of Asia. Later speculations came nearer the mark. For instance, the anthropologist, Paul Schebesta, thought that Zimbabwe was a colony established by ancient Kushites of the Upper Nile country. Another investigator, Hugo Bernatzik, regarded it as a prehistoric culture having its genesis in one of the coastal regions of the Indian Ocean. Still later, Drs. David Randall-MacIver and Gertrude Caton-Thompson dated the ruins back only to the medieval period (the ninth century C.E.), and regarded them as the outcome of an indigenous African culture.

The German writer on popular science and history, Herbert Wendt, thinks that the original Zimbabwe civilization was created by the ancient Egyptians, and that it was annexed in medieval times by the Bantu-speaking Shona people. "In the early Middle Ages," asserts Wendt, "this civilization was taken over by black conquerors; they were Bantu of the Shona tribe. These Shona, after whom Mashonaland is called, constructed on the ruins of the ancient Rhodesian gold state the greatest Negro empire of all times, an empire covering two hundred and fifty thousand square miles and with a central population of three millions." (*It Began in Babel*, p. 214.) In another passage in the same book, Mr. Wendt shows a parallel between the customs of the ancient Egyptians and the Medieval Shona, as follows:

> The Shona encountered obviously an ancient civilization in Zimbabwe, which they developed to fit their own requirements. The dynasty of the "Rulers of the Mines" was a Negro one, but its culture, customs and civilization clearly show foreign influences—particularly Egyptian. Worship of the sun and moon, marriage between royal brothers and sisters, the princesses' complete freedom in love, the sacrifice of first fruits—these are only a few parallels between Egypt and the Shona kingdom. . . . The connections between the Nile and the Zambesi are so striking, between the land of Punt and the mining area of the later Zimbabwe are so numerous, that it is difficult to discount the former existence of Egyptian contacts with South Africa [*It Began in Babel*, pp. 76–77, by Herbert Wendt].

The ruins of Zimbabwe are in a region of gold-fields extending 600 by 700 miles. The first Europeans to visit this area found remains of old mines extending to a depth of 150 feet. The ancient miners worked in rocks and extracted millions of tons of ore. This accounts for the numerous theories of non-African aliens as the operators of these gold mines; for it was difficult for Europeans to imagine native Africans engaged in such activities in the distant past. But when Dr. Gertrude Caton-Thompson explored the area she concluded: "Instead of a degenerate offshoot of a higher Oriental civilization, you have, I believe, a vigorous native civilization unsuspected by all but a few students, showing a national organization of a kind, of originality and amazing industry." (Cited by Ian D. Colvin in *Zimbabwe's Ruins of Mystery*, in *Wonders of the Past*, Vol. II, p. 970, edited by Sir J. A. Hammerton.)

Mr. Colvin agrees with Dr. Caton-Thompson that some of the ruins date back only to the Middle Ages, but he argues that other relics are far more ancient. His position is that:

> It may be taken as established that the buildings were already there and already old—when the Portuguese first went to East Africa. It may also be taken for certain that the fragments of Chinese and Saracenic pottery were found, as asserted, under the floor of Zimbabwe, which dates that particular building as medieval. But that does not end the controversy, any more than the date of the building of St. Paul's fixes the period of London. The stone and flint implements found in the debris, and the enormous extent of the gold mines, which must have been worked by the slow process of hand labor, alike suggest an occupation not of centuries merely but of thousands of years [*Ibid.*, pp. 975–76].

The first Bantu people settled in Southern Rhodesia between 1000 and 1200, C.E. They had come from overcrowded lands further north; and it was these people who built the first stone walls at Great Zimbabwe. Another group of Bantus, the Rozwi, about the year 1440, gained control of the goldmining territories of Southern Rhodesia and also the routes utilized by the gold traders for exporting this metal through the Indian Ocean seaports. After subduing the original Shona rulers, the Rozwi king and his son who succeeded him on the throne established the empire of Monomotapa. The ruler of this empire was likewise called the Monomotapa, which means "Lord of the Mines." In 1499, when the Portuguese rounded the Cape of Good Hope for the first time, the Emperor of Monomotapa ruled over an extensive territory and traded gold for manufactured goods with the ships of all the nations engaged in the Indian Ocean commerce. We learn from the Portuguese historian João de Santos: "The Portuguese had to approach the king, not crawling flat on the ground like the Kaffirs, but barefooted all the same. When they reached him, they lay down on the ground, reclining on their sides, and spoke to him without looking at his face. After every few words they reverently clapped their hands."

The people of Monomotapa had a matriarchal social system similar to that of ancient Egypt, since the emperor or king always married one of his sisters. The most influential member of the royal court was the mother of the monarch, who was called upon to make the decision in case of a dispute as to the succession to the throne. Among the other features of this ancient land were two-story houses, a feudal landed aristocracy, and a standing army. The Portuguese were properly impressed by all this; but one thing that made them marvel the most was the palace of the emperor of Monomotapa. João de Barros, Portuguese annalist, writing in the middle of the sixteenth century, gives the following description:

The inside consists of a great variety of sumptuous apartments, tapestry, the manufacture of the country. The floors, ceiling, beams and rafters are all either gilt or plated with gold and curiously wrought, as are all the chairs of State, tables, benches, etc. The candlesticks and branches are made of ivory inlaid with gold, and hang from the ceiling by chains of the same metal or silver gilt. The plates, dishes and bowls belonging to the Emperor's table are made of a sort of porcelain, curiously wrought on the edges with sprigs of gold resembling those of coral. In short, so rich and magnificent is this palace, that it may be said to vie with that which distinguishes a monarch of the East [cited by J. C. deGraft-Johnson in his *African Glory*, p. 146].

Around 1485, a civil war broke out between the Monomotapan ruler and one of his most powerful chiefs, named Changa. Chief Changa won the war, and it was his dynasty that dominated the empire with its capital at Zimbabwe for about three centuries. This Changamir Empire ruled over the southernmost part of Southern Rhodesia and Mozambique; while in the northernmost part of the same territory the monarchs of Monomotapa still remained in power. Early in the seventeenth century, the ruler of Monomotapa, being unable to control some of his powerful chiefs, called in Portuguese mercenaries armed with muskets to give him assistance. This was a fatal blunder; for the Portuguese turned their guns against him in the year 1628. Two Monomotapan armies were defeated and the Monomotapans, after that, were merely puppets of the Portuguese usurpers.

The Changamir Empire had better luck; for they managed to elude the clutches of European invaders. The Changamir chiefs lived in stone houses which dotted the countryside, and their people practiced animal husbandry, and mined various metals which they traded to the cities of the coast for commodities which they found needful. This life of ease and tranquillity lasted until about 1800. Then African invaders came in from South Africa and, crossing the Limpopo River, invaded the cities of the Changamirs, looting them and destroying the stone palaces. These African conquerors ruled for less than a century; for they were then displaced by armies of invaders from Europe.

Uganda, in the Great Lakes region of Central Africa, was invaded from the north by the Bachwezi. These people, between the thirteenth and fifteenth centuries, established the Kitwara Empire. The Bachwezi were very tall in stature and possessed great skill in trading and hunting. Throughout the fifteenth and sixteenth centuries new invaders entered Uganda and drove the Bachwezi southward into the territories of Karagwe, Ruanda, Urundi, and Ankole. The newcomers established the new kingdoms of Bunyoro, Busoga, Buganda, and Toro. In the beginning, the kingdom of Bunyoro was dominant, but the Buganda monarchy forged to the forefront of political power in the eighteenth century. By the middle of the nineteenth century, Buganda was the greatest state and the most advanced society of Central Africa. The ruler of Buganda was called the Kabaka, who was assisted in his governmental duties by a council of feudal chiefs. The feudal government of Uganda was a special kind; for the wealth of the country was its cattle. Here wealth and economic power were measured not by land or money, but by the amount of cattle which an individual owned. In Uganda the biggest man was the one who owned the largest number of cattle.

In ancient and medieval times there were several large states in the Congo region. Of the early days of these kingdoms there are no surviving records, but when the first Portuguese explorers visited Africa they found an imposing Bantu state, the kingdom of Kongo, in a flourishing condition. A contemporary student of African affairs gives us a description of this medieval Bantu kingdom, as follows:

> This covered a large area of the coast across the mouth of the Congo River (which was known by the Africans as the Zaire until it was renamed after the kingdom of the Kongo) and stretched far inland. The royal capital city of Kongo lay over 150 miles inland. Whenever the king reviewed his army, he rode, according to one report, upon an elephant surrounded by slaves and nobles, and followed by a man whose special task was to talk loudly and continuously about the king's courage

and bravery. How, or when, this kingdom of Kongo began we do not know, but it greatly impressed the Portuguese [*Africa South of the Sahara*, p. 13, by G. W. Kingsnorth].

Duarte Lopez, a native of Benevento, in April of 1578, set sail for Loanda, a port city of the kingdom of Kongo. Lopez spent twelve years in this country and, though he wrote no account of his adventures himself, his story was recorded by Fillipo Pigafetta, an official of the Vatican, and published in Rome in 1591. An English translation by Abraham Hartwell was published in 1597. A more recent English translation appeared in 1881, and was the work of Thomas Fowell Buxton. The title of this book is: *History of the Kingdom of Congo*. In this book we find that, when Lopez was in the kingdom of the Kongo, that nation had a circumference of 1,685 miles. The ruler was called Dom Alvarez, king of Kongo, and of Abundo, and of Matama, and of Quizama, and of Angola, and of Angri, and of Cacongo, and of the seven kingdoms Congere Amoloza, and of the Panelungos, and the Lord of the river Zaire (Congo), and of the Anzigiros, and of Anziquara, and of Loango, etc. The monarch had lost control of some of his minor kingdoms, but he clung to all his regal titles, though some of them related to vanished glories.

During the time when Duarte Lopez was in Kongo, that kingdom was composed of six provinces, namely: Bamba, Batta, Pango, Pemba, Sogno, and Sundi. The governors of the provinces were called "Mani," a title which meant "Lord." The Bamba province was the largest and wealthiest and was under the governorship of Dom Sebastian Manibamba. The governor of the island of Loanda was called, for instance, Mani Loanda. We learn from Lopez, as recorded by Pigafetta, that Bamba was the stronghold of the armed forces of Kongo. The sovereign could recruit four hundred thousand welltrained soldiers and put them into the field of military service.

The capital of the kingdom of Kongo was in the province of Pemba, which was under the jurisdiction of the Mani Pemba, but the capital, San Salvador, with all surrounding territory within a radius of twenty miles, was regarded by the king as his private estate.

A missionary from Portugual converted the Mani Sogno to the Christian faith in 1491. Soon afterward King Emmanual of Kongo was converted and took the name of Dom João, and his sons were educated in Portugal. We learn from an African anthropologist, Dr. R. E. G. Armattoe, that:

> Early in the sixteenth century it became a Christian land, whose wealth and pomp dazzled all Christendom. Its emperors and courtiers vied in their splendor with the grandees of Spain and Portugal, and its native prelates were ordained by Rome. Never again will an African kingdom exhibit so much refinement and so much grace. We have it on the authority of the ancient chroniclers that in their deportment and attire, in their manners and in their conversation, they had nothing to learn from the illuminati of Europe [*The Golden Age of Western African Civilization*, p. 30, by R. E. G. Armattoe].

King Dom João ceded to the Portuguese a private estate within the twenty-mile limit of his own enclave around San Salvador. The Europeans were permitted to erect a wall around their settlement. The royal palace was surrounded by a wall, as were the homes of other members of the royal family. The Portuguese settlement covered an area of almost one square mile, and the residences of royalty covered about the same amount of territory. The country possessed a good supply of various grains, but occasionally grain was imported by the overland route from Egypt. There was an abundance of agricultural products in Kongo, such as rice, citrus fruits, bananas, coconuts, cola, watermelons, cucumbers, pineapples, and palms of different varieties, including the date palm. From one variety of palm tree, there were extracted wine, vinegar, oil, fruit, and bread. The cola nut was chewed by the natives; and it was said to quench the thirst, to strengthen the stomach, and to exercise a therapeutic effect on a pathologic liver.

From the observations of Lopez, Ogilby, and others, the dwellers of the eastern part of the kingdom of Kongo and regions adjacent are known to have been very skilled makers of cloth. They specialized in velvet, both cut and uncut, and in the making of satins, taffeta, damasks, sarcenets, etc. The yarn for these cloths was made from a certain species of palm, from which by a special process they drew fine threads. They were expert weavers, and turned out attractive damasks decorated with leaves and figures. Their brocades were considered finer than those of the contemporary Italians, and were generally reserved for the king and other members of the royal family.

In 1642 a group of Dutch ambassadors visited Dom Alvarez II, king of Kongo. The monarch received the foreign emissaries at night. The ambassadors from Holland walked through a long gallery lined on both sides by men holding large wax candles. Their audience with the sovereign was described by a contemporary, whom we quote:

His Majesty sat in a small chapel, hung with rush mats, from the top of which hung a branch with wax candles. He was dressed in cloth of gold coat and drawers and had about his neck three gold chains. His right thumb was adorned with a very large granite or ruby ring, and his left hand with two great emeralds. On the left sleeve of his coat a gold cross was fastened, richly enclosed in a piece of well-polished crystal. He wore on his head a fine white cap, and on his legs a pair of russet boots. At his right side stood an officer, who sometimes gently fanned the air with an handkerchief; and at his left side another holding a Tin Bow, and a Tin Sceptre, covered with fine striped cloth. His seat was a red velvet Spanish Chair over which, upon a border, was embroidered in letters, Dom

Alvarez Rex Kongo. Right before him lay spread a great Turkey carpet, and over his head hung a canopy of white satin, wrought with gold, and trimmed with a deep fringe. Lastly, a little on his right hand kneeled Dom Bernado de Menzos, his Interpreter and Secretary [Astley's *Voyages and Travels*, p. 257; cited by J. C. deGraft-Johnson in *African Glory*, p. 140].

The picture we get today of Africa in past ages from the history taught in our schools is that Africans were savages and that, although Europeans invaded their lands and made slaves of them, they were in a way conferring a great favor on them; since they brought to them the blessings of Christian civilization. How false this picture is we shall see in the next chapter, which deals with the destruction of African culture. One of the few modern scientists who tried to tell the truth about the African past was the German anthropologist, Professor Leo Frobenius. Unfortunately his works, for the most part, have not been translated into English. A short passage from *Histoire de la Civilisation Africaine* gives an example of what Frobenius was trying to convey to the misinformed of modern Europe and America:

What was revealed by the navigators of the fifteenth to the seventeenth centuries furnishes an absolute proof that Negro Africa, which extended south of the desert zone of the Sahara, was in full efflorescence, in all the splendor of harmonious and well-formed civilizations, an efflorescence which the European conquistadors annihilated as far as they progressed. For the new country of America needed slaves, and Africa had them to offer, hundreds, thousands, whole cargoes of slaves. However, the slave trade was never an affair which meant a perfectly easy conscience, and it exacted a justification; hence one made of the Negro a half-animal, an article of merchandise. . . . The idea of the "barbarous Negro" is a European invention which has consequently prevailed in Europe until the beginning of this century [cited by Dr. W. E. Burghardt DuBois in *The World and Africa*, p. 79. The passage quoted above was translated by Dr. DuBois from the French edition of *Civilisation Africaine* by Leo Frobenius].

In the Central African region which we have been discussing in this chapter, the ancient institution of divine kingship is widely prevalent. For illustrative purposes we select Uganda; here the divine kingship pattern has survived in a fine state of preservation. The Reverend P. Hadfield has written a scholarly treatise on the sacred kingship in Africa; and in discussing this institution in Uganda we learn from the Reverend Hadfield that: "Sana, the King of Ganda during the middle of the nineteenth century, had the title 'Llare,' which probably means 'the Almighty One.' He was regarded as a god incarnate, and consequently, his subjects were compelled to pay homage to him as a divine being. Moreover the king not only owned the land of Ganda, but he also controlled the forces of nature." (*Traits of Divine Kingship in Africa*, p. 12, by the Rev. P. Hadfield, M.A., B.D., F.R.A.I.)

A more elaborate study is that of Tor Irstam, the title of which is *The King of Ganda: Studies of the Institution of Sacred Kingship in Africa*, Stockholm, 1944). Dr. Raphael Patai, Director of the Israeli Institute of Folklore and Ethnology in his *Hebrew Installation Rites*, Cincinnati, 1947, shows that, of the twenty-seven coronation rites in the African systems investigated by Irstam, no less than twenty-one are found in Old Testament accounts of the coronation of the kings of Israel and Judah. The scheme of Dr. Patai, using the numbers of Irstam's tabulation, are reproduced and discussed by Robert Graves and Joshua Podro in that work of profound scholarship, *The Nazarene Gospel Restored*, pp. 107-8, London, 1953. According to Graves and Podro, Dr. Patai missed two of Tor Irstam's parallels; namely No. 3, "The king received a new name," and No. 13, "The king drew on his shoes." We list the twenty-three rites as recorded by Graves and Podro in their restoration of the Nazarene Gospel; but we have taken the liberty of rewording the statements of some of the parallels for the sake of clarity of expression. The complete list of the twenty-three rites is as follows:

1. The king was regarded as being reborn at the time of his coronation as the Son of God.
2. He was dressed in robes of royal purple.
3. The king was given a new name.
4. The official who anointed the king addressed him. The king replied. He then was proclaimed the new monarch.
5. The ritual called for a fight preceding the final installation of the king. This ritual victory of the king over his enemies was an essential part of the ceremony.
6. After an initial stage, the rite of installing the ruler was postponed for a week.
7. The king received communion by the eating of a sacrificial meal.
8. The king was baptized.
9. The king climbed to the top of a hill called the Bamah or "pillar."
10. A memorial pillar was erected by the king.
11. He was admonished by the prophet, or anointer, and he promised to heed the sacred instructions.
12. The monarch was anointed with oil.
13. The king drew on his shoes.
14. As part of his regalia the king was given a shield, a spear, etc.
15. The king ascended the throne.
16. He was then crowned.
17. A rite involving fire took place.
18. Baked goods were distributed to the people by the king.
19. The king traveled around his dominion.
20. Festivities to celebrate the coronation were held.
21. The king was made the butt of ridicule by the people.

22. Human sacrifices were indulged in.
23. A temporary substitute king was recognized.

Rituals similar to those listed above are found in tribes and nations all over Africa, in both ancient and modern times; and European and American scholarship always assume that the practices are of non-African origin; but there are no facts to support such a conclusion. "In dealing with the origin of divine kingship in Egypt and among African tribes," we are told by the Reverend Hadfield, "we are largely in the realm of conjecture. Some traits may be ultimately assignable to the culture of the Old Orient, . . . while a direct diffusion across the Indian Ocean to the coasts of Africa cannot be excluded. On the other hand, it does not appear that the Old Orient will answer all the questions. Some traits of this complex pattern may have developed on African soil, and additions to it may have come from Egypt in historic times." (*Traits of Divine Kingship in Africa*, p. 127, by the Rev. P. Hadfield.)

We hold that the rites and ceremonies connected with the institution of divine kingship are mainly if not entirely of African origin. There is a large literature dealing with this subject and, besides the references cited above, we recommend *Kingship, Kings and Councillors*, and *Social Origins* by the late Professor A. M. Hocart. There is much valuable material in the thirteen volumes of Sir J. G. Frazer's *Golden Bough*, dealing with the origin and evolution of the sacred kingship. For readers who might find it difficult to consult the complete *Golden Bough*, there is a one-volume abridgment which may be recommended as quite adequate.

Chapter Nine

THE DESTRUCTION OF
AFRICAN CULTURE

Much knowledge of the culture of Africa has been lost because of the destruction of ancient records. Great libraries in several African cities were burned and looted, and their literary treasures were lost to posterity. The ancient Egyptian city of Thebes possessed a magnificent library. Its ceiling was painted sky-blue decorated with the images of sparkling stars; and on its walls were allegorical pictures relating to current religious doctrines and portraits of the sacred animals connected with ancient ritual. This library, with all its precious records, was destroyed by an invading Assyrian army in 661 B.C. Egypt at the time was ruled by kings of the 25th dynasty —rulers of Kushite or Ethiopian origin. The events leading up to the looting of Thebes have been well described by the late Professor Breasted:

> Taharka had now been ruling twenty-five years and he was growing old, when in 663 B.C. he accepted as coregent, perhaps not voluntarily, a son of Shabaka, named Tanutamon, whom he appointed over Upper Egypt. Tanutamon probably resided at Thebes, where Mentemhet, the prince of the Theban principality, was still in control, while Taharka himself, worn out with the unequal struggle against Assyria, had long before retired to Napata. There he survived the appointment of Tanutamon less than a year, dying in 663 B.C., whereupon the latter hastened to Napata to assume the sole kingship. Before these events, Tanutamon had been informed in a dream that he was to gain the sovereignty of both the North and the South, and in response to this vision, he now immediately invaded Lower Egypt (663). . . . The Assyrian garrison and doubtless some of the Delta lords, who now stood in great fear

of their Ninevite suzerain, gave him battle; but he defeated them and succeeded in taking Memphis. . . .

Content with the appearance of unchallenged supremacy in Lower Egypt, Tanutamon settled himself in Memphis as Pharaoh of all Egypt, in fulfillment of his divine vision. Meanwhile, on the first news of his departure from Napata, the Assyrian officers in the Delta had sent with all haste to Nineveh to notify Ashurbanipal, and in 661 B.C. the great king's army drove the Ethiopian for the last time from Lower Egypt. The Assyrians pursued him to Thebes, and as he ingloriously withdrew southward, they sacked and plundered the magnificent capital of Egypt's days of splendor [*A History of Egypt*, pp. 467–68, by James Henry Breasted].

The Hebrew prophet, Nahum, predicting the destruction of Nineveh, half a century later, refers to the fall of Thebes in the following passage from the Old Testament: "Art thou better than No-Amon [Thebes], that was situate among the rivers, that had the waters round about her; whose rampart was the sea, and her wall was of the sea? Ethiopia and Egypt were her strength and it was infinite. . . . Yet was she carried away, she went into captivity: her young children also were dashed to pieces at the top of all the streets: and they cast lots for her honorable men, and all her great men were bound in chains." (Nahum, III, 8–10.)

In the fourth century B.C., the great Library of Alexandria was founded in Egypt by the first king of the Ptolemaic Dynasty. A half century later this library housed a fine collection of about one million volumes. In these books was gathered the knowledge of the ancient world; and it included valuable works in science, mathematics, technology, literature, and history. In the first century B.C., a Roman army under Julius Caesar invaded Egypt. The citizens of Alexandria resisted the incursion of the Romans, and in the resulting battle about a third of the library was destroyed. Julius Caesar called a meeting of the leading citizens of Alexandria, and he blamed them for the damage to the library. His position was that they should not have resisted him.

After the days of Julius Caesar, the Library of Alexander was rebuilt and enlarged, and as far as possible the lost manuscripts were restored. Then came the rise to power of the early Christian church. The leaders of the primitive Christian Church were, for the most part, ignorant and bigoted religious fanatics who embarked on a course of promoting faith and destroying knowledge. The leader of the Christian party in Alexandria in 389 A.C. was Bishop Theophilus, who at the head of a mob of Christian monks destroyed what was left of the great Library of Alexander. On the death of Theophilus, he was succeeded in the bishopric of Alexandria by his nephew, St. Cyril, who was even worse than his late uncle. In the early part of the fifth century of the Christian era, Hypatia, the daughter of Theon, the mathematician, conducted an academy in Alexandria. This talented lady gave lectures on the philosophies of Plato and Aristotle, and instructed her students on the works of Appolonius and other geometers. Bishop Cyril decided that such knowledge must be suppressed, and he proceeded to take the necessary steps to achieve that objective. The great tragedy that befell Hypatia is best described by an eminent historian of science, who informs us:

> Each day before her academy stood a long train of chariots; her lecture rooms were crowded with the wealth and fashion of Alexandria. They came to listen to her discourses on those questions which man in all ages has asked, but which never yet have been answered: "What am I? Where am I? What can I know?" Hypatia and Cyril! Philosophy and bigotry. They cannot exist together. So Cyril felt, and on that feeling he acted. As Hypatia repaired to her academy, she was assaulted by Cyril's mob—a mob of many monks. Stripped naked in the street, she was dragged into a church, and there killed by the club of Peter the Reader. The corpse was cut to pieces, the

flesh was scraped from the bones with shells, and the remnants cast into a fire. For this frightful crime Cyril was never called to account. . . . Henceforth there was to be no freedom for human thought. Everyone must think as the ecclesiastical authority ordered him, A.D. 414. In Athens itself philosophy awaited its doom. Justinian at length prohibited its teaching, and caused all its schools in that city to be closed [*History of the Conflict between Religion and Science,* pp. 55–56, by Professor John William Draper].

There is a story that the remains of the Library of Alexander were destroyed by Arab invaders in the seventh century; but this charge is entirely unfounded. The first library was burned in 48 B.C., by the invading Romans, and the second great library was looted by fanatical Christian monks in 389 A.C., and was never restored; hence there was no library for Amru and his Moslems to destroy. We have referred to the Roman conquest of Carthage in 146 B.C., when its library of five hundred thousand volumes was burned. In the medieval Moorish Empire of the Two Shores, there were many cities housing fine libraries. Besides the royal libraries of the rulers in such cities as Cordova, Morocco City, and Fez, many universities and colleges possessed fine libraries—not to mention the book and manuscript collections owned by scientists, scholars, and educated men in general, who had a taste for fine literature. Due to wars and other catastrophes, very little of this literary heritage of the past has survived.

The University of Sankore in Timbuktu enjoyed high prestige as a seat of higher education during the reign of Askia the Great of the Songhay Empire, in the sixteenth century. Its professors corresponded with and visited other universities in Morocco and Egypt. At an earlier period under the rule of the Mali monarchs, this same university maintained contacts with similar institutions in Moorish Spain. In the middle of the sixteenth century a large and learned society of literati flourished in Timbuktu; and in addition the city was filled by numerous Sudanese students, eager in their pursuit of knowledge and virtue. The most scholarly and celebrated professors established schools, where they lectured to bodies of students. Proficient students on finishing their courses of study received diplomas issued by their masters. Professor Ahmed Baba of Timbuktu, a great scholar of his day, has left us a sketch of one of the masters under whom he had studied in his youth. This learned professor, Mohammed Abu Bekr of Wankore, we learn from his former pupil, was "one of the best of God's virtuous creatures." We are further informed:

> He was a working scholar, and a man instinct with goodness. His nature was as pure as it was upright. . . . Calm and dignified, with a natural distinction and a modesty that rendered intercourse with him easy, he captured all hearts. Everyone who knew him loved him. . . . His whole life was given to the service of others. He taught his pupils to love science, to follow its teachings, to devote their time to it, to associate with scholars, and to keep their minds in a state of docility. He lavishly lent his most precious books, rare copies, and the volumes that he most valued, and never asked for them again, no matter what was the subject of which they treated.

Ahmed Baba, in his undergraduate days, asked this professor to lend him a rare treatise on grammar. The great master gladly complied with his request and furthermore searched through his library for other books that would be of service to his pupil. "It was astonishing to see him," Ahmed Baba remembered, "and he acted thus notwithstanding the fact that he had a passion for books, and that he collected them with ardor, both buying and causing them to be copied." We are not surprised to hear that "in this way he lost a great quantity of his books." "His like," we are assured by Professor Baba, "will never be found again." The mind of this great teacher is described as "subtle, sagacious, ready, swift to comprehend.

His intelligence was broad and luminous. His usual manner was taciturn and grave, but he would occasionally break into sallies of wit."

We have already referred to the Moorish invasion of the Songhay Empire in the latter part of the sixteenth century. Unhappily, at this time the scholarly society of Timbuktu was brought to ruin. The best citizens of Timbuktu were rounded up and deported to Morocco on March 18, 1594. In the words of Lady Lugard:

All that was cultivated, all that was enlightened, all that was rich, refined, and influential, was driven out, and the greater number, men, women and children, were taken in chains across the desert. . . . Amongst the exiles were the most distinguished men of letters of the Sudan, and the most delicately nurtured women and children of the town. Ahmed Baba, the biographer and historian, . . . was among them. Fortunately for him, his fame was so widespread as to command respect in all centers of learning. When he arrived in Morocco he was treated with the respect due to his great reputation, and though he was not permitted to return to Timbuktu for many years, he was given practical freedom in Morocco, and allowed to form a school, where he continued the life of study and of teaching which he had led in the Sudan. . . . It is interesting, in the midst of all that the exiles had lost, to find them chiefly concerned for the destruction of their libraries. "I," said Ahmed Baba afterwards to the Sultan of Morocco, "had the smallest library of any of my friends, and your soldiers took from me 1600 volumes." Others, those who in the happier days had so generously lent their books to all who needed them, lost every volume that they possessed. Unfortunately, while other forms of wealth were appropriated, the contents of the libraries were destroyed. The sack of Timbuktu was the signal for the letting loose of all the evils of lawless tyranny upon the country. From this time the history of the Sudan becomes a mere record of riot, robbery and decadence [A Tropical Dependency, pp. 309–10, by Lady Lugard].

The destruction of libraries is only one phase of the despoiling of African culture. We must now move on and discuss the even more tragic story of the rape of a continent— of the murder and enslavement of its peoples and the degradation and destruction of its civilization.

In the year 1498, when King al Fudail reigned over Kilwa, we learn from the *Kilwa Chronicle* that news was received from Mozambique of the appearance of three ships; and that on these ships were men from the land of the Franks. Actually these craft were manned by Portuguese sailors, and were under the command of Admiral Vasco da Gama. In those days the East Africans generally called all Europeans Franks, just as the Europeans referred to all Africans as Moors. The ships of Da Gama in a few days passed by Kilwa and docked at Mafia, an island city a little north of Kilwa. "The lord of Mafia rejoiced," we read in the *Kilwa Chronicle*, for the ruler of Mafia thought that these European interlopers were honest and upright men.

> But those who knew the truth [the *Kilwa Chronicle* continues] confirmed that they were corrupt and dishonest persons who had only come to spy out the land in order to seize it. And they determined to cut the anchors of their ships so that they would drift ashore and be wrecked by the Muslims. The Franks learnt of this and went on to Malindi. When the people of Malindi saw them, they knew they were bringers of war and corruption, and were troubled with very great fear. They gave them all they asked, water, food, firewood, and everything else. And the Franks asked for a pilot to guide them to India, and after that back to their own land—God curse it! [*The East African Coast, Select Documents*, pp. 47–48; translated by G. S. P. Freeman-Grenville].

Duarte Barbosa, a Portuguese royal commercial agent, visited the trading cities of the Swahilis early in the sixteenth century before they were invaded and looted by later compatriots. The following description is of Kilwa:

> Going along the coast from this town of Mozambique, there is an island hard by the mainland which is called Kilwa, in which is a Moorish town with many fair houses of stones and mortar, with many windows after our fashion, very well arranged in streets, with many flat roofs. The doors are of wood, well carved, with excellent joinery. Around it are streams and orchards and fruit gardens with many channels of sweet water. It has a Moorish king over it. From this place they trade with Sofala, whence they bring back gold, and from here they spread all over Arabia Felix, which henceforth we may call by this name (even though it be in Ethiopia) for all the seacoast is well peopled with villages and abodes of Moors. Before the king our Lord sent out his expedition to discover India, the Moors of Sofala, Cuama, Angoya and Mozambique were all subject to the King of Kilwa, who was the most mighty king among them. And in this town was great plenty of gold, as no ships passed towards Sofala without first coming to this island [*The Book of Duarte Barbosa*, translated by Mansel Longworth Dames; Hakluyt Society; 2 vols., London: 1918. Cited by Basil Davidson in *The African Past*, pp. 131–32].

The Portuguese were bent on taking over the Indian Ocean trade, and on exacting tribute from the cities of the Swahilis, whom they mistakenly called Moors, and finally on a program of pillage and looting. A Portuguese fleet, in 1505, under the leadership of Francisco d'Almeida, captured the cities of Kilwa and Mombasa, and proceeded to sack them. On board d'Almeida's flagship, the *San Rafael*, was a German, Hans Mayr, who has left us a description of these nefarious events.

In reference to Kilwa, we are told that: "As soon as the town had been taken without opposition, the Vicar-General and some of the Franciscan fathers came ashore carrying two crosses in procession and singing the Te Deum. They went to the palace, and there the cross was put down and the Grand-Captain prayed. Then everyone started to plunder the town of all its merchandise and provisions." (Cited by Basil Davidson in *The African Past*, p. 136.) Two days later d'Almeida ordered the city to be set on fire, and the greater part of it was destroyed.

The German observer, Hans Mayr, gives the following description of the fate of Mombasa:

> The Grand-Captain ordered that the town should be sacked, and that each man should carry off to his ship whatever he found: so that at the end there would be a division of the spoil, each man to receive a twentieth of what he found. The same rule was made for gold, silver and pearls. Then everyone started to plunder the town and to search the houses, forcing open the doors with axes and iron bars. There was a large quantity of cotton cloth for Sofala in the town, for the whole coast gets its cotton cloth from here. So the Grand-Captain got a good share of the trade of Sofala for himself. A large quantity of rich silk and gold embroidered clothes was seized, and carpets also; one of these, which was without equal for beauty, was sent to the King of Portugal, together with many other valuables [English translation by Freeman-Grenville; cited by Basil Davidson in *The African Past*, p. 136].

Soon after the onslaught on the trading centers of the East African coast, a systematic traffic in slaves in West Africa was inaugurated by European invaders. A few Africans were reduced to slavery and transported to Europe early in the fifteenth century; but the African slave trade did not begin in earnest until about a century later. This evil enterprise was the outcome of the Spanish conquest of Mexico and Peru. The natives of Peru and Mexico were reduced to slave status and forced to work in mines. Their death rate was so high that their European masters were impelled to look elsewhere for slave labor; but the question was where? Bartolome de las Casas, Bishop of Chiapa, in 1517 came to their rescue by proposing that each Spanish gentleman be permitted to import twelve African slaves. This advice was adopted by the king of Spain, who issued a patent to one of his friends giving him the authority to import four thousand black slaves annually to Cuba, Hispaniola, Jamaica, and Puerto Rico. This patent was sold soon afterward to Genoese merchants, who allotted a share of the business to the Portuguese; and in a short while nearly all of the nations of Europe were participants in the traffic. By this time there was no limit on the number of slaves to be exported to the Americas. To quiet their consciences, the European enslavers of Africans invoked the endorsement of the Christian Church.

> The peculiar and damning fact in the history of slavery [as is pointed out by a careful student of the institution], so far as the Christian Church is concerned, is this. . . . It was created by Christians, it was continued by Christians, it was in some respects more barbarous than anything the world had yet seen, and its worst features were to be witnessed in countries that were most ostentatious in their parade of Christianity. It is this that provides the final and unanswerable indictment of the Christian Church. . . . It should be added that, according to Livingstone, slavery was unknown to the Africans until it was introduced by Christians—the Portuguese [*Christianity, Slavery and Labour*, pp. 52–53, by Chapman Cohen].

Lest Mr. Chapman Cohen be suspected of an anti-Christian bias, we must say that his opinions are supported by the authentic records of history. In discussing the African slave trade, an outstanding Christian apologist, the Reverend Loring Brace, says, in his famous book, *Gesta Christi*, page 365, that "the guilt of this great crime rests on the Christian Church as an organized body." (Cited by Joseph McCabe in *The Social Record of Christianity*, p. 94.)

The first African slaves were shipped from the coast of

Guinea to Haiti in 1510; and by 1576 there were 40,000 black slaves in Latin America. By the year 1800 this number had increased to 776,000. In Jamaica, in 1767, there were 140,000 slaves; by 1800 the number had reached 300,000. In the new colony of Virginia, in 1620, a group of 20 slaves were imported; but by the year 1760, the number of slaves had reached 200,000. It has been estimated that the total number of African slaves imported into the English colonies of America and the West Indies was at least 40,000,000. The mortality rate of this sordid traffic was high. Livingstone estimated that one slave in three was killed in raids or on the trip to the coast, and slave merchants lost one out of three of their human cargo on the voyage across the sea. All told, the slave trade was responsible for the death of about 100,000,-000 Africans. The modern reader may find it hard to imagine the desolating impact of the slave trade on African society. An accurate picture of a raid by enslavers on a peaceful west coast village is given by a scholarly modern writer, as follows:

> From the black men digging in the fields about the village, a cry of sudden fear went up. Women shrieked and children scurried for hiding as if pursued by lions. One of the men, standing on a little eminence, pointed vehemently out to the sea, whose blue serenity was broken by approaching masts. Then all the men, in terror, dashed to their huts, seized spears and any other weapons they could grab, and, herding their families into the shelter of the surrounding forest, swore by all the tribal gods to sell themselves dearly. . . .
>
> They knew that other Africans, multitudes of them, had been captured; that villages had been left desolate and empty; that children had been orphaned, mothers wrested from their sons, sons from their mothers, husbands from their wives; and that the lives of whole communities had been devastated as by volcanic blasts. For these strangers from across the waters were pitiless hunters—hunters of men [*The Long Road to Humanity*, p. 325, by Stanton A. Coblentz].

These kidnapers and enslavers of their fellow human beings were not inhibited by any pangs of conscience. From their own records we infer that they considered themselves to be very pious people. In the *Conquests and Discoveries of Henry the Navigator*, we have the following discourse from a slave raider:

"And at length Our Lord God, who rewardeth all that is well done, ordained that in return for the work of this day done by our men in His service they should have the victory and the reward of their fatigues and disbursements, in the taking of one hundred and sixty-five captives, men, women and children, without reckoning those that died or that killed themselves." (Cited by Chapman Cohen in *Christianity, Slavery and Labour*, p. 55.)

The first Englishman of importance to engage in the slave traffic was John Hawkins, who was later made a knight by Queen Elizabeth I and appointed Treasurer of the Navy. Hawkins started out by assembling a fleet of five ships, which was soon augmented by three more, bringing the total to eight. Such a venture required capital, and such notables as Queen Elizabeth, the Earl of Pembroke, and the Earl of Leicester bought shares. The flagship of the fleet was owned by the queen, who obligingly lent it to Hawkins, and the name of this vessel was the good ship *Jesus*. Captain Hawkins was a pious man, who admonished his sailors to "Serve God daily," and to "Love one another." On disembarking at Cape Verde, and finding the natives to be of "a nature very gentle and loving," Hawkins and his party proceeded to kidnap some of them. Then after sailing along, "burning and spoiling" as he went, he visited settlements in Latin America, where he compelled the settlers to purchase slaves at his price. Sir John Hawkins was rewarded by a grateful sovereign by the granting of a coat of arms consisting of "a demi-Moor in his proper colors, bound and captive," as a fitting token of the new and lucrative trade which he had opened up to England.

The chief ports of the British slave trade were London, Bristol, and Liverpool, with Liverpool carrying on the bulk of the business. In 1795 one-fourth of the ships sailing out of Liverpool were engaged in the slave trade. There was an increase from 15 vessels in 1730 to 136 in 1792. From January of 1806 to May of 1807, 185 ships operating from Liverpool sailed from Africa with a total slave cargo of nearly 50,000. Mr. G. F. Cooke, a well-known tragedian, was hissed by certain members of the audience, while playing at a theater in Liverpool; and he retorted: "I have not come here to be insulted by a set of wretches, of which every brick in your infernal town has been cemented by an African's blood."

In 1781, a case was brought before an English court, in which the captain of a slave ship was charged with throwing 132 slaves overboard. The captain was not charged with murder; the court was only called upon to decide whether the action of the captain was justified or not, and who should be responsible for the financial loss. A well-known English historian calls our attention to a case that shows the way in which the slave trade was conducted:

"During the hearing of a case for insurance, the following facts were brought out. A slave ship with 442 slaves was bound from Guinea to Jamaica. Sixty of the slaves died from overcrowding. The captain, being short of water, threw ninety-six more overboard. Afterwards, twenty-six more were drowned. Ten drowned themselves in despair. Yet the ship reached port before the water was exhausted." (*The United Kingdom: A Political History*, Vol. II, p. 247, by Goldwin Smith.)

Anyone who is familiar with the history of black slavery will note that the strongest bulwark of the slave system was organized Christianity; or in other words, the various denominations of the Christian Church. The abolitionists of the eighteenth and nineteenth centuries were fought by the churches tooth and nail. The only Christian body that took a firm stand against the slaveocracy was the Quakers. As late as the middle of the nineteenth century the Reverend James Wilson referred to slavery as: "That gracious and benevolent system which elevates the heathen cannibal into the contented, civilized, intelligent domestics we see around us. Nay, more, into humble, faithful and most joyous worshippers of the true and everlasting God. Bless God for such a system. We don't apologize for slavery, we glory in it, and no society shall exist within our borders that disqualifies or stigmatizes the slave trade." (*Report of the Anti-Slavery Society*, p. 281.)

We recall reading of a slave ship which landed on the West African coast and kidnapped a number of men, women, and children; then headed for the New World with its human cargo. The captain of this vessel in checking his records was shocked to find that these hapless Africans had been kidnapped on a Sunday; so the ship was turned around and headed back to the African coast. Here the captives were turned loose, and then recaptured on a weekday. In the eyes of the captain, God approved of his slaving activities, but frowned upon the desecration of the Sabbath Day.

Of how African culture was destroyed by the Atlantic trade, we have a brilliant and concise summary by modern students of African affairs:

> Year after year, for more than three centuries tens of thousands of African farmers and craftsmen were shipped away to work in American plantations, mines and cities. With their labor they created vast wealth and profits, but seldom for themselves and never for Africa. . . . West Africa, like other parts of Africa, possessed its own craftsmen. Often they were highly skilled. They produced goods that were sold from one end of West Africa to the other. But they produced them by old-fashioned hand-methods. Increasingly they had to face the competition of much cheaper goods made by machinery in Europe.
>
> Cheap foreign goods, produced by Europeans or Indians

forced to work for very low wages, began to ruin the market for cotton stuffs produced by self-employed and often prosperous African craftsmen. Cheap European metalware, machine-made, competed with the handwork of African metal-smiths. Understandably, African craftsmen suffered from this rivalry. Yet they were unable to meet it by going over to European factory methods, since they had neither the necessary money nor the knowledge, while their way of life kept them faithful to traditional methods. So the slave trade removed African labor from Africa, and did much to ruin the livelihood of African craftsmen [*A History of West Africa*, pp. 294–95, by Basil Davidson, with F. K. Buah, and the advice of J. F. Ade Ajayi].

After the abolition of the slave trade, Africans were not given a chance to recover from centuries of bondage. Instead the European powers got together, invaded the continent, and reduced the majority of African peoples to colonial status. This caused further destruction of African culture. A good example of this brigandage is the history of the so-called Congo Free State under the control of King Leopold II of Belgium. An international African Association was formed by Leopold; and, at the Berlin Conference of 1884, the several European powers interested in the stealing of African territories handed over to the Belgian monarch the greater part of the Congo basin—an area covering about one million square miles. The Berlin Conference opened its proceedings "in the name of Almighty God" and turned over this vast territory to King Leopold's International African Association. In August, 1885, the king gave notice that his Association would from then on be known as the "Congo Free State," with himself as the sovereign of the realm. Leopold issued decrees declaring all land, ivory, and rubber as property of the state—namely, himself. Then the Belgian Secretary of State ordered the Governor-General of the so-called Congo Free State to "neglect no means of exploiting the forests." This was done with murderous cruelty; and Leopold derived a profit of about $1,500,000 a year from the operation. In the words of Lord Russell:

> The methods by which these vast profits were accumulated were very simple. Each village was ordered by the authorities to collect and bring in a certain amount of rubber—as much as the men could bring in by neglecting all work for their own maintenance. If they failed to bring the required amount, their women were taken away and kept as hostages in compounds or in the harems of government employees. If this method failed, native troops, many of them cannibals, were sent into the village to spread terror, if necessary by killing some of the men; but in order to prevent a waste of cartridges they were ordered to bring one right hand for every cartridge used. If they missed, or used cartridges on game, they cut off the hands of living persons to make up the necessary number. The result was, according to the estimate of Sir H. H. Johnston, which is confirmed from all other impartial sources, that in fifteen years the native population was reduced from about twenty million to scarcely nine million [*Freedom and Organization: 1814–1914*, p. 453, by Bertrand Russell].

For years the world knew nothing of these atrocities. "Enormous pains were taken," to quote Lord Russell again, "to keep secret the large scale systematic murder by which the royal capitalist obtained his profits. The officials and law courts were both in his pay and at his mercy, private traders were excluded, and Catholic missionaries silenced by his piety. Belgium was systematically corrupted, and the Belgian government was to a considerable extent his accomplice. Men who threatened disclosures were bought off, or, if that proved impossible, disappeared mysteriously." (*Ibid.*, p. 454.)

The story was finally revealed to the world by Mr. Edmund D. Morel, a shipping clerk in the office of a Liverpool trading company which was in partnership with King Leopold. Of course, Mr. Morel lost his position of shipping clerk as a result of his disclosures; and then, although practically penniless, he took up his pen and, by way of the British press and publishers, enlightened the world as to the tragic happenings in the Congo. Morel fought a long uphill battle before he could get a hearing, but finally he managed to arouse the conscience of the world. As Chapman Cohen has told us:

> So long as possible, both governments and missionary societies burked investigations of the atrocities reported. The matter was first raised in our own Parliament by Sir Charles Dilke in 1897. Some sort of an official report was prepared, but no further Parliamentary notice worth recording was taken until 1903. . . . The silence of the missionary societies was equally striking. Mr. Morel points out that, although plenty of information was available, the executives of the missionary societies took no action, and, "with three exceptions," no missionary gave public expression to his experiences until October, 1903. The Roman Catholic Missionaries were altogether silent until 1903—was not Leopold a devout Catholic? And when Mr. Morel visited the United States of America in 1904 to ventilate the Congo horror, he was bitterly opposed by Cardinal Gibbons, the leading Catholic ecclesiastic in the United States [*Christianity, Slavery and Labour*, p. 144, by Chapman Cohen].

In 1906, King Leopold II donated a fund of $60,000 to encourage scientific research for the prevention of sleeping sickness. In a manifesto he stated that: "If God gives me that satisfaction [victory over sleeping sickness] I shall be able to present myself before His judgment-seat with the credit of having performed one of the finest acts of the century, and a legion of rescued beings will call down upon me His Grace." (Cited by E. D. Morel in *Red Rubber*, p. 151.)

The African peoples were vulnerable to conquest by European invaders on account of a profound difference in cultural outlook. Among Africans, society has a matriarchal basis. The cultivation of peaceful pursuits is a way of life; egalitarianism between the sexes is practiced; the fundamental approach to life is hedonistic; religious beliefs are idealistic in form; and the concept of sin is conspicuous by its absence. On the other hand, the Europeans developed a patriarchal society with an inferior status for women; the cultivation of warfare was adopted as their way of life. Associated with these traits are a materialistic type of religion and a highly developed sense of sin. The Europeans, being warlike, had a distinct advantage over the peaceful Africans. Another factor that aided the European whites in their destruction of African institutions was a strange mixture of race prejudice and Christian theology. A good example of how this type of propaganda is put across has been clearly presented by the late Chapman Cohen, who related that:

> In nearly every case the conquering white professes the Christian religion, and that nearly always the conquest of the colored people by the whites is justified on the grounds that they are the carriers of purer religion and a higher civilization. In passing, it may be noted that the color bar is a question that belongs essentially to Christian times. No such distinction appears to have existed in antiquity. The Greek might take pride in his superior culture, the Roman in his higher degree of salvation, or in the power of the Empire to which he belonged, but I cannot recall any case in which the claim was made of superiority merely on account of a difference of color. To an ancient Greek or Roman nothing would have appeared stranger than to find a ruffianly, illiterate, uncultured white asserting superiority over another man, merely because of a difference in the color of his skin. . . . It was left for this to develop under the influence of the Christian religion, and for Christians to provide a religious ground for the distinction in the curse that God had pronounced on the children of Ham. And as the religious basis weakened, Christianity effected here what it effected elsewhere. It provided a rationalization of the color bar on the grounds of here a biological, there an ethical, else-

where a cultural difference—all of which owed whatever force they possessed to the very distinction that had been created. The white said it was impossible to mix with colored people on grounds of equality. Having said so he proceeded to make it impossible. Having made it impossible he produced the manufactured impossibility as proof of the soundness of the generalization [*Christianity, Slavery and Labour*, pp. 135–36, by Chapman Cohen].

When the first European navigators landed on the West African coast at Vaida, on the shore of the Gulf of Guinea, they found well-constructed streets and roads, lined for miles on end by rows of shade trees; they traveled for days through vast fields producing valuable crops, in a country whose inhabitants wore magnificent costumes of their own manufacture. When they sailed further to the south in the Congo region, they found great states directed by powerful rulers. The dwellers in this area were tastefully clad in fine silk and velvet; they were well endowed with industrial wealth and were thoroughly civilized. On the eastern coast, similar conditions were found. After the onslaughts of slave trade and the invasions of the colonial era, this culture was reduced to a shambles; then the perpetrators of this destruction issued propaganda declaring that Africans had never been civilized.

A moving account of how African civilization was deliberately wrecked was penned by Dr. W. E. B. DuBois, in the following words:

There came to Africa an end of industry, especially industry guided by taste and art. Cheap European goods pushed in and threw the native products out of competition. Rum and gin displaced the milder native drinks. The beautiful patterned cloth, brocades and velvets disappeared before their cheap imitations in Manchester calicos. Methods of work were lost and forgotten.

With all this went the fall and disruption of the family, the deliberate attack upon the ancient African clan by missionaries. The invading investors who wanted cheap labor at the gold mines, the diamond mines, the copper and tin mines, the oil forests and cocoa fields, followed the missionaries. The authority of the family was broken up; the authority and tradition of the clan disappeared; the power of the chief was transmuted into the rule of the white district commissioner. The old religion was held up to ridicule, the old culture and ethical standards were degraded or disappeared, and gradually all over Africa spread the inferiority complex, the fear of color, the worship of white skin, the imitation of white ways of doing and thinking, whether good, bad, or indifferent. By the end of the nineteenth century the degradation of Africa was as complete as organized human means could make it. Chieftains, representing a thousand years of striving human culture, were decked out in second-hand London top hats, while Europe snickered [*The World and Africa*, p. 78, by W. E. B. DuBois].

The African people fought valiantly to preserve their ancient ways, but the odds against them were overwhelming.

In 1906 when I penetrated into the territory of Kassai-Sankuru [states Frobenius], I found still, villages of which the principal streets were bordered on each side for leagues, with rows of palm trees, and of which the houses decorated each one in charming fashion, were works of art as well. . . . Everywhere velvets and silken stuffs. Each cup, each pipe, each spoon was an object of art perfectly worthy to be compared to the creations of the Roman European style. But all this was only the particularly tender and iridescent bloom which adorns a ripe and marvellous fruit; the gestures, the manners, the moral code of the entire people, . . . were imprinted with dignity and grace, . . . I know of no northern people who can be compared with these primitives for unity of civilization. Alas these last Happy Isles! They, also, were submerged by the tidal wave of European civilization. And the peaceful beauty was carried away by the floods [Professor Leo Frobenius in

Histoire de la Civilisation Africaine. Cited by Dr. W. E. B. DuBois in *The World and Africa,* pp. 156–57].

The prospects for the future of Africa looked very dark at the beginning of the present century. Now the picture is considerably brighter as a new Africa looks toward the future. The past ten years have been a time of momentous happenings in Africa, but what of the future? A wise statement on this question has been made by a contemporary African scholar: "It is perhaps too early to pass judgement on a decade which has been full of excitement, promise and frustration for the African continent. Nevertheless it can still be maintained that the progress so far made in Africa's decade of achievement can be sustained if honest, sincere and intelligent leadership is always forthcoming." (*African Glory,* p. 193, by J. C. deGraft-Johnson.)

That the Christian missionary enterprise has been used to keep Africans in a state of bondage may come as a shock to some readers, but there is an abundance of documentary material which places the fact beyond all doubt. We call attention to a statement of Henri Junod, a prominent Swiss Protestant missionary:

> I speak of resignation. It is necessary to the Blacks, for despite all that has been written on the fundamental axiom of the absolute equality of mankind, they are an inferior race, a race made to serve. It would be harmful to them to cover up this evident fact under a pile of sentimental eloquence. . . . Christianity alone will make out of the Black a servant satisfied with his lot, for it alone can bring him to a free and voluntary submission to the plans of Divine Providence. . . . Everyone, I will even say the whole of humanity, is deeply concerned that the Negro should accept the position assigned to him by his physical and intellectual faculties. Without the arms of the natives, the gold mines of Johannesburg, which have built up the prosperity of South Africa, would cease to exist from one day to the next, for it is these arms which accomplish the entire manual labor in the extracting of gold. Then again, when we consider the immense plains on the coast of Delagoa, the valleys of the Nkomati, the Limpopo and the Zambesi, how could these fertile territories be exploited if the blacks refused their aid? In these tropical latitudes the European dies of fever, especially if he starts working the soil himself . . . and the white man's role is that of the organizer, the master, under whose watch must work the million arms of the native population [Cited by J. C. deGraft-Johnson, in *African Glory*, pp. 51–52].

The outstanding labor leader in modern Africa is Mr. Isaac Wallace-Johnson. He was forced to leave Nigeria in 1933,

317

on account of his work in organizing labor unions. He settled in Accra, in the Gold Coast colony, where he organized labor and engaged in literary activities. In May of 1936, Mr. Wallace-Johnson wrote an article, published in the *Africa Morning Post*. The title of this article was: "Has the African a God?" In this discourse he said: "Personally, I believe the European has a God in whom he believes and whom he is representing in his churches all over Africa. He believes in the God whose name is Deceit. He believes in the God whose law is 'Ye strong you must weaken still further the weak.' Ye 'civilized' Europeans you must 'civilize' the 'barbarous' Africans with machine-guns. Ye 'Christian' Europeans you must 'Christian-ize' the 'pagan' Africans with bombs, poison gases, etc."

Wallace-Johnson was promptly arrested and tried for seditious libel. He was found guilty and fined $250. Taking the case to the African Court of Appeals, he again lost. An appeal was then made to the Privy Council in England. This court, presided over by the Lord Chancellor, Lord Caldecott, returned a strange verdict. The article was declared to be entirely free of sedition, in either act or content, but the conviction of the author was upheld, because he had violated the Gold Coast Criminal Code, which held that an attack on religion was an attack on the government of the colony.

Chapter Ten

AFRICA RESURGENT

Most of the African nations at the present time enjoy political autonomy, but this is a very recent state of affairs. Two happenings of great import mark the beginning of this trend. The first occurrence was the convening of the 6th Pan-African Congress in Manchester, England, in 1945. The principal organizer of this convocation was Dr. W. E. B. DuBois. Among the delegates were Mr. George Padmore, Chief Akintola, Mr. H. O. Davies, Mr. Jomo Kenyatta, and Dr. Kwame Nkrumah.

"The delegates believe in peace," was the proclamation of the Manchester meeting. "How could it be otherwise, when for centuries the African people have been the victims of violence and slavery? . . . We are determined to be free. . . . We demand for Black Africa autonomy and independence. . . . We will fight in every way we can for freedom, democracy and social betterment."

The second event of great importance in this movement was another Pan-African conclave, which met in 1946 at Bamako, now capital of the Republic of Mali. The Bamako conference heralded the organization of the Rassemblement Democratique Africaine (African Democratic Alliance, or RDA), a movement which aimed at home rule for all the African colonies under French domination.

The first colony to attain self-governing status was the Gold Coast, which was renamed **Ghana**. The great African statesman who led this movement was Dr. Kwame Nkrumah. His Convention Peoples Party, in a general election held in 1951, won over the opposition by an overwhelming popular vote. At the time, Dr. Nkrumah was in jail for sedition. Sir Charles Arden-Clarke, the British governor, ordered the release of Nkrumah from prison so that he could head the new Administration.

Complete independence was attained in 1957, and the new state enjoyed dominion status until 1960, when it became a republic within the British Commonwealth. President Nkrumah remained in office for nine years, and his plans for economic improvement seemed to be working; but by 1966 the economic condition of the nation had taken a turn for the worse, and opposition politicians charged widespread corruption in the ranks of the ruling party, the Convention Peoples' Party (CPP). So on February 24th, a coup d'état was brought about by the army and supported by the police. This coup, led by General Joseph A. Ankrah, deposed President Nkrumah, outlawed the CPP, suspended the republican constitution of 1960, and established a National Liberation Council (NLC). The NLC is composed of seven members, three from the army and four from the police. The chairman of the Council is Lieutenant General J. A. Ankrah; and the vice chairmanship is held by John W. K. Hartley, Inspector-General of Police. The National Liberation Council possesses complete legislative power, exercised by decree; and all executive functions formerly exercised by the president, the Cabinet, or by ministers are now controlled by the Council, which promises eventually to return the government of the country to civilian rule.

A coup d'état in May, 1958, placed General Charles de Gaulle into the French presidency. This event reflected dissatisfaction with the way previous governments had treated the problem of independence in the African territories under French control. The supporters of DeGaulle in the RDA looked to him for a solution of this problem. Mr. Félix Houphouet-Boigny, a secretary of state of France in the first DeGaulle cabinet, was a prominent African statesman from the Ivory Coast, and a leader of the RDA, and he was hopeful that DeGaulle would come up with a workable plan. The scheme proposed by President DeGaulle was the establishment of a French Community similar to the British Commonwealth. In this organization all member states were to have equal rights, though for an indefinite period the central government in Paris would make decisions on problems of defense and foreign affairs, with the advice of the prime ministers of the self-governing members of the French Community.

In the summer of 1958, DeGaulle toured French West Africa to present his plan to the leaders of the various states in that area. The response was favorable until he reached Conakry, the capital of **Guinea.** Prime Minister Ahmed Sékou Touré was against the French Community, which he regarded as a trick to perpetuate French rule under the pretense of granting independence to the colonies. So he told DeGaulle that he would vote against the Community and work for complete independence. Therefore, on September 28, 1958, Guinea voted in favor of independence from France; and on October 2nd of the same year Guinea was proclaimed a republic, with Sékou Touré as president. General DeGaulle invoked economic sanctions against Guinea by attempting to shut off its export trade in bauxite and bananas, and by persuading the allies of France to refuse recognition to the new republic. This put Guinea in a difficult economic position, but the new nation was not defeated.

Shortly before Christmas in 1958, President Nkrumah of Ghana offered President Sékou Touré a loan of ten million pounds and a political union with Ghana to create the nucleus of a United States of West Africa. Encouraged by offers of aid from Nkrumah, and by the backing of the people of Guinea, Sékou Touré was able to keep his ship of state afloat. By the end of 1959 the Republic of Guinea had received the recognition of the principal governments of the world. In the meantime it had become a member of the United Nations and had survived successfully its economic difficulties.

Mr. Roy MacGregor-Hastie, an American foreign correspondent, who has an expert acquaintance with modern African political developments, has penned an accurate account of what happened to the French Community after Guinea survived its bid for freedom:

> Sékou Touré's survival meant the end of the French Community, almost before it had begun its uncertain life in West Africa. Senghor, the president of Senegal which was within the French Community, tried to form a union with the French South Saharan Sudan (Mali) in 1959, as a counterweight to Nkrumah and Sékou Touré's Guinea-Ghana union, but this was not a success. Nobody could afford to be less than Sékou Touré, and one by one the states within the French Community gave notice to deGaulle that they would leave and claim complete independence. By the end of August, 1960, Senegal, Mauritania, Mali, the Upper Volta, Niger, Chad, the Ivory Coast, Togo, Dahomey and the Cameroons were all independent and members of the United Nations [*Africa: Background for Today*, p .128, by Roy MacGregor-Hastie].

Nigeria was not slow in following Ghana and Guinea in the quest for independence. The people of Nigeria, however, had a special problem. Within its boundaries there are about 250 different tribes; and the goal of uniting all of them under the rule of a central government has not yet been attained. In 1900, while a British dependency, the country was divided into three administrative districts: the Southern Protectorate, the Northern Protectorate, and the Colony of Lagos. In 1906 the Colony of Lagos was affiliated with the Southern Protectorate, and in 1914 the two protectorates were merged under the rule of the Governor-General, Lord Lugard. But the territory was still far from being united, since it was divided into three regions. The Northern Region, inhabited mainly by Moslems, was under the jurisdiction of their Emirs; the Western Region was dominated by the Yoruba people;

whereas in the Eastern Region, the Ibos were the chief tribal group. In 1946 the Legislative Assembly of Nigeria was made more democratic, and Houses of Assembly were established in each of the three regions.

The founding of the Federation of Nigeria occurred in 1954. Under this set-up, general matters, such as foreign affairs, were handled by the Federal Legislature at Lagos, to which body each region sent representatives. Aside from the general matters, each region enjoyed autonomy in the management of its internal affairs.

When Nigeria became independent on October 1, 1960, the dominant political figures were Sir Abubakar Balewa; Chief Obafemi Awolowo; Dr. Nnamdi Azikiwe; and Sir Ahmadu Bello, Sardauna of Sokoto. Chief Awolowo was most powerful in the Western Region, the Sardauna of Sokoto in the Northern Region, and Dr. Azikiwe in the Eastern Region. These three supreme political leaders agreed to endorse Sir Abubakar Balewa as Federal Prime Minister of the new government. With Nigerian independence established, the British Governor-General, Sir James Robertson, retired. He was followed in that office by Dr. Azikiwe, who became the first Governor-General of the new Nigeria. Unfortunately the efforts of these leaders failed to unify the various regions of the country. Tensions and conflicts developed, especially during the elections in 1964 and 1965. Finally in January, 1966, a coup by young army officers led to the overthrow of the established regime and the death of Prime Minister Balewa. The Federal Cabinet then surrendered the political power to the commander of the army, General Agai-Ironsi, who thereupon established a military government and assigned military governors to the three regions, while attempts were made to draft a new constitution for the nation.

All this was bad enough, but much worse was to come. In the middle of 1967, the Eastern Region attempted to establish itself as the independent state of **Biafra.** This led to a civil war which raged until early 1970, when an uneasy peace was achieved. Nigeria is now ruled by a Supreme Military Council, headed by Major General Yakubu Gowon.

A British Commission for Peace in Nigeria was organized to help bring the tragic civil strife to an end. Lord Fenner Brockway and James Griffiths, MP, as agents of this peace commission, visited both Nigeria and Biafra in an effort to set in motion peace negotiations between the warring factions. Lord Brockway made a report of the mission in the pages of the *New Statesman,* a well-known London weekly. In discussing the difficulties of achieving a peace settlement between Nigeria and Biafra, Lord Brockway pointed out the grave international hazards involved:

> Both James Griffiths and I were gravely disturbed by the real possibility that the war (which will be long-lasting unless the opportunities of a cease-fire are now seized) could become a Great Power conflict rather than an African conflict. Russia as well as Britain is supplying military equipment to Nigeria, and there is British concern at the growth of Russian influence. France, despite denials, is indirectly supplying arms to Biafra through Gabon and the Ivory Coast. We saw arms manufactured in seven European countries which are provided to both sides through a highly-financed black market. We have asked the British government to invite all governments to place an embargo on the export of arms and the Council of Europe to investigate the black market deals ["Our Nigerian Peace Mission," in the *New Statesman,* January 3, 1969, by Lord Fenner Brockway].

It is to be hoped that the peoples of Nigeria may soon settle their differences and unite their efforts in the pursuits of peace and progress; for Africans, of whatever nation, cannot afford the costly luxury of internecine strife.

The preamble to the new Constitution adopted on October 31, 1960, by **The Republic of the Ivory Coast** declares that nation to be "one and indivisible, secular, democratic and social." The motto of the country is "Union, Discipline and Work." The official language is French. Under the able leadership of President Houphouet-Boigny, the country has enjoyed a high level of prosperity. The budget has been balanced and there are small surpluses available for capital development. The Ivory Coast is an associate member of the European Common Market, and the basis of its currency is the overseas franc. The capitol city, Abidjan, the chief port of the nation, is a thriving center of commerce and industry. Recently factories for the assembly of motor cars and the production of soluble coffee have been established there. The building of a chemical industry is planned for the near future. The economic future looks promising. In food products the Ivory Coast is self-sufficient; and its wealth of natural resources guarantees an extensive export trade. There are over twelve million acres of forest in the southern part of the country. Among the timber exports are mahogany, iroko, and other high-quality woods. The total timber export figure for 1964 was one and a half million tons. Among other important exports were cocoa (124,000 tons), coffee (204,282 tons), bananas (130,000 tons), manganese (104,000 tons), and diamonds (198,000 carats).

The Ivory Coast is a modern democratic state and its policy for the future was stated by President Felix Houphouet-Boigny on July 14, 1960, as follows:

The Ivory Coast is, and must remain, not only the land of liberty, but above all, the land of fraternity. If we know how to unite, if we know how to prove to the world our political maturity, if we know how to meet the new responsibilities that are ours, if we know how to keep the friendships that are precious for our development—then the future will indeed be, as is the earnest wish of all of us in this beautiful Ivory Coast with such great potentialities, a radiant future, in harmony with the fiery sun of our beautiful country.

Sierra Leone became independent on April 27, 1961, with Sir Milton Margai as Prime Minister. The country, as a member of the British Commonwealth, was regarded as a constitutional monarchy, with the Queen of England as sovereign. On the death of Sir Milton Margai in 1964, his brother Sir Albert Margai became prime minister. The new prime minister favored a republican-type government based on a one-party regime. The opposition to this scheme resulted in political discord, which finally resulted in a military coup d'état on March 23, 1967. Since that date Sierra Leone has been controlled by the National Council of Reformation (NCR), composed for the most part of army and police officers, headed by Colonel A. T. Juxon-Smith. The NCR is attempting to eliminate internal strife in the nation and to revive the national economy by reducing its debts and fighting corruption in the civil service. It is hoped that the NCR will succeed in its objectives and then return the government to civilian control.

Gambia is a narrow strip along the Gambia River, and has a population of only 350,000. Gambian independence was attained on February 18, 1965. It is a British Commonwealth state with Queen Elizabeth II of Great Britain as head of state, represented by Alhaji Sir Farimang Singhatch as Governor-General. The prime minister at present is Sir David Jawara. The principal export of Gambia consists of groundnuts, which was not large enough in 1965 to keep the economy on a self-supporting basis. So the new state had to depend on financial assistance from Great Britain. The economic situation is now improving. "Wholly dependent on its groundnut harvest, Gambia seemed at the time of independence, condemned to live eternally off British aid. But the country has succeeded better than expected. In 1967, she was able to cut down on her consumption of British aid, and the positive results of this exercise seem to have strengthened Gambian confidence." (*Africa 1968*, p. 175.)

Congo-Kinshasa (formerly the Belgian Congo) proclaimed itself an independent state on June 30, 1960. The first prime minister, Mr. Patrice Lumumba, attempted to promote political unity of the various regions of the country, but he soon faced a secessionist movement in the Katanga district. Lumumba gained a majority of the Congolese Parliament, but he was outmaneuvered by his political enemies. The Belgian vested interests did not desire to lose control of the copper mines of Katanga, so they managed to place Kasavubu in the presidency. President Kasavubu, after being made an officer in the Belgian army, usurped power and dismissed Lumumba from his post without a parliamentary vote. In addition, a secessionist movement arose in Katanga led by a man named Tshombe; and, fearing the power of Lumumba to oppose this movement, the partisans of Tshombe assassinated Lumumba on January 17, 1961. The Tshombe government stayed in power until November 24, 1965, when it was ousted by a coup. General Joseph D. Mobutu, commander of the Congolese army, was placed in the presidency by the High Command of the army, so that law and order could be restored. A policy of Congolization was adopted by the Mobutu regime. The mainstay of the Congo economy is copper. Three hundred thousand tons of this valuable metal are mined annually. Export of copper amounts to 40 percent of the total of all exports of the country and accounts for 70 percent of earnings in foreign exchange. The Congo-Kinshasa government held title to 17 percent of the shares of the Union Minière du Haut Katanga, the corporation in control of copper mining; but in actual practice it had no control over the managerial policies of the Union. A series of crises developed between the Union and the government. To cite a contemporary authoritative reference work:

> Tension reached a high point when the Union refused to move its headquarters to Kinshasa in accordance with Congolese law. The Union was Congolized and on January 1, 1967, became the Societe General Congolaise des Minerais (GECOMIN). This move had been prepared for by the adoption in May 1965 of the Bakadjika law, named after its author, stipulating the restitution of the ownership of its soil and underground resources to Congo-Kinshasa. . . .
> On November 24, 1967, the Chief of State took stock of what had been done to clean up public finances and announced the adoption of a Development Plan. There were indications in this speech that the leaders had arrived at the conclusion that all their problems stemmed from a shortage of qualified personnel—there were only 13 university graduates when independence was proclaimed on June 30, 1960—and that efforts should be directed towards the overcoming of this shortage [*Africa 1968*, p. 157].

At the present time in Congo-Kinshasa, 2,500 students are pursuing courses in higher education in the following schools: Lovanium University, Lubumbashi University, the National Teaching Institute, the National School of Law and Administration, and the Congolese Political Institute. With a vigorous educational program tied in with the control of the natural resources of the Congo-Kinshasa Republic by the Congolese people, this vast region should eventually enjoy an era of great progress.

Congo-Brazzaville (formerly known as the French Congo) is noted for its small population; all told, only 882,900. Yet this nation is one of the most advanced in all Africa. The enrollment in primary schools is close to 100 percent. Over 200,000 students are attending schools, with one Congolese out of four either attending a school or a university. Besides this, there are almost 700 students studying in foreign lands. Industrial development is brisk and extensive in the fields of agriculture, forestry, and animal husbandry. This nation became independent on August 15, 1960. The first president, the Abbe Fulton Youlou, was deposed in a mid-August revolution in 1963. A new constitution adopted after the August Revolution declared the Congo-Brazzaville Republic to be "indivisible, secular, democratic and social." The incumbent president is Mr. Alphonse Massamba-Debat, who was elected December 19, 1963.

In the East African region, **Uganda** holds an enviable position; since its lands are blessed with great natural wealth. The chief agricultural products are cotton and coffee, and these staples are owned and controlled by Africans. The years 1966 and 1967 were highly prosperous: Over 400,000 bales of cotton were produced and a coffee crop of about 150,000 tons was realized. The chief mineral resource is copper, of which 16,150 tons were mined in 1966. A hydro-electric power plant at the Owen Falls Dam, located at Jinja, has a capacity of 150,000 kilowatts. This facility serves both Uganda and Kenya.

Education in Uganda is well organized, with a large number of primary and secondary schools. The University College of Makerere was established in 1939 at Kampala for the benefit of students from all over East Africa. In 1963 it became part of the University of East Africa.

In 1962, Uganda became an independent state, affiliated with the British Commonwealth. A constitution was adopted, which provided for a federal coalition between the central government and the kingdoms of Ankole, Buganda, Bunyoro, and Toro, and the territory of Busoga. In 1963 the governor-generalship was abolished, and the Kabaka of Buganda became the Head of State. He was subsequently elected president by the National Assembly. The federal constitution was suspended in 1966 by the Prime Minister, Dr. A. Milton Obote, who suspected the Kabaka of a plot against the government involving outside military intervention. The Kabaka was forced out of the presidency, and went into exile in Great Britain. "In 1967, Obote consolidated his coalition with a new Constitution which gave strong powers to the President, abolished the entrenched powers of the traditional rulers in the Bantu south, and divided Buganda into four provinces." (*Africa 1968*, p. 295.) The incumbent president is Dr. Obote, who possesses all executive authority, and who governs the country with the assistance of an appointed cabinet, selected from a National Assembly with a total membership of ninety-two.

Up until 1920, **Kenya** was called British East Africa, and the first African member did not enter the Legislative Council until 1944. A railroad from Mombasa, the chief port, was extended into the interior of the country at the turn of the century. The High Commissioner, Sir Charles Elliot, encouraged European settlers to enter the country and develop its natural resources. The European settlers did help to make the railroad profitable by their agricultural production, but this led to serious problems over landownership with the African peoples, especially the Kikuyu and Masai. An English army officer, Colonel R. Meinertzhagen, visited Nairobi, the capital of Kenya, in 1902. He tells of meeting the High Commissioner, and of discussing governmental policy with him. This incident is of sufficient importance to call for notice. The story is best related in the words of the Colonel:

> Apparently Charles Elliot, the High Commissioner, learned that Beatrice Webb was my aunt, so he asked me to dine with him this evening. . . . He amazed me with his views on the future of East Africa. He envisaged a thriving colony of thousands of Europeans with their families, the whole of the country from the Aberdares and Mount Kenya to the German border [i.e., of Tanganyika] divided up into farms; the whole

of the Rift Valley cultivated or grazed, and the whole country of Lumbwa, Nandi to Elgon and almost to Baringo under white settlement. He intends to confine natives to reserves and use them as cheap labor on farms. I suggested that the country belonged to Africans and that their interests must prevail over the interests of strangers. . . . I said that some day the African would be educated and armed; that would lead to a clash. Elliot thought that that day was so far distant as not to matter and that by that time the European element would be strong enough to look after themselves; but I am convinced that in the end the Africans will win and that Elliot's policy can lead only to trouble and disappointment [*Kenya Diary, 1902–1906* by Colonel R. Meinertzhagen, London, 1957. Cited by Basil Davidson in *The African Past*, pp. 365–66].

The reader may recall the Mau Mau uprising in the early 1950's by some members of the Kikuyu tribe. This movement was anti-European and anti-Christian and was based on the maldistribution of land among the African peoples of Kenya. The movement was led by Mr. Jomo Kenyatta. The rebellion was aimed against European settlers, but it turned into a civil war, since most of the Kikuyu did not support the Mau Maus. From hideouts in the forests of the Aberdare Mountains, the Mau Mau raided farms in the Kenya highlands. By 1955, the worst of the rebellion was over; but, all in all, about 2,000 Africans, 32 Europeans, and 26 Asians had been slain. Some changes for the better were made as a result of the Mau Mau troubles, since scattered plots of land were rearranged so as to give African farmers compact land plots, which were easier to work than the hitherto scattered parcels.

Kenya became an independent nation on December 12, 1963, with Jomo Kenyatta as prime minister. At the present time (1969), Mr. Kenyatta is president of Kenya. He is an able and cultured man, having specialized in the study of anthropology under the tutelage of Professor Bronislaw Malinowski, at the University of London. For the past thirty years

Kenya has maintained, for the most part, a steady pace of progress. Its developments in agriculture, trade, industry, and education have been encouraging—especially since World War II. About 1,300 Kenyan students attend three colleges in East Africa, and about 4,000 are in schools in Great Britain and the United States. The Royal College, established in Nairobi in 1956, is an outstanding institution of higher learning.

Like many other new African nations, **Tanzania** has a rather involved history. The territory known as German East Africa became a British mandate colony in 1918, after the end of World War I. Then its name was changed to Tanganyika. Up until 1886 nearly all of Tanganyika, as well as Kenya, was under the dominion of the Sultan of Zanzibar. At that time Great Britain annexed Kenya, and Germany seized Tanganyika. The method by which the Sultanate of Zanzibar was carved up has been well described by Carveth Wells, whose account we quote:

As for the wretched Sultan of Zanzibar, he had to be thankful that he was permitted to retain a narrow strip of the east coast about six hundred miles long and ten miles wide plus a few islands close to the coast. . . .

But even so, it soon became evident that great inconveniences were likely to arise if the sultan was allowed to have real sovereignty over any part of his former possessions, so in 1890 Germany made the sultan sell outright the Tanganyika portion of his coastal strip for four million marks, while England generously consented to lease the rest.

By this time the real estate of the Sultan of Zanzibar had diminished from an area much larger than France, Germany and England combined, to a few little islands, including Zanzibar, with a total area less than Rhode Island. Even this was too much of an inconvenience for Great Britain to bear. Once again the three Great Powers (England, Germany and France) put their heads together; and in November 1890, in return for not objecting to her proclaiming the Sultanate of Zanzibar a British protectorate, England gave Germany the island of Heligoland and recognized the claims of France to the enormous island of Madagascar [*Introducing Africa,* pp. 140–41, by Carveth Wells].

Under the British mandate, Tanganyika was ruled by a governor. In 1925, Sir Donald Cameron became governor of Tanganyika, and he set about reorganizing the government. Cameron had been an official in Nigeria under Lord Lugard and had been favorably impressed by the policy of indirect rule. He recognized the authority of the various African chiefs, who were given a voice in the government of the nation. A Legislative Council was instituted in 1926, but elections were not held until 1958. In 1959 a Council of Ministers was organized as advisors to the governor. The 1960 elections gave the elected members a majority in the Legislative Council, with the African leader of the majority party, Mr. Julius Nyerere, occupying the post of Chief Minister. Near the end of 1961 Tanganyika became an independent nation, with Nyerere as president.

Zanzibar was a protectorate under British rule until the end of 1963, when it became independent. Shortly afterward, a revolution was staged and the Sultan and his government were abolished. On April 23, 1964, Zanzibar and Pemba merged with Tanganyika to become a United Republic. On October 29, 1964, the new state was named the United Republic of Tanzania.

Education is an important factor in the development of Tanzania. About 750,000 pupils attend primary schools. The secondary schools have 25,000 students enrolled. In 1961, the University College of Tanganyika opened at Dar es Salaam; and in 1963 this institution became a part of the University of East Africa. There are now 300 Tanzanian students in attendance at the University of East Africa and about 1,500 are registered in outside colleges and universities. The 1967–68 budget allocated 17.6 percent for education. President Julius Nyerere is not only a statesman, but also a distinguished scholar; he has translated Shakespeare's play *Julius Caesar* into Swahili, the official language of Tanzania.

The British protectorate of Nyasaland became independent, under the name of **Malawi** in 1964, and in July, 1966, it attained the status of a republic, with Dr. Hastings Kamuzu Banda as president. Being a landlocked nation, the country is not as free as it would like to be. Its exports and imports must pass mainly through the port of Beira in Mozambique. Large quantities of meat and sugar are purchased from Rhodesia; while 100,000 natives of Malawi work in mines and on farms in the Union of South Africa. The economic situation, however, is improving. At present, the chief exports are tea, tobacco, and cotton; but fishing and forestry resources are being developed and factories of various sorts are being constructed. The people of Malawi are for the most part farmers, fishermen, and herdsmen. Education is being developed as rapidly as possible. In 1965, 337,720 students were attending primary schools; 7,985 were enrolled in secondary schools; and 1,387 were engaged in teacher training courses of study. The British government made a one-million-pound grant for the establishment of the University of Malawi, which opened its doors in October, 1965, at Zomba, the capital of Malawi. In 1966, 300 students were attending the new institution. Six hundred pupils are in residence in foreign colleges and universities.

Until 1964, **Zambia** (formerly Northern Rhodesia) was part of a federation whose other members were Malawi and Rhodesia. Efforts are now being made to cut contacts with South Africa and Rhodesia to a minimum: Dependence on export outlets controlled by neighboring nations is not a healthy economic situation, so the present aim is to develop trade contacts with Congo-Kinshasa and Tanzania. In February, 1967, Zambia arranged with Tanzania for the construction of a 1,000-mile oil pipe line to link the two countries. In the same year, President Kenneth Kaunda of Zambia paid an official visit to Peking, China. The Chinese government, President Kaunda reported, agreed to finance the construction of a 1,000-mile Zambia-Tanzania railroad line, to be known as the Tanzambia Line. The economic outlook of Zambia seems to be favorable, for: "Zambia enjoys a favorable trade balance; her mineral resources have increased considerably, with copper taking a clear lead among exports. Zambia therefore has in prospect a spectacular economic spurt forward— provided she can find ways to solve the problems imposed on her by her environment and her lack of direct access to the sea." (*Africa 1968*, p. 313.)

Educational improvement policies are being vigorously pursued. There are now over 400,000 students in primary schools and about 16,000 in secondary institutions. Lusaka University was established in 1966, with faculties in Science, Medicine, Literature, and Sociology. Administration and Polytechnic Institutes are planned for the near future.

Alongside and within the Union of South Africa were three regions, known as Basutoland, Bechuanaland, and Swaziland. These were called High Commission Territories, and each was presided over by a Resident Commissioner assisted by the local chiefs.

Basutoland declared independence on October 4, 1966, under the name of **Lesotho**. It is a small country with an area of less than twelve thousand square miles. It is entirely surrounded by the apartheid state of South Africa. Lesotho is a constitutional monarchy, with King Moshoeshoe II as ruler. Like most constitutional monarchs, the king is mainly ornamental; since the power behind the throne is in the hands of the prime minister: Chief Leabua Jonathan. In order to survive, Lesotho must get along with the South African government. This caused trouble right from the start. There was a conflict between the Basutoland Congress Party, with Panafrican and Socialist orientation, and Prime Minister Leabua Jonathan, with the king caught in the middle. After some violent incidents in December, 1966, the sovereign was placed under house arrest. Chief Leabua Jonathan declared that: "We are not indifferent to the ideal of Panafricanism and African unity, but our own country's interests dictate our present course."

The Republic of **Botswana** (formerly the British protectorate of Bechuanaland), achieved freedom in 1966. "This is a flat, dry country," Mr. Kingsnorth notes, "where the main occupation is cattle rearing. Its great interest lies in its main tribe, the Bamangwato. Their reputation was made by Khama III, who ruled from 1872 until 1923. . . . It was at his request that Bechuanaland became a British Protectorate in 1885. Unfortunately confusion arose over the succession when Seretse Khama aroused opposition in 1949 by marrying an English girl; but in 1961 he was permitted to return to political life, and his Democratic party won the first general election in 1965. When Bechuanaland became independent as the Republic of Botswana in 1966, Seretse Khama became President." (*Africa South of the Sahara*, p. 153, by G. W. Kingsnorth.) Botswana has a common border with the independent state of Zambia; and this has given rise to an interesting situation. South African nationalists, in flight from the apartheid police, escape into Botswana, where they are sheltered in a camp at Francistown. From there they travel northward across the Zambezi River into Zambia, where the International Refugees' Council of Zambia gives them sanctuary. From a reliable work of reference, we learn that:

Recently, however, the flow of political refugees into the former British protectorates has dwindled considerably. At the same time, Botswana has acquired another problem: the reverse flow into South Africa of trained South African guerrilleros. Bots-- wana can apparently not afford to displease its powerful neighbors, South Africa and Rhodesia, by encouraging this freedom transit. In 1967, the Botswana police arrested a number of guerrilleros; the judges sentenced them only for illegal entry and illegal possession of firearms [*Africa 1968,* p. 127].

After the Boer War, **Swaziland** came under British control, and was made a High Commission protectorate in 1907. There was an election in 1967, which was won without opposition by the National Council Party of King Sobhuza II. Independence was finally achieved in Swaziland in September, 1968. The Africa correspondent of the *Christian Science Monitor* visited this area a few years back and noted that:

> Progress is on the way. Swazi soil will soon be bearing the biggest man-made forests in the world. Britain's Colonial Development Corporation has a big scheme under way in Swaziland's Usutu Forest and there are other company projects. Next must come the railway to ship the timber out and open the country to development.
>
> Backed by a council of chiefs and headmen, Sobhuza wields extensive rule over his countrymen, dispensing tribal justice and controlling a Swazi national treasury. . . . Inevitably there must come a legislative council and the paraphernalia of parliamentary rule [*The New Face of Africa: South of the Sahara,* p. 219, by John Hughes].

Of the North African countries, **Libya** was the first to gain independence. It was a self-governing colony under Italian control from 1911 to 1943. This territory adopted a constitution and declared itself free in October, 1951. The constitution, modified on December 8, 1962, declared Libya to be an independent Islamic kingdom, with Arabic the official language. The ruler of the United Kingdom of Libya is King

Idris I. The wealth of the country is concentrated in its petroleum industry. The first oil well was drilled in 1957. Now Libya holds seventh rank among the petroleum-producing nations of the world. In 1961 over 5 million barrels of petroleum were produced; by 1966 the total for that year had climbed to over 550 million barrels. Men who were formerly shepherds are now becoming clerks in banks under the new regime created by oil. Operators of caravans are transforming themselves into oil entrepreneurs, and the rising class of businessmen work in modern buildings fitted out with fluorescent lighting. Education is not being neglected. The Libyan University was established on December 15, 1959, at Benghazi and includes the following Faculties: Arts, Law, Business, Economics, and Science.

In 1934, a movement for the liberation of **Tunisia** was started by Mr. Habib Bourguiba, the leader of the Neo-Destour (New Constitution) party. Within a four-year period Bourguiba was in prison and his party suppressed. After the collapse of France in World War II, Bourguiba regained his liberty; though trouble with the French after the war caused him to flee to Egypt. From this base he organized a resistance movement against France. After two years of guerrilla war, the French forces agreed to political autonomy for Tunisia in 1955, and Bourguiba returned from exile to head the new government. Independence was announced on March 20, 1956, and the new Republic of Tunisia was officially proclaimed on July 25, 1957, with President Habib Bourguiba as Head of State. The Tunisian Constitution, as approved by the Constituent National Assembly, June 1, 1959, declares the nation to be: "A free, independent sovereign state, with Islam as its religion and Arabic as its official language." The course of events in Tunisia for the first decade of the new regime was most encouraging. At the beginning of 1968 Tunisia embarked on the second decade of a new age.

At the threshold of this second decade, Tunisia appears as a model of political stability achieved without any waste of human energy, and with hardly any emigration of qualified personnel. It provides the rest of the world with the image of a country hard at work pursuing without ostentation a policy of austerity, building a cooperative form of socialism in a climate which is deliberately constructive and evolutionary. . . . Tunisia has also achieved a harmonious symbiosis of her Arabic and African roots, of her Mediterranean location and her resolutely modernistic posture [*Africa 1968,* p. 289].

The educational system of the country is flourishing on all levels. The University of Tunis has Faculties of Arts, Humanities, Law, Economics, Science, Engineering, Agriculture, and Medicine, as well as a group of specialized institutes. In 1966–67 the University of Tunis had a student body of nearly 7,000; and there were nearly 3,000 Tunisian students in foreign universities.

After many years under French and Spanish domination, the ancient kingdom of **Morocco** regained independence on March 2, 1956. The new constitution of Morocco, adopted by referendum, December 7, 1962, states in its preamble: "The Kingdom of Morocco is a sovereign Moslem State, its official language is Arabic. . . . In its capacity as an African state, one of its objectives is the achievement of African unity." The present ruler of Morocco is King Hassan II. The monarchical succession is hereditary, the crown being transmitted to direct male descendants in order of primogeniture.

"Among the countries of Africa," according to *Africa 1968* (page 225), "Morocco is one of those with the greatest potential. Its exceptional geographical situation which places it at the crossroads of major cultural and economic trends enables it to trade with America, Europe, sub-Saharan Africa and the other nations of the Maghreb. It has numerous and varied natural resources, a well developed infra-structure, an industry which is already large and diversified, as well as incomparable tourist attractions."

Its educational program is extensive and well developed. In 1966–67, over 1,120,000 students were enrolled in primary schools and over 211,000 in secondary schools. For higher education, the figures were as follows: Law—3,330 students; Arts—2,000; Science—673; Medicine—588; and Miscellaneous—approximately 1,500.

> By the end of 1960 [we are told by a well-informed foreign correspondent], **Algeria** was the only country in North Africa which had not achieved independence . . . pressure from Tunisia and Morocco on both the French government and the Algerian native politicians was especially great because the three North African countries together form the Mahgreb, an area with a single heritage of custom and civilization, and there was even a movement devoted to the re-creation of a single Mahgreb community. To the south of Algeria, the French-speaking states of Mali and Niger gloated over their neighbor's political backwardness [*Africa: Background for Today*, pp. 145–46, by Roy MacGregor-Hastie].

General DeGaulle and the French settlers in Algeria frowned on any liberation movement in that country. Oil had been discovered in the Sahara Desert, and the French element did not wish to lose this new source of wealth. The Soviet Union and the Peoples Republic of China had friends among Algerian leaders who sought freedom from French domination. When a provisional government was formed by Algerians in 1959, the Peking regime gave it diplomatic recognition and donated funds to help it along.

A Pan-African Congress was convened in Tunis in February, 1960, which planned the formation of an African Liberation Army which was to "sweep the white man into the sea." Before such a scheme could be realized, the Algerian National Liberation Front organized its own army, which was generously financed and furnished with arms by the Soviet Union and Communist China. From the end of 1960 to the middle of 1962 the provisional government of Algeria waged war against France. Finally a cease-fire was arranged between the rebels and the DeGaulle regime at a meeting at Evian, Switzerland, in March, 1962. An agreement was arrived at for Algerian independence on July 2, 1962; and on September 15, 1963, Mr. Ahmed Ben Bella became president of the Algerian Republic. The Ben Bella regime was terminated by an army coup on June 19, 1965. The country is now governed by the National Council of the Algerian Revolution, under the chairmanship of Colonel Houari Boumédienne.

The natural resources of the nation are being exploited and expanded. The rich petroleum resources point to future progress in the national economy. The educational system is still in a rudimentary stage of development, but the number of pupils attending the schools has doubled since independence was declared in 1962.

The ancient land of **Egypt** (now known as the **United Arab Republic**), after flourishing for thousands of years under its native kings, finally succumbed to foreign domination. Since the seventh century B.C., the country has been ruled by Assyrians, Persians, Greeks, Romans, Arabs, Turks, and Englishmen. Native rule returned in 1922.

Modern Egypt was created during one of Napoleon Bonaparte's famous military expeditions. It was another man of genius, Mohammed Aly, who took charge at the beginning of the 19th century and decided to effect its recovery. His achievements included dams, land tenure legislation, communication networks and the training of administrative personnel. In 1869, the opening of the Suez Canal made Egypt a crossroad of international commerce. The British occupation, in 1882, favored monoculture by the development of cotton plantations. Today, one of Egypt's biggest problems is to reduce this acreage to more competitive proportions.

Between 1920 and 1950, upon the initiative of the Misr Bank and of its founder, Talaat Harb, an active bourgeoisie created viable industries; in 1961 the Nasser regime nationalized 85% of the country's economy. After years of militant Pan-Arabism, the country has now been obliged to concentrate on domestic development. For Egyptians today, the word Misr (Egypt) has an almost mystical resonance; that of Ourouba (Arabism) has receded to only a secondary significance [*Africa 1968*, p. 301].

Education, particularly higher education, is extensive and well organized. The University of Al Azhar, is a thousand years old, having been founded in the year 970. It consists of eight Faculties, 750 professors, and 8,100 students. Cairo University, founded in 1908, has thirteen Faculties, two Institutes for Higher Studies, and a branch at Khartoum, in the Sudan. The teaching staff numbers 2,379, and the total of enrolled students is 57,440. Alexandria University, founded in 1942, has a student body of 30,000 pupils, and the eight Faculties are manned by a teaching staff of 825 members. Ain Shams University, established in 1950 at Heliopolis, has nine Faculties, a teaching staff of over 1,000, and a student body of over 31,000. The newest institution for higher studies, founded a few years ago, is Assiut University, with six Faculties, 700 professors, and 7,345 students. In Cairo, there is the American University, which was founded in 1919. It is a private institution with a professorial staff of 65 and a student body of 732. Besides these institutions, there are the following higher Institutes in Egypt: The Electronics Institute in Menouf, the Petroleum Institute in Suez, The Institute of Technology in Helouan, and The Cancer Institute in Cairo.

From 1899 to 1955 **The Sudan** was governed by an Anglo-Egyptian Condominium. In 1953 Great Britain and Egypt offered The Sudan a choice between union with Egypt or independence. In January, 1954, elections were held for the formation of a Constituent Assembly. A majority was gained by the Nationalist Union Party, led by Mr. Ismail el-Azhari;

and on December 19, 1955, the Parliament, by unanimous vote, proclaimed The Sudan to be an independent democratic republic. National Independence Day was celebrated on January 1, 1956. There was a military coup in 1958, which suspended the 1955 Constitution; but this military government was overthrown in 1964, and the 1955 Constitution is now back in force. The Sudan Republic has three very valuable assets, listed below:

1. An administrative elite, thanks to which the state is able to function.
2. Vigilant and militant trade unions, the solidarity of which has been cemented by many trials and substantial successes.
3. Its student youth, which is impatient, occasionally turbulent, but thirsting for culture and responsibility. These three factors make up an enviable capital: they presage important achievements to come [*Africa 1968*, p. 273].

The latest data on education in The Sudan are given in *Africa 1968*, p. 274, in the following table:

(1964–65)	Student Totals
Nursery Schools	2,210
State Primary	466,873
Private Primary	12,802
Intermediary	27,283
State Secondary	15,955
Private Secondary	9,217
Technical (1966)	5,934
Teacher Training	2,310
University Level (1966)	3,060

His Imperial Highness, Haile Selassie, presides over the destinies of **Ethiopia,** the world's oldest empire. Driven from his throne by the Italian invasion in 1936, he was able to return in 1941, after the liberation of his dominions during

World War II. Eritrea, a neighboring country, became independent in 1952, but formed a federation with Ethiopia. By 1962 the Eritreans admitted that political autonomy was not practical for them, so Emperor Haile Selassie dissolved the federation and made Eritrea a province of Ethiopia. Somalia (formerly the territories of British and Italian Somaliland) declared for independence in 1960. In 1950, when Italian Somaliland became a U.N. Trust Territory, Selassie protested that the land actually belonged to Ethiopia. By producing maps, the Emperor was able to prove title to the Somalia province of Ogaden, which he then incorporated into the Ethiopian Empire.

Ethiopia is in the forefront of the new African revolution. It was noticed by Mr. John Hughes, Africa correspondent for the *Christian Science Monitor*, that:

> African leaders from Kwame Nkrumah to Tom Mboya are welcomed in the Ethiopian capital. African students have been offered scholarships at Addis Ababa's University College. Important African anniversaries and freedom days are celebrated with publicity in the capital. . . .
>
> The Emperor has aligned with African states in condemnation of South Africa's apartheid policy, and dedicated Ethiopia to assisting the achievement of independence of "our African brothers who are still under mandatory rule.". . .
>
> All this indicates that Haile Selassie is leading his country, with its longest history of independence in Africa, to what he hopes will be a position of stature and influence in the new black councils of the continent [*The New Face of Africa: South of the Sahara*, pp. 268–69, by John Hughes].

The Ethiopian emperor made a tour of the Soviet Union in 1959, and the Communist leaders gave him a royal welcome. As Mr. Hughes described it:

> During his visit to Leningrad, the Emperor was escorted to

the Museum of Anthropology and Ethnography to be shown drawings of himself and his father, together with pictures of nineteenth and twentieth century Russian and Soviet hospitals in Ethiopia, and a display of Ethiopian newspapers and a modern Ethiopian Bible. There was even some talk of a merger between the Ethiopian Coptic Church and the Russian Orthodox Church which had first been mooted in Czarist days.

The Emperor paid handsome tribute to Soviet achievements and at the end of his visit it was announced that Mr. Khrushchev would pay a return visit to Ethiopia, and that the Soviet Union would grant a long-term, low-interest loan to Ethiopia of $100,000,000. The Soviet Union was to build a technical school in Addis Ababa, would send machinery and other items to Ethiopia in terms of a trade pact, and would make the Emperor a personal gift of an Ilyushin 14 aircraft. Since then the Soviets have followed up with an agreement to make a geological survey of Ethiopia for minerals, to establish gold-mining plants and to build a big oil refinery at Assab on the Red Sea [*The New Face of Africa: South of the Sahara*, pp. 269–70, by John Hughes].

In some of the Western bloc powers, there was fear that Ethiopia might be engulfed by the Communist bloc; but, as John Hughes noted, "it is difficult to believe that the Lion of Judah is inviting the Russian Bear to share his lair." (*The New Face of Africa*, p. 270.)

The Emperor's palace in the Ethiopian capital city of Addis Ababa is a superb example of African-Oriental grandeur, and it contains within its walls many ancient treasures of high artistic merit. Not far from the Imperial Palace, on a hilltop, is the site of Africa Hall, the headquarters of the Organization of African Unity. This imposing edifice, done in modernistic style, is graced with great scenes in stained-glass, depicting Ethiopian life, reminiscent of the illuminated manuscripts of medieval days.

The Ethiopian people are fortunate to have a man like Haile Selassie to guide the destinies of their country. He is indubitably a great man. The well-known journalist, Karl von Wiegand, declared: "I know of no king or emperor who surpassed him in natural dignity, graciousness, refinement and ease. I have seen a number of white monarchs who do not even approach him in those qualities or, perhaps even in intelligence." (*Cosmopolitan* Magazine, March, 1936.)

Mr. J. A. Rogers, journalist, anthropologist, and historian, knew Emperor Haile Selassie well. "No picture of him," said Mr. Rogers, "has ever been able to capture the essence of his spirit. So far as a general impression of him is concerned, he has been truly described as a 'black edition of the pictured Christ.' His beard and curly hair provide unmistakable proof of his African ancestry. In color he is a lightish black-brown and considerably darker than the published pictures of him. (*World's Great Men of Color*, Vol. I, p. 289, by J. A. Rogers.)

If the Ethiopian emperor has made a favorable impression on world opinion, the same may be said of the Ethiopian people. An American globetrotter, Mr. Don Carl Steffen, gives his impression of the people of Ethiopia, as follows: "Today's 'typical' Ethiopian is a proud man, seemingly without complexes—either superior or inferior—ranging in color from light tan to blueblack ebony, handsome and of a regal carriage in movement." (*The Splendour of Africa*, p. 15, by Don Carl Steffen.)

There is a great demand for education in Ethiopia, and the school system is doing its best to cope with the situation. Over 400,000 students are enrolled in primary schools, with instruction conducted in the Amharic language. The secondary schools have enrolled more than 35,000 pupils. In the realm of higher education the University College of Addis Ababa is the outstanding institution. It has about 2,500 students, with an additional 2,000 in an extension division. Among its Faculties are the Institute of Ethiopian Studies and the College of Theology. The last-mentioned institution is a university center for all the Oriental Apostolic Churches.

Another country, not among the newly liberated nations, which must be mentioned, since it is now a part of Africa resurgent, is **Liberia**. This West African state became an independent state on July 26, 1847. For more than a century Liberia just jogged along, seemingly on the highroad to nowhere. But now there are the hustle and bustle of progress in the land. As recently as 1954 it could be said that: "Liberia is still one of the most backward of West African countries. It has no railroads and very few roads worthy of the name." (*Introducing Africa*, p. 77, by Carveth Wells.) By the end of the 1960's, the picture was quite different. From an authoritative work of reference we learn that:

Liberia should be regarded as a rather special case among African nations, if economic expansion and political stability are valid indices. . . . Thirteen years ago, there was one bank in Liberia. There are seven now. Twenty years ago, there were no roads, no railways, no airports and no industry; now the road, rail and air networks are serving a growing industry. With its economy booming, Liberia enjoys a rare privilege; that of having a substantial trade surplus. . . . An improvement in living standards, the development of hygiene and the systematic elimination of illiteracy are part of Liberia's daily life and efforts.

In foreign affairs, the country's desire to intensify the process of integration with other African nations has led the government to seek a rapprochement with its neighbors. Liberia was one of the founders of the OAU Charter and the initiator of a free exchange zone founded in August 1964 with Sierra Leone, Guinea and the Ivory Coast. President Tubman would like his country to become a link between anglophone and francophone Africa. He is one of the most determined adversaries of Portugal (against which he has declared a total embargo), as well as South Africa and Rhodesia [*Africa 1968,* p. 203].

Liberia's principal exports are rubber and iron ore, which together account for 90 percent of the nation's exports. Its iron ore production is exceeded only by the outputs of Canada and Sweden. Plans are under way for establishing an iron industry complex in the port city of Buchanan and for the construction of an oil refinery in Monrovia. Diamond and gold mines are now being worked. In 1965, 244,000 carats of diamonds were produced, and in 1966 the total number of carats rose to 555,000. Gold production in 1965 was 116 pounds, which in 1966 rose to 297 pounds. Liberia has nearly 14,000 square miles of forests, which will prove to be a source of great wealth when properly developed.

The latest nation to join the forward march of free Africa is **Equatorial Guinea,** which became independent in December, 1968. This tiny territory, formerly known as Spanish Guinea, borders upon Gabon, Cameroon, and the Atlantic Ocean. Equatorial Guinea is comprised of the Rio Muni territory, the island of Fernando Po, and a few nearby smaller islands. Its chief exports are cacao and coffee.

Although not on the African mainland, we may consider **Madagascar** as an African country. On October 14, 1958, Madagascar was proclaimed a republic, and on January 26, 1960, it became an independent nation. The president of the Republic of Madagascar is Mr. Philibert Tsiranana. The party in power is the Parti Social Démocrate (Social Democratic Party). In early September, 1967, the annual congress of the Parti Social Démocrate was held; and the question arose as to whether the drive for socialism should be rapid or gradual. The viewpoint of President Tsiranana was adopted. He came out in favor of a "practical and human socialism which lives and prospers without being mesmerized by lofty doctrines which all too often have little relevance to the actual reality with which we have to deal."

Education is well organized in Madagascar. The enrollment of students is as follows: Primary—650,000; Secondary and Technical—60,000; Higher Education—3,100. The University of Madagascar includes Faculties of Science and Technology, Law and Economics, Medicine, Legal Studies, and Business. There are also institutes for Social Welfare and Public Works, a Teacher-Training School for Advanced Agronomy, a National School of Telecommunications, a National Institute of Administration, and an Isotope Laboratory.

The apartheid **Union of South Africa** has not joined the new African revolution, and has no intention of doing so. Africans, who form 69 percent of the population of the country, are being kept down by a European minority of 18 percent. (The remaining 13 percent is composed of "Coloureds" [a mixture of black Africans and white Europeans] and Asians [mainly migrants from India].) This has turned the nation into a potential powder keg, since the Africans are determined to be free, and the government is equally determined to keep them in bondage. Eventually conditions must change. "It is impossible to believe," as Mr. Hughes states, "that South Africa can escape the African revolution which has swept across most of the continent. . . . For the moment South Africa seems a bastion of white rule, out of character with the rest of the changed map of Africa. Yet if all the lessons of the African revolution mean anything, Africans will guide the force of change here too. And it will come quicker than any of us imagine." (*The New Face of Africa*, pp. 210–11, by John Hughes.)

Rhodesia is theoretically a British colony, but in practice the government is independent. With a population of 4,000,000 Africans and 200,000 Europeans, the Europeans control the state and the Africans are held in a condition of serfdom. This sort of thing must change, but it is hard to say just when change will come. Prime Minister Ian Smith proclaimed a unilateral declaration of independence on November 11, 1965, after a split with the British government over political rights to be granted to Africans.

The African colonies under Spanish rule are **Ceuta, Ifni, Melilla** and **Spanish Sahara.** These territories possess little value from an economic viewpoint. All are just dots on the map of Africa, except Spanish Sahara, which is mainly desert.

There is only one French colony left on the African mainland: the tiny territory **Afars and Issas,** on the Red Sea Coast, bordered by Somalia and Ethiopia. The **Comores Archipelago and Réunion,** islands off the coast of Africa, are still dependencies of France.

The chief African colonies under Portuguese rule are **Angola** on the Atlantic coast and **Mozambique** on the Indian Ocean strand. Another colony is **Portuguese Guinea,** on the Atlantic coast, bordered by Senegal and Guinea. Besides these, there are the **Cape Verde Islands,** and **São Tomé** and **Principe,** also island territories still under the heel of Portugal. These colonies will sooner or later join the African revolution.

South-West Africa, a former German colony, is now nominally under the control of the United Nations. In actuality, it is an annex of the Union of South Africa. African nationalist groups are carrying on a resistance movement in this territory, which is larger than France and Great Britain combined. Eventually even this backward land, where there is no college or university, will join the African revolution and become part of Africa Resurgent.

NOTE: The reader who would like to bring himself up to date on what is currently going on in Africa should consult: *Africa 1968.* This is a reference volume on the African continent, prepared by Jeune Afrique, and published as a special annual issue. The publisher is planning *Africa 1969* as an even more comprehensive work. The editor of this excellent and valuable work is Mr. Bechir Ben Yahmed.

BIBLIOGRAPHY

CHAPTER I

Asimov, Isaac. *The Universe from Flat Earth to Quasar*. Walker & Co., New York, 1966.

Brodrick, Alan Houghton. *Man and His Ancestry*. Newly revised with an introduction by M. F. Ashley Montagu. Fawcett Publications, Inc., Greenwich, Conn., 1964.

Brooke, F. A. *The Science of Social Development: A Study in Anthropology*. Watts and Co., London, 1936.

Broom, Robert. *Finding the Missing Link*. Watts and Co., London, 1950.

Calverton, V. F. (Editor). *The Making of Man: An Outline of Anthropology*. The Modern Library, New York, 1931.

Carrington, Richard. *A Million Years of Man*. Mentor Books, New York, 1964.

Churchward, Albert. *The Origin and Evolution of the Human Race*. G. Allen and Unwin, London, 1921.

Darwin, Charles. *The Origin of Species and Descent of Man*. Modern Library Edition. Random House, New York.

Davidson, Basil. "Mother Africa." In *West Africa*, No. 2611, June 17, 1967.

Hapgood, Charles H. *Maps of the Ancient Sea Kings: Evidence of Advanced Civilization in the Ice Age*. Chilton Book Co., New York and Philadelphia, 1966.

Herskovits, Melville J. *Man and His Works*. Alfred A. Knopf, New York, 1948.

Lehrman, Robert L. *The Long Road to Man*. Fawcett Publications, Inc., Greenwich, Conn., 1965.

Lyttleton, Raymond A. *The Modern Universe*. Harper & Bros., New York, 1956.

Montagu, Ashley. *The Human Revolution*. The World Publishing Co., Cleveland and New York, 1965.

Montagu, Ashley. *Man: His First Million Years*. Mentor Books, New York, 1958.

Montagu, Ashley. *Man: His First Two Million Years.* Columbia University Press, New York, 1969.

Morgan, Lewis Henry. *Ancient Society.* Henry Holt & Co., New York, 1878.

Read, Carveth. *Man and His Superstitions.* Cambridge University Press, Cambridge, 1925.

Reinert, Jeanne. "The Man Dr. Leakey Dug Up," *Science Digest,* Vol. 60, No. 5, November, 1966.

Robertson, Archibald. *Morals in World History.* Watts and Co., London, 1945.

Romer, Alfred Sherwood. *Man and the Vertebrates.* 2 vols. Penguin Books, Baltimore, 1968.

Silverberg, Robert. *Man Before Adam: The Story of Man in Search of His Origins.* McCrae Smith Co., Philadelphia, 1964.

Thomson, George. *Aeschylus and Athens.* Second edition. Lawrence and Wishart, London, 1946.

Thomson, George. *Studies in Ancient Greek Society: The Prehistoric Aegean.* Third edition. Lawrence and Wishart, London, 1961.

Wendt, Herbert. *In Search of Adam.* Houghton Mifflin Co., Boston, 1956.

White, Andrew Dickson. *A History of the Warfare of Science and Theology in Christendom.* 2 vols. D. Appleton & Co., New York, 1896.

CHAPTER II

Baldwin, John D. *Pre-Historic Nations.* Harper & Bros., New York, 1869.

Barnes, Harry Elmer. *An Intellectual and Cultural History of the Western World.* Random House, New York, 1937.

Boas, Franz. *The Mind of Primitive Man.* The Macmillan Co., New York, 1944.

Braghine, Alexandre. *The Shadow of Atlantis.* E. P. Dutton & Co., New York, 1940.

Breasted, James Henry. *Time and Its Mysteries.* Series I. New York University Press, New York, 1936.

Briffault, Robert. *Rational Evolution.* The Macmillan Co., New York, 1930.

Budge, E. A. Wallis. *A History of Ethiopia.* 2 vols. Methuen & Co., London, 1928.

Budge, E. A. Wallis. *From Fetish to God in Ancient Egypt.* Oxford University Press, London, 1934.

Chamberlain, A. F. "The Contribution of the Negro to Human Civilization," *Journal of Race Development,* April, 1911.

Churchward, Albert. *The Signs and Symbols of Primordial Man.* Second edition. George Allen & Co., London, 1913. E. P. Dutton & Co., New York, 1913.

Donnelly, Ignatius. *Atlantis.* Edited by Egerton Sykes. Harper & Bros., New York, 1949.

Dorsey, George A. *The Story of Civilization.* New York, 1931.

Dorsey, George A. *Why We Behave Like Human Beings.* New York, 1925.

DuBois, W. E. Burghardt. *Black Folk Then and Now.* Henry Holt & Co., New York, 1939.

Durant, Will. *Our Oriental Heritage.* New York, 1935.

Ferris, William H. *The African Abroad.* 2 vols. The Tuttle, Morehouse & Taylor Press, New Haven, 1913.

Frazer, James George. *Man, God and Immortality.* The Macmillan Co., New York, 1927.

Frazer, James George. *Totemism and Exogamy.* 4 vols. Macmillan & Co., London, 1910.

Frobenius, Leo. *The Voice of Africa.* 2 vols. Hutchinson & Co., London, 1913.

Georg, Eugen. *The Adventure of Mankind.* E. P. Dutton & Co., New York, 1931.

Glanville, S. R. K. (Editor). *The Legacy of Egypt.* The Clarendon Press, Oxford, 1942.

Haddon, Alfred C. *History of Anthropology.* Watts and Co., London, 1934.

Hall, H. R. *The Ancient History of the Near East.* Methuen & Co., London, 1916.

Hammerton, J. A. (Editor). *Wonders of the Past.* 2 vols. Wise and Co., New York, 1937.

Herodotus. *The History of Herodotus.* 4 vols. Translated by George Rawlinson, with essays and notes by Sir Henry Rawlinson and Sir J. G. Wilkinson. Harper & Bros., New York and London, 1858.

Herodotus. *The History of Herodotus.* Translated by George Rawlinson. Edited by Manuel Komroff. Dial Press, New York, 1928. Tudor Publishing Co., New York, 1939.

Higgins, Godfrey. *Anacalypsis.* 2 vols. University Books, New Hyde Park, New York, 1965.

Johnston, Harry H. *The Negro in the New World.* Methuen & Co., London, 1910.

Lugard, Lady Flora Shaw. *A Tropical Dependency.* Barnes & Noble, New York, 1964.

McCabe, Joseph. *Lies and Bunk About Racial Superiority.* E. Haldeman-Julius Co., Girard, Kansas, 1943.

McCabe, Joseph. *Life Among the Many Peoples of the Earth.* E. Haldeman-Julius Co., Girard, Kansas, 1927.

Morgan, Lewis Henry. *Ancient Society.* Henry Holt & Co., New York, 1878.

Perry, W. J. *The Children of the Sun.* E. P. Dutton & Co., New York, 1923.

Perry, W. J. *The Growth of Civilization.* Second edition. Penguin Books, Ltd., Harmondsworth, 1937.

Pine, Tillie S., and Levine, Joseph. *The Africans Knew.* Pictures by Ann Grifalconi. McGraw-Hill Book Co., New York, Toronto, London, Sydney, 1967.

Raglan, Lord. "Anthropology and the Future of Civilization." In *The Rationalist Annual,* London, 1946.

Raglan, Lord. *How Came Civilization?* Methuen & Co., London, 1939.

Rawlinson, George. *The Five Great Monarchies of the Ancient Eastern World.* Fourth edition. 3 vols. Scribner & Welford, New York, 1880.

Rawlinson, George. *The Origin of Nations.* Scribner, Welford & Armstrong, New York, 1878.

Rogers, Joel A. *Africa's Gift to America.* New York, 1961.

Seignobos, Charles. *History of Ancient Civilization.* T. Fisher Unwin, London, 1910.

Thomas, Bertram. *The Arabs.* Doubleday, Doran & Co., Garden City, New York, 1937.

Thorndike, Lynn. *Short History of Civilization.* F. S. Crofts, New York, 1936.

Wells, H. G. *The Outline of History.* 3 vols. Triangle Books, New York, 1940.

Wells, H. G. *A Short History of the World.* Watts and Co., London, 1948.

CHAPTER III

Allen, Richard H. *Star Names and Their Meanings.* G. E. Stechert Co., New York, 1899.

Braghine, Alexandre. *The Shadow of Atlantis.* E. P. Dutton & Co., New York, 1940.

Breasted, James Henry. *Ancient Times.* Ginn and Co., Boston, 1916.

Breasted, James Henry. *A History of Egypt.* Bantam Books, New York, Toronto, London, 1967.

Breasted, James Henry. *Time and Its Mysteries.* Series I. New York University Press, New York, 1936.

Briffault, Robert. *The Mothers.* 1-vol. edition. The Macmillan Co., New York, 1931.

British Association Report, Glasgow Meeting, 1876. London, 1877.

Brodeur, Arthur G. *The Pageant of Civilization.* R. M. McBride & Co., New York, 1931.

Brown, Brian. *The Wisdom of the Egyptians.* Brentano's, New York, 1923.

Budge, E. A. Wallis. *The Book of the Dead.* An English translation of *The Papyrus of Ani.* University Books, New Hyde Park, New York, 1960.

Budge, E. A. Wallis. *The Gods of the Egyptians.* 2 vols. Methuen and Co., London, 1904.

Budge, E. A. Wallis. *Osiris: The Egyptian Religion of the Resurrection.* 2 vols., bound in one. University Books, New Hyde Park, New York, 1961.

Bury, J. B.; Cook, S. A.; and Adcock, F. E. (Editors). *The Cam-*

bridge Ancient History. Vols. I and II. Cambridge University Press, Cambridge, Vol. I, 1923, Vol. II, 1926.

Busenbark, Ernest. *Symbols, Sex and the Stars*. The Truth Seeker Co., San Diego, California, 1949.

Carpenter, Edward. *Pagan and Christian Creeds*. Harcourt, Brace and Co., New York, 1920.

Carus, Paul. "Zodiacs of Different Nations," *Open Court*, August, 1906.

Casson, Stanley. *Progress and Catastrophe*. Harper & Bros., New York, 1937.

Churchward, Albert. *The Signs and Symbols of Primordial Man*. Second edition. George Allen & Co., London, 1913. E. P. Dutton & Co., New York, 1913.

Cooke, Harold P. *Osiris: A Study in Myths, Mysteries and Religion*. Bruce Humphries, Inc., Boston, 1931.

DeGraft-Johnson, John Coleman. *African Glory*. Walker & Co., New York, 1966.

Del Grande, Nino. "Prehistoric Iron Smelting in Africa," *Natural History*, Sept.–Oct., 1932.

Doane, T. W. *Bible Myths and Their Parallels in Other Religions*. The Truth Seeker Co., San Diego, California.

Dorsey, George A. *The Story of Civilization: Man's Own Show*. Halcyon House, New York, 1931.

DuBois, W. E. Burghardt. *The World and Africa*. International Publishers, New York, 1965.

Durant, Will. *Our Oriental Heritage*. Simon and Schuster, New York, 1935.

Eichler, Lillian. *The Customs of Mankind*. Nelson Doubleday, Inc., Garden City, New York, 1924.

Finger, Charles J. *Lost Civilizations*. Haldeman-Julius Co., Girard, Kansas, 1922.

Frazer, James George. *Adonis, Attis, Osiris*. 3rd edition. 2 volumes bound in 1. University Books, New Hyde Park, New York, 1961.

Frazer, James George. *The Golden Bough*. Abridged edition. The Macmillan Co., New York, 1940.

Frazer, James George. *The Worship of Nature*. The Macmillan Co., New York, 1926.

Freud, Sigmund. *Moses and Monotheism.* Alfred A. Knopf, New York, 1939.

Gould, F. J. *A Concise History of Religion,* Vol. 1. Watts and Co., London, 1907.

Graves, Kersey. *The World's Sixteen Crucified Saviors.* The Truth Seeker Co., San Diego, California.

Hadfield, P. *Traits of Divine Kingship in Africa.* Watts and Co., London, 1949.

Hammerton, J. A. *The Encyclopedia of Modern Knowledge.* The Amalgamated Press, London, 1936.

Hammerton, J. A. (Editor). *Wonders of the Past.* 2 vols. Wise and Co., New York, 1937.

Hapgood, Charles H. *Maps of the Ancient Sea Kings: Evidence of Advanced Civilization in the Ice Age.* Chilton Book Co., New York and Philadelphia, 1966.

Harding, Arthur M. *Astronomy.* Garden City Publishing Co., Garden City, New York, 1935.

Heckethorn, Charles William. *The Secret Societies of All Ages and Countries.* 2 vols. University Books, New Hyde Park, New York, 1966.

Herodotus. *The History of Herodotus.* Translated by George Rawlinson. Edited by Manuel Komroff. Dial Press, New York, 1928. Tudor Publishing Co., New York, 1939.

Higgins, Godfrey. *Anacalypsis.* 2 Vols. University Books, New Hyde Park, New York, 1965.

Laing, Samuel. *Human Origins.* Chapman and Hall, London, 1892. A revised edition, edited by Edward Clodd, published by Watts and Co., London, 1913.

Lockyer, J. Norman. *The Dawn of Astronomy: A Study of the Temple Worship and Mythology of the Ancient Egyptians.* The M.I.T. Press, Cambridge, Mass., 1963.

MacNaughton, Duncan. *A Scheme of Egyptian Chronology.* Luzac and Co., London, 1932.

McCabe, Joseph. *The Golden Ages of History.* Watts and Co., London, 1940.

Maspero, Gaston Camille. *The Dawn of Civilization.* Second edition. Society for the Promotion of Christian Knowledge, London, 1896.

Massey, Gerald. *A Book of the Beginnings*. 2 Vols. Williams and Norgate, London, 1881.

Massey, Gerald. *The Natural Genesis*. 2 Vols. Williams and Norgate, London, 1883.

Massey, Gerald. *Ancient Egypt: The Light of the World*. 2 Vols. T. Fisher Unwin, London, 1907.

Moret, Alexandre. *Kings and Gods of Egypt*. G. P. Putnam's Sons, New York and London, 1912.

Olcott, William Tyler. *Sun Lore of All Ages*. G. P. Putnam's Sons, New York and London, 1914.

Parsons, Geoffrey. *The Stream of History*. Charles Scribner's Sons, New York and London, 1932.

Petrie, W. M. Flinders. *Social Life in Ancient Egypt*. Houghton Mifflin Co., Boston and New York, 1923.

Plutarch. "Isis and Osiris." A Treatise in Plutarch's *Moralia*, Vol. V. The Greek text, with an English translation by Frank Cole Babbitt. The Loeb Classical Library, Harvard University Press, Cambridge, Mass., 1962.

Reade, Winwood. *The Martyrdom of Man*. Watts and Co., London, 1934. A new edition published by Pemberton Publishing Co., London, 1968.

Robertson, John M. *Christianity and Mythology*. Second edition. Watts and Co., London, 1936.

Rylands, L. Gordon. *The Beginnings of Gnostic Christianity*. Watts and Co., London, 1940.

St. Clair, George. *Creation Records Discovered in Egypt: Studies in the Book of the Dead*. David Nutt, London, 1898.

Silverberg, Robert. *Empires in the Dust*. Bantam Books, New York, London, Toronto, 1966.

Thompson, D'Arcy Wentworth. "The Science of Astrology," a book review, *Nature*, Oct. 23, 1937.

Volney, C. F. *The Ruins of Empires*. Peter Eckler, New York, 1890. Reissued by The Truth Seeker Co., San Diego, California.

Weigall, Arthur. *Personalities of Antiquity*. Doubleday, Doran & Co., Garden City, New York, 1928.

Wendt, Herbert. *It Began in Babel*. Houghton Mifflin Co., Boston, 1962.

Yarker, John. *The Arcane Schools*. William Tait, Belfast, Ireland, 1909.

CHAPTER IV

DeGraft-Johnson, John Coleman. *African Glory*. Walker & Co., New York, 1966.

Haldane, J. B. S. *Heredity and Politics*. W. W. Norton & Co., New York, 1938.

Herodotus. *The History of Herodotus*. Translated by George Rawlinson. Edited by Manuel Komroff. Dial Press, New York, 1928. Tudor Publishing Co., New York, 1939.

Lugard, Lady Flora Shaw. *A Tropical Dependency*. Barnes & Noble, New York, 1964.

Johnston, Harry H. *The Uganda Protectorate*. 2 vols. Hutchinson & Co., London, 1902.

Lane-Poole, Stanley. *The Story of the Moors in Spain*. G. P. Putnam's Sons, New York, 1886.

McCabe, Joseph. *The New Science and the Story of Evolution*. Hutchinson & Co., London, 1931.

McCabe, Joseph. *The Golden Ages of History*. Watts and Co., London, 1940.

McCabe, Joseph. *The Splendour of Moorish Spain*. Watts and Co., London, 1935.

Oman, Charles. *The Dark Ages*. Rivington & Co., London, 1954.

Parker, Richard. *A Moor of Spain*. Penguin Books, Melbourne, London, Baltimore, 1953.

Rocker, Rudolph. *Nationalism and Culture*. Freedom Press, London, 1937.

Rogers, J. A. *World's Great Men of Color*. Vol. I. Author's publication, New York, 1947.

Thompson, James Westfall. *Economic and Social History of the Middle Ages*. The Century Co., New York and London, 1928.

Toynbee, Arnold J. *A Study of History*. Vol. I. Oxford University Press, London, 1934.

CHAPTER V

Chu, Daniel, and Skinner, Elliott. *A Glorious Age in Africa.* Zenith Books, Doubleday & Co., Garden City, New York, 1965.

Davidson, Basil. *A Guide to African History.* Revised and edited by Haskel Frankel. Zenith Books, Doubleday & Co., Garden City, New York, 1965.

Davidson, Basil. *The Lost Cities of Africa.* Little, Brown & Co., Boston and Toronto, 1959.

Davidson, Basil, and Buah, F. K. *A History of West Africa to the Nineteenth Century.* Anchor Books, Doubleday & Co., Garden City, New York, 1966.

Dobler, Lavinia, and Brown, William A. *Great Rulers of the African Past.* Zenith Books, Doubleday & Co., Garden City, New York, 1965.

Durant, Will. *The Story of Philosophy.* Simon and Schuster, New York, 1933.

Jeffreys, M. D. W. "The Negro Enigma," *West African Review,* Sept., 1951.

Johnston, Harry H. *A History of the Colonization of Africa.* Cambridge University Press, London, 1899.

Lugard, Lady Flora Shaw. *A Tropical Dependency.* Barnes & Noble, New York, 1964.

Ratzel, Friedrich. *The History of Mankind.* 2 Vols. 2nd ed. London, 1904.

Reade, Winwood. *The Martyrdom of Man.* Watts and Co., London, 1934. A new edition published by Pemberton Publishing Co., London, 1968.

Smith, Grafton Elliot. *The Ancient Egyptians and the Origin of Civilization.* Revised edition. Harper & Bros., London and New York, 1923.

Wendt, Herbert. *It Began in Babel.* Houghton Mifflin Co., Boston, 1962.

CHAPTER VI

Bershadsky, Rudolph. "Atlantis," an article in *On the Track of Discovery*, Series 2, Progress Publishers, Moscow, U.S.S.R., 1964.

Braghine, Alexandre. *The Shadow of Atlantis*. E. P. Dutton & Co., New York, 1940.

Churchward, Albert. *The Signs and Symbols of Primordial Man*. Second edition. George Allen & Co., London, 1913. E. P. Dutton & Co., New York, 1913.

Davidson, Basil. *The Lost Cities of Africa*. Little, Brown & Co., Boston and Toronto, 1959.

DeRoo, Peter. *History of America Before Columbus*. 2 vols. J. B. Lippincott, Philadelphia and London, 1900.

Donnelly, Ignatius. *Atlantis*. Edited by Egerton Sykes. Harper & Bros., New York, 1949.

Draper, John William. *History of the Intellectual Development of Europe*. New York, 1861. Revised edition, 1876.

Herodotus. *The History of Herodotus*. Translated by George Rawlinson. Edited by Manuel Komroff. Dial Press, New York, 1928. Tudor Publishing Co., New York, 1939.

Lawrence, Harold G. *African Explorers of the New World*. Published in *The Crisis* Magazine, June–July, 1962. Republished as a monograph by Haryou-Act, Inc., New York, 1962.

Lugard, Lady Flora Shaw. *A Tropical Dependency*. Barnes & Noble, New York, 1964.

Radin, Paul. *The Story of the American Indian*. Garden City Publishing Co., Garden City, New York, 1937.

Reinert, Jeanne. "Secrets of the People of the Jaguar," *Science Digest*, Vol. 16, No. 3, September, 1967.

Rogers, J. A. *Africa's Gift to America*. Author's publication, New York, 1961.

Silverberg, Robert. *Lost Cities and Vanished Civilizations*. Bantam Books, New York, 1963.

Silverberg, Robert. *Mound Builders of Ancient America*. New York Graphic Society, Ltd., Greenwich, Conn., 1968.

Smith, G. Elliot; Malinowski, Bronislaw; Spinden, Herbert J.; and Goldenweiser, Alexander. *Culture: The Diffusion Controversy.* W. W. Norton & Co., New York, 1927.

Spence, Lewis. *The Religion of Ancient Mexico.* Watts and Co., London, 1945.

Verrill, A. Hyatt. *Old Civilizations of the New World.* Tudor Publishing Co., New York, 1938.

Von Hagen, Victor Wolfgang. *The Aztec: Man and Tribe.* New American Library, New York, 1961.

Wiener, Leo. *Africa and the Discovery of America.* 3 Vol. Innes & Sons, Philadelphia, 1920–22.

Wiener, Leo. *Mayan and Mexican Origins.* Author's publication, Cambridge, Mass., 1926.

CHAPTER VII

Baldwin, John D. *Pre-Historic Nations.* Harper & Bros., New York, 1869.

Budge, E. A. Wallis (Translator). *Kebra Nagast.* Oxford University Press, London, 1923.

Davidson, Basil (Editor). *The African Past.* Universal Books, Grosset & Dunlap, New York, 1967.

Davidson, Basil. *A Guide to African History.* Revised and edited by Haskel Frankel. Zenith Books, Doubleday & Co., Garden City, New York, 1965.

Davidson, Basil. *The Lost Cities of Africa.* Little, Brown & Co., Boston and Toronto, 1959.

Freeman-Grenville, G. S. P. (Translator). *East African Coast, Select Documents.* London, 1962.

Gibbon, Edward. *The Decline and Fall of the Roman Empire.* 2 vols. A Modern Library Giant. Random House, New York.

Hapgood, Charles H. *Maps of the Ancient Sea Kings: Evidence of Advanced Civilization in the Ice Age.* Chilton Book Co., New York and Philadelphia, 1966.

Rawlinson, George. *The Origin of Nations.* Scribner, Welford & Armstrong, New York, 1878.

Steffen, Don Carl. *The Splendour of Africa.* Walker & Co., New York, 1965.

Wells, Carveth. *Introducing Africa.* G. P. Putnam's Sons, New York, 1954.

CHAPTER VIII

Armattoe, R. E. G. *The Golden Age of Western African Civilization.* Lomeshie Research Center, Londonderry, Ireland, 1946.

Davidson, Basil (Editor). *The African Past.* Universal Books, Grosset & Dunlap, New York, 1967.

DeGraft-Johnson, John Coleman. *African Glory.* Walker & Co., New York, 1966.

Draper, John William. *History of the Conflict Between Religion and Science.* No. 12 of the International Scientific Series. D. Appleton & Co., New York, 1889.

DuBois, W. E. Burghardt. *The World and Africa.* International Publishers, New York, 1965.

Frazer, James George. *The Golden Bough.* Abridged edition. The Macmillan Co., New York, 1940.

Graves, Robert, and Podro, Joshua. *The Nazarene Gospel Restored.* Cassell & Co., London, 1953.

Hadfield, P. *Traits of Divine Kingship in Africa.* Watts and Co., London, 1949.

Hammerton, J. A. (Editor). *Wonders of the Past.* 2 Vols. Wise and Co., New York, 1937.

Hocart, A. M. *Kings and Councillors.* P. Barbey, Cairo, Egypt, 1936.

Hocart, A. M. *Kingship.* H. Milford, London, 1927.

Hocart, A. M. *Social Origins.* Watts and Co., London, 1954.

Irstam, Tor. *The King of Ganda: Studies of the Institution of Sacred Kingship in Africa.* Stockholm, 1944.

Kingsnorth, G. W. *Africa South of the Sahara.* Cambridge University Press, Cambridge, 1966.

Wendt, Herbert. *It Began in Babel.* Houghton Mifflin Co., Boston, 1962.

CHAPTER IX

Breasted, James Henry. *A History of Egypt.* Bantam Books, New York, Toronto, London, 1967.

Coblentz, Stanton A. *The Long Road to Humanity.* Thomas Yoseloff, New York and London, 1959.

Cohen, Chapman. *Christianity, Slavery and Labour.* The Pioneer Press, London, 1936.

Davidson, Basil (Editor). *The African Past.* Universal Books, Grosset & Dunlap, New York, 1967.

Davidson, Basil, and Buah, F. K. *A History of West Africa to the Nineteenth Century.* Anchor Books, Doubleday & Co., Garden City, New York, 1966.

DeGraft-Johnson, John Coleman. *African Glory.* Walker & Co., New York, 1966.

Draper, John William. *History of the Conflict Between Religion and Science.* No. 12 of the International Scientific Series. D. Appleton & Co., New York, 1889.

DuBois, W. E. Burghardt. *The World and Africa.* International Publishers, New York, 1965.

Freeman-Grenville, G. S. P. (Translator). *The East African Coast: Select Documents.* The Clarendon Press, Oxford, 1962.

Lugard, Lady Flora Shaw. *A Tropical Dependency.* Barnes & Noble, New York, 1964.

McCabe, Joseph. *The Social Record of Christianity.* Watts and Co., London, 1935.

Morel, Edmund D. *Red Rubber.* T. Fisher Unwin, London, 1906.

Report of the Anti-Slavery Society. New York, 1860.

Russell, Bertrand. *Freedom and Organization: 1814-1914.* George Allen and Unwin, London, 1934.

Smith, Goldwin. *The United Kingdom: A Political History.* 2 vols.

Wallace-Johnson, Isaac. "Has the African a God?" *Africa Morning Post,* May, 1936.

CHAPTER X

Brockway, Fenner. "Our Nigerian Peace Mission," *New Statesman,* January 3, 1969.

Davidson, Basil (Editor). *The African Past.* Universal Books, Grosset & Dunlap, New York, 1967.

Hughes, John. *The New Face of Africa: South of the Sahara.* Longmans, Green & Co., New York, London, Toronto, 1961.

Kingsnorth, G. W. *Africa South of the Sahara.* Cambridge University Press, Cambridge, 1966.

MacGregor-Hastie, Roy. *Africa: Background for Today.* Criterion Books, New York, 1967.

Rogers, J. A. *World's Great Men of Color.* Vol. I. Author's publication, New York, 1947.

Steffen, Don Carl. *The Splendour of Africa.* Walker & Co., New York, 1965.

Wells, Carveth. *Introducing Africa.* G. P. Putnam's Sons, New York, 1954.

Yahmed, Bechir Ben (Editor). *Africa 1968.* A reference book on the African continent. Published by Jeune Afrique.

NEW BIBLIOGRAPHICAL APPROACH
TO AFRICAN HISTORY
by John Henrik Clarke

In the last ten years, there has been some notable improvement in books relating to African history. The best known of the new books on this subject have been written by the English writer, Basil Davidson. Mr. Davidson is not a historian in the general sense. He is a journalist who brings to the study of African history astute research and new insights into an old subject that has been universally distorted. The purpose of this essay is to call attention to his books and those of other writers that should be considered by students and teachers who are interested in developing a new approach to African history.

The Lost Cities of Africa (Atlantic-Little, Brown, Boston, Massachusetts, 1959) is Mr. Davidson's first book on general African history. The revelations in this book disturbed the historical establishment, which likes to think, and teach, that all Africa dwelled in darkness waiting for the Europeans to bring the light.

This book told of the great kingdom of Kush, with its splendid cities of Meroe and Napata that represented an advanced African culture of the upper Nile several centuries before Christ. He shows that the great flowering of African civilization in western Africa was mainly medieval and is reflected in the rise and fall of the great states of Ghana, Mali, and Songhay. East Africa presented another picture of splendor and state-building. The thriving Africa-Asia trade and the evidence of a civilization that rose and fell in the southeastern part of Africa are reflected in the interior cities of Zimbabwe and Mapungubwe. In the book *Black Mother: The Years of the African Slave Trade* (Little, Brown and Company, Boston, Massachusetts, 1961), Mr. Davidson examines the African slave trade and shows the role that this trade played, economically, in the rebirth and expansion of Europe.

Mr. Davidson supported his inquiry into African history in the book *The African Past: Chronicles from Antiquity to Modern Times* (Little, Brown and Company, 1964). In the book *Africa: History of a Continent* (Macmillan and Company, 1966), the writer, Basil Davidson, and the photographer, Werner Forman, have combined their respective talents to produce a long photo-essay on African history that complements the subject. In this book, Basil Davidson continues to show growth and depth in his knowledge of this subject that has so long been neglected or distorted. The text of the book is a perfect wedding of first-hand knowledge and prodigious research—the result of years of study, travel, and experience. In addition to evaluating the most recent historical research and archaeological findings, Basil Davidson offers a clear and scholarly account of the growth and development of old civilizations in Africa and traces their internal development as well as their varied links with Asia, Europe, and America.

The book presents the essence of African history and calls attention to the need for further study. The author, properly, begins at the beginnings by showing: Africa's importance in the development of early types of minial and of homo sapiens; the forgotten world of the "green Sahara," 5000–2000 B.C., as the cradle of early cultures; some consequences of Saharan desiccation; and the beginnings of the African Iron Age north and south of the Sahara.

In dealing with the old myths and new truths about Africa, Basil Davidson has asked for a reconsideration of the entire field of African studies in the following statement:

> Whether in the field of scientific archaeology, the study of languages or the movement of ideas, the assembly of historical tradition or the elucidation of records written by Africans, Europeans, Asians and Americans, fruitful labour and learning in several countries over the past few decades have produced a

large body of explanatory work, and have proved that the writing of African history need be neither the repetition of romantic legend nor the mere listing of faceless names and battles long ago. These historical advances have swept away some old myths and established some new truths.

Werner Forman's brilliant photographs complement the text without intruding upon it. In both words and pictures the book is a record of African achievement from prehistoric times to the present.

African Kingdoms (1966), by Basil Davidson and the editors of Time-Life Books, is part of the series "Great Ages of Man," a history of the world's cultures. This volume represents the continuation of the trend toward publishing books on Africa that can be understood by the lay reader who has no prior knowledge of the subject. It is, frankly, a popular treatment of the topic, and such a treatment is needed. The reader needs a simplified overview of this subject that had been made difficult by distortions and omissions. African history is no more than the missing pages of world history. Honest historians like Basil Davidson are attempting to put these missing pages back into their proper place.

The remarkable thing about the retelling of the histories of the old African kingdoms is that we learn that, at certain periods, these kingdoms were far ahead of the nations of Europe in their state organization and in attention to the welfare of their people. Here are some of the insights into the Golden Age of African History that are reflected in the pages of this book:

Eight thousand years ago, while vestiges of the Ice Age chilled Europe, the Sahara we know today as an empty, arid desert was a fertile region whose flowing rivers and grassy valleys teemed with fish and wild animals. During the next 6,000 years in this inviting land, waves of migrants developed a series of increasingly advanced societies, which they recorded in a collection of remarkably beautiful scenes carved and painted on native rock—the most complete record of early African civilizations and Stone Age life to be found anywhere.

For many centuries, Africa and its people seemed mysterious and even perverse to the rest of the world. Generations of traders anchored their ships on the continent's glittering surf line and pushed their caravans through its dry, abrasive plains. They knew and valued Africa's gold and ivory, but the continent itself remained a puzzle. Where had Africans come from? Why were they so different from other men?

This and many other new books on Africa are answering some of the long-outstanding questions. As Basil Davidson has said:

> Africa has not been, after all, a land of unrelieved savagery and chaos. On the contrary, its people have had a long and lively history, and have made an impressive contribution to man's general mastery of the world. They have created cultures and civilizations, evolved systems of government and systems of thought, and pursued the inner life of the spirit with a consuming passion that has produced some of the finest art known to men.

The Growth of African Civilization, a history of West Africa, 1000–1800 (Doubleday Anchor Book, 1966), written by Basil Davidson in collaboration with F. K. Buah and the advice of Professor J. F. A. Ajayi, was planned for students of history in West Africa who were preparing for the General Certificate of Education and similar public examinations. The writers and their adviser have written this book to dispel the idea that there was no African history before the coming of the Europeans. In their research for the book they discovered that, until very recently, those writings designated as textbooks on African history were nothing more than accounts of Africans' encounter with the Europeans, written by merchants, missionaries, and colonial servants.

The book covers the five hundred years, 1000 to 1500, before the Europeans started to come into Africa in large numbers, and it continues through 1800, the period when the Western slave trade was converted into the modern colonial system. Because of this approach, the reader is able to see what was accomplished in Africa before the slave trade and what, in Africa and in Europe, set in motion this tragic era in African history.

This book is recommended as an introduction to the history of West Africa.

One of the most encouraging aspects of the new approaches to African history is reflected in the work of young African historians who are, at last, beginning to present African history from an African point of view. This point of view is best reflected in the following books:

A Thousand Years of West African History, edited by Dr. J. F. Ade Ajayi, Professor of History, University of Ibadan, and Ian Espire (Nelson and Company, 1965). It was produced in response to the urgent needs of African teachers and students for a handbook which offers an up-to-date account of major themes of West African history interpreted by a group of scholars currently working in the field. The book is one outcome of a workshop on the teaching of African history held at Ibadan in 1965.

All the themes in West African history taken up in this book are important enough to deserve a separate book by themselves. In the foreword to this book, Dr. K. Onwuka Dike has said:

> In the last ten years or so, the study of African History has made progress, especially in focusing attention on the history of African peoples as distinct from the activities of their invaders. . . . European history and the activities of Europeans have remained the dominant themes for too long. To improve this situation, the West African Examinations Council has recently approved new syllabuses devised by its professional committees

and, as a result, for the first time, the systematic study of West African History in the nineteenth and twentieth centuries is now available. . . . The history of Africa is a new and exciting field of study.

Some of the most able of Africa's young historians and some enlightened Europeans are now putting the best of their talents into this "new and exciting field of study."

African Glory, the story of vanished Negro civilizations, by Dr. J. C. de Graft-Johnson, was first published in 1954. It is a short general history of Africa, and one of the best books on the subject. For a number of years this book has been out of print. It has been reissued at a time when the approaches to African history are improving. When Dr. de Graft-Johnson's book was first published, he was in a class by himself. There has been a flood of books on African history since 1954; most of them have been bad, in both structure and content.

In the writing of this book, Dr. de Graft-Johnson draws on many sources and gives a vivid account of the grandeur of precolonial Africa and the personalities in Africa who created great states and empires, and, in most cases, ruled them exceptionally well. Dr. de Graft-Johnson writes about the history of Africa as a total geographical area and not just about what some writers call tropical Africa or Africa south of the Sahara.

In the early chapters of his book he shows the relationship of North Africa to the other parts of the continent and takes certain aspects of African history into consideration that are still being neglected by other historians. In addition to the revealing chapters on North Africa, Dr. de Graft-Johnson writes of the great empires of western Africa which flourished during the Dark Ages of Europe and achieved a level of culture comparable to any in the world. He describes the highly developed system of government introduced by the Ashantis of the Gold Coast (now Ghana), and outlines the careers of such wise and humane rulers as Mansa Musa, whose contributions to the fourteenth century Mali Empire earned him a brilliant reputation not only in Africa, but in Europe and Asia as well.

This is only one of many biographies of great African personalities that can be found in this book. These are the new lessons in old African history that are giving many present-day African nation builders a new consciousness of past achievement and limitless possibilities as they discover their forgotten heritage and learn to use it to make their future.

Africa in the Nineteenth and Twentieth Centuries (Nelson and Company, 1966), edited by Joseph C. Anene and Godfrey Brown, is a companion book to *A Thousand Years of West African History*. This is one of the many books recently sponsored by the University of Ibadan, in Nigeria, that is in the early stages of earning a reputation as a major center for the advancement of historical scholarship on Africa. These books are meant to fulfill the need for good intermediate textbooks on the history of Africa essential for teaching in African schools.

Since the end of World War II, a number of African countries, especially Gambia, Ghana, Nigeria, and Sierra Leone, have been attempting to develop textbooks for their schools that reflect a more African point of view. In the main, the contributors to this volume have fulfilled this need.

In the foreword to the book, Dr. K. Onwuka Dike has said: "This book epitomises a number of significant developments in Africa at the present time. It reflects the twentieth century renascence of African culture."

In his essay, "The Place of African History in Education in Africa," Godfrey N. Brown seemed to have been extending Dr. Dike's remarks when he said:

> To argue again the case for African History as an academic study is unnecessary. Only those who have either no first-hand experience of contemporary Africa or have made no attempt to study the continent's history can support such statements as

"Africa has no history," or "African History is nothing more than the story of European activities. . . ." The great asset of the study of African History in African educational institutions is that it is a first-pronoun subject; it is concerned with learning about people like us (admittedly a matter of degree). This is particularly important in a continent that is emerging from a period of colonial rule during which the history of aliens was endowed with unwarranted prestige.

SELECTED BIBLIOGRAPHY OF NEW BOOKS REFLECTING A NEW APPROACH TO AFRICAN HISTORY

TOPICS IN WEST AFRICAN HISTORY
by Adu Boahen, Longmans, New York and London, 1964. A clear and readable history of West Africa. Very useful for teachers.

A NEW HISTORY FOR SCHOOLS AND COLLEGES, Books One and Two
by F. K. Buah, Macmillan and Company, New York and London. Basic textbooks for lower grades, prepared for the schools of Ghana, but they could be useful for any school.

AFRICA IN THE ANCIENT WORLD
by G. O. Onibonaje, Onibonaje Press, Ibadan, Nigeria, 1965. Distributed in the U.S.A. by the University Place Book Shop.

AFRICA: RISE OF ISLAM TO END OF SLAVE TRADE
second volume of above-mentioned book, same author and publisher.

THE DAWN OF AFRICAN HISTORY
edited by Roland Oliver, Oxford University Press, New York, 1961. This book is useful and is used selectively. Some of the old misconceptions relating to African history are repeated here.

THE MIDDLE AGE OF AFRICAN HISTORY
edited by Roland Oliver, Oxford University Press, New York, 1967. Same comment as above.

THE REVOLUTIONARY YEARS: WEST AFRICA SINCE 1800
J. B. Webster and A. A. Boahen, Longmans, New York and London, 1968.

THE MAKING OF MODERN AFRICA
by J. D. Omer-Cooper, E. A. Ayandele, A. E. Afigbo, and R. J. Gavin, Longmans, New York and London, 1968. This book is basically good, though a little too kind to the colonialists.

AFRICA SINCE 1800
by Roland Oliver and Anthony Atmore, Cambridge University Press, 1967. A good preface to the history of modern Africa.

ANCIENT AFRICAN KINGDOMS
by Margaret Shinnie, St. Martin's Press, New York, 1965. Short and very useful histories of the great empires and kingdoms in precolonial Africa.

KINGDOMS OF THE SAVANNA
by Jan M. Vansina, University of Wisconsin Press, Madison, Wisconsin, 1965. This is a good general history of Central African states before the coming of the Europeans.

AFRICAN BEGINNINGS
by Olivia Vlahos, Viking Press, 1967. This book is an introduction to the origins of African history.

AFRICA IN HISTORY
by Basil Davidson, The Macmillan Company, New York, 1968. Revised edition of the book, AFRICA: HISTORY OF A CONTINENT. This is a good basic textbook on African history.

A HISTORY OF EAST AND CENTRAL AFRICA
by Basil Davidson, Doubleday Anchor Books, New York, 1969.

INDEX

Abdallah, Abu, 188
Abd-er-Rahman III, 183–84
Abidjan, 325
Abulfeda, 234
Abyssinia, 66–67. *See also* Ethiopia
Addis Ababa, 345
Adonis, 133
Adule, 265, 266
Afars and Issas, 350
Africa Hall, 345
Africa 1968, 327, 328, 330, 335, 337, 339, 341–42, 343, 350 n.
African culture, destruction of, 26, 29–30, 296–318
Africa Romana, 160, 164, 165–66
Afro-American Freedom Struggle, 34
Afro-American literature and history, 20
Agai-Ironsi, General, 323
Ahmed, Mohammed, 33
Ahmose II, 116–17
Ajaya, J. F. Ade, 220, 309–10
Akhnaton, 125
Akintola, Chief, 319
Alexander the Great, 116, 117, 118
Alexandria, 96, 117–18, 119–20, 121, 162, 266, 297–99
Alexandrian Museum, 118–19, 120
Algeria, 161, 340–41
Ali, Sunni the Great, 19, 214–15
Allen, Richard H., 123
Al-Mamun, Caliph, 180, 181
Almeria, 192
Almohades, 186–87
Almoravides, 184, 186–87, 206–7
Alphabet, Egyptian origin, 149–51
Alphonso VI, King, 185
Alvarez, King Dom II, 291–92
Aly, Mohammed, 341
Amasis, 116–17
Amen, 125, 136
Amenemhet I, 107
Amenhotep III, 109, 110
America, discovery of, 22–25, 232–60
Ammon, 117
Anaximander, 117
Andalusia, 177–80, 186, 191–92
Angola, 350
Ankrah, Joseph A., 320

Ansika Kingdom, 28
Apollonious, 80, 120
Arabia Felix, 266, 303
Arabs, 17, 26, 166–95, 201, 265–66, 280–81
Aradus, 147
Archaic Civilization, 83–89, 276
Archimedes, 120
Armattoe, R. E. G., 290
Arnq-Amen, 276
Asantewa, Queen Yaa, 32
Ashantis, 31–32
Askia dynasty of Songhay, 216
Askia Mohammed I, 216–17
Assyrians, 73, 116, 257
Atlantis, 81–82, 256–59
Aton, Atonism, 110, 111, 125
Australoids, 89
Australopithecus africanus, 42
Australopithecus Prometheus, 44
Avicenna of Bokhara, 182
Awolowo, Obafemi, 323
Axum, 266, 267, 268
Azab, 265, 266
Azikiwe, Nnamdi, 323
Aztecs, 245, 253–54

Baba, Ahmed, 21, 217, 300–1
Babylonia, 71–72, 91, 139
Bachwezi, 287–88
Bakuba Kingdom, 28–29
Baldwin, John D., 69–70, 265, 277
Balewa, Abubakar, 323
Bamako conference, 319
Banda, Hastings Kamuzu, 334
Bantu, 27, 285
Barbosa, Duarte, 302–3
Barlow, G. W., 43
Barnes, Harry Elmer, 91
Basutos, 28
Batuta, Ibn, 205, 251–53, 279
Bekr, Abu, 168, 169, 184
Bekr, Mohammed Abu, 300–1
Bekri, El, 202
Belgian atrocities, 310–12
Belisarius, General, 165–66
Bello, Ahmadu, 323
Ben Bella, Ahmed, 341
Berbers, 160, 198, 200, 213
Berlin Conference, 310
Bernatzik, Hugo, 283

Bershadsky, Rudolph, 243–44, 257–58
Biafra, 323–24
Bilal ibn Rahab, Hadzrat, 16
Bizerte, 148
Black Belt, 225
Black Christ, 256
Black Guaninis, 233
Black race, *passim*. *See also* Negro race
Boas, Franz, 63, 90
Bolongongo, Shamba, 29
Boniface, Count, 164–65
Boobooboo, 282
Botswana, 336–37
Boumédienne, Houari, 341
Bourguiba, Habib, 338
Bowelle, Behanzin Hossu, 33
Brace, Loring, 305
Braghine, Alexandre, 80–81, 82, 102, 241–43, 255
Breasted, James Henry, 64–65, 78, 106, 108–9, 112, 113, 121, 296–97
Brenans, Lieutenant, 157, 158
Briffault, Robert, 94–95
Brockway, Fenner, 324
Brodeur, Arthur G., 93
Brooke, F. A., 48
Broom, Robert, 42–44
Brown, Brian, 198
Brown, William A., 220
Buah, F. K., 220, 309–10
Budge, E. A. Wallis, 64, 66–67, 122, 123, 133–34, 136, 137–38, 139, 268
Buganda, 288
Bunsen, Baron, 270
Bunyoro, 288
Bushmen, 28
Bushongo culture, 28–29
Busoga, 288
Byblos, 147–48
Byzantine Empire, 163, 165–66

Cabeza colosal, 237–38
Cadiz, 148
Caesar, Augustus, 161
Caesar, Julius, 120, 121, 161–62, 297–98
Cairo, 209–10
Calendar: Egyptian, 121–22; Mayan, 246–48, 249; Zapotec, 248; similarities in, 257–58

Calendar-Round, 247
Callimachus, 119–20
Cambodia, 278
Cameron, Donald, 333
Cameroons, The, 322
Cape Verde Islands, 350
Carpenter, Edward, 135, 145
Carthage: destruction of, 148–49, 160; rebuilding of, 161–62; under Byzantine rule, 165–66; captured by Arabs, 170
Carus, Paul, 140
Casson, Stanley, 104
Cato, 149
Caton-Thompson, Gertrude, 283, 285
Cattle, 288
Caucasian race, 225
Central Africa, 26–29
Ceuta, 170, 349
Chad, 322
Chaka, 34
Chaldeans, 71, 72
Chamberlain, Alexander F., 63
Changa, Chief, 287
Changamir Empire, 287
Chard, Chester, 50
Christian Church: African influence on, 15–16, 145–46; in Ethiopia, 16; and slavery, 30, 305, 307, 308–9; invasion of Spain, 187, 194–95; war with Jews, 271; in Kongo, 289; crimes against Alexandria, 298–99; and Belgian atrocities, 312; and racism, 313–14, 318
Christian missionaries, and African bondage, 311–12, 317
Church of Africa, 16
Churchward, Albert, 41, 79, 89, 139–40, 246
Civilization: beginnings of, 9–16, 22–25, 48–49; defined, 60–61
Clapperton, Hugh, 222
Classificatory system of relationship, 84–89
Cloves, 282
Coblentz, Stanton A., 306
Coe, Michael, 239
Cohen, Chapman, 305, 307, 312, 313–14
Colchis, 92
College of Fez, 251–52

Colonialism: European, 4, 5, 7, 19, 232–34, 310–13, 319–50 *passim;* and cultural alienation, 8–9; Arabian, 26, 167–70; British, 31–33, 307–9; French, 33; Moorish, 170–87, 218; Portuguese, 302–4, 305; Belgian, 310–12. *See also* Slavery

Colton, Joel, 4–5

Columbus, Christopher, 234, 235–36, 241, 261, 262

Colvin, Ian D., 285

Comores Archipelago, 350

Congo-Brazzaville, 328–29

Congo Free State, 310

Congo-Kinshasa, 327–28

Constantinople, 180

Cooke, G. F., 308

Cooke, Harold P., 133

Coppen, Yves, 44

Copper, 211, 327

Cordova, 175–80, 182, 187, 188, 192

Coronation rites, 293–95

Crete, 77

Ctesibius, 120

Cultural alienation as a weapon of domination, 8–9

Culture-stage classifications, 57–58

Cyril, Bishop, 298–99

Da Gama, Vasco, 302

Dahomey, 33, 322

D'Almeida, Francisco, 303

Dark Ages, 17, 163–65

Dart, Raymond, 42, 43, 44

Darwin, Charles, 40

Davidson, Basil, 25, 49, 198, 219–20, 234–35, 261–63, 267, 268, 273–74, 277, 279, 280, 303, 304, 309–10, 331

Davies, H. O., 319

De Barros, João, 286

DeGaulle, Charles, 320–21, 322, 340

DeGraft-Johnson, J. C., 15–16, 147, 161–62, 165, 166–67, 169–70, 174–75, 286–87, 292, 316, 317

Denham, Dixon, 222

Deniker, 90

DeRoo, Peter, 234

De Santos, João, 286

Devonian era, 39

Diodorus Siculus, 10, 94

Dionysus, 133

Diop, Cheikh Anta, 7

Divine Kingship, 294–95

Doane, T. W., 146

Dobler, Lavinia, 220

Donnelly, Ignatius, 82, 258–59

Dorsey, George A., 72, 90–91, 94

Draper, John William, 236–37, 299

Dravidians, 75, 92

DuBois, Felix, 21, 197

DuBois, W. E. Burghardt, 34, 115, 293, 314–15, 316, 319

Dupuis, Charles F., 140

Durant, Will, 75, 147, 231

Earth, origin of, 37–38

East Africa, 25–26, 33

Eastern Roman Empire, 163, 165–66

Edfu Text, 93

Education: in ancient Africa, 24; in West Africa and Songhay Empire, 217; mentioned *passim. See also* Libraries, Universities

Egypt: Africanness of, 4, 11–14; ancient, 64, 79–80, 93–156, 257, 259, 260, 296–97; dynasties of, 96; and alphabet, 149–51; cultural influence on world, 150–54; origin of name, 153; annexed by Rome, 161; link to West Africa, 196–97; racial origins, 228; mythology, 245–46; modern, 341–42

Eichler, Lillian, 150, 151

El-Azhari, Ismail, 342–43

Elliot, Charles, 330–31

"El Rey," 239

Equatorial Guinea, 348

Eratosthenes, 120

Eritrea, 344

Es-Saheli, 210

Estevanico, 25

Ethiopia: and origin of civilization, 10–12, 65–92, 158–59, 265–72; and Christianity, 16; invasion of Egypt, 97; and worship of Rameses, 112; material features, 269–70; modern, 343–46

Ethiopian Dynasty, 115

"Ethiopoids," 230

Euclid, 120

European backwardness, 3

European versions of African history, 3–9
Evans-Pritchard, Professor, 275–77
Exogamy, 85–89

Falashas, 269
Fanti Confederation, 31
Finger, Charles J., 149–50
Frazer, James George, 84, 85, 115, 130–31, 132, 133, 295
Freeman-Grenville, G. S. P., 280, 302, 304
French Community, 321–22
Frobenius, Leo, 81–82, 157, 292–93, 315–16
Fulah (Fulani), 224
Funan, 278

Gadwal, 248–50
Gambia, 233, 326
Gao, 196, 197, 211, 212, 213–14, 217, 218, 222
Garvey, Marcus, 34
Genii of Hades, 141
Genseric, 165
Geological ages, 49, 59
Georg, Eugen, 81, 91–92
Ghana, 20, 31, 199, 201–7, 319–20, 321
Ghartey, King, 31
Gibbon, Edward, 272
Gibraltar, 171
Gillen, F. J., 89
Gold, 202–4, 207, 209–11, 281, 285–86, 303
Golden Age of West Africa, 18, 196–231
Golden Stool, 32
Goldenweiser, Alexander, 233
Gould, F. J., 132
Gowon, Yakubu, 324
Granada, 188, 192
Graves, Kersey, 146
Graves, Robert, 293–94
Great Pyramid, 63, 95, 98–104
Great Sphinx, 95, 117, 140
Greece, 4–5, 77–78, 158–59, 160
Griffiths, James, 324
Groundnuts, 326–27
Group marriage, 85
Guinea, 33, 321–22, 347
Gundel, Wilhelm, 142

Haab, 247
Habashan, 267–68
Hacen, Abu el, 251–52
Haddon, Alfred C., 52–53, 64, 73
Hadfield, P., 134, 293, 295
Hafside dynasty, 187–88
Hajib, Ibn Amir, 234, 261, 262
Haldane, J. B. S., 189
Hall, H. R., 74
Ham, Hamites, 68, 153–54, 158–59
Hamilcar Barca, 148
Hammerton, John, 76
Handicrafts, 309–10
Hannibal, 148
Hansberry, William Leo, 9
Hapgood, Charles H., 58, 149, 264
Harding, Arthur M., 135
Harith, Zid Bin, 16–17
Harrison, Jane, 134
Hartley, John W. K., 320
Harun-al-Rashid, Khalif, 17, 180
Hassan II, King, 339
Hassen, Mohammed Ben Abdullah, 33
Hat Benben, 114
Hausa States, 216, 218, 220–22, 224
Hawkins, John, 307
Hayford, Casely, 32
Heckethorn, Charles William, 147
Heeren, Arnold Hermann, 11, 12, 79–80, 265
Hejira, 167
Hekaptah, 153
Heliolithic Neolithic culture, 68
Heliopolis, 114
Hercules, 135–38, 173
Hermopolis, 113
Hero, 121
Herodotus, 63–64, 65–66, 92, 94, 98, 100, 103, 115, 117, 135, 158, 159–60, 259
Herskovits, Melville, 5
Hieroglyphic system, 232
Higgins, Godfrey, 69, 142, 151–52
Higgs, Eric, 50
Hipparchus, 120
Hippo, 165
Hobbes, Thomas, 50
Hocart, A. M., 295
Homo habilis, 47, 49

Horus, 93, 124–29 *passim*, 133, 141–43, 145, 245–46
Hottentots, 28
Houphouet-Boigny, Félix, 320, 325
Huddite dynasty, 187–88
Hughes, John, 337, 344–45, 349
Huxley, Thomas Henry, 67
Hyksos, 108, 110
Hypatia, 298–99

Ibos, 322
Idris I, King, 337–38
Idris, Mai, 220
Idrisi, Abu Adullah Mohammed el, 278–79, 181–82, 203, 278–79
Ifni, 349
Ikhnaton, 110
Imhotep, 13–14, 106
India, 75–76, 92, 277–78
Inquisition, 192
International African Association, 310
Iron, 62–63, 93–94, 278–79
Iron Age, 62–63, 93–94, 274
Irstam, Tor, 293
Irving, Washington, 174
Isis, 117, 127, 128–29, 145
Ivory, 277
Ivory Coast, 322, 325–26, 347

Ja Ja, 33
Jawara, David, 326
Jeans, James, 37
Jeffreys, M. D. W., 225, 227
Jenne, 196–97, 212, 214–15, 217
João, King Dom, 290
Johnston, Harry H., 72–73, 159, 226–27
Jonathan, Leabua, 335–36
Julian, Count, 170
Junod, Henri, 317
Justinian, 165, 166, 167
Juxon-Smith, A. T., 326

Kabaka of Buganda, 329–30
Kam, Kamites, 153–54
Kanem, 221, 222
Kanem-Bornu Empire, 199, 218–20
Kangaba, 207
Kano, 216, 221–22
Kasavubu, President, 327

Kaunda, Kenneth, 335
Kebbi, 217
Kenya, 330–32
Kenyapithecus wickeri, 47–48, 49
Kenyatta, Jomo, 319, 331
Khaldun, Ibn, 186, 272
Khama, Seretse, 336
Khayyám, Omar, 181
Khmers, 277–78
Khonsu, 123, 136
Khufu, Pharaoh, 95, 98, 103
Kilwa, 279–80, 281, 302, 303–4
Kingsnorth, G. W., 288–89, 336
Kolon, Prince Ali, 211, 212, 214
Kongo Empire, 27–28, 288–92
Kroeber, Alfred L., 91
Kromdraai Man, 44
Kumbi, 202, 205, 206, 207
Kush, Kushites, 10, 14, 66–67, 68, 70, 73, 91, 109, 112–13, 115, 198, 260, 266–67, 270, 276

Lagos, 322, 323
Laing, Samuel, 95–96, 100
Lane-Poole, Stanley, 174, 190–93
Lawrence, Harold G., 234, 241
Leakey, Louis S. B., 10, 45–49, 50, 225
Leakey, Mary, 45–47, 225
Leon, Nicolas, 254–55
Leopold II, King, 310–12
LePlongeon, Augustus, 240–41
Lepsius, Karl Richard, 11
Lesotho, 335–36
Lhote, Henri, 158
Liberia, 347–48
Libraries: of Ahmed Baba, 21; of Alexandria, 96, 119–20, 121, 297–99; of Carthage, 149; of Constantinople, 180; of Cordova, 192; of Thebes, 296; destruction of, 299–302
Libya, 148, 158–60, 337–38
Lightfoot, John, 37
Linnaeus, 90
Liverpool, 308
Loango Kingdom, 27
Lockyer, Norman, 123
Lopez, Duarte, 289
Lugard, Lady Flora Shaw, 65–66, 185, 187, 196, 197, 198

99, 203, 215, 224, 253–54, 260, 266, 301
Lugard, Lord, 322, 333
Lumumba, Patrice, 327
Lyttleton, Raymond, 38

MacGregor-Hastie, Roy, 321–22, 340
Macnaughton, Duncan, 14
Madagascar, 333, 348–49
Mahgreb, 339–40
Mahomet, 70
Malawi, 334
Mali, 20, 199, 207–13, 234, 235, 252–53, 261–63, 322, 340
Malinowski, Bronislaw, 233
Man: prehistoric, 9–12, 37–59; early civilizations, 12–15, 22–25; primordial human group, 51–54
Mandingoes, 33, 234, 236, 249
Manetho, 96, 111, 115
Margai, Albert, 326
Margai, Milton, 326
Marquez, C. C., 254–55
Maspero, Gaston, 95
Massamba-Debat, Alphonse, 329
Massey, Gerald, 14, 79, 150, 153–54
Masudi, Al, 198, 272–77 passim
Matriarchal society: in Egypt, 94–95, 107–8; of Berbers, 160; in Ghana, 201; in Mali, 252; in Monomotapa, 286; in African culture, 312–13. See also Mother-right
Mauch, Karl, 283
Mau Maus, 331
Mauritania, 160, 161, 322
Mayas, 82, 232–41, 257
Mayr, Hans, 303–4
Mazrui, Ali A., 4
Mboya, Tom, 344
McCabe, Joseph, 78, 119, 177–78, 189, 190, 305
McMichael, Edward V., 244–45
Mecca pilgrimage, 209–10, 216
Meinertzhagen, R., 330, 331
Melgar, J. M., 237
Melilla, 349
Menelik, 269
Menes, 96–97, 259
Merinite dynasty, 187–88
Meroe, 197–99, 266–67
Mesopotamia, 72–73, 188

Metal ages, 61–64
Meyer and Breasted, 96–97
Misr Bank, 342
Mithra, 133
Mobutu, Joseph D., 327
Moeshoeshoe II, King, 335
Mohammedanism, 16–17, 167–69, 208–9, 215, 219, 221, 322
Mombasa, 303, 304
Monomotapa, 26, 286–87
Montagu, Ashley, 50
Moore, Richard B., 6–7
Moors. See Morocco
Moreaux, Thomas, 98–99
Morel, Edmund D., 311–12
Moret, Alexandre, 125–26
Morgan, Lewis Henry, 51–52, 57–58, 62
Morocco, 15, 19, 21, 161, 166–95, 218, 301, 339–40
Moses, 111–12
Mother-right, 51, 52, 55–56, 84. See also Matriarchal society
Mound Builders, 244
Mozambique, 350
Musa, Governor, 170–71
Musa I, Mansa, 208–12, 234–35, 261–63
Musa, Mohammed Ben, 181
Mut, 136
Mutammed, Al, 184–85

Nahum, 297
Napata, 266–67
Nar, Prince Sulayman, 211, 212, 214
Nasamonians, 159–60
Nasser regime, 342
Negro race: unsuitability of term, 6; Nilotic, 41; origin of, 225–27; definition of, 228–30; in pre-Columbian America, 233–60; mentioned passim
Nephthys, 129
Niani, 207, 211, 212, 252–53
Niger, 322, 340
Nigeria, 32–33, 322–24
Nkrumah, Kwame, 319–20, 321, 344
Nubia, 14, 15
Numidia, 149, 160, 161
Nun, Joshua ben, 17, 180
Nut, 126, 127

Nyerere, Julius, 333–34
Nyikang, 275

Obote, A. Milton, 330
Ogaden, 344
Oil, 340
Old Stone Age, 22, 24
Olduvai Gorge, 44–47
Olmec culture, 239–41, 244, 246
Oman, Charles, 163
Omari, Al, 234–35, 261
Omayyad dynasty, 168, 183, 186, 189
Oppert, Julius, 258
Osiris, 117, 124–34

Padmore, George, 319
Palace of Minos, 77
Palermo, 148
Palmer, R. R., 4–5
Pan-African Congress, 340
Paranthropus crassidens, 44
Paranthropus robustus, 44
Parker, Richard, 194–95
Parsons, Geoffrey, 93
Pasha, Zebehr, 198–99
Patai, Raphael, 293
Peake, Harold, 17
Peet, T. Eric, 144
Pemba, 333
Perry, W. J., 73, 75, 82
Petrie, W. M. Flinders, 96–97, 98, 101–2, 103–4
Phoenicians, 146–48, 149–50, 158–59, 160, 264, 265
Phratries, 53–54, 86–88
Piankhi, King, 112–15
Plate of the Bacabs, 249
Plato, 256–57
Plesianthropus transvaalensis, 43, 44
Plutarch, 129, 131
Podro, Joshua, 293–94
Portuguese, 302–4, 305
Portuguese Guinea, 350
Prejudice, unknown in ancient world, 160
Prempeh, King, 32
Principe, 350
Proconsul africanus, 46
Procopius, 166–67
Proctor, Richard A., 100
Ptolemy I, 117, 119, 120
Ptolemy II, 119
Ptolemy Euergetes, 120, 122

Ptolemy Philadelphus, 96
Punic War, 148
Punt, 147
Pygmies, 41, 159–60
Pyramids, 13, 123
Pythagoras, 117

Quakers, and slavery, 308–9
Queen of Sheba, 268–69

RDA. *See* Rassemblement Democratique Africaine
Ra, 124, 125, 126, 129
Races: classifications of, 90–92; origins of, 225–27. *See also* Caucasian race, Negro race, White race
Radin, Paul, 232, 245, 247, 248
Raglan, Lord, 61, 78–79
Ramses II, 112
Randall-MacIver, David, 283
Rassemblement Democratique Africaine, 319, 320
Ratzel, Friedrich, 229
Rawlinson, George, 72, 270–71
Rawlinson, Henry, 73–74, 270
Read, Carveth, 53
Reade, Winwood, 106, 222–23
Reck, Hans, 45
Reinert, Jeanne, 239
Religion: in Egypt, 122–46, 151, 153–56; in North Africa, 165; in Ghana, 206; in Mali, 207–9; in Songhay Empire, 215–16; of Kanem-Bornu, 219; of Mayas, 245, 255–56; in America, African influence on, 255; in Ethiopia, 267–68; in Yemen, 271–72; mentioned *passim*. *See also* Atonism, Christian Church, Christian missionaries, Mohammedanism, Totemism, Zodiac
Republic of the Ivory Coast, The, 322, 325–26, 347
Réunion, 350
Rhodes, 273
Rhodesia, 349
Ripley, William Z., 228
Riva-Palacio, 254
Robertson, Archibald, 55, 56–57
Robertson, James, 323
Robertson, John M., 132–33
Robinson, John T., 44
Rocker, Rudolph, 182

Roderick, King, 170–74
Rogers, Joel A., 63, 83, 185, 254, 346
Roman, Father, 233
Rome: conquest of Carthage, 148–49; rebuilding of Carthage, 160–61; defects of system, 162–63; reasons for fall, 163–64
Romer, A. S., 39
Rozwi, 285–86
Russell, Bertrand, 230
Ruzo, Daniel, 243–44

Sahara region, 157–58
Said, Ibn, 187, 189, 273
St. Clair, George, 136, 141
Salt, 202, 204–5, 207, 211, 218
Salvian, 166
San Salvador, 290
Sao Tomé, 350
Saramaccas, 242–43
Sardinia, 148
Schebesta, Paul, 283
Scipio, Cornelius, 148
Seb, 126
Sebeknefrure, Queen, 107–8
Seignobos, Charles, 68
Sékou Touré, Ahmed, 321–22
Selassie, Haile, 270, 343–46
Sena, 273–74
Senegal, 322
Set, 127–28, 131
Sewell, J. W. S., 65
Sheba, Queen of, 269
Shekkarau, Sarki, 221
Shilluk, 275–76
Shona, 284
Sicily, 148
Sidon, 147
Sierra Leone, 233, 326, 347
Silverberg, Robert, 47, 107, 148, 244–45, 247, 278
Singhatch, Farimang, 326
6th Pan-African Congress, 319
Slavery: and colonialism, 5, 18–20, 26, 302–10; and Arabs, 26; and Vandals, 165; in Ghana, 205; and Saramaccas, 242; justified by "barbarous Negro" concept, 292–93
Sleeping sickness, 312
Smith, Goldwin, 308
Smith, Grafton Elliot, 68, 228–29, 233

Smith, Ian, 349
Smyth, Piazzi, 100
Sobhuza II, King, 337
Societe General Congolaise des Minerais, 328
Sofala, 273, 304
Solomon, King, 268–69
Solon, 117
Somalia, 344
Somaliland, 93, 266
Songhay Empire, 19, 20, 199, 207, 211, 212–18, 221–22, 224, 234, 299, 301
Soninkes, 200, 207
Sosigenes, 120
Southern Africa, 33
South-West Africa, 350
Soviet Union, 344–45
Spain, 175–83, 191–95
Spanish Sahara, 349
Spence, Lewis, 245–46
Spencer, Baldwin, 89
Spinden, Herbert J., 232–33, 247
Spinoza, 231
Steffen, Don Carl, 269, 346
Stephanus of Byzantium, 11
Stirling, Matthew W., 237–39
Stubbs, S. G. Blaxland, 76
Sudan, 33, 342–43
Sumer, 260
Sumerians, 71–72, 73, 91, 139
Sundiata, King, 207–8
Sunni dynasty, 214–15
Susu, 207
Swahili, 279–80, 281, 302–3
Swaziland, 337

Tachefin, Yusuf, 184–86
Taghaza, 202, 205, 211, 218
Taharka, 115–16
Takedda, 211
Tamrin, 269
Tanganyika, 332–33
Tanzania, 332–34
Tarifa, 170–71
Tarik, General, 171, 174–75
Tarikh-es-Sudan, 196, 197
Tassili-n-Ajjer, 157–58
Taung ape-man, 41–42
Tchadanthropus uxoris, 44
Tekrur, 207
Telanthropus capensis, 44

Temple of Ptah, 153
Temple of the Sphinx, 140–41
Terblanche, Gert, 43
Thales, 117
Thebes, 109–10, 136, 296–97
Theophilus, Bishop, 298
Thomas, Bertram, 70
Thompson, D'Arcy Wentworth, 143
Thompson, James Westfall, 164
Thomson, George, 54
Thorndike, Lynn, 75
Thoth, 123–24, 126–27, 129, 144
Thutmose I, 108
Timbuktu, 21, 212–22 *passim*, 299–300, 301
Togo, 322
Toledo, 170–71, 176, 189, 192
Torday, Emil, 63
Toro, 288
Totemism, 52–54, 84, 88–89, 96
Touré, Muhammed, 19
Toure, Samory, 33
Toynbee, Arnold, 189–90
Trade: in iron, 62–63, 93–94, 278–79; in gold, 202–4, 207, 209–11, 281, 285–86, 303; in salt, 202, 204–5, 207, 211, 218; in copper, 211, 327; in ancient Africa, 264–82; in ivory, 277; in cloves, 282; in cattle, 288; in handicrafts, 309–10; in groundnuts, 326–27; in oil, 340
Tres Zapotes, 238
Tripolitania, 161
Tshombe, Moise, 327
Tsiranana, Philibert, 348
Tubman, President, 347
Tunisia, 161, 338–39
Tutankhamen, 110
Tyre, 147
Tzolkin, 246–47

Uganda, 287–88, 293, 329–30
Union Minière du Haut Katanga, 327–28
Union of South Africa, 349
United Arab Republic, 341–42
Universities: of Baghdad, 17; of Sankore, 21, 299; of Jenne, 215; of Tunis, 339; of Al Azhar, 342; of Madascar, 348–49; mentioned 20–21

University College of Addis Ababa, 344, 346
Upper Volta, 322
Utica, 148, 160, 162

Vandals, 164–66
Venus Calendar, 248
Verrill, A. Hyatt, 255–56
Vespucci, Amerigo, 241
Volney, C. F., 11, 154–56
Von Hagen, Victor Wolfgang, 240
Von Wiegand, Karl, 346

Walata, 252
Wali, Mansa, 208
Wallace, Alfred Russel, 100–1
Wallace-Johnson, Isaac, 317–18
Wangara, 203–5, 209, 211
Waqlimi, 273, 275
Waq Waq, 273
West Africa, 18–22, 26, 31, 196–231
Weatherwax, John M., 22
Wells, Carveth, 281–82, 332–33, 347
Wells, H. G., 67–68, 91–92
Wendt, Herbert, 117, 225–26, 227, 284
White race: inferiority of, 3, 189–90; mentioned *passim*
Wiener, Leo, 232–33, 235–36, 241, 248–50
Wilson, James, 309
Wootz steel, 279
World history, 3–7
Worldwide ancient culture, 264–65

Yahia, Emir, 184
Yahmed, Bechir Ben, 350 n.
Yasin, Ibn, 184
Yemen, 271–72
Yoruba, 81–82, 322
Youlou, Abbe Fulton, 329

Zabaj Islands, 278–79
Zambia, 334–35
Zanj, 272–77, 279
Zanzibar, 281–82, 332–33
Zati, 194–95
Zimbabwe, 26, 283–85
Zinjanthropus boisei, 46
Zodiac, 134–46, 154–56, 258–59
Zoser, King, 13, 106
Zulus, 28, 34

Free Catalog!
Books of African-American Interest
From Carol Publishing Group

Thank you for buying this book!

Carol Publishing Group proudly publishes dozens of books of African-American interest. From history to contemporary issues facing Black Americans and popular culture, these books take a compelling look at the African-American experience.

Selected titles include: • The African Cookbook • African Names: Names From the African Continent for Children and Adults • Afro-American History: The Modern Era • The Autobiography of Jack Johnson • Black Hollywood: The Black Performer in Motion Pictures, Volumes One & Two • Black Is the Color of My TV Tube • The Black 100: A Ranking of the Most Influential African-Americans, Past and Present • Black Robes, White Justice: Why Our Legal System Doesn't Work for Blacks • Break It Down: The Inside Story From the New Leaders of Rap • Call Her Miss Ross: The Unauthorized Biography of Diana Ross • Caroling Dusk: An Anthology of Verse by Black Poets • Clotel: Or, the President's Daughter • A Documentary History of the Negro People in the United States, Volumes One through Four • Good Morning Revolution: Selected Poetry and Prose of Langston Hughes • Harriet Tubman: The Moses of Her People • Introduction to African Civilizations • Langston Hughes: Before and Beyond Harlem • Life & Times of Frederick Douglass •Lyrics of Lowly Life: The Poetry of Paul Laurence Dunbar • Man, God & Civilization • Michael Jackson: The Magic and the Madness • Muhammad Ali: A View From the Corner • Negro in the South • The Negro Novelist: 1940-1950 • Negrophobia: An Urban Parable • Negro Slave Songs in the United States • Paul Robeson Speaks: Writings, Speeches and Interviews 1918-1974 • Prisoners of Our Past: A Critical Look at Self-Defeating Attitudes Within the Black Community • Racism and Psychiatry • Repeal of the Blues: How Black Entertainers Influenced Civil Rights • Thurgood Marshall: Warrior at the Bar, Rebel on the Bench • To Be Free: A Volume of Studies in Afro-American History • Up From Slavery • The Way It Was in the South: The Black Experience in Georgia • What Color is Your God?: Black Consciousness and the Christian Faith • The Whole World in His Hands: A Pictorial Biography of Paul Robeson • Why Black People Tend to Shout: Cold Facts and Wry Views from a Black Man's World • Work, Sister, Work: How Black Women Can Get Ahead in the Workplace • Zulu Fireside Tales

Ask for these African-American Interest books at your bookstore. Or for a free descriptive brochure, call 1-800-447-BOOK or send your name and address to Carol Publishing Group, 120 Enterprise Ave., Dept. 420, Secaucus, NJ 07094.

Books subject to availability